Mary Tudor

A Life

To Judith,
wife and colleague

Mary Tudor
A Life

DAVID LOADES

Basil Blackwell

First published 1989

Basil Blackwell Ltd
108 Cowley Road, Oxford OX4 1JF, UK

Basil Blackwell Inc.
3 Cambridge Center
Cambridge, Massachusets 02142, USA

British Library Cataloguing in Publication Data

A CIP catalogue record for this book is available from the British Library.

Library of Congress Cataloging in Publication Data

Loades, D. M.
Mary Tudor: a life/David Loades.
p. cm.
Bibliography: p.
Includes index.
ISBN 0-631-15453-1
1. Mary I, Queen of England, 1516-1558. 2. Great Britain-King and rulers-Bibliography. 3. Great Britain-History-Mary I, 1553-1558. I. Title.
DA347.L579 1989
942.05'4'092-dc20 89-7163 CIP

Typeset in 11 on 12 pt. Baskerville
by Setrite Typesetters Ltd, Hong Kong
Printed and bound in Great Britain at
The Camelot Press Ltd, Southampton

Contents

Preface

When I first began to interest myself professionally in mid-sixteenth-century England, thirty years ago, the best available biography of Mary Tudor was the recent revision by H. F. M. Prescott of her pre-war work, *Spanish Tudor*. Since then three popular lives have appeared – *The Lady Mary* by Milton Waldman (1972), *Mary Tudor* by Jasper Ridley (1973), and *Bloody Mary* by Carolly Erickson (1978) – but none of them has superseded Prescott. At the same time a great deal of work has been done on Mary's reign, particularly by Michael Graves, Jennifer Loach, Robert Tittler and myself. Excellent biographies of other closely related figures have also been published; *Henry VIII* by J. J. Scarisbrick (1968), *Mary Tudor, the White Queen* (Henry's sister) by W. C. Richardson (1970), *Anne Boleyn* by Eric Ives (1986), and *Charles Brandon, Duke of Suffolk* by S. J. Gunn (1988), to mention but a few. A further biography of Mary from an academic base is therefore long overdue, and recent work on the court by David Starkey, Simon Adams and others has suggested an additional dimension to explore. Hence this book, which does not pretend to be any more than another brick in the edifice of Tudor history, but which expresses a long-standing concern of my own with personal motivation and the roots of policy. Having lived with Mary and the events of her reign for so long, a fuller examination of her life was a debt of honour to be paid.

Many friends and colleagues have contributed in one way or another, by encouragement and by sharing their own ideas, over a much longer span than this book has taken to write, particularly Mrs Jane Pakalski, Dr Christopher Haigh, Miss Helen

Miller, Dr Mia Rodriguez Salgado and Professor Sir Geoffrey Elton. On this occasion, however, my principal debt is to my wife, who has urged me on, and who has read the whole text with a keen and critical eye, suggesting many improvements. To her this work is affectionately dedicated.

David Loades
University College of North Wales
Bangor

Glossary

ATTAINDER – condemnation for felony or treason by due process of law. This could be achieved either by trial under the common law, or by Act of Parliament.

ACATRY – that department of the domestic household which managed the supply of butchers' meat to the kitchens.

ADVOWSON – the right to present to an ecclesiastical benefice.

AFFINITY – those bound to a lord by ties of blood or special allegiance; also called 'well willers'. The term was used to include both those formally employed or retained and those whose association was one of friendship, dependence or common interest.

CAESAROPAPIST – the belief that full ecclesiastical authority in respect of jurisdiction is, or should be, vested in the person of the king.

DOT – the sum of money involved in a dowry. Dower lands were normally involved as well.

FREE AND CUSTOMARY TENANCIES – free tenures were held under the common law, and were pleadable in the king's courts. Customary tenures were unfree in origin (villein tenures), and could only be pleaded in the manorial or honour court of the lord.

MANRED – an old word meaning those men who would answer a lord's summons to arms. 'Affinity' included families as well.

OBIT – an endowment in memory of a deceased person. Normally used of small or occasional sums rather than foundations in perpetuity.

PURSUIVANT – a herald of inferior status to a king of arms. Later used to mean an official seeking out malefactors and serving warrants of arrest.

RECOGNISANCE – a bond to guarantee good behaviour or the satisfactory discharge of some specific duty.

REVERSION – the receipt of a benefit or office after the present holder. A guaranteed succession.

TAIL MALE – an unalterable succession in the male line. Normally used of the inheritance of land.

ULTRA VIRES – literally 'beyond the strength'. An action or process outwith the lawful competence of the person or institution performing it.

VENIRE FACIAS – a writ of instruction to cause the appearance of an accused party.

WYVERN – a mythical beast in the form of a winged dragon with eagles' feet. Used in heraldry.

ESTATES GRANTED TO MARY IN 1547

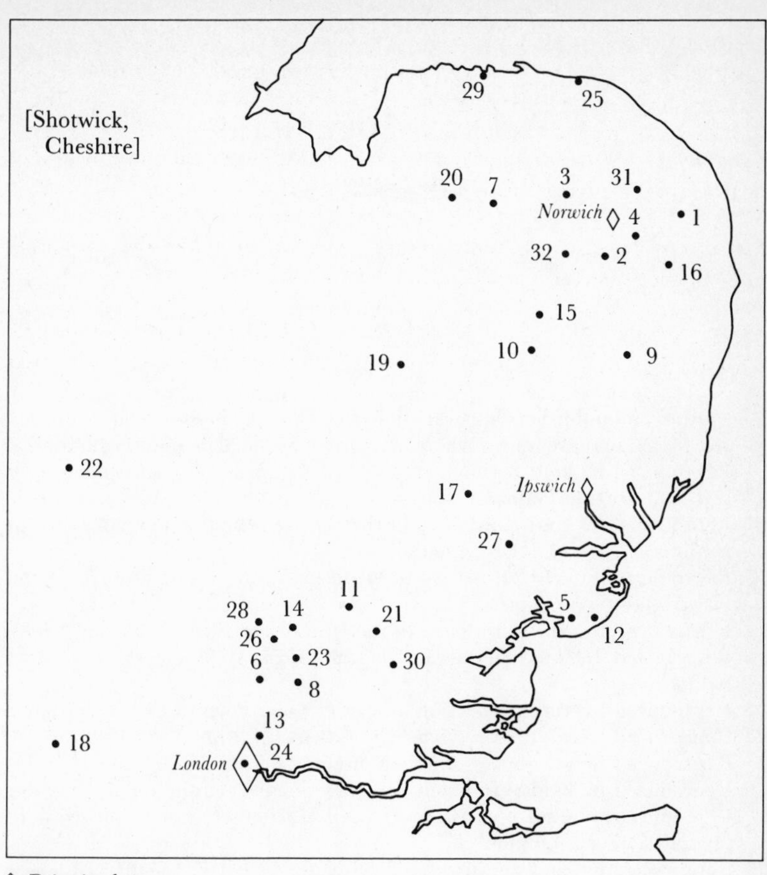

◇ Principal towns

Estates identified by the principal seat or manor; many minor lands are not marked.

1 Acle	12 Gt Clacton	23 Roydon
2 Aslacton	13 Highbury	24 St John of Jerusalem (Clerkenwell)
3 Barningham	14 Hunsdon	25 Sheringham
4 Brooke	15 Kenninghall	26 Stansted Abbot
5 Chiche St Osyth	16 Loddon	27 Stoke by Nayland
6 Copped Hall	17 Long Melford	28 Ware
7 East Bradenham	18 Marlowe	29 Wells
8 Epping	19 Mildenhall	30 Writtle
9 Fressingfield	20 Necton	31 Wroxham
10 Garboldesham	21 Newhall	32 Wymondham
11 Greenstead	22 Olney	

Acknowledgements

The author and publishers are grateful to the following persons and institutions for permission to reproduce works of art printed as the plate numbers indicated.

1 Reproduced by kind permission of the Earl of Scarsborough (photograph: National Portrait Gallery, London)
2 Reproduced by kind permission of the Earl of Scarsborough (photograph: National Portrait Gallery, London)
3 Reproduced by kind permission of Windsor Castle, Royal Library © 1988 Her Majesty The Queen
4 Reproduced by kind permission of the Kunsthistorisches Museum, Vienna
5 Reproduced by kind permission of the Board of Trustees, The Royal Armouries
6 Reproduced by kind permission of the National Portrait Gallery, London
7 Reproduced by kind permission of The British Library
8 Reproduced by gracious permission of Her Majesty The Queen
9 Reproduced by kind permission of the National Portrait Gallery, London
10 Reproduced by kind permission of Lord Hastings (photograph: National Portrait Gallery, London)
11 Reproduced by kind permission of the National Portrait Gallery, London
12 Reproduced by kind permission of Collection du Musée Granvelle – Musée du Temps, Besançon.
13 Reproduced by kind permission of the National Portrait Gallery, London
14 Reproduced by kind permission of the National Portrait Gallery, London
15 Reproduced by kind permission of The Duke of Buccleuch and Queensberry
16 Reproduced by kind permission of the Museo del Prado, Madrid
17 Reproduced by kind permission of The British Library
18 Reproduced by kind permission of the Royal Commission on Historical Monuments
19 Reproduced by kind permission of the Ashmolean Museum, Oxford
20 Reproduced by kind permission of the Bodleian Library, Oxford
21 Reproduced by kind permission of the Bodleian Library, Oxford
22 & 23 Reproduced by courtesy of the Trustees of the British Museum
24 & 25 Reproduced by kind permission of The British Library

26 Reproduced by kind permission of the Trustees of Sudeley Castle, Gloucestershire
27 Reproduced by kind permission of the Bodleian Library, Oxford
28 Reproduced by kind permission of the Victoria & Albert Museum, London
29 Reproduced by kind permission of The British Library
30 Reproduced by kind permission of the Ashmolean Museum, Oxford
31 Reproduced by kind permission of the National Portrait Gallery, London
32 Reproduced by kind permission of the Museo del Prado, Madrid
33 & 34 Reproduced by kind permission of the Ashmolean Museum, Oxford
35 Reproduced by kind permission of the National Portrait Gallery, London
36 Reproduced by kind permission of the Ashmolean Museum, Oxford
37 Reproduced by kind permission of the Ashmolean Museum, Oxford
38 Reproduced by kind permission of Trinity College, Oxford
39 Reproduced by kind permission of The British Library

Introduction

In the second parliament of Mary's reign an Act was passed 'declaring that the Regall Power of this Realme is in the Queenes Matie as fully and absolutely as ever it was in any of her most noble progenitors, Kinges of this Realme'. There has been a good deal of debate about the exact reason for this statute, and why it came in the second parliament rather than the first, but its general purpose is clear enough.[1] A ruling queen was an anomaly, and in the case of England unprecedented.[2] Mary's accession, welcome though it was in the circumstances of 1553, represented the failure of twenty-five years of intense and often disruptive struggle to preserve the kingdom from a female ruler. The reasons for that struggle, and for the strength of the feelings which it aroused, lay in the social and legal status of contemporary women. How far that status would affect a ruler was untested. Married women were particularly vulnerable, and it

Unless otherwise stated, the place of publication of printed works is London.

[1] 1 Mary, session 3 cap.1. It was claimed in Elizabeth's reign that the matter had been raised because some of Mary's councillors (Rochester was suspected) were urging her that the common law limitations on the English Crown applied only to kings, and that she could therefore rule absolutely. BL Harleian MS 6234; J. Loach, *Parliament and the Crown in the Reign of Mary Tudor*, 96–7. The Imperial ambassador Simon Renard believed that some English lawyers had claimed that Mary had only a 'woman's estate' in the Crown, which would thus pass to her husband on marriage. *Calendar of State Papers, Spanish*, XII, 15. Renard's view, as well as being contemporary, also seems more plausible.

[2] Matilda, Henry I's daughter, had maintained her claim against Stephen for a number of years in the twelfth century, but had never enjoyed full possession of the Crown.

was not known to what extent the marriage of a ruling queen might affect the autonomy of her realm. Mary's whole adult life has to be seen against this background, which profoundly affected not only the attitudes of her subjects, but also her own mentality.

The traditional role of women was either religious or domestic. Nunneries absorbed not only those whose sense of vocation might prevail over the wishes of their families; but also many, particularly in the middle and upper ranges of society, who either could not, or would not, find suitable marriages. Apart from the vow of chastity, marriage offered the only route to a secure and respectable life. Marriage brought important functions to a woman of substance, not only as a mother, but also as a manager of her husband's interests. In the case of a lady or gentlewoman this might involve both the running of a substantial household and the supervision of his estates during periods of absence, which might be prolonged by warfare, official business or imprisonment. Married women were no strangers to responsibility, but their legal status was low. Control over their property passed to their husbands, and they had only limited rights of access to the courts. For those with a taste for independence, widowhood was much to be preferred. A widow could expect to be provided for by her late husband, but she could also function in her own right. It is by no means uncommon to find in the records both free and customary tenements in the hands of widows; and the relicts of craftsmen and merchants often took over their establishments, joining the appropriate guild or fraternity in the process. Most widows remarried within the same community after a short time, because the social pressures to do so were strong; but some did not. Jane Wyatt, for example, widowed by Sir Thomas's execution in 1554, received a modest estate in her own right in the following year, brought up her children, and lived until 1610.[3] Several of Mary's leading household servants, most notably Susan Tonge (or Clarencius), were widows when they joined her service, and were well rewarded with lands and annuities.

Titles of nobility were normally transmitted in tail male, and although a woman could be granted a peerage in her own right, such grants were very uncommon before the seventeenth cen-

[3] George Wyatt, *The Papers of George Wyatt*, ed. D. M. Loades, 11.

tury. Property could, and frequently did, descend through the female line, and litigation between the heir male (in possession of the title) and the heir general (in possession of the estate) was commonplace. One such dispute in the fifteenth century, between the descendants of Lionel, duke of Clarence, and those of John, duke of Lancaster, had raised, but not resolved, the question of whether the Crown was a title or a property. This dispute is normally known as the Wars of the Roses. A peer's widow continued to hold her late husband's rank and title as a matter of courtesy until she remarried, and sometimes even thereafter. Henry VIII's sister Mary continued to be known as the queen of France after her marriage to the duke of Suffolk, and Katherine Willoughby, the same duke's widow, was still called the duchess after her marriage to the commoner, Richard Bertie. Similarly a title forfeited by attainder could still be borne by the widow – Gertrude, marchioness of Exeter, and Jane, duchess of Northumberland, being cases in point. Nevertheless, the widow of a tenant in chivalry did not have a legal right to the custody of her husband's heir, even if it was her own child. Such wardships belonged to the overlord – in the case of tenants in chief, the Crown. The dowager might be, and often was, granted the wardship, but it had to be purchased and success in such a bid was by no means assured.[4]

An unmarried woman of full age (over twelve) possessed the same legal status as a widow, but in practice seldom enjoyed much independence until she came into possession of her inheritance. A strong-minded or much indulged daughter might be allowed a major say in the choice of her own husband, but it was not to be counted upon, and wilful disobedience could result in disinheritance. In this respect a royal princess was even less free than the heiress to a normal estate, because it was a treasonable offence for a member of the royal kindred to marry without the monarch's consent. The elder Mary Tudor ran that risk when she married Charles Brandon in 1515, although she was already a widow; and Catherine Grey was imprisoned by Elizabeth when she secretly married the earl of Hertford in 1561. In the case of Henry VIII's daughters, he laid down in his will that

[4] L. Stone, *The Crisis of the Aristocracy, 1558–1640*, 600–5. Wards, particularly young heiresses, could be bought and sold without regard either to their own welfare or that of their estates, which was why many dowagers were prepared to pay dearly to protect their family interests.

neither was to marry without the consent of his son's council, it being assumed that those marriages would take place during Edward's minority. However, Mary was already queen when she came to make her choice, and her father's will was effectively ignored in that respect, although not without contention.[5] A princess, like the daughter of any other aristocratic house, could expect to be married for the benefit of her male relations, but in her case the desired benefits would be political, and probably international. If she was wise, an independent heiress would consult her kindred over such a step, but no one knew what constraints might apply to a ruling queen. The Crown was the only magisterial office open to a laywoman. Women were to be found in paid employment and service at all levels, particularly at court,[6] but the only offices which they held were private and domestic. Both Mary and Elizabeth had lady governesses in their youth, and as queen, Mary appointed Susan Clarencius mistress of the robes, which effectively meant being chief gentlewoman of the privy chamber, but none of these positions carried jurisdictional responsibility. The offices which carried such responsibility, even within the household, such as the lord chamberlain and lord steward, were always held by men of suitable rank. In France the so-called Salic law debarred women from the throne, and even precluded the transmission of a claim through the female line, but no other monarchy was similarly exclusive. The Imperial title was elective, and it would have been unthinkable for a woman to have held the premier secular office in Christendom, but ruling queens did appear from time to time on Europe's other thrones.

At the beginning of the sixteenth century the most important example was Isabella of Castile, and after the death of her son Juan in 1499 the lawful heir to that kingdom was her daughter Juana. However, Juana's fate provides a good example of the hazards which could beset a female succession. She had been

[5] Both Wyatt and Dudley claimed that Mary had forfeited the throne by marrying without the consent of the council. D. M. Loades, *Two Tudor Conspiracies*, 196–7.

[6] Several of the instrumentalists of the king's music were women, and Mary had two female jesters in her household before her accession – Jane 'the Fool', and Lucretia the tumbler. As queen she appointed Levina Teerlinc, the wife of George Teerlinc, one of her gentlemen pensioners, and niece of Lucas Horenhout, to be her court painter.

married before her brother's death, and in accordance with conventional dynastic wisdom, to Philip of Burgundy, the son of the emperor Maximilian. When her mother died in 1504, she was consequently settled in the Netherlands with her husband and two small sons. Despite the oaths of the Castilian Cortes and Philip's support, she never succeeded in making good her claim, except on paper. Her father, Ferdinand, who had no hereditary title to Castile, established himself as regent, and after Philip's death in 1506, excluded Juana completely on the dubious grounds of insanity.[7] When he died in 1516, he was succeeded by Juana's elder son, Charles, later the emperor Charles V. The English were not particularly sensitive to distant precedents, but the relevance of Juana's experience to the possible marriage of Elizabeth would not have been missed, particularly as the unfortunate woman lived in retirement, and virtual captivity, until 1555.

Sixteenth-century women had, of course, their own ways of subverting the male dominance of public affairs. Theoretically a wife was completely subservient to her husband, but in practice she had a number of effective weapons for influencing him. One of these was a persuasive tongue (often known by a less flattering description); another was sexual – the eternal wiles of the bedchamber; and a third was by calling upon the assistance of her male kindred. Even when the husband was a king he could be vulnerable to such pressures, as both Anne Boleyn and Catherine Howard demonstrated. At the height of her power the former was as dominant as Cardinal Wolsey had been, but it was a fragile triumph, because the same leverage which she had used against Catherine of Aragon could be used against her. It was partly for this reason that the stereotypes of wife and ruler were completely incompatible, and confronted any ruling queen with a crisis of identity. Maitland of Lethington identified this dilemma neatly to Elizabeth when he told her that she had 'ane highe stomack' and would brook no master. The image of a married queen was particularly difficult to resolve, even when her consort was of equal status, and in such circumstances it

[7] Juana certainly seems to have behaved in a deranged manner immediately after Philip's death, but it is by no means certain that her reason was permanently impaired. In theory she shared the Crown with her son after 1516.

tended to be assumed that the inferiority of the wife to her husband also extended to their respective realms. As the Scottish commissioners pointed out to their English equivalents in 1544, if their lad had been a lass, the English might have been less keen on the marriage of Edward and Mary Stuart. And even an unmarried queen could not escape the stigma expressed in contemporary assumptions about the 'natural imbecility' of women in general.

The view that women were intellectually and morally inferior to men had a long history, and one which it is not necessary to discuss in this context. John Knox's *First Blast of the Trumpet against the Monstrous Regiment of Women* (1558) was a classic statement of received prejudice dressed up as the will of God. Normally no woman, however high her social status, had an opportunity to challenge such assumptions directly, but she could do so by implication. One of the methods of doing this was through education. Humanist scholars such as More and Vives were beginning to express the view, not that women were of equal capacity to men in general, but that some women were exceptionally gifted, and worthy of the attention of the serious teacher.[8] It was in this advanced tradition that Mary was brought up, and given an intellectual training to match her royal status. In her case the result was uncertainty rather than emancipation; she knew that she was a princess and the heir to a throne, but although her education could give her a good grasp of the theoretical responsibilities of government, it could give her no practical guidance whatsoever. Consequently as queen she continued to accept the 'natural' opinion that many matters were not amenable to a woman's judgement, and needed to be resolved either by her ministers or by her consort. A second, and quite different, method of challenging male supremacy was provided by the traditional culture of courtly love, in which the woman was exalted, pure and unattainable; the knightly lover loyal, diligent and humble. It was not quite a 'world turned upside down' in the same tradition as a boy-bishop or a Lord of Misrule, but it offered the normally subordinate woman a position of superiority and of self-respect. As its name suggests, this was an aristocratic pastime, and its benefits were not available to

[8] *De Institutione Foeminae Christianae*, trs. R. Hyrde; reprinted in Foster Watson, ed., *Vives and the Renasence Education of Women*, 29–138.

the wives of the bourgeoisie, let alone those of humbler status. It flourished in the royal court, particularly the court of Henry VIII, where it combined with other aspects of chivalric culture, such as the joust, to produce a series of potent images. For eighteen years Catherine of Aragon presided over festivities which were designed to project in visual form the representation of power in the service of virtue. That the queen had come to symbolize virtue was a fact which Henry was regretting by 1530, because it was one of the strongest cards in the hand which she played with such determination until her death in 1536. Courtly love may not have helped to promote the intellectual or legal equality of women, but it certainly gave them a different moral status from that which had been customarily presented by the church.

The courtly tradition also helped in another way. Thanks partly to Castiglione's extremely influential manual for courtiers, *Il Cortegiano*, a lady could be respected not only for her beauty and virtue, but also for her wit. At the court of Urbino, presided over by Elisabetta Gonzaga, Aemilia Pia conceded not an inch to her male antagonists, and although this could be dismissed as a lightweight performance, it represented another small step away from the image of Griselde, which had so frequently in the past been held up (by men) as a feminine ideal. Powerful women, such as Eleanor of Aquitaine, had long since learned to use the civilizing influences of courtly love to enhance their positions, but the person who raised this political exploitation to an art form was Elizabeth Tudor. Thanks to the work of Roy Strong and Frances Yates, the cult of Gloriana is now a thoroughly familiar concept,[9] but it is worth remembering how extraordinary Elizabeth's achievement was. She was able to turn the handicap of her sex into an asset, converting her councillors, nobles and courtiers into putative lovers in such a way that they must often have wondered whether they were in the real world or in some kind of chivalric romance. By not marrying she was able to become the symbolic bride of her country and use the characteristic subtlety of her mind to baffle and dominate the men with whom she had to deal. The late sixteenth century was suddenly replete with powerful women; Mary of Guise, Margaret of

[9] R. Strong, *The Cult of Elizabeth*, and other works; F. A. Yates, *Astraea: The Imperial Theme in the Sixteenth Century* (1975).

Parma, Catherine de' Medici, Mary Stuart and Elizabeth herself. Only Elizabeth did not marry, and as a ruler she was by far the most successful. How far this was calculated, it is difficult to say, and as was repeatedly pointed out at the time, she jeopardized the succession by her wilfulness or negligence. Whatever one thinks of Elizabeth's political skills, she was an unusual and original woman who, by refusing to accept female stereotyping, secured her own freedom of action, and a unique niche in English history.

It would hardly be fair to blame Mary for failing to do the same. Her sister, after all, had the benefit of Mary's experience. Nevertheless, Mary's limitations as a ruler were largely those which were imposed by her sex. She was well educated, and as intelligent and strong-minded as most noblemen of her generation. But she was physically and emotionally weakened by physiological defects, and by the frustration of her natural instincts. More important, she allowed herself to become dependent because that was considered a proper thing for a woman to be. By comparison with Elizabeth, Mary was a profoundly conventional woman, and ill-adapted to cope with the stresses which royal rank imposed. In order to understand her life and its historical significance, one has to start from the personal nature of sixteenth-century monarchy, where birth and death, marriage and sickness, were essential ingredients of politics. This was a world in which the normal function of women was as dynastic instruments, and in which all the trappings and conventions of sovereignty were designed for men. All this Mary accepted, not as a regrettable fact of life, but as something willed by God, and therefore binding upon her conscience. Whether by nature or upbringing, she had no guile, and if the misfortunes of her youth had left her any sense of humour, history has failed to record it.

1

The Token of Hope

(1516–1525)

The Tudors were haunted by the twin spectres of infertility and dynastic failure. From the death of Arthur in 1502 to that of Elizabeth just over a hundred years later, scarcely a month passed in which the succession was not a matter of debate, speculation or controversy. The prompt birth of a son in September 1486 had set the seal of divine approval upon Henry Tudor's acquisition of the throne, and upon his subsequent marriage to Elizabeth of York. For a few brief months, from February 1499 to June 1500, the royal couple had three living sons, but thereafter the face of God became increasingly veiled, and His will inscrutable. Edmund, the third son, died on 19 June 1500, and Arthur, the eldest, on 2 April 1502. Less than a year later, in February 1503, the queen also died, and in spite of many urgings, Henry did not remarry. For the last six years of his life his whole achievement hung by a thread, and the deterioration of character which both contemporaries and historians have commented upon, has to be seen in that context. The king's uncle, Jasper Tudor, duke of Bedford, had died without lawful issue in 1495, and there was no cadet branch of the Tudor family. Had his remaining son predeceased him, the strongest claim on Henry's own death would have lain with his elder daughter, Margaret, married to James IV of Scotland. There was no Salic law in England. Both the Yorkist claim and the Tudor claim (such as it was) had been transmitted through the female line. However, if a woman succeeded to the throne by hereditary right, it was assumed that her husband would enjoy an equal right, as well as all the real power and responsibility of government. It was by no means certain that the English nobility would have been willing to accept a Scottish king at that point, even if Henry had specifically enjoined it. Nor could it be taken for granted that his own son would be accepted as a minor, if the dice of mortality should fall that way. As Henry was well aware, when rumours of his deteriorating health were circulating, shortly after Elizabeth's death, the names which had been canvassed in at least one significant discussion had not included 'my lord Prince'. 'Some spake of my lord of Buckingham, saying that he was a noble man and would be a royal ruler. Other there were that spake ... in like wise of your traitor Edmund de la Pole.'[1] The report may have referred to an isolated and unrepresentative incident, but the implications were sinister enough. One more dynastic misfortune and the wars of the previous century could easily recommence, with a similar cast and for the same reason.

The rejoicing which greeted the accession of Henry VIII on 21 April 1509, without dispute and without the necessity for a regency, was thus particularly justified. The Crown of England had changed hands peacefully and legitimately for the first time since 1422, and for only the second time since 1327 was the lawful heir an adult capable of assuming immediate responsibility. 'Heaven and earth rejoices,' wrote lord Mountjoy to his friend Erasmus with pardonable exaggeration, 'everything is full of milk and honey and nectar.' The young king was not merely healthy and *compos mentis*, he was brimming with physical and mental energy, and determined to be the epitome of a renaissance prince. He was unmarried, but not entirely unspoken for. On 23 June 1503, at the age of twelve, he had been contracted to marry the seventeen-year-old Catherine, daughter of Ferdinand and Isabella of Spain, who was already the widow of his elder brother, Arthur. It had been a typical dynastic arrangement between two hard-headed statesmen. Ferdinand wanted to keep the English alliance, and Henry wanted to keep Catherine's dowry. But there were doubts and difficulties from the start. A papal dispensation was needed because of Catherine's first marriage, but a sordid and acrimonious dispute then ensued over the nature of the impediment. Catherine swore that the marriage had never been consummated, and that she therefore

[1] *Letters and Papers Illustrative of the Reigns of Richard III and Henry VII*, ed. J. Gairdner (1861), I, 233–4.

had no blood relationship with Henry. In this she was supported by her Spanish attendants, but the English believed otherwise, and the dispensation eventually obtained was from full affinity. The terms of the contract also bound Ferdinand to pay a further dowry of 100,000 crowns, and this he was extremely reluctant to do.[2] Consequently the stipulated date for the wedding in 1505 passed, and nothing happened. Henry VII then began to negotiate with Philip of Burgundy for a marriage between his heir and Philip's daughter Eleanor, a girl of a rather more suitable age. For a while the unfortunate Catherine was wanted neither in England nor in Spain. Henry grudged the cost of keeping her, and Ferdinand, who was struggling to hold on to power in Castile after Isabella's death, had no desire to see her complicating the succession question there. However, Philip died in 1506 without committing his daughter, and the status of the unfulfilled contract of 1503 was still doubtful when the intended bridegroom succeeded to the throne.

Meanwhile Catherine, whose life in England had been nothing if not chequered and unpredictable, had convinced herself that it was the will of God that she should marry her former husband's brother, and that the constancy of her intention was being tested by divine purpose. This view was not shared by Ferdinand's ambassador in England in 1509, Gutierre Gomez, count of Fuensalida, or indeed by anyone else, as far as can be discovered. On 27 April Fuensalida reported that he understood on good authority that the dying king had absolved his son of any obligation towards the six-year-old treaty, and that also seems to have been the understanding of such senior councillors as Warham and Fox.[3] However, within a few days Henry had confounded all predictions by sweeping aside the accumulated difficulties and announcing that he would marry Catherine at once. His own explanation for this sudden decision was that it represented an act of filial piety, enjoined by his father for the discharge of his own conscience. If Catherine ever heard this ungallant story, she paid no attention to it, and it was probably not true. The king's decision seems to have been spontaneous and emotional, but he may well have been urged to protect himself against any charge of irresponsibility by posing

[2] Mattingly, *Catherine of Aragon*, 54.

[3] *Correspondencia de Gutierre Gomez de Fuensalida* ed. El Duque de Alba (Madrid, 1907), 515–17.

as a dutiful son. Whatever his motive, and despite the glamorous dimension which it added to his image, Henry's marriage to Catherine was an ill-considered move. She was five years his senior, and at least his equal in both intellect and determination. The strength of her character effectively foreclosed his options in foreign policy for almost a decade, and she never ceased to regard him as an agent of that divine providence which was shaping her own life. In 1509 the darker implications of that devotion lay far in the future, and for the time being they were a happy and brilliant couple. As long as Henry's main ambition was to levy war against France, there were no political tensions to disturb their relationship, and at first (in spite of his later reputation) he was a loyal husband.

Like Elizabeth of York, Catherine conceived promptly after her marriage, apparently a good omen, demonstrating the fertility of both partners. But there the similarity ended. On 31 January 1510, the queen miscarried of a female child. Such misfortunes were commonplace, and neither took the setback too much to heart. Within a few weeks she was pregnant again, and on New Year's Day 1511, gave birth to a son. The scale of the rejoicing indicated the importance of the event. A great tournament was held to please the king, and a pilgrimage to Walsingham to please the queen. There were bonfires in the streets of London, and the fountains ran with wine. Another life now lay between the kingdom and political confusion, a third Henry Tudor, who might grow up to rival his father and grandfather. The joy, however, was as short-lived as the child himself. Just over seven weeks later he died in his splendid nursery at Richmond, and this time the grief and anxiety of his parents was deep and prolonged. There were no recriminations, as far as we know, but a good deal of pious heart-searching to discover in what way God could have been offended, for such a sharp blow could only be seen as a corrective for major sin – either the kingdom's or their own. Catherine was not given to sin, and Henry was not given to recognizing it. Over the next four years the situation deteriorated further. The queen conceived at least twice, and probably miscarried on both occasions.[4] The king, partly as a diversion from the anxiety of his

[4] The chronology of Catherine's pregnancies is not easy to reconstruct. After her marriage in June 1509, she must have conceived promptly, and miscarried in January 1510. She was reported to be pregnant again by the end of May, which would be consistent with the birth of Henry on 1 January 1511. There were no further such reports in 1511 or 1512, but on 8 October

continued childlessness, and partly because Catherine's pregnancies necessitated long periods of sexual abstinence, began to find other women attractive. Fact is hard to disentangle from malicious gossip. Don Luis Caroz, the Spanish ambassador, reported a furious quarrel over a sister of the duke of Buckingham, a quarrel which also involved the duke himself and the king's favourite, Sir William Compton. However, Caroz was not close to Catherine, let alone to Henry, and his source was probably unreliable. It was normal for kings to take mistresses – Catherine's own father had begotten several bastards – and such behaviour, apart from attracting the formal censures of the church, might even be welcomed by the population at large as evidence of continued vitality. If there were serious quarrels between Henry and Catherine, on this or any other ground, they have gone unrecorded. In public he was conspicuously gallant. *Cœur Loyal* was his favourite *nom de guerre* in the lists, and he never wore any token other than hers in a jousting career which lasted from 1510 to 1527.

Nevertheless, their continued childlessness cast a shadow over the relationship as time went on, and when Henry was bitterly angry with Ferdinand for the latter's betrayal of their alliance in the summer of 1514, it was rumoured that Catherine would be discarded in favour of a French princess. There was probably no truth in the report, because it was followed within a fortnight by another letter to Italy containing news of a further pregnancy. Moreover, it was the queen who held the regency while Henry campaigned in France, and who sent him the tokens of victory from Flodden field. Henry may have dallied in Hainault, but when he returned to England at the end of September, with a typically romantic gesture he galloped straight to Richmond to lay at Catherine's feet the keys of Tournai and Thérouanne, the trophies of his own conquests. Such knight errantry can have been of little comfort. In January 1515 the queen was delivered of a stillborn son 'of eight months' 'to the very great grief of the whole court' as the Venetian ambassador reported.[5] The king

1513 the Imperial agent James Banisius reported that she had been delivered of a son. If he was right, the child was almost certainly stillborn, and probably premature, since there are no recorded preparations for a lying-in. On 14 September 1514, in a letter describing the betrothal ceremony of Mary Tudor and Charles XII of France, Nicolo di Favri described the queen as being pregnant, and that would be consistent with her bearing a stillborn son 'of eight months', as Andrea Badoer reported on 8 January 1515.

[5] *Calendar of State Papers, Venetian*, ed. R. Brown et al., II, 555.

was already consoling himself with Elizabeth Blount, although it is not certain that she had yet become his mistress. Catherine's star had also waned in another sense. Henry may not have considered revenging her father's treachery by repudiating his wife, but he certainly distanced himself from her politically. For the first three or four years of their marriage she was, in effect, his most trusted counsellor. By 1514 that role was filled by Thomas Wolsey, and Wolsey's influence extended to every aspect of royal policy. With her beauty fading and her piety becoming obsessive, time was running out. Only by bearing an heir to the throne could the queen hope to recover either her personal or her political influence.

In spite of starting so badly, the year 1515 saw some improvement in Catherine's position. After the crisis of the previous year, her husband and her father were once again allies, and she had played some part in bringing that about. Also, some time in April or early May, she conceived again. After so many false hopes, the expectancy of the court was subdued, and the comments of diplomatic observers guarded. A Venetian who saw the queen for the first time in this year, described her as 'rather ugly than otherwise', and Francis I unfairly but perceptively contrasted her with her still youthful and magnificent husband. Catherine was only thirty, and had been married for six years, but the strain of repeated abortive pregnancies had told on her both physically and mentally, and the complimentary asides which had once accompanied every mention of her name were a thing of the past. Nevertheless, on this occasion the omens were defied, and on 18 February 1516 in the palace at Greenwich she was delivered of a healthy child. The rejoicing was genuine, but restrained, for the child was a girl. Seldom can the sex of an infant have been of greater significance, for a female heir created almost as many problems as she solved. As the princess of England lived and grew strong over the following weeks, her main significance was as a token of hope. Henry was defiantly optimistic, perhaps because of the need to keep up his own spirits. 'The queen and I are both young,' he told the Venetian Giustinian a few days later, 'and if it is a girl this time, by God's grace the boys will follow.' Lord Mountjoy, writing from Tournai on 5 March allowed his loyal enthusiasm to overrun the limits of tact: 'our Lord send you as much rejoicing of my lady princess, and make you as glad a father as ever was king, and after this good beginning to send you many fair [children] to your Grace's comfort and all your true subjects.'[6] It is to be hoped that Catherine did not see her fifth pregnancy and third confinement described as 'a good beginning'! However, the cruel fact remained that her main task was still to be performed, and her capacity to perform it was diminishing year by year.

Meanwhile, a daughter was a political and social asset. On Wednesday 20 February, two days after her birth, the child was borne with great pomp and solemnity to the Church of the Observant Friars in Greenwich, and christened Mary. Virtually the whole nobility of England seems to have been in attendance. The countess of Surrey carried her, supported by the dukes of Norfolk and Suffolk, 'the Lord Cardinal was her Godfather, the Lady Catherine and the duchess of Norfolk were her Godmothers at the font, and the Countess of Salisbury was her Godmother at the bishop.' As the procession emerged from the church, the heralds proclaimed the name and style of the new princess, 'God send and give good life and long unto the right high, right noble and excellent Princess Mary, Princess of England and daughter of our most dread sovereign lord the king's highness.'[7] Henry awaited their return in the presence chamber of Greenwich palace, and received the rich baptismal offerings which expressed the loyalty of his peers and their ladies to the Tudor dynasty. The magnificent pageantry for which Mary was the pretext made its own political point, as such events commonly did in a renaissance court. A king could be crowned only once, but each of his children made their own contribution to his prestige and security by undergoing the first of the rites of passage. Over the next few months, the underlying tension at court relaxed. The queen recovered well, and the Maying which followed was unusually elaborate, with the royal couple being entertained to a venison breakfast by 'Robin Hood' in the greenwood 'under shoters hil'.[8] However, no further pregnancy followed, and Catherine's habitual piety became increasingly pronounced. She had always led her own life to some extent, conversing with her Spanish attendants, patron-

[6] *Letters and Papers, Foreign and Domestic, of the Reign of Henry VIII*, ed. J. Gairdner et al. II, 1621.

[7] BL Harleian MS 3504, f. 232.

[8] Edward Hall, *The union of the two noble and illustre famelies of Lancaster and York*, ed. H. Ellis, 582.

izing scholars and managing her own estates. Her attitude towards Henry's more vigorous amusements was dutiful and tolerant, but unenthusiastic. While he hunted she visited neighbouring shrines, and while he danced late into the night, she frequently sought an early bed.

How long Henry's public optimism survived, we do not know. It was early in 1518 before Catherine conceived again, and it is hard to discover how her condition was regarded. The summer and early autumn were largely occupied with complex diplomatic negotiations for a general European peace. On 29 July the Papal legate, Cardinal Campeggio, arrived in London to urge upon Henry the duty of all Christian princes to crusade against the infidel. More immediately, Wolsey was negotiating directly with the French. On 2 October the Anglo-French plan, usually known as the Treaty of London, was unveiled. Altogether it embraced over twenty powers, great and small, in a scheme of perpetual non-aggression to be guaranteed by all the signatories. So bland a formula presented few difficulties, and most of the intended participants signed over the next few months – to the immediate benefit of Wolsey and Henry, and to no lasting effect whatsoever. However, within this general scheme was included a much more specific treaty between England and France, providing for the return of Tournai, and the marriage of the Princess Mary to the infant dauphin, a child even younger than herself. This agreement was signed on 4 October, and on the following day in the queen's chamber at Greenwich, Admiral Bonnivet, representing the dauphin, was solemnly betrothed to the two-year-old princess.[9] The whole scheme hinged upon this betrothal, and the French had insisted (for understandable reasons) that Mary should be explicitly recognized as her father's heir in default of male issue. Given the age of the parties, and the normal duration of such treaties, it is possible that the English did not take the implications of this statement too seriously, but the astute Giustinian believed that it would never have been agreed to if the queen of England had not been pregnant, and hopes of a son revived. If that was the case, disappointment soon followed. On 9 November Catherine was delivered of a daughter 'to the vexation of everyone'. Never had the kingdom desired anything so passionately as it had a prince at this time, reported

[9] *L&P*, II, 4480.

Giustinian, no doubt reflecting English anxiety at the remote prospect of a French king.[10] So preoccupied was he with this sentiment that he neglected to say whether the child was born alive or dead; it really did not matter.

Although she was only thirty-three, Catherine did not conceive again. The hope so strongly revived by Mary's birth, and still alive in the autumn of 1518, ebbed away over the following years. To make matters worse, in 1519 Elizabeth Blount, the king's mistress for some two years, bore a healthy son whom he immediately acknowledged, naming him Henry Fitzroy. There was not to be a royal nursery again for fifteen years, and Mary grew up as the heir of England. Her whole upbringing, as well as her role in international diplomacy, was strongly influenced by that fact. No sooner had the news of the Anglo-French treaty become public, than Henry began to receive warnings of its hostile reception in the Low Countries and in Spain. Even the most distant hint of a dynastic union of England and France was sufficient to stir the wrath and alarm of the Habsburgs. Catherine had been in no position to protect her nephew's interests, a fact which sharply underlined the extent of her own eclipse by Wolsey, but young Charles was rapidly emerging as a powerful figure in his own right. He had been duke of Burgundy since his father's death in 1506, and had gained undisputed possession of the Crowns of Spain with the death of Ferdinand ten years later. In 1519 he was to become Holy Roman Emperor and the most powerful ruler in Christendom. With a patience and caution which were to be typical of his whole career, he set out to unravel the moral and legal obligations which bound his young cousin to the Valois prince. Although he was to see her only once, Mary was to be a constant presence for the remainder of his life, until they died within a few months of each other forty years later.

At first, Henry paid no attention to the warnings from Bruges and Saragossa. His treaty with Francis was ratified in Paris on 15 December, and both parties were speaking of an interview between the two kings in the summer of 1519. This did not take place because, when it came to the point, both were too preoccupied with the Imperial election. But the plan was postponed, not abandoned, in circumstances which serve to illustrate

[10] *Cal. Ven.*, II, 1103.

the extremely personal nature of renaissance politics. In order to emphasize his good faith, Henry vowed not to shave his beard until the meeting had taken place; not to be outdone in a romantic gesture, Francis reciprocated. Catherine, however, had other ideas. Not liking either beards or the French alliance, she reminded Henry that she had made frequent representations to him on the subject in the past, and persuaded him to shave the beard off.[11] Francis was offended – how seriously it is hard to tell – and there were a few ruffled feathers (or hairs) before the incident was shrugged off. In March 1519 there was a brief alarm in the French court that the princess had died, and Sir Thomas Boleyn's letters from Paris are liberally sprinkled with references to her well-being. Henry might have been young, and in apparently rude health, but life was uncertain, and as long as the betrothal lasted, Francis had a legitimate interest in the English succession. The French had good reason to be anxious, not because Henry was likely to die, but because he was playing a double game. Although Tournai was duly returned (much to Charles's annoyance), and the meeting between Henry and Francis arranged for June 1520, at the same time an invitation was extended to the emperor to visit England on his way from Spain to the Low Countries – a voyage which he was expected to make in April 1520. The plan almost failed, because Henry could not delay his departure from England beyond the end of May, and on 15 May Charles was still held up at Corunna by adverse winds. The extent of his anxiety in this situation is revealed by letters to Wolsey and other English councillors which he drafted in anticipation of missing his rendezvous – letters warning against French deception, and offering his own financial inducements. However, the wind changed at the critical moment, and he reached England late on May 26. For three days he was lavishly entertained, and in the intervals between hunting and dining contrived to deliver his political message to both the king and the cardinal. By the time that he left on 29 May, and Henry set off for Ardres to meet the king of France, the balance had tilted slightly, but decisively, against the success of that encounter.

The Field of Cloth of Gold is one of the most celebrated events of the century, and has been described many times. Given the

[11] *L&P*, III, 416, 514.

deep distrust and almost instinctive hostility with which the nobility of the two kingdoms regarded each other, it did not go at all badly. Chivalric competitiveness was stopped short of bloodshed, and the magnificent entertainments brought the jousting rivals together in a spirit of conviviality. More important, the treaty of October 1518 was confirmed, the financial arrangements consequent upon the return of Tournai were agreed, and an understanding was reached over French relations with Scotland. In fact Wolsey's part of the proceedings were much more successful than the king's – or the queen's. In spite of the frequent and profuse expressions of brotherly love, Henry and Francis were too much alike to entertain any real affection for each other, and Henry in particular seems to have left the field less well-disposed than he approached it. Catherine discharged her duty as gracious ornament and object of knightly devotion. She may even have had some genuine rapport with Queen Claude, but neither she nor her ladies impressed the French gentlemen. They were collectively condemned as neither beautiful nor well dressed, and the freedom of their manners (a criticism which did not extend to the queen) was much condemned.[12] It is hard to believe that Catherine enjoyed herself much, as she must have realized that her nephew would be the victim of any possible Anglo-French co-operation which might result. For some unexplained reason the four-year-old Mary, who could have added significantly to the human warmth of these celebrations, was left behind in England. When the meeting had originally been intended for 1519, she was included on the list which Henry had drawn up. Moreover, in December 1519, when the plans for the 1520 meeting were already well advanced, Queen Claude had taken the trouble to send her secretary to London with presents for her affianced daughter-in-law, a jewelled cross 'worth six thousand ducats' and a portrait of the dauphin.[13] The timing suggests that this may well have been a hint that she would like to see the child, but if so, it was not taken up. Francis, however, had no intention of allowing Mary's significance to be forgotten, and on 2 July 1520, before Henry got back from Calais, three of his gentlemen paid a formal call upon the princess at Richmond. She received them, as

[12] J. G. Russell, *The Field of Cloth of Gold*, 126.
[13] Antonio Surian to the signory, 6 December 1519. *Cal. Ven.*, II, 1298.

her father was informed, 'with the most goodly countenance, proper communication, and pleasant pastime in playing at the virginals'. The visitors professed themselves suitably impressed, 'her young and tender age considered', and no doubt went back to report to Francis that her absence had not been occasioned by illness or by any hitherto undisclosed defect.

Henry, meanwhile, had held further discussions with Charles, first at Gravelines and then at Calais. The young emperor did his best to break what he saw as the Anglo-French *entente*, but the most that he could achieve was a repetition of England's commitment to the general treaty of 1518. Since he was convinced that Henry and Francis were scheming to attack him, and his suspicion of Francis was justified, Charles probably regarded the outcome of these talks as reassuring. For the time being, under Wolsey's guidance, Henry was refusing to be drawn into any aggressive alliance – so it was Francis, rather than the king of England or the emperor, who failed to get what he wanted out of the 'summit conferences' of 1520. On the central issue of the marriage, however, the French retained the advantage because Henry, in spite of his mounting anxiety about the succession, would not budge. Charles apparently followed up his personal efforts in that direction with a diplomatic approach through his ambassador in London, because in August 1520 Sir Richard Wingfield was instructed to inform Francis that such an attempt had been made, but that 'the king will remain true to his oaths'. However, in the latter part of 1520 relations between France and the Empire were steadily deteriorating. Francis was the aggressor, and although Henry retained his public posture as a neutral and potential arbitrator, behind the scenes his position on the marriage began to change. By January 1521 he was responding positively to the emperor's persistent overtures, in spite of the fact that the suggested bridegroom was Charles himself – who was sixteen years older than Mary and would have had to wait for eight years for his bride to attain the lawful age of cohabitation. Henry was under no illusions about this, as his instructions to his ambassador, Cuthbert Tunstall, make clear. A treaty of the type in question 'will not prevent the Emperor from marrying any woman of lawful age before our daughter comes to mature years, as he will only be bound to take her if he is then at liberty.'[14] Such a situation would have its advantages from the English point of view.

[14] *L&P*, III, 1150.

> 'We are willing', Henry's instructions went on, 'that the dote and dower be appointed in the treaty; and it is to be considered that she is now our sole heir; and may succeed to the crown. So we ought rather to receive from the emperor as large a sum as we should give with her if she were not our heir. But if we have an heir male hereafter, we are willing to give with her as great a dote as was assigned to our sister Mary, which did not exceed £50,000.'

Having changed his ground, the king was now anxious to extract the maximum advantage from the negotiation, and reminded Charles unnecessarily that if the match between Mary and the dauphin were to go ahead, and the latter were to become king of both France and England, the combined navies of England and France would sweep him off the seas.

By the early part of 1521, Wolsey was struggling hard to preserve the peace of 1518. It was a losing battle, but Mary's second major marriage negotiation has to be seen in that context. The emperor was insistent that the French had attacked his territories, and invoked English assistance under the terms of the existing treaty. Henry, under Wolsey's guidance, offered arbitration, partly out of a genuine desire to avoid bloodshed (and expense) and partly in the hope of obtaining more favourable terms for his eventual intervention. In February Tunstall reported a predictable wrangle over the dowry. Gattinara, the Imperial chancellor, had dismissed the £50,000 offered as inadequate, and indicated that the princess of Portugal was on offer with a million crowns (about £200,000).[15] His riposte was a bluff, because a Portuguese alliance would have been little use to Charles at that point, and Tunstall countered by emphasizing Mary's place in the succession, which he claimed was worth far more than a million crowns. By May Francis had got wind of what was afoot, and a game of cat and mouse ensued. Expressions of outrage or indignation would only have precipitated an Anglo-Imperial alliance, so the French confined themselves to mild incredulity. Henry responded with equal disingenuousness, assuring Francis that, although he had indeed been solicited from such a quarter, he had paid no attention to the overtures. Wolsey even went so far as to tell Sir Richard Jerningham, the ambassador in Paris, that the duke of Buckingham had conspired against Mary's right to succeed because of his 'displeasure' at the French marriage. A few days later Jerningham reported the king's response: 'he had liever have my lady

[15] Ibid., 1162.

princess, and though the king's grace had ten other children, than the king of Portugal's daughter with all the spices her father hath.'[16] Francis had no intention of conceding, and a Portuguese union at that point would have been no more use to him than it was to Charles.

In the event, the political situation settled the marriage, rather than the other way round. By July the pope had moved decisively onto the Imperial side, and this was important since both Charles and Mary had need of dispensation from earlier contracts before they could be betrothed. On 29 July Wolsey was formally commissioned to conclude an agreement, and on 2 August he crossed over to Calais. In the negotiation which followed, Gattinara's hand was strengthened by the fact that Wolsey was simultaneously staging a last-ditch attempt to persuade the French to accept arbitration. He tried to insist that Mary should be handed over at seven years of age, and that her dowry should be a million ducats (about £330,000). In the circumstances this could only be a bargaining position, and Wolsey countered by offering custody at full age (twelve), and £90,000 – out of which the emperor's debts to England were first to be paid. By the end of August agreement had been reached, and the treaty was ratified on 14 September. If the French had not ceased hostilities by the end of November, England was to join the emperor in arms, but would not be bound to mount a full-scale campaign until May 1523. Mary was to be betrothed to the emperor, and to marry him with a dowry of £80,000 if she was still Henry's heir at the time, and £120,000 if she was not – although it was secretly stipulated that this supplement would not be insisted upon.[17] The treaty of Bruges was not published, because in spite of the collapse of negotiations with France, England was not bound to enter the war until May 1522, and Wolsey was still hoping against hope to find a formula of reconciliation. The one card which he could still play for that purpose was Francis's continuing enthusiasm for the English marriage. Either French intelligence was seriously defective, or Francis was trying to embarrass Henry with a display of injured innocence. At the end of November he insisted to his ambassadors in England that the treaty of June 1520 was in full force,

[16] 15, 20 and 24 May 1521. *L&P*, III, 1283, 1293, 1303.
[17] *L&P*, III, 1508, 1571.

and even attempted to renew it, an overture which Wolsey evaded. As late as the middle of January 1522, he was still claiming to disbelieve the reports which his spies had brought to him, on the grounds that he refused to believe that his 'good brother' the king of England would go back on his word. He did not, however, suspend hostilities and put the honesty of Wolsey's brokerage to the test.

Throughout the spring the cardinal maintained his efforts to renew the peace, but neither side was interested. The treaty of Bruges had provided for Charles to pay another, and longer, visit to England, and he timed his arrival to coincide with the end of the period of grace. He landed at Dover on 28 May, and stayed until 6 July. In the course of these six weeks the emperor was generously entertained with hunting, masking and jousting. On 6 June he rode into London beside his host, to be received with magnificent pageantry and lodged in the new palace of Bridewell, which had been specifically prepared for his comfort. Before that, on 2 June, he had enjoyed a more personal and significant greeting at Greenwich. When he arrived by water in the early evening, 'at the halle doore the Quene and the Princes and all the Ladies received and welcomed hym ... and the Emperor had great ioye to se the Quene his Aunte, and in especiall his young cosyn germain the Lady Mary.'[18] Later in the evening the six-year-old princess had danced very gracefully for her solemn betrothed, and he had treated her with a kindness and courtesy which lingered in her mind. The discrepancy in their ages can only have been emphasized by this encounter, but Charles was intent upon the business in hand, and gave no sign of the reservations which he must have felt. On 19 June at Windsor he signed a fresh treaty with Henry, confirming the treaty of Bruges, and settling on Mary at the time of their marriage the lordships formerly allotted to Margaret, the sister of Edward IV, at the time of her marriage to Charles the Bold. By the end of the month Clarencieux, king of arms, had denounced Francis as a violator of the peace of 1518, and declared Henry's war upon him. When he left for Spain, the emperor had every reason to be satisfied with his stay in England – but nothing could add the necessary ten years to Mary's age.

[18] Hall, *The union of Lancaster and York*, 635.

Despite the cordiality of relations between Charles and Henry, Wolsey's lack of enthusiasm for hostilities continued to be apparent, and for the time being his eyes were on Scotland rather than on France. There the Francophile duke of Albany spent the summer endeavouring to motivate the Scottish lords for a march south. By September he had failed, and Wolsey seized the diplomatic initiative. If the 'auld alliance' had worn so thin, perhaps the time was ripe for a revolution in Anglo-Scottish relations. James V was a boy of nine, and Henry's nephew through his mother, Margaret, who was now the countess of Angus. Margaret's relations with her brother were not of the best, but she was consistently anxious to undermine French influence in Scotland, and responded favourably to the cardinal. It was a pity that Henry had only one daughter, because she could be publicly betrothed to only one person at a time. However, it was a long way from betrothal to marriage, especially for one so young. And given the fact that Charles was most unlikely to honour his commitment once the present war had run its course, Wolsey did not scruple to draft Mary into the service of this new policy. By January 1523 an 'arrangement' was being talked of, which would have included a sixteen-year truce, and the permanent exclusion of the duke of Albany from Scotland.[19] Albany himself was soon aware of this development, and in March contrived to have some of his letters, which made unambiguous reference to the scheme, intercepted by servants of the emperor. Charles made light of the matter, and at first he seems to have been justified. Throughout the summer of 1523 the northern war continued in desultory fashion, with a succession of English raids on Kelso and Jedburgh. As a military effort it did not amount to much, but it was considerably more than the English had so far achieved in France, despite Henry's renewed talk of his claim to the French throne. However, late in the season there was a change. The duke of Bourbon, at odds with Francis over a personal matter, offered his services to the emperor. Suddenly, in August, there was a tripartite agreement for a combined attack upon Paris, and by early September an English army under the duke of Suffolk had invaded the north of France. Shortly after, the duke of Albany arrived back in Scotland with 5000 French troops, and it looked as though the familiar pattern of southward invasion was about to be repeated.

[19] *L&P*, III, 2765.

All expectations were disappointed. Suffolk's campaign, inadequately supported by Bourbon and the emperor, collapsed in the wintry weather of early December, and Albany was once again unable to persuade the Scots to support his intended thrust. There was talk of renewing the allied campaign in the spring, but liaison was poor, and Wolsey was already thinking in terms of a truce. In these circumstances the earlier talk of a Scottish marriage was revived, and at the end of August 1524, having received some encouragement to do so, Margaret wrote to her brother with an elaborate plan for reconciliation and union. The Scottish lords, she claimed, earnestly desired a marriage between Mary and their young king; and in view of the terms they had in mind, their sincerity need not be doubted. In the first place, they wanted any resulting treaty to be ratified by the English parliament; secondly, James was to be declared the second person in England and receive estates appropriate to a prince of the realm. Should he then be disappointed of the succession by the birth of a son to Henry, Scotland was to receive Berwick and the Debatable Land.[20] This was, of course, a bargaining position. Negotiations followed over the next two months, and by the end of October 1524 it looked as though an agreement was in sight. On 24 October Wolsey sent word to Margaret that Henry intended to dissolve his marriage treaty with the emperor, and proceed immediately to a betrothal between Mary and James, so that the latter might be 'trained in the devotion of England'. On 18 November the bishop of Dunkeld, the earl of Cassilis and the abbot of Cambuskenneth were commissioned in the name of James V to negotiate peace with England, and a marriage between James and Mary. How seriously Wolsey intended such a treaty is a matter of doubt. He had been quietly trying for some months to distance Henry from the emperor, and had been negotiating secretly with the French. In October the English envoys with Charles at Mechlin reported that another Scottish dispatch had been intercepted, and that they feared the emperor's distrust of Henry might lead him to conclude a separate peace.

The Scottish marriage has to be seen against this European background, and it is often ignored in discussions of the wider

[20] Queen Margaret to Henry VIII, 31 August 1524. *L&P*, IV, 600. The Debatable Land was an area in the west March, north-east of Carlisle, the sovereignty of which had never been determined.

issues, but for a few months it seems to have been a real option. Although it would have involved an unpopular Scottish succession, in the long run the advantage would have accrued to England as the major partner, and the exclusion of French influence from Scotland was a great inducement. However, in February 1525 this political pattern was dramatically altered. Margaret felt that her commitment was not matched on the English side, and one of Wolsey's envoys reported that her influence was rapidly declining. On 14 February Francis was defeated and captured at the battle of Pavia, and the barren Imperial alliance suddenly promised a rich crop. Wolsey was temporarily swept along by Henry's enthusiasm to exploit the situation, and the Scottish marriage lost its attractiveness at the very moment when a convincing display of purpose was required. Henry, however, quickly realized that he was in no position to move decisively against his weakened enemy, and Charles, having endured English prevarication and half-heartedness over the previous twelve months, had no desire to exert himself further for the benefit of his ally. A French attempt in March, therefore, to revive the project for marriage between Mary and the dauphin was slightly less desperate than it must have seemed. The nine-year-old princess was at the very centre of the complicated diplomatic game which followed. At the end of March, when Henry was still hoping to persuade the emperor to mount a combined offensive, he instructed his ambassadors to deny that he had entertained any alternative marriage scheme for his daughter, and even offered to allow her to be placed in Charles's care – although under the strictest safeguards. A few days later Wolsey followed this up with the gift of an emerald, ostensibly from the princess, and a message that 'her grace hath devised this token for a better knowledge to be had when God shall send them grace to be together, whether his Majesty do keep himself as continent and chaste as by God's grace she will.'[21] The emperor was unimpressed by the jealous pangs of a pre-adolescent, and had already decided that he needed a bride of full age without further delay. On 7 June, when his own negotiation for the hand of Isabella of Portugal was already well advanced, he called Henry's bluff. He would raise an army for the invasion of France, provided that Henry would pay for it,

[21] Wolsey to Tunstall and Wingfield, 3 April 1525. Ibid., 1240.

hand over his daughter at once, and pay her full dowry within four months.

It was these terms, spelling the end of any hope which the English may have entertained of reaping a fruitful harvest from Francis's unprecedented weakness, which so offended Henry. He did not particularly mind the abandonment of the Imperial marriage – that had been anticipated – but the way in which it was done wounded his pride by deliberately exposing his limitations. He tried to extract some advantage from the situation by using his knowledge of the Portuguese negotiation to blame Charles for the breakdown of the treaty of Windsor. He would not try to hold Charles to his treaty obligations, provided that he paid his debts to the English Crown, and that the treaties were publicly annulled. This response gained him little advantage. In Italy it was reported that Henry had released the emperor from his obligation willingly, because Mary was destined for the king of Scots, but the truth was less satisfactory. Louise of Savoy, the regent of France, had urged the Scots at the end of June not to trust the English. 'As to the princess Mary, she has already been promised to the Dauphin and to the Emperor, and in like manner they will break the promise made to the Scots.' By then such warnings were unnecessary, because no marriage was in prospect. On 30 August England and France concluded the peace treaty of the More, so called from having been signed at Wolsey's residence of that name, in Hertfordshire, and brought three years of futile and expensive war to an end. Mary was again a disposable asset, but her deployment had so far brought her father no very tangible gains, and the fact that she was still his heir made her future use increasingly hazardous. In November 1524, from a vantage point in Rome, Giovanni Sangi had commented: 'it does not seem very probable that the daughter of the king of England will bring that kingdom with her as dower' to either Charles or the dauphin.[22] Not only was he right in his immediate prophecy, he also expressed one of the major diplomatic imponderables of the period.

Mary herself had so far played only a very small part in these complex manœuvrings. She can be glimpsed here and there in the diplomatic correspondence, displaying her childish talents for music and dancing, and chatting briefly to official visitors

[22] Giovanni Batista Sangi to the bishop of Capua. Ibid., 843.

under the watchful eyes of her governess and ladies. At two she had been solemnly betrothed to the dauphin, and at six she had met her other fiancé on two brief occasions. Although it is unlikely that either of these episodes made much impression on her, she must have been conscious of her royal dignity as soon as she was conscious of anything beyond physical comfort. No subject, however exalted, was permitted to be covered in her presence, or to kiss her, except on the hand. On formal occasions she was knelt to, as was the king himself, and treated with more deference than her mother. This sense of status must also have been increased by the fact that she lived for the most part surrounded by her own household and away from the court. Although not many of them survive, she had her own 'giestes', or itineraries, which show her moving in her own orbit, usually around the lesser royal residences in the Home Counties, intersecting the orbit of the court at major festivals such as Christmas – or whenever the king decided that it should be so.[23] In July and August 1518 she moved from Bisham to the More, and thence to Enfield and Haringey, although her stay at Enfield was cut short by infection. This must have been typical of many summer migrations. In July 1517 she carried out her first official duty, as godmother to her cousin Frances Brandon, but a proxy acted in her stead as it would hardly have been seemly for one infant to answer for another. In these early days her extreme youth was often blandly ignored, as when Cuthbert Tunstall delivered a homily on matrimony for her benefit on the occasion of her betrothal in October 1518. Each New Year she received gifts; not, on the whole, the sort to delight the heart of a child, but gold cups, spoons and pomanders. Lady Mountjoy, who gave her two smocks on 1 January 1518, perhaps came the nearest to making any concession to childish tastes.

Mary's household must have been constituted within a few days of her birth, although there is no actual record of the event. Her first governess, or 'Lady Mistress', appears to have been Elizabeth Denton, who had received an annuity of £50 in May 1515 'for services to the late king and queen'. Margaret Brian, who later claimed to have been the original 'Lady Mistress' is listed in the accounts of November 1517 as receiving an annuity of 40 marks 'during the life of Elizabeth Denton, widow, who has

[23] Pace to Wolsey, 18 July 1518, Ibid., II, 4326.

the fee of Lady Mistress to the Princess', and at that point clearly held the office in reversion.[24] Thereafter, Lady Denton disappears from the records, and Margaret Brian probably claimed her reversion some time during 1518. She did not hold the office for long, and her replacement may have been connected with the death of her husband, Sir Thomas Brian, and her remarriage during the early summer of 1519. By May 1520 the princess's household was headed by no less a person than Margaret Pole, countess of Salisbury, who was also her godmother. This lady was the daughter of George, duke of Clarence, the younger brother of Edward IV, and held her title in her own right. Her appointment probably indicated Henry's recognition of the fact that Catherine was unlikely to bear more children, and that Mary was consequently his heir in more than a formal and temporary sense. It was Lady Salisbury who presided over the princess's reception of her French visitors in July 1520, an occasion at which the duchess of Norfolk and her daughters were also present. Only a person of the highest rank and dignity was suitable to have the custody of a child who might one day be queen of both England and France.

The lady governess was supported, in the original establishment, by a treasurer (Richard Sydnor, dean of Totnes), a chaplain (Henry Rowle), one gentlewoman, four 'rockers' and a laundress. Mary's nurse at this stage was Catherine Pole, the wife of Leonard Pole, one of the gentlemen ushers of the king's chamber.[25] In October 1519, before the household was augmented, Mary's chamber was allocated sixteen liveries during a period of residence at court. During the previous year, the overall cost of her establishment was estimated at £1400, and the records show that a full set of service departments, including wardrobe, kitchen, *acatry* and stables was in operation. Sometimes, particularly during the winter, the princess spent several weeks at a time in the company of her parents, and during those periods her own servants would have worked alongside those of the king and queen, perhaps on a shift system to avoid overcrowding and confusion. The reorganization which took place

[24] Ibid., II, 3802.

[25] Ibid., 1473. On 2 July 1517 Catherine Pole received a grant of two annuities of £10 each from the issues of the lordship of Cheshunt. These provided half her annual wage of £40. Ibid., 3429.

towards the end of 1519 left Richard Sydnor, Henry Rowle and Catherine Pole in their former places, but promoted three of the 'rockers' to be gentlewomen of the chamber, and added a male staff of six gentlemen, nine valets and four grooms.[26] One of these last was David ap Rice; his wife Beatrice, who became laundress at this point, was eventually to be the longest serving of Mary's attendants. In 1522 the number of gentlemen and valets was slightly increased, and fifteen pages added, but apart from that, the size and shape of the princess's household seems to have remained substantially unchanged until her removal to Wales in 1525. During those periods when Mary was resident at court, the services of the lady governess were not required, and she was free to go about her own business. In July 1521, when the court was about to move from Windsor to the less spacious residence at Easthampstead, where there was no 'convenient lodging' for the princess, Lady Salisbury was not allowed to return to duty. She had fallen under suspicion because of her close association with the duke of Buckingham, and although no other action was taken against her, her connection with Mary lapsed for about four years. On 21 July Richard Pace, the king's secretary, wrote to Wolsey that Henry considered the dowager countess of Oxford to be a suitable replacement 'if she could be persuaded' – or failing her, Lady Jane Calthorpe. Wolsey moved swiftly, but to no avail. The dowager countess pleaded ill-health, and by the beginning of September Sir Philip and Lady Calthorpe had been approached. Sir Philip was an experienced courtier, who had accompanied the king to the Field of Cloth of Gold, and also to his meetings with the emperor, but it is not clear what particular qualifications Jane had for so responsible a post. By the middle of October they had been appointed, at a joint wage of £40 a year,[27] and in the following September both of them signed the household book for the preceding year, along with Richard Sydnor, the treasurer. Sir Philip's position was

[26] Wages of the princess's household from 1 October 11 Henry VIII to 1 September 12 Henry VIII. Ibid., III, 970. Ibid., Addenda, 259.

[27] Pace to Wolsey, 13 October 1521. Ibid., III, 1673. Sir Philip Calthorpe came from Ewerton in Suffolk, and served on the commissions of the peace for both Norfolk and Suffolk. His daughter later married Sir Henry Morley, and also served in Mary's household. *Burke's Dormant and Extinct Peerages* (1846), 417. D. MacCulloch, *Suffolk and the Tudors*, Appendices II, III.

probably that of chamberlain, although he is nowhere specifically described as such. By August 1524 the princess's establishment included a steward, and a controller, as well as a chamberlain and a treasurer. Together they were commissioned to collect the subsidy from her household, but were not identified by name.

One officer who is conspicuous by his absence from any of these fragmentary early lists is a schoolmaster. For the first three or four years of her life Mary would have been exempt from the pressures of formal education, 'brought up among the women' as her half-brother was later to put it, but by 1521 at the latest, some process of instruction must have been taking place. Garrett Mattingly believed that Catherine herself 'taught her her ABC, guided her childish pen, ordered her reading and corrected her latin exercises',[28] but, as we have seen, Mary spent long periods in each year away from her mother. Perhaps it was her chaplain, Henry Rowle, who provided the day by day supervision of those early lessons. The king was spasmodically interested in his daughter's progress, particularly when he wanted her to make a good impression, but was directly involved only with her music. Her precocity in that discipline may well have been the result of the attentions of one or more of the numerous talented performers whom he had attracted into his service. Mary's early education is something of a mystery, but must have involved the active collaboration of both her parents. Catherine had herself received an excellent humanist training in Spain, and through her mother was familiar with the idea of women being educated to rule in their own right. Henry, for understandable reasons, faced this concept only with great reluctance. Consequently, we have more evidence of the queen's hopes and intentions than we do of their actual realization, which would have depended upon the king's appointment and authority. In 1523 Catherine commissioned her fellow countryman Juan Luis Vives (who visited England by her invitation in that year) to write a general treatise on the education of women, *De Institutione Foeminae Christianae.* 'Your dearest daughter Mary', Vives wrote in his preface, 'shall read these instructions of mine, and follow in living. Which she must needs do if she is to order herself after the example that she hath at home with her.' Vives's ideas were advanced, even

[28] Mattingly, *Catherine of Aragon*, 140.

revolutionary, but they did not go anywhere near suggesting an intellectual equality between the sexes. Not only were women far more prone to be led astray by unsuitable literature, they also needed protection against contaminating male company. A diet of scripture, the Fathers, and certain 'acceptable' pagan classics was consequently prescribed, to be consumed at home.

De Institutione was followed by a number of other treatises, similarly commissioned. Vives himself contributed *De ratione studii puerilis* and *Satellitium sive Symbola*; Erasmus *Christiani matrimonii institutio*; Thomas Linacre *Rudimenta grammatices*; and Giles Duwes *An Introductorie for to lerne to rede, to pronounce, and to speke French trewly*. The first of these was a detailed guide to good reading, varying from the New Testament to Paulinus, Aratus and Prosper. Everything to be studied had a moral as well as an academic purpose: 'Let her be given pleasure in stories which teach the art of life . . . stories which tend to some commendation of virtue, and detestation of vice.'[29] The *Satellitium* was a collection of proverbs and adages designed to fortify the 'princely mind' of the future queen; and the *Christiani matrimonii institutio* a guide to the proper conduct of a wife and mother of exalted station. Vives discussed Mary's education with Catherine when he visited the English court, but the belief that she was entirely in charge of her daughter's upbringing, which seems to be expressed in his prefaces and dedications, was probably disingenuous. She was, after all, his patron. Those who actually taught the child were less intellectually distinguished, although there is no reason to doubt their competence, and they had no easy task. Shaping the mind of the heir to the throne was a great responsibility, and if they followed Vives's guidance as to reading, they may well also have heeded his caution against over-indulgence: 'the daughter should be handled without any cherishing. For cherishing marreth sons, but it utterly destroyeth daughters.'[30] By 1525 Mary could read and write, both in English and in simple Latin, had some command of French, and could probably understand the Spanish in which her mother conversed with her physician and apothecary. She could also play competently upon the lute and virginals, sing, dance, and ride in a manner appropriate to her status, and behave with

[29] M. Dowling, *Humanism in the Age of Henry VIII*, 225.
[30] Foster Watson, ed., *Vives and the Renasance Education of Women*, 133.

becoming gravity on formal occasions. She had also begun to be aware of the uncomfortable tension in her life, for which there was no ultimate remedy. As the king's heir she outranked her mother, and received the homage of all her father's subjects, but she also knew, or thought she knew, that she was destined for a royal marriage. Vives might recommend the reading of Plato, More's *Utopia*, and Erasmus's *Institutio christiani principis*, as appropriate for a woman who might ultimately bear rule, but he did not encourage her to believe that she possessed the intellectual resources of a man. At the same time Catherine held the strongest views about the nature of wifely duty, and had learned by hard experience that neither blood nor intelligence could compensate the married woman for the disadvantage of her sex. Even Isabella had provided a different education for her son, Juan, from that which her daughters had enjoyed, excellent though that had been. It is therefore an exaggeration to say that Catherine brought Mary up to be a ruler. Nobody, not even Vives, knew quite how that could be done. Mary was educated to be a queen, but it was naturally assumed that her husband would govern England if she ever ascended the throne. Piety, chastity and humane letters were the objectives of those who guided her lessons from the very first, and the prospect of marriage dominated the schoolroom as much as it did her role in the political life of her father's court.

Vives urged that no child should be taught alone, and both Elizabeth and Edward later had schoolfellows; but if anyone shared Mary's lessons, we have no knowledge of it. Apart from the occasional comments of diplomats and courtiers, our main source for the knowledge of Mary's early life is the accounts of Richard Sydnor. Here we can even trace the monthly consumption of sheep, grain and stockfish, the purchase of cloth and other material for the wardrobe, and the regular migrations of a peripatetic household. In 1522/3, which was probably a typical year, Sydnor received £1100 from Sir Henry Wyatt, the treasurer of the king's chamber, and accounted minutely for the disbursement of £1097 9s. 6¾d.[31] The only children who feature in these accounts are those who received casual rewards for small services, or bringing presents: 'To a man and three boys, playing before [the princess], 6s 8d; To two girls of Tollys, bringing

[31] *L&P*, III, 3375.

oranges and cakes, [ ]'. Occasional payments of this kind are both informative and amusing. One day in December 1521, *en route* from Richmond to Ditton, an unspecified sum was given in alms to the poor 'by order of the Princess'. It would be interesting to know how much discretion of this kind was allowed to a five-year-old. Christmas that year was spent at Ditton, away from the court, and the clerks of St George's chapel, Windsor, came and sang 'ballets' for Mary's entertainment on Christmas day. The following Christmas was spent in the same place, and the accounts suggest frolics of a much more boisterous and hazardous kind, presided over by John Thurgoode, 'Lord of Misrule'. There was an interlude of some kind, featuring a friar and a shipman, a disguising which apparently required twelve men to appear as haystacks, and a firework display which consumed a quantity of gunpowder. At the end there is a note of expenditure 'for mending Adam's garments' – but whether as a result of the gunpowder is not clear.[32] On a more serious note, we have a record of the New Year gifts which Mary received; a silver standing cup from her father, a gold salt from Cardinal Wolsey, a gold cross from the countess of Devon, and twelve pairs of shoes from Sir Richard Weston, who clearly had a practical mind. At other times we can catch a glimpse of the young princess being ferried along the river from Richmond to London in the queen's barge, or from Richmond to Syon to visit the countess of Oxford. Her council (the senior officers of her household) received official letters both from the king and the queen, and duly rewarded the messengers who brought them. On 12 September 1523 one such messenger brought copies of the statutes of the last parliament, and a commission to collect the first installment of the subsidy from the household – but he got his reward just the same![33]

From what we can observe, Mary's life in these early years seems to have been varied, healthy and interesting. Her schooling grew more purposeful and time-consuming as she became older, but there was no shortage of recreation and entertainment. Her health was assiduously cared for, probably by the king's own physicians as there is no record of her employing her own, and she was often moved to avoid infections such as small-

[32] Ibid., 2585.
[33] Ibid., 3375.

pox and plague. Henry was pathologically nervous of disease, and his daughter was a valuable commodity. He was also genuinely fond of her, and Mary probably had more attention and affection from both her parents than was common with royal or aristocratic children of the period. Nevertheless, she spent far more time away from court than at it, and the occasional visits which can be detected (particularly to her mother) when her household was within easy reach, cannot have made much difference. She seems to have been brought up in an entirely adult world, and to have been treated from the start as though she was a diminutive adult rather than a child. This may be an impression created by deficiencies in the evidence, but there are no signs of schoolfellows, playmates, or even toys. These last must have existed in some form, but the regular company of other children cannot be assumed. She had no brothers or sisters, and her cousins Frances and Eleanor Brandon do not seem to have featured at all in her life. Her education seems to have been enlightened, if somewhat austere, but of play in the ordinary childish sense, there is no mention – unless we count the well-known incident in which she pursued Dominic Memo crying 'Priest! Priest!' She would have had little opportunity to be lonely, and later in life is known to have enjoyed sewing and playing cards, both of which occupations she probably learned at an early age, and both of which were gregarious activities in an aristocratic household. The offices of the church were strictly observed in the princess's own chapel, and regular offerings and almsgiving were conducive to an early sense of *noblesse oblige*, as the incident on the road to Ditton makes clear. By modern standards, Mary was painfully short of emotional outlets as a small child, but as Ralph Houlbrooke has written of the family in this period: 'It was the truly solicitous parent's responsibility to make sure that his offspring were not pampered, but strictly controlled for the good of their bodies and souls.' There is no reason to suppose that Henry and Catherine had so far fallen short in any way of the highest standards of parenthood.

2

The 'Princess of Wales'

1525–1533

The summer of 1525 saw a major change of emphasis in Mary's life, the exact reasons for which are not easy to reconstruct. While diplomacy was still disentangling the consequences of the emperor's decision to marry Isabella of Portugal, during July and August, Mary was equipped with a lavish entourage, and dispatched to the marches of Wales. Ostensibly the reason lay in the urgent needs of the Principality itself:

> forasmuch as by reason of the longe absence of any Prince making continual residence either in the Principalitie of Wales or in the marches of the same, the good order quiet and tranquilitie of the countrys theraboute hath greatly been altered and subverted, and the due administration of Justice by means of sundry contrarieties hitherto hindered and neglected.[1]

No doubt Wolsey was keen to extend the jurisdiction of his court of Star Chamber into the Marches by means of the princess's council, but there was more to this development than an improvement in provincial administration. At the same time the king's natural son, the six-year-old Henry Fitzroy, was given an even larger household and sent to the north of England as titular lieutenant. Both these establishments were largely selected by the cardinal, and should be seen as extensions of his influence and patronage, but the policy which their creation represents was the king's. The creation of honours and titles was a matter with which Henry greatly concerned himself, and 18 June 1525

[1] BL Cotton MS Vitellius C.i, f.23.

saw a dramatic concentration of activity. On that day Henry Courtenay, earl of Devon, became marquis of Exeter, Thomas Manners, Lord Ros, became earl of Rutland, Henry Clifford became earl of Cumberland, and Henry Brandon, the nine-year-old son of the duke of Suffolk, was created earl of Lincoln. These simultaneous promotions were no coincidence, and were clearly designed to support, and focus attention on, the young Henry Fitzroy, who on the same day became earl of Nottingham and duke of Richmond. Fitzroy's sudden emergence from relative obscurity to the highest honour indicated another attempt on the king's part to deal with the intractable and unsettling issue of the succession. Catherine was furious, and revealed her anger with unaccustomed indiscretion, but apart from the affront to her susceptibilities, no great harm had been done. Indeed, had her reaction been political rather than moral she might have spared herself and her daughter a great deal of anguish. It had been clear since at least 1521 that the queen would bear no more children, so Henry had three courses of action open to him. He could accept that Mary would be his only heir, and that her husband would rule England after his own death; he could recognize Fitzroy, and settle the succession on him; or he could repudiate Catherine and marry again.

The first course, which was much the simplest legally and morally, was fraught with political problems. If she married the ruler of another kingdom, or his heir, the independence of England would be compromised, and this was something which neither Henry nor his subjects wanted. If she married 'within the realm', as had once or twice been hinted, not only would it be a disparagement, but factional strife would have been a serious risk. Only a union with a cadet of one of the major royal families could have satisfied both honour and security to some extent – an extremely difficult balance to strike. In the summer of 1525 the king was keeping his options open. A period of intense diplomatic activity focusing upon Mary had come to an end, and there is no evidence that he had yet contemplated the third option. The ostentatious advancement of Fitzroy stopped short of any legal moves to include him in the succession; and the princess's new and honourable role was also less than conclusive. Although Mary was sent to the Marches in much the same way as Prince Arthur had been sent in 1501, and although she was frequently referred to as the princess of Wales, neither that title nor any of its accompanying perquisites, was ever bestowed upon her. Henry was thirty-four, and sexually active, but by no means promiscuous. He had almost certainly stopped sleeping with Catherine by this time, and his mistress for the previous three years had been Mary Boleyn, a daughter of his servant and courtier Sir Thomas Boleyn. The fact that she bore him no children may indicate that she was a good deal more cautious than her subsequent career would indicate, or that he was less active than he liked to pretend. Henry's sexual psychology was to be of great importance over the next decade, so the point is not without significance. Catherine seems to have accepted the situation with resignation, and in public remained very much the dutiful wife. However, the king's waning affection had the result of concentrating her considerable energies upon works of piety and charity – and upon her daughter.

Catherine's view of the succession problem was different from Henry's in one very important respect. She did not appreciate the English desire for autonomy, and consequently could see no valid argument against Mary's right.[2] The orthodox dynastic position which she held concentrated less upon the princess than upon her heirs. If Mary married at the normal age (between sixteen and twenty-two), there was every prospect that she would have sons of her own before Henry died, and the eldest of those sons would have Imperial prospects on the grand scale. When he was in a confident mood, or particularly anxious to press a marriage treaty, this was a view which Henry sometimes shared, but it was becoming an old-fashioned concept by 1525. The king might talk grandly of 'winning his ancient right' in France, and had actually sought election as Holy Roman Emperor in 1519, but the basic fact remained that England would have been the minor partner in any prospective marriage alliance except that with Scotland; and would have been doubly disadvantaged by coming in on the female side. Even if Henry had been directly succeeded by a Habsburg or Valois grandson, there would have been no chance of the English extending an imperial sway over a major part of western Europe. Catherine's perception of English attitudes may well have been coloured by

[2] This view was also shared by Charles, although he was well enough aware of the general English hostility to foreigners. *L&P*, v, 265, no.15. Vives also wrote to Henry directly, urging him to solve the dynastic problem by making a suitable marriage for Mary. Vives to Henry VIII, 13 January 1531. *L&P*, v, 46.

her own popularity, or she may have treated such attitudes with the contempt of a Spanish grandee. She could not have been altogether unaware of the seething hatred of the Londoners for the Flemings, nor of the animosity which had caused one nobleman at the Field of the Cloth of Gold to imperil his career by declaring that if he had one drop of French blood in his veins, he would cut it out.[3] Understandably, Henry's political sensitivities were more attuned to his subjects' prejudices, and he was poised uneasily between the desire to gamble on a dynastic opportunity, and the fear of leaving his realm in the hands of a foreign king.

Mary's departure for Thornbury in August 1525 therefore served a number of purposes. It confirmed that she was the king's only legitimate child, signalled her temporary withdrawal from the marriage market, and got her well away from her mother. The breakdown of the Imperial marriage alliance, and Wolsey's desire for another *rapprochement* with France gave the cardinal a strong motive for wishing to diminish Catherine's influence. At the same time Henry's increasing realization that he might wish to use his daughter in ways of which Catherine would not approve, prompted him in the same direction. The separation was a relative matter, but would have been clear enough to those directly involved. Whereas Mary had been in and out of the court every few weeks, and seldom more than a day's ride away, she was now on the other side of England, and her visits were special events. Both her honour and her welfare were thoroughly provided for. The countess of Salisbury, her former lady governess, was recalled to service, having shaken off the suspicions of 1521. Edward Sutton, Lord Dudley, a man who had been in and out of royal favour since the turn of the century, became chamberlain; and Walter Devereux, Lord Ferrers, steward of the household.[4] The chamber establishment numbered sixteen ladies and gentlewomen, plus fifty-seven male servants, varying in status from the chamberlain to the messengers. The ladies and gentlemen were allowed servants of their own to the number of over ninety, so the full complement of this side of the household was approximately 165 persons. The domestic household numbered eighty-six, from the steward to the

[3] On Catherine's intercession for the Evil May Day rioters in 1517, see Mattingly, *Catherine of Aragon*, 136. The incident of the indiscreet nobleman was reported by a Venetian observer. *Cal. Ven.*, III, 108.

[4] BL Harleian MS 6807, f.3.

footmen, but because of its lesser dignity provided for only thirty-seven private servants – a total of 123. Attached to the princess's household, and serviced by it, was a refurbished council in the Marches, presided over by John Voysey, bishop of Exeter. Apart from its president, the council consisted of a chancellor, six learned counsel and a secretary. These officers were supported by a herald, a pursuivant, and two sergeants at arms, in addition to the forty-one personal servants allowed by the 'check roll'. The distinction between the household and the council was not intended to be clear cut. Lord Dudley, Lord Ferrers, Sir Ralph Egerton (treasurer of the household), Sir Giles Greville (controller), Sir William Morgan (vice-chamberlain) and other officers acting as councillors when the need arose.[5]

The original establishment, drawn up in July 1525 provided for a total of 304 persons, and an annual wage bill of £741 13s 4d. The straightforward appearance of this list is, however, deceptive. As late as January 1526 Lord Ferrers was writing to Voysey as though he had no connection with the council; and the offices of steward, and chamberlain of South Wales, were not formally granted to him until May of that year. Similarly, Sir Philip and Lady Jane Calthorpe, Mary's former chamberlain and governess, are not mentioned in the July list, yet in August 1525 they were both receiving funeral liveries from the great wardrobe as members of the princess's household.[6] By 20 July 1526 Calthorpe had succeeded Sir William Morgan as vice-chamberlain, and by March 1527 was chamberlain in place of Lord Dudley. Apart from the countess of Salisbury (and presumably the Calthorpes) only a handful of Mary's Welsh household had served her before. Catherine Pole and Alice Baker had been with her since 1516, as had Richard Sydnor, now treasurer of the chamber. Among her gentlemen, John and Thomas Morgan, Anthony Coton, Hugh Pennington and Richard Baker were survivors from the 1519 list, as was her laundress, Beatrice ap Rice. Perhaps a dozen of her chamber staff were familiar faces, out of a total of some seventy-five, but one or two of them would have been very important in diminishing the strangeness of her new surroundings. She may also have known her schoolmaster,

[5] BL Cotton MS Vitellius C.i, f.23.
[6] Wolsey to Sir Andrew Windsor, 14 August 1525; *L&P*, IV, 1577.

Dr Richard Fetherstone, although there is no positive evidence that he had taught her before.[7] At least a quarter of her new establishment, and probably more, came from Welsh or Marcher families, including the steward, treasurer, vice-chamberlain, and master of the horse. The last named, Francis Vaughn, hailed from a remote corner of Merioneth, where, in June 1527 he was granted the lordship of Glyndyfrydby. In 1526 some changes were apparently made because in addition to the replacement of Morgan by Calthorpe, the marquis of Dorset then appears as master, and Sir Thomas Denys as controller in place of Sir Giles Greville.[8] The full cost of this establishment, including the household, the expenses of the council, and building work to the various royal residences and other houses in the Marches, ran at about £4500 per annum, and it was not long before a reappraisal was felt to be necessary.

In February 1528 a number of gentlemen and yeomen were sent home 'to renew their attendance upon her grace at a future warning', because the diets were felt to be running at an unreasonable level. On 3 May Voysey wrote anxiously to Lord Ferrers about the difficulty of protecting Mary against infection in view of the number of suitors to the council who thronged her court, and shortly thereafter the whole project seems to have been abandoned. By the summer the princess, whose movements are very difficult to track at this point, had apparently moved back to the Home Counties. Lord Ferrers had been replaced as steward by Henry Jerningham, and the whole household had presumably been reduced from viceregal magnificence to the rather more modest proportions which it still retained five years later. The council continued to function, but Voysey was not a particularly effective president, and after his authority had been shaken by the conspiracy of Rhys ap Griffith in 1531 he was replaced by the tougher Rowland Lee. Whether Mary's 'recall' had anything to do with the development of the king's 'great matter' is impossible to determine. Probably the true causes were much less dramatic. The gesture had made its point.

[7] Dowling, *Humanism in the Age of Henry VIII*, 227.

[8] It does not seem at all certain that Dorset's appointment ever took effect. *L&P*, IV, 2331; ibid., Addenda, 458. Denys was Wolsey's servant, and chamberlain of his household during his visit to France in 1527. Ibid., IV, 3216.

As a working body the council had never had any need of the princess's presence, and her stately establishment was unnecessarily expensive. Nevertheless, the fact that the king had begun to explore the third of his possible options cast a haze of doubt over the prospects of both Mary and Henry Fitzroy, and perhaps suggested that a dimming of their splendour was in the best interest of his freedom of action.

Mary's life during the two and a half years which she spent mostly in the Marches, can only be very imperfectly reconstructed. The instructions originally issued in July 1525 were sufficiently explicit, but in no way remarkable. The countess of Salisbury 'according to the singular confidence that the king's highness hath in her' was to oversee the princess's moral and academic education:

> That is to say at due tymes to serve God, from whom all grace and goodness proceedeth. Semblably at seasons convenient to use moderate exercise for taking open air in gardens, sweet and wholesome places and walkes which may confer unto her health, solace and comfort . . . And likewise to pass her tyme most seasons at her virginals or other instruments musical, so that the same be not too much and without fatigation or weariness. To intend to her learning of latin tongue or French. At other seasons to drawe [and to take great care with her diet and personal cleanliness].[9]

Richard Fetherstone, her schoolmaster, was a noted scholar, and one in whose skill and integrity both Henry and Catherine had confidence. At the end of July, just before she set off, Mary received a letter from her mother, urging her to diligence in her lessons. 'As for your writing, I am glad ye shall change from me to Master Fetherstone, for that shall do you much good.' Although she would be too far away for part-time supervision, Catherine still intended to keep an eye on this vital aspect of her daughter's development, particularly her skill in Latin. This application on both sides was apparently rewarded, for it was during her residence in the Marches, in 1527 when she was twelve years old, that Mary translated into English that prayer of St Thomas Aquinas which later earned her such praise from Lord Morley.[10] In 1529 Erasmus was to testify that she also wrote

[9] BL Cotton MS Vitellius C.i., f.23.

[10] BL Royal MS 17 C. xvi; Add. MS 17012. Dowling, *Humanism in the Age of Henry VIII*, 228 and n.

'fine latin epistles', but this was probably based on hearsay and referred to the formal exercises which her mother had asked to see. The competence of Mary's instruction in good humanist Latin, and her aptitude for it, are well attested, although none of her own writings from this period survive. The other language upon which much stress was laid was French, and her tutor for this purpose was Giles Duwes, one of the gentlemen waiters of her chamber and a former royal librarian. Duwes subsequently published a French grammar and conversation manual based on his experience during this service, which features the princess in a number of dialogues about piety, philosophy, courtly love and household management. If his *Introductory* is a fair reflection of his skill, then he had a light touch, a lively imagination, and a sense of humour. French was a common aristocratic accomplishment, but was no longer generally spoken at court, and if Duwes's somewhat tongue-in-cheek comments are to be trusted, not heard at all in the Marches of Wales outside his own classroom.

The evidence for Mary's educational progress during these formative years is mainly circumstantial, and not entirely consistent. When she was appraised by another French embassy in May 1527, they reported that she spoke to them in good French and Latin, and played the harpsichord skilfully. By other visitors she was variously described as speaking Italian, and as understanding it but not speaking it; and there is similar uncertainty about the level of her skill in Spanish. The Greek recommended by Vives does not seem to have been attempted, and is referred to only once, in a much later encomium. Probably she was never taught either Italian or Spanish in any formal sense, but picked up a working knowledge from her mother and her mother's servants. A Mary Fernando, who may have been a kinswoman of the queen's long-serving physician, was among Mary's attendants in 1525, and later on, when secrecy was needed, Catherine was to write to her daughter in Spanish. However, there is no conclusive evidence that she ever spoke it fluently. Music was always her most conspicuous accomplishment, and the lute, harpsichord and virginals are all mentioned at various times in accounts of her skills. Whether she ever made any progress with the drawing mentioned in the governess's instructions is not apparent, but at some point during all this pious and purposeful activity, she must also have acquired the taste for bowls, card games and the casting of dice which feature so frequently in the surviving chamber accounts of her later years.

It is hard to imagine Vives approving of such frivolity, and this too was probably picked up from her servants when the governess was otherwise engaged.

Around this nurtured but isolated little girl, the great household revolved in ordered hierarchy. At 'principal seasons, when there shalbe access or recourse of noblemen or other strangers repayring unto the Courte', then 'all the principal officers and ministers of the Chamber' were to be in continual attendance. But on other days, when the ceremony was less pressing, a proportion were permitted to 'take some honest solace' near at hand, provided that they were within call if needed. The minimum daily attendance was to consist of 'ii gentlemen ushers, ii yeomen ushers, xii yeomen and ii gromes', organized in shifts by the chamberlain or vice-chamberlain 'with condign punishment of such as shall offend'. Similarly the steward, treasurer and controller were to take care that 'all gross empiracions and provisions may be politiquely and profitably made' and the service of the hall and chambers 'in due manner ordered'. The almoner was to see that all broken meats were distributed to the poor, and that beggars and sturdy vagabonds were 'punished and avoided'. The instructions did not differ in substance from those governing the royal household itself, and their purpose was the same. In addition to her natural person, Mary was for the time being also a political person, representing the authority and magnificence of her royal father, and no item of order or protocol could be neglected. Even her dietary scheme was laid down in minute detail, with five different grades of menu served at every meal.[11] The princess herself could be offered anything up to thirty-five dishes in the two courses of her dinner. Her major officers, the lord president of the council, chamberlain, steward etc. chose from a maximum of about twenty-five. Lesser officers, such as the cofferer and clerk controller, received twenty; the ladies and gentlemen of the chamber fifteen, and the rest ten. The number of dishes, and their nature, varied from one season of the year to another, but the carefully graded hierarchy remained the same. This had nothing at all to do with the dietary needs of a nine-year-old girl, and everything to do with protocol and courtly etiquette.

Mary used a number of different residences during her 'tour of

[11] BL Cotton Charter XIV, f.8.

duty' in the Marches. Ludlow was the main base of the council and substantial sums were spent on refurbishing the castle as a viceregal palace, but it was far from being her permanent headquarters. Thornbury, the duke of Buckingham's former seat near Bristol was also used, as was Tickenhill in Shropshire, and Hartlebury, near Bromsgrove in Worcestershire. The princess also made her own progresses; on one occasion as far as Coventry, and in September 1526 via Tewkesbury to Langley in Oxfordshire, to rendezvous with her father. Henry was coming up from Winchester, and had originally intended to meet his daughter at Woodstock, which was one of his favourite lodges, but rumours of plague caused the 'geistes' to be hastily reorganized. The king reached Langley on 1 September, and the princess on the 3rd 'well accompanied with a goodly number of persons of gravity', as Richard Sampson noted approvingly.[12] Together they then travelled by easy stages, via Bicester and Buckingham to Ampthill. On 1 October Mary took her leave and returned to the west. In addition to this carefully planned encounter, the princess visited her father's court on a number of occasions during this period. The original plan seems to have been for her to pay the first such visit at Christmas 1525, but at some time during the autumn the plan was changed, and Voysey wrote anxiously to Wolsey for advice on the protocol of so great a feast in the context of the Marches.[13] In early May 1526 she was at Greenwich, where her attendance at a great banquet in 'the gallery within the tiltyard' is recorded, but it is not known how long she stayed. During the autumn of the same year negotiations were resumed for a French marriage, and by April 1527 were far enough advanced for Mary to be summoned back to court for a further inspection. This took place on St George's Day, again at Greenwich, and in addition to the usual praise of her accomplishments produced the sober judgement that she was 'so thin, spare and small as to make it impossible to be married for the next three years'. She was eleven, and the minimum age of cohabitation was twelve, so the comment was a pointed one. Her aunt Margaret had gone to Scotland to marry

[12] *L&P*, IV, 2407, 2452. Her visit to Coventry is recorded in the city annals, which also mention the gift of £100 and a kerchief. R. W. Ingram, ed., *Records of Early English Drama, Coventry* (1981), 125. I am indebted to Mr Neil Samman for this reference.

[13] 27 November 1525, *L&P*, IV, 1785.

James IV at that age, but Mary was an undergrown child. Two weeks later she was still at court, taking part in the masking and revels, and again we do not know the date of her departure.

Although quite a lot is known about her circumstances, and we have several descriptions of her appearance, the Mary who was emerging from childhood to adolescence during these years in the Marches of Wales is inaccessible as a personality. There are no stories about her, and no subsequent memoirs of youthful companions. The use of the word 'maidens' in a general description of her chamber establishment suggests that some at least of her gently born attendants may have been close to her in age, but there are no obvious candidates in the surviving lists. Her chief lady in 1525 may well have been an interesting companion, but for a quite different reason. She was none other than Catherine Douglas, daughter of the earl of Huntly, who had married Perkin Warbeck in her youth. Middle-aged by this time, and married to her third husband, Sir Matthew Craddock of Glamorgan, her career had been sufficiently chequered and unusual to make her company an education in itself, but there is no hint of her actual relationship with Mary.[14] Most of the other ladies had either served at court for some years, or were married to gentlemen of the household. The countess of Salisbury was not entrusted with the upbringing of the daughters of any other noble families, so as far as we know Mary continued during these years to be without the companionship of other girls of suitable age and social status.

Among the Stowe MSS in the British Library, there is a curious postscript to Mary's residence in the Marches. When her household was reduced during the summer of 1528, her superfluous servants were not simply dismissed, or transferred to other households. Some had already been sent home on full pay to await a subsequent recall which never came; others were apparently sent to neighbouring monasteries, with instructions that they should be employed and supported. On 9 November 1532 the king and the council (which was still known as the princess's council) wrote to the abbot of Bardesley, reminding him that he had at that time received one Humphrey Andrews 'until such time as [he] should be called to [his] service and

[14] BL Harleian MS 6807, f.3; *Dictionary of National Biography*, ed. Stephen Lee et al. (1885–1986).

attendance again'. 'And accordingly ye thereupon, as the said Humphrey saith, promised him meat and drink, with twenty shillings of wages and livery yearly.' Four years later Andrews complained that these promises had not been fulfilled, and the council ordered the abbot to remedy the situation forthwith.[15] As well as revealing a high-handed attitude towards religious houses, this episode suggests a lingering ambivalence with regard to Mary's role and status. Clearly, in 1528 the decision to bring the princess back from Wales was not regarded as final. By 1532 the progress of the king's 'great matter' had made her return a very remote possibility, but the council had received no instructions to bring the interim arrangements to an end.

On 17 March 1526 Francis I of France crossed the Bidassoa, and re-entered his kingdom after thirteen months of honourable but hazardous confinement.[16] He had signed a treaty with Charles V which he had no intention of observing – a dangerous gamble in view of the fact that he had been constrained to place both his sons in Imperial custody as pledges of his good faith. Wolsey had been preparing for this moment for several months, and in May 1526 his patient diplomacy aligned with Francis's incautious desire for revenge to produce the league of Cognac. England was not a party to this alliance, which consisted of France, the Papacy, Venice, Milan and Florence, because Wolsey's intention was to force Charles to moderate the terms of the treaty of Madrid; and he wanted (as usual) to be in a position to mediate. He also had a more effective plan for bringing England and France together than by membership of an ephemeral Italian league. On 31 May he confided to Gasparo Spinelli, the Venetian ambassador in London, that this consisted of a renewal of the marriage proposals dropped in 1522. The proposed bridegroom was now Henry, duke of Orleans, Francis's second son, a boy three years younger than Mary. He was not available in person, being inadvertently resident in Spain at the time, but in view of his tender years that scarcely mattered. Negotiations were proceeding firmly in that direction by July, when Spinelli reported that John Clerk, the bishop of Bath and Wells had been sent to France with instructions to that effect.

[15] BL Stowe MS 141, f.13.

[16] In September 1525 he had fallen so gravely ill that the physicians had given him up for lost. R. J. Knecht, *Francis I*, 187–8.

However, two months later the discussions were taking a quite different direction, and one that strongly indicates Henry's personal intervention. By September he was offering to join the league of Cognac, and to give up his ancient title to France, provided that Francis paid him a pension, ceded Boulogne and married Mary himself.[17] This last suggestion, although somewhat grotesque, considering that Francis was only two years younger than Henry himself, and a notorious lecher, made sound political sense from the English point of view. Francis had been a widower since 1524, and his health appeared to have been seriously undermined by his months of captivity. If he predeceased Henry, leaving children by Mary, the English and French successions would be separated, since he already had two sons. If Henry died first, then Francis would claim England in right of his wife, but his reign would probably be brief, and thereafter the two countries would again go their separate ways. In a sense Henry was gambling on his own life, but there is no reason to suppose that he was not serious in making the suggestion.

At first Francis was sceptical, believing that the main point of the proposal was the securing of Boulogne, but by November he was changing his position. Clerk reported that he was 'much minded' to the match, and by the end of December, when Henry had decided to drop the Boulogne demand, well-informed opinion in France thought that the marriage would take place. The main argument against it was that Francis was contracted by the terms of the treaty of Madrid to marry the emperor's sister Eleanor, the widowed queen of Portugal. Therein lay both the difficulty and the temptation of the English match, so the negotiations continued through the early months of 1527. The pope was reported to be much in favour, an opinion which may have been considerably influenced by a judicious gift of 30,000 crowns from Henry in mid-January. On the other hand Wolsey felt constrained to insist that Mary could not be handed over until she was of full age – a judgement which the French envoys admitted to be fully justified when they saw the princess for themselves in April. Consequently, when an agreement was finally signed on 30 April, the options were left open, but the main emphasis had returned to the duke of Orleans. Wolsey was

[17] Gasparo Spinelli to the signory, 11 September 1526; *Cal. Ven.*, III, 1406.

anxious to ensure that the boy should come to live in England (once he was retrieved from Spain) 'and become popular there', in order to reassure the English that this Valois prince would be their own king.[18] However, when the treaty of Amiens was concluded on 18 August, no such stipulation was made. By then the world had been changed by two momentous events. On 6 May a mutinous Imperial army had sacked the city of Rome and imprisoned the pope, a dramatic event which horrified Europe and put an end to any likelihood of English involvement in an anti-Imperial war. Also a few weeks later, during July, the first reports began to circulate that the king of England intended to repudiate his wife. These rumours, and the doubt which they aroused over Mary's legitimacy, did not prevent the marriage treaty from being ratified, but they did make it impossible for Wolsey to play a strong hand, and made the eventual implementation of the treaty extremely dubious. The security of Mary's early years had come to an end, and both her status and her function were matters of uncertainty and debate.

When she returned from the Marches in the summer of 1528, Mary disappeared into relative obscurity. In mid-May she was at Greenwich, and was reported to be suffering from smallpox. At the beginning of October Luis Vives returned to England, at Catherine's instigation, ostensibly to teach her Latin. If he ever took up such a charge at all it can only have been for a very brief period, because by November he was in trouble with the council for advising Catherine on the subject of her marriage. His intervention pleased neither Wolsey nor the queen herself, and shortly after he left, having accomplished nothing. The summer progress and all the other activities of the court were disrupted by the sweating sickness; only Wolsey stuck grimly to his diplomatic task, attempting to find some leverage against Imperial influence in a papal *Curia* still shaken and intimidated by the sack of Rome. It must have been a tense and difficult summer for all the leading actors in the unfolding drama. Anne Boleyn, who had succeeded her sister in the king's affection, and was obviously the intended beneficiary of the annulment, was seriously ill of the sweat in June, a circumstance which caused Henry grave concern – but not grave enough for him to run the risk of joining

[18] Wolsey had expressed this view at the outset of the negotiation. *Cal. Ven.*, III, 1297.

her. Anne at this stage was still confident of Wolsey's ability to secure the king's release, and maintained a delicate relationship with the cardinal. 'As for the coming of the Legate' she wrote, 'I desire that much, and if it be God's pleasure, I pray him to send this matter shortly to a good end, and then I trust, my Lord, to recompence part of your great pains.'[19] Having a much clearer perception of the difficulties in which he was enmeshed, and few illusions about the consequences of failure, Wolsey responded by exercising his professional charms upon her – graceful compliments, and 'rich and goodly presents'. Meanwhile the queen was entering a curious limbo. She was often present at court, and accompanied the king in public, but was personally and politically isolated. Although her nephew's formidable support protected her interests in Rome, only the Imperial ambassador, Inigo de Mendoza, could occasionally reassure her of the effectiveness of that support. In her daily life she fell back increasingly upon the company and consolation of her remaining Spanish servants, and began to detach herself from the English context in which she had been immersed for almost thirty years.[20] Mary, under the watchful eyes of Richard Fetherstone and the countess of Salisbury, pursued her studies and was protected as far as possible, both from the sweating sickness and from her mother's troubles. As an intelligent thirteen-year-old, she must have had some notion of what was afoot, but we have no direct evidence of her reaction, and it does not seem to have affected her material well-being in any way at all.

The king's 'great matter' has been frequently and thoroughly discussed, and the canonical intricacies of the case need not concern us here.[21] It is, however, important to appreciate that Catherine's position was not quite as reasonable and blameless as is usually assumed. The morality of Henry's relationship with Anne Boleyn was a complicating factor, but the real issue was the succession, and Catherine either could not or would not see the difficulty of the king's position. Unless he had more legitimate children the realm was very likely to fall into foreign hands, either through Mary's marriage or through her death and

[19] G. Burnet, *History of the Reformation* (1688–1714), I, 104; E. W. Ives, *Anne Boleyn*, 133.

[20] Mattingly, *Catherine of Aragon*, 185, 201.

[21] See J. J. Scarisbrick, *Henry VIII*, 163–98; G. de C. Parmiter, *The King's Great Matter*; H. A. Kelly, *The Matrimonial Trials of Henry VIII*.

the succession of the king of Scots. An honourable retreat was available to her, because if she had taken the veil her marriage could have been automatically dissolved, without reference to its original validity.[22] Such a possibility may have been suggested at any time after 1521, and declined, but there is no evidence that it was. Instead, either Wolsey or Henry was guilty of a grievous error of judgement in deciding to seek an annulment on grounds of consanguinity, the so-called 'Levitical prohibition'. The error was compounded by feeble attempts at secrecy, and finally by a clumsy confrontation in July 1527 in which Henry attempted to justify himself in terms of learned opinion. In the circumstances, the queen's reaction was completely predictable. She knew that doubt had been cast upon her marriage when it was first contracted, but not only did she have complete faith in the efficacy of the pope's dispensation, her own conscience was perfectly clear. Her marriage had been effected by the mysterious providence of God in recompense of her faith and constancy. To call it in question again was not only an outrage to her own honour, it was also a form of blasphemy. Within a few weeks of her disastrous interview with the king, Catherine sent one of her Spanish servants, Francisco Felipez, post-haste to the emperor of Valladolid, and Charles reacted with unwonted promptness. He was not particularly fond of his aunt, whom he had met only once, but family honour and political interest pointed in the same direction. With Mary already contracted to the duke of Orleans, if Henry should become free to marry again his ties with France might well be strengthened. Wolsey was actually in France for that purpose at the time when Charles received the queen's message. He therefore sent a personal expostulation to Henry, and instructed his agents in Rome to block any move which the English might make to obtain a canonical annulment. For reasons which we have already noticed, his word was law in the *Curia* in the summer of 1527, and it appeared that the king's attempt to dissolve his marriage had been aborted almost before it began.

Unfortunately for the prospect of a negotiated settlement, Henry's conscience was just as committed as Catherine's. Contemporary and subsequent accounts of his manœuvres which

[22] The canon law on this was not entirely clear, but it was an acceptable canonical proposition, and in the circumstances would almost certainly have sufficed. Scarisbrick, *Henry VIII*, 214 and n.

represent them as a mere vulgar intrigue to secure the woman of his choice are very much beside the point. Henry knew that his marriage was unlawful, and that was why God had refused to bestow upon Catherine the healthy son whom he had successfully begotten upon Elizabeth Blount. He knew that it was the Levitical prohibition which he had broken, and therefore Wolsey's hopeful and highly relevant suggestion, that if Catherine's marriage to Arthur had never been consummated then the original dispensation was incomplete, was not followed up. If Henry had deliberately chosen to make his course as difficult and dangerous as possible, he could not have gone about it more effectively. Royal marriages had been annulled in the past for political reasons and upon trivial pretexts; they would also be so annulled in the future; but Henry had chosen to fight upon an important issue of canonical principle, which would not have been readily conceded even if the political obstacles had been less formidable. It was his commitment to Leviticus which prevented his acceptance of Catherine's repeated assertion that she had come to him as a virgin. Similarly, if Leviticus was the word of God, and could not be dispensed by the pope, then Julius II had acted *ultra vires*, a proposition which no subsequent pope was going to accept lightly. In England reactions to the news of the king's proceedings were illogical, but entirely predictable. Those same gentlemen, citizens and artisans who would have complained bitterly and threatened rebellion at the prospect of a French or Scottish king were loudest in their professions of outrage. How could Henry discard his virtuous and noble queen of eighteen years, and bastardize his innocent and hopeful daughter?[23] Surely the wrath of God would light upon him for such conduct! The blame was laid, particularly by women, on 'that whore Nan Bullen' and upon the unpopular Wolsey. Catherine was genuinely popular, partly because of the conscientious manner in which she had carried out most of her royal duties, and partly because of her exemplary piety. At a time when the public observance of religious duties by the king was judged to be an essential element in attracting divine favour to the realm, Catherine had greatly enhanced her husband's reputation. There was consequently a general unwillingness to believe

[23] *Cal. Span.*, IV, 27; Mattingly, 184. Leviticus (20:21) forbade a man to marry his deceased brother's wife.

that her marriage had been offensive to God, in spite of her frequent misfortunes in child-bearing. Moreover, Mary was a living proof that the king's allegations were unfounded. Leviticus pronounced a sentence of childlessness against the guilty couple; it was Henry's selective interpretation which applied this to the absence of a son.[24]

In spite of his underlying political objectives, the king's case did not look any stronger in England than it did in Italy, and his strenuous efforts to recruit learned support were largely a waste of time and effort. It was never very likely that Clement VII would genuinely accept the validity of his arguments. On the other hand there were shifts and changes in the political circumstances which offered occasional opportunities. After his escape to Orvieto early in December 1527, Clement was temporarily free from Imperial supervision, and quite willing to obtain some small revenge upon the authority which had subjected him to such humiliation. A generous and timely offer of financial support might have been the only inducement required, but the chance was unexpected and no advantage was taken of it. At the same time the pressure being mounted by the league of Cognac for the release of Francis I's sons might bring the emperor to a wider settlement, and, as a contribution to that objective, England delivered a formal declaration of war at Burgos on 21 January 1528. By March Wolsey was hopeful of a general peace, which might have persuaded Charles to give the pope a free hand in the resolution of Henry's marriage – but his hopes were deceived, and English involvement in the war remained only on paper. Throughout the summer of 1528 Wolsey and his various agents in Rome, John Clerk, Edward Fox and Stephen Gardiner, pursued a definitive solution to the king's cause like a will-o'-the-wisp. What he eventually gained was a joint commission, along with cardinal Lorenzo Campeggio, the protector of England, to try the case in England, and a verbal understanding that the pope would confirm the verdict. When Campeggio eventually arrived in London, on 9 October, he quickly discovered two things: first that the king was utterly and passionately convinced of the rightness of his cause, 'an angel from heaven could not dissuade him'; and second that the political pressure for a

[24] Henry seems to have been convinced by the humanist Robert Wakefield that the original Hebrew said 'without sons' rather than 'without children'. E. Surtz and V. Murphy, eds., *The Divorce Tracts of Henry VIII*, xiii.

decision was overwhelming. If Henry did not get what he wanted, not only would Wolsey's position be destroyed, but the authority of the papacy in England would be destroyed as well.[25] Whether Campeggio took these representations seriously or not, we do not know. Even if he did, there was little he could do to respond to them, since his own instructions were to play for time, and in no circumstances to come to a decision. In fact Campeggio was little more than the victim of Clement's duplicity and his urgent desire to escape from English importunity.

Both Henry and Catherine expected the issue to be joined publicly once Campeggio had arrived, and the queen justifiably believed herself to be at a crippling disadvantage. In spite of Mendoza's honest efforts, she could obtain no proper legal advice. Of her English friends and counsellors, only John Fisher was willing to take her part in public, and he could offer little at this stage beyond encouragement. But both sides were framing their expectations in ignorance of Campeggio's instructions, and his first effort was to find a solution which would not involve the implementation of his commission. He suggested that Catherine should take the veil. This would give Henry what he wanted without offending Habsburg family sensibilities, and without affecting Mary's legitimacy, or her claim to the throne in default of further heirs. Henry was enthusiastic. He had no real desire to disinherit his daughter, and was fully convinced of his ability to beget healthy children upon a new wife. Unfortunately, the proposal came too late for Catherine to be able to accept it without losing face, and the king made the situation worse by blustering and threatening force. The only solution which could have avoided an open conflict was consequently refused, and at the same time the queen demonstrated that it was not primarily concern for Mary's rights and status which motivated her. Catherine's defence of her marriage was a personal statement of her own integrity and faith – innocent of political content, and consequently not accessible to compromise. Henry was a bully, and as blind to the legal and moral strength of Catherine's case as she was to the political imperative of his, but he was not the ruthless tyrant of catholic and Imperialist myth. Not only did he permit the queen to name her own counsel, he allowed her to

[25] Stefan Ehses, *Romische Dokumente zur Geschichte der Ehescheidung Heinrichs VIII von England* (Paderborn, 1893), 54; Scarisbrick, *Henry VIII*, 213.

recruit a formidable team, led by Warham, Tunstall and Fisher. Her Spanish confessor, George Athequa, the bishop of Llandaff, was also permitted to serve, and several of these men distinguished themselves in her defence, both when the legatine court finally assembled at Blackfriars, and also subsequently in print.

By November 1528 Wolsey was clearly aware that the king had chosen his ground badly, and could see no hope in a formal judicial procedure. Either the pope must exercise his plenitude of power to make a political ruling on Henry's behalf, or there was a real risk that the papal authority in England would be destroyed. 'I close my eyes before such horror . . . I throw myself at the Holy Father's feet . . . I beg him to look on his royal majesty's holy and unchangeable desire', he wrote.[26] Henry would not be deflected from his purpose, and the irresistible force was about to collide with the immovable matter. As Professor Scarisbrick has observed, to have succeeded the king's cause would have required flawless management and great good fortune – neither of which it received.[27] Wolsey did his best, but Henry's personal intervention handicapped him, and with the exception of Stephen Gardiner his agents in Rome were not up to their formidable task. The emperor's personal interest in the case, the strength of his political and military position in the early part of 1529, and the diplomatic talent at his disposal lengthened the odds still further. Far from being a friendless victim, Catherine held all the best cards by the time that Wolsey and Campeggio opened their court on 18 June. Within two weeks she had inflicted a decisive and humiliating defeat upon the king by appealing to Rome, and having her case revoked to the Rota where a judgement in her favour was a foregone conclusion. The queen's personal courage was impeccable. She had resisted all attempts at intimidation and blandishment, and in the process had created an explosive situation which put the authority of the English Crown to a searching and unexpected test. For the time being, the real nature of this crisis was concealed by Henry's search for a scapegoat, which resulted in the dramatic fall of Cardinal Wolsey, but it remained close beneath the surface, and was not to be finally resolved until 1537. Wolsey's fall was occasioned by his failure to obtain a

[26] *L&P*, IV, 4897; Scarisbrick, *Henry VIII*, 216.
[27] Scarisbrick, *Henry VIII*, 227.

favourable verdict from the legatine court, but the underlying reasons were deeper, and of longer standing. To some extent he was the victim of his own success, and presumed upon his relationship with the king in a manner which Henry had come to resent; but more important, he had offended the great aristocracy by monopolizing the power to which they aspired.

The upsurge of jealousy and intrigue which finally poisoned the king's mind against his long-serving chancellor, also had the somewhat paradoxical effect of weakening the political position of the queen, even as she scored her judicial triumph. Ostensibly, Wolsey had fallen, not for attacking Catherine's marriage, but for failing to attack it effectively. Consequently the great nobles who had engineered that fall, particularly the dukes of Norfolk and Suffolk, found themselves inexorably committed to upholding the king's 'scruple', and supporting his search for a new marriage to Anne Boleyn. Catherine and Wolsey were old adversaries, but Anne was the third corner of a triangle, opposed to both. If we are to believe George Cavendish, Wolsey's gentleman usher, Anne had begun her relationship with the king as an aristocratic cat's-paw against the cardinal.[28] This seems to have been the opinion of long hindsight, because as late as the summer of 1528 she was still relying upon him to make the king available to her. But by the autumn of 1529, when that hope had failed, she was his enemy, and took her advantage along with the rest. So Wolsey was hated by the nobility for his power over the king, and by Anne Boleyn for his lack of power over the pope. At the same time he was widely unpopular with ordinary people, particularly in London, for promoting the king's annulment suit at all, and was commonly blamed for having initiated it. His failure and fall consequently left Henry and Anne in direct and explicit conflict with Catherine, and exposed those who might be inclined to take the queen's side to the perils of high treason. By the end of 1529 Anne's influence over the king was as unchallengeable as Wolsey's had once been. The French ambassador, du Bellay, reported, 'The Duke of Norfolk is made chief of the council, and in his absence the Duke of Suffolk, and above everyone Mademoiselle Anne.' Her father was created earl of Wiltshire on 8 December, and bore himself with a high

[28] George Cavendish, *The Life and Death of Cardinal Wolsey* in *Two Early Tudor Lives,* ed. R. S. Sylvester and D. P. Harding, 38.

hand; her brother George was sent as ambassador to France. A new regime had been created, which placed power in the hands of the Boleyns and their allies – stifling Wolsey's last hopes of rehabilitation, and leaving Catherine without any effective political support.

Her victory had been decisive, but purely negative. She could remain Henry's wife in the eyes of the law and the Church, but she could not compel him to treat her as such. On the same day that Thomas Boleyn became earl of Wiltshire, his allies George Hastings and Robert Radcliffe were created earls of Huntingdon and Sussex. As he had done before, Henry signalled a change of policy with a distribution of honours; and on the following day there was a grand celebration, attended by the entire court, over which Anne presided at the king's side. Nevertheless, a remarkable feature of the next two years was to be the king's failure to take decisive action against Catherine, and his apparent inability to resolve the intolerable situation of having an official and unofficial queen. Her household and her formal dignity were undiminished; she spent long periods at court, dined with the king in public, and celebrated major festivals with him, including Christmas 1529. Inevitably, Henry found himself reproached from both sides. Dining with Catherine on 1 November, he was taxed with neglect, and informed that his case in canon law was hopeless. Taking refuge with Anne, he was greeted with a passionate tirade:

> Did I not tell you that whenever you disputed with the queen she was sure to have the upper hand? I see that some fine morning you will succumb to her reasoning, and that you will cast me off. I have been waiting long and might in the meanwhile have contracted some advantageous marriage ... But alas! Farewell to my time and youth spent to no purpose at all.[29]

Caught between two such tough and determined women, the king appeared vacillating and often somewhat ridiculous. On the one hand he was in love with Anne, and frequently infuriated by Catherine's self-righteousness and propensity to martyrdom. On the other hand he had a scrupulous, almost obsessive, respect for the forms of law, and in spite of occasional outbursts, had not yet seriously thought of taking the law into his own hands. Little as

[29] Ives, *Anne Boleyn*, 154.

he might like it, the law still meant appeal to Rome, and a mixture of ingenious argument with whatever political pressure he could bring to bear. For the time being there seemed little prospect of the latter. The peace of Cambrai in August 1529 had temporarily brought to an end the war which Wolsey had hoped to use for such a purpose, leaving the emperor in the ascendant. Given the relationship between Charles and Catherine, the Boleyn faction was bound to be pro-French, but the hopes which were to be placed in French pressure on the *Curia* to resolve the king's 'great matter' were exaggerated and misplaced. When Francis again needed an ally against the emperor, the pope was likely to be more useful than the king of England.

It was to be over two years before any significant change took place in this situation – two years of restless political activity, endless frustration and periodic personal crisis. Inevitably the coalition which had removed Wolsey broke up, and as the Boleyns began to make enemies at court, the queen's political isolation lessened. By 1530 the duke of Suffolk was expressing serious reservations about the whole annulment project, and the duke of Norfolk might have followed suit if his wife (with whom he was on very bad terms) had not emerged as an ardent partisan of Catherine. John Fisher cautiously published his *De causa matrimonii serenissimi Regis Angliae* in Alcala, but by the spring of 1531 even court preachers were beginning to urge the king to think again. Leading courtiers such as Sir Henry Guildford and Sir William Fitzwilliam were talking behind the scenes about the need to 'unseat the king from his folly', and the council discussed the possibility of an Imperial trade embargo with grave and justified alarm.[30] One of the reasons for this shift was Anne Boleyn's personal unpopularity. That same strength of character which captivated Henry alienated his friends, and reminded them of her relatively humble origins. Another was the subtle and persuasive skill of the Imperial ambassador, Eustace Chapuys. Chapuys, a Savoyard gentleman and one of the most professional diplomats of his generation, had arrived in August 1529, with instructions to protect the queen's interests, and, if possible, to break up Henry's relationship with Anne. Everyone who disliked the Boleyns, or feared the consequences of a rupture with the emperor, talked to Chapuys, whose meticulous

[30] *Cal. Span.*, IV, 177; Ives, *Anne Boleyn*, 172–3.

dispatches over the next seven years constitute the largest single source collection available to the historian of the period. Unfortunately, his commitment to Catherine, and later to Mary, coloured Chapuys's observations, and distorted his judgement, so that he consistently exaggerated both Henry's maltreatment of his wife and the weight of her political support. Nor could all the ambassador's threats and blandishments alter the underlying situation – that both Henry and England needed a male heir.

A further crisis was reached at the end of May 1531. All the king's diplomacy had achieved in Rome was a postponement of the sentence against him – a delay which angered both Catherine and Anne, but which suited the emperor's ambivalent position to perfection. He was willing to give the queen verbal and diplomatic support, but most unwilling to get involved in conflict with Henry. Chapuys misled him into believing that the English themselves would rebel in Catherine's favour, and such an outcome would have pleased him well enough, so delay and frustration had much to commend them. However, early in 1531 it began to appear likely that the revocation of the case to the Rota, decreed in July 1529, would be implemented, and that Henry would be summoned to appear in Rome. On 31 May a final attempt was made to persuade the queen to give way. She received a delegation of some thirty councillors and others in her privy chamber at Greenwich, listened courteously to their pleas on behalf of the king and the realm, and made her habitual reply:

> I say I am his lawfull wyfe, and to hym lawfully maryed and by the ordre of holye Churche I was to hym espowsed as his true wyfe, although I was not so worthy, and in that poynte I will abyde tyll thecowtre of Rome which was prevy to the begynnyng have made therof a determinacion and finall endyng.

As Garrett Mattingly observed, they might as well have been talking to Castilian limestone.[31] On receipt of this news, Henry went off on a prolonged hunting trip, either to think or to build up his courage for a decisive move, and Anne went with him. Catherine remained with the court at Windsor. On 14 July, shortly after rejoining the court, the king departed suddenly for

[31] Mattingly, *Catherine of Aragon*, 241.

Woodstock, leaving orders for the queen to remain where she was. When she sent him a message of complaint, he exploded with rage, declaring that he did not wish to see her again, or to receive any further letters. This was the end of the *ménage à trois*, and a victory for Anne. It also put an end to those lingering hopes of reconciliation which Catherine's friends in the court had persisted in harbouring. But it made no difference to the legal situation, and impartial observers like the Venetian Mario Savorgnano shared Chapuys's conviction that no annulment would take place, not only because of the likely judgement in Rome, but also because 'the peers of the realm, both spiritual and temporal, and the people are opposed to it'.[32] By the autumn of 1531 the queen was keeping her own court, undiminished in scale, and had become, perhaps unwillingly, a focus of political opposition. Henry's kingship was being put to the test. Whatever the rights and wrongs of the substantive issue, by the end of 1531, he had to destroy Catherine, or his own authority would be fatally impaired.

Throughout the period of the *ménage à trois*, Mary seems to have been a frequent and welcome visitor to the court. She was there at Christmas 1529, when the king made her a present of £20 'for to disporte her wt', and the Venetian ambassador's secretary noted that she had accompanied her father and mother to mass on 2 January. Similar presents of £10 or £20 appear at irregular intervals over the following two years in the privy purse accounts, but are kept in proportion by the much larger and more frequent sums expended on 'lady Anne'.[33] For the time being there was no serious talk of Mary's marriage. She was contracted to the duke of Orleans, and nothing had happened since 1528 to weaken Henry's pro-French orientation; but the marriage could not really be expected to take place until the duke attained the minimum canonical age, which would not be until 1533. In the autumn of 1529 the newly arrived Chapuys picked up a rumour that she was to be given to her half brother, the duke of Richmond. Such a horrific idea, he decided, could only have emanated from Anne Boleyn, but in fact it appears to have been a desperate suggestion by Clement VII, and was

[32] 25 August 1531; *Cal. Ven.*, IV, 682.

[33] *The Privy Purse Expenses of King Henry VIII*, ed. N. H. Nicholas, 13, 55, 70, 98, 127, 146, 148, 162, 183, 202, 221, 262, 281; for Anne, 222–3, 274–7; Ives, *Anne Boleyn*, 195.

never seriously considered. In the summer of 1530 she sent her father a buck, and her servants were suitably rewarded, but it was only in the autumn of that year, when she was fourteen and a half, that Mary began to reappear in the diplomatic correspondence. At the end of June a Milanese envoy, Augustino Scarpinello, arrived in London, and reported that 'the princess occupies herself with her very becoming studies in her usual residence' – which seems to have been Richmond. Her father visited her there at about the same time, but there were few interruptions to her tranquil routine. In November the emperor's agent in Rome reported that overtures were being made by the Milanese for a marriage between Mary and the duke, Francesco Sforza, which may explain Scarpinello's presence, but if such was his errand nothing came of it. He does not even seem to have seen the princess, because he reported from Hampton Court in mid-December that she was 'always apart, at a distance of ten or fifteen miles, with a suitable establishment, and is said to be already advanced in wisdom and stature'.

The early part of 1531 was something of an Indian summer to Mary's childhood. In March she visited her mother 'for five or six days', and they stayed together for nearly a month.[34] In June the king came to Richmond and 'made great cheer' with her. The previous Christmas she had spent at court as usual, and received the same £20 allowance as in the previous year. However, the shadows were now beginning to close about her. In February she was fifteen, and in early April, shortly after parting from her mother, she fell ill. Chapuys described the symptoms as stomach pains and sickness, and added 'from what her physician tells me, I expect she will be well again very soon'. Scarpinello, slightly franker, reported that she had been very ill 'from what the physicians call hysteria'. Three weeks later she was still not fully recovered from what was plainly a menstrual disorder of some kind. Whether this ordeal marked the onset of puberty, or a malfunction induced by the high and very obvious level of tension at that time between her mother and Anne Boleyn, is not clear. On 12 July Henry paid a certain Dr Bartelot £20 for his attendance upon her, in addition to the services of her own physician, which suggests that the matter was not regarded as

[34] Chapuys to Charles V, 8 March, 22 March, 2 April; *L&P*, v, 124, 148, 171.

routine. Also, as is commonly the case with more ordinary matrimonial breakdowns, Mary became a bone of contention between her parents. In May 1531, before the final breakdown of relations, when she and Henry were together at Greenwich, Catherine suggested that the princess should visit them. The king refused, and added bitterly that she could go to her daughter if she wished – and stay there. Yet in June he visited Mary himself, and in July, after he had banished Catherine from the court, he allowed her to go to her mother at Windsor, where they consoled themselves with hunting, and with visiting the other royal residences in the area.[35] The queen must have known that this apparent indulgence was deceptive, because she had already received a harsh and unambiguous message from Henry that he did not wish to see her again. She was ordered to retire to the More, and Mary to Richmond before he returned to Windsor. Catherine was to choose a permanent place of retirement, and was not to see her daughter again.

At this stage neither Henry nor his advisers knew what to do next, and he was inclined to ease his frustration by being abusive to the queen. However, it is important to distinguish between what he said and what he did. Since he had declared as early as 1527 that he did not regard her as his wife, it is remarkable that he did not dismiss her from the court until 1531. Indeed, an Italian visitor in 1530, who knew perfectly well what was going on, was amazed at their mutual courtesy and restraint in public, and considered their behaviour 'more than human'.[36] Similarly, when she was finally dismissed, according to Chapuys, Henry announced his intention to make drastic reductions to her household, but he does not appear to have done so. Another Italian, visiting the More at the end of August 1531, described her court as numbering 200, which included fifty chamber servants and thirty 'maids of honour' – which would have been a full complement for a queen consort. Catherine's behaviour at Christmas that year was a perfect example of her skill in exploiting her moral advantage, and goading the king into a kind of miserable frenzy. She had been exiled from the court, and forbidden to write to the king – so she sent him a lavish New Year gift!

[35] Chapuys to Charles V, 31 July 1531; *L&P*, v, 361.

[36] Augustino Scarpinello to the duke of Milan, 16 December 1530; *Cal. Ven.*, IV, 642.

Henry, who had sent her no gift, and had ordered his courtiers to ignore her, was reduced to embarrassing expedients to avoid receiving it. Even Edward Hall admitted that Christmas 1531 was miserable. Mary received her usual allowance, but was not at court, and Anne was not yet strong enough to take Catherine's place. At the same time the news from Rome was as bad as possible. All attempts to claim English immunity from certain types of papal jurisdiction (including matrimony) had been met with incredulous rejection, and it could only be a matter of time before definitive sentence was given against the king.

In theory, Mary's relations with her father remained unchanged, but in practice she must already have been committed to her mother's side of the dispute. We have no direct evidence of her attitude to Anne Boleyn (or to anyone else) at this time, but Chapuys was probably right in describing it as hostile. In April 1531, when she was recovering from illness, the princess requested permission to visit her parents at Greenwich, which was refused 'to gratify to lady [Anne], who hates her as much as the queen, or more so because she sees the king has some affection for her'. At Christmas she received a much larger gift than Anne. That probably had more to do with protocol than affection, but several warrants to Lord Windsor, the master of the great wardrobe, to supply cloth and liveries to her household suggest that her normal requirements were being generously met. In November the question of her marriage was raised again. Francis I was now angling for a match between the duke of Orleans and the pope's niece, Catherine de' Medici, and Henry, who scented an advantage for himself, did not attempt to insist upon the four-year-old treaty of Amiens. Consequently Mary was available again, and the chamberlain of the duke of Cleves arrived in London to solicit her for his master's son. In January 1532 Chapuys thought the match a possibility, but nothing came of the initiative. Her dubious status and political position must have made the princess less attractive as a partner, although she was by this time of marriageable age; not very tall, according to a contemporary description, but pretty and well proportioned, with a very beautiful complexion.[37] In fact Mary was not very high in anyone's priorities, except her mother's, to whom she

[37] Mario Savorgnano, 25 August 1531; *Cal. Ven.*, IV, 682. There is no portrait of her as early as this.

represented an emotional lifeline. Forbidden to meet, they seem to have corresponded regularly by means of loyal and discreet servants. If Henry had seriously intended to negate Catherine's influence over his daughter, he had certainly not gone about it very thoroughly or efficiently.

By this time the Roman *Curia* was beginning to take the possibility of some desperate and irresponsible action by the king of England seriously. As early as November 1530 Rodrigo Niño had reported to the emperor that he feared Henry would obtain his annulment *de facto* from the bishops of his own kingdom, rather than continue to litigate in the Rota. His own agents were threatening as much, but it was difficult to know how much was bluff, and they probably did not know themselves.[38] On 25 January 1532 another Imperial agent, Dr Ortiz, reported that the pope had prepared a bull of excommunication against Henry, but for the time being intended it only as a threat. Should the king of England have a son by 'this Anna', he went on 'it is to be feared he will attempt some greater iniquity', and it would be better if the queen and the princess could be got out of his power. Charles did not take the hint, but Ortiz had struck a note which was to recur frequently in Imperialist correspondence over the next few years. However, those who anticipated personal violence did Henry an injustice; what he and his advisers had in mind was a great deal more original and far-reaching. The ingredients of this new policy had been assembled piecemeal. Some had come from William Tyndale's *The obedyence of a Chrysten man*, published in 1528 and 'discovered' by Anne herself. Some had come from the 1531 edition of Christopher St German's 'Doctor and Student' dialogues; and some from Edward Fox's 'Collectanaea satis copiosa', which was in Henry's hands before the end of 1530.[39] The king had been using parliament to put pressure upon the English church since 1529, but the main intention at first seems to have been to compel Clement to come to the rescue by making concessions. If so, the policy was a failure, and a fresh mind was needed to give shape and direction to the ideas and ambitions which lay ready to

[38] *L&P*, IV, 6742.

[39] J. Guy, 'Thomas More and Christopher St. German: the battle of the books', and 'Thomas Cromwell and the intellectual origins of the Henrician Reformation' in *Reassessing the Henrician Age*, ed. J. Guy and A. Fox, 121–50, 151–78.

hand. That mind was provided by Thomas Cromwell, a former servant of Wolsey, who was recruited to the council during 1531. As late as October of that year no plan of action had been prepared, and the intended recall of parliament was postponed until January. The potential opposition to any overt attempt to settle the king's 'great matter' in parliament was very great, as the duke of Norfolk had already discovered when he raised the matter with a group of his supporters. Catherine's friends were powerful, particularly in the House of Lords. However, by January 1532 Cromwell had realized that, with the possible exception of Sir Thomas More, the lord chancellor, they were defending too narrow a front.

The 'Supplication against the Ordinaries' was an outflanking manœuvre. Exploiting the widespread and genuine dissatisfaction with the manner in which the clergy had gone about their recent campaign against heretics, it invited the king as 'the only sovereign lord, protector and defender' of both clergy and laity to legislate in parliament to 'establish not only those things which to your jurisdiction and prerogative royal justly appertaineth, but also reconcile and bring into perpetual unity your said subjects, spiritual and temporal'.[40] When asked for their comments, the clergy in convocation walked into a trap. Their response was framed by Stephen Gardiner as an unequivocal assertion of clerical independence: 'We your most humble subjects may not submit the execution of our charges and duty, certainly prescribed by God, to your highness's assent.' Henry exploded with rage, and on this issue the bulk of the laity in parliament supported him. Threatened with a statutory attack upon their privileges, or a large-scale renewal of the *praemunire* proceedings of 1530, the bishops gave way and agreed to surrender their legislative independence to the king. Sir Thomas More resigned the Great Seal, and at court the religious conservatives, including Stephen Gardiner, began to run for cover. Professor Scarisbrick was probably right when he argued, in his major study of the reign, that neither Henry nor Cromwell had planned this major coup simply for the purpose of outflanking the queen's supporters.[41] Nevertheless, it had that effect. Henry had been toying with *Caesaropapist* ideas for some time, and

[40] Ives, *Anne Boleyn*, 190.
[41] Scarisbrick, *Henry VIII*, 297–300.

might well have launched a jurisdictional attack upon the church sooner or later, even without Anne Boleyn's intervention, but the timing of the 'supplication' has to be seen in the context of the king's imminent defeat in the Rota. The ecclesiastical autonomy which had protected Catherine since 1527 had been decisively breached by subsuming the particular issue in the general, and by claiming that the Crown enjoyed an exclusive right to its subjects' allegiance.

By June 1532 it was clear that the surrender of the bishops was a decisive victory for the Boleyn faction. Thomas Audley replaced More as chancellor, and William Paulet became controller following the death of Anne's old enemy, Sir Henry Guildford. On 23 August Archbishop William Warham also died. Warham had been at Canterbury since 1503, and was a statesman bishop of the old school. Nevertheless, during the controversy over the 'Supplication' he had emerged as a principled opponent of royal encroachments, and his death was thus doubly convenient to the king. Not only did it reduce the risk of a stubborn episcopal rearguard action, it also opened the way for the appointment of a new metropolitan who would have no qualms about alleviating the pangs of Henry's conscience. Within a few weeks Thomas Cranmer, a man already publicly committed to the king's proceedings, had been nominated to succeed him. By August Henry was talking openly of marrying again, and planning to take Anne with him to his second rendezvous with Francis I, scheduled for October. Since there was no prospect of effecting his marriage before that date, the king decided to give Anne the status necessary for such an encounter in a different way. On 1 September he performed the unprecedented ceremony of creating her a peeress in her own right, as marquis of Pembroke, and settled upon her a landed income of £1000 a year.[42] There was nothing that Catherine could do about this sequence of events. Her defences were intact, and the righteousness of her cause recognized throughout Europe – even Martin Luther acknowledged it – but this was becoming increasingly irrelevant as the political situation in England unfolded. The armed truce which had lasted from 1527 to 1531 had now been replaced by cold war. When Henry

[42] No peeress had previously been created in her own right. Several women had inherited peerage titles, where the terms of creation so permitted, and the countess of Salisbury had been restored to such a title in 1513.

requested her jewels, she replied that it would be a sin on her part to allow them to adorn 'the scandal of Christendom'. It was not yet high treason to use such language, and Henry simply rephrased his request as an order, which was complied with.

If Anne was a scandal to the Imperialists, she was also something of an embarrassment to Francis I. For obvious reasons she and her supporters were ardently pro-French, but Francis was also angling for a papal alliance, and could not afford to upset that negotiation by receiving Anne on French soil as *de facto* queen. It was therefore agreed that the first meeting between the two monarchs, at Boulogne, would be a 'stag party'; only when Francis visited Calais for the second meeting would the ladies appear. Both meetings were amicable, and to that extent successful, but the strains created by the ambiguous position of the marquis of Pembroke were clearly visible. None of the ladies of his own family accompanied Francis to Calais, and Anne's companions and attendants were all of her own kin or faction. Henry could command a massive presence of his nobility and gentry, however unsympathetic some of them may have been to the Boleyns, but he seems to have been unable to command their wives and daughters. Nor, indeed, could he command his own daughter. One of the main objectives of the meetings had been propaganda, and within a few weeks of the king's return Wynkyn de Worde published *The maner of the tryumphe at Caleys and Bulleyn.* In a detailed description of the festivities, the second name in the list of ladies, after Anne herself, is 'my lady Mary'. The only Mary actually present was Anne's sister, who could not have claimed such a description – or such precedence. Either Cromwell had deliberately falsified the record in order to make it appear that Mary had countenanced the triumph of her mother's rival, or Henry had attempted to enforce her compliance and had failed. The return from Calais was disrupted by storms, and Henry and Anne spent over a week weatherbound in the Exchequer, the large and convenient house which was normally used for royal visits. It may have been during this period, while they were occupying interconnecting bedrooms, that Anne finally decided her prospects of marriage to be sufficiently assured for her to yield to the long frustrated passion of her royal lover.

By this time Catherine was almost as great an embarrassment to the emperor as Anne was to Francis. She wrote to him persistently, urging him to force the pope into deciding her case.

Henry VIII was as big a threat to the church as the Turkish infidel, she declared in September:

> Your Majesty knows that God gives the victory to those who do in his service works good and deserving of merit, and that among the most deserving is to try, as you have been doing, to end this case, which is no longer mine alone, but concerns all those who fear God.[43]

Eustace Chapuys was her enthusiastic and energetic friend, adding his pleas and predictions of disaster to hers, and writing direct to Charles's agents in Rome to the same effect. Neither the emperor nor the pope were much moved by this extravagance. Clement continued to believe in delay, and encouraged every initiative which seemed likely to spin the case out. Charles was keenly aware that the political balance in England had tilted decisively in favour of France, and would stay that way unless he could soften the intransigence of one or both of the parties. The pope did not need Chapuys to tell him what was going on in England. He had his own nuncio, Andrea del Borgho, at the English court, and Del Borgho understood the nature of his master's dilemma. By January 1533 the danger of England going into schism, if not outright heresy, was real and imminent. Catherine's moral and legal case was irrefutable, and her political support in Rome overwhelming. At the same time, a decision in her favour would precipitate the impending crisis with Henry. So Del Borgho withheld the brief which was already in his hands ordering the king to cease cohabiting with Anne and return to his lawful wife. Clement then made a mistake. He knew perfectly well that the archbishop designate, Thomas Cranmer, was a supporter of the king. Chapuys had also written to Dr Ortiz accusing him of being 'a servant of the concubine' (which he was not) and 'devoted heart and soul to the Lutheran sect' (which he was not either), and begging Ortiz to use his influence to stop the pope from issuing the bulls of consecration. Clement took a different view believing, apparently, that Cranmer would not dare to meddle with such an important issue immediately after his appointment, and would in any case proceed with great deliberation. So the bulls were issued, and Cranmer annulled the king's marriage on his own authority on 23 May.

[43] *Cal. Span.*, IV, 510.

If Catherine felt betrayed by the emperor, she took care not to say so. Right up to the last minute, if Chapuys is to be believed, she continued in the conviction that Henry would obey a definitive papal sentence against him, and the ambassador added 'the majority of the people here are still such good catholics that they would compel the king to obey.'[44] Given the unprecedented nature of the steps which Henry was taking, such illusions are understandable, but they were illusions nonetheless. By January Anne was pregnant, and it was imperative that the child should be born in wedlock. Before the end of the month they were secretly married, and when parliament reassembled in February it was immediately confronted with Cromwell's carefully drafted bill to prohibit appeals to the spiritual jurisdiction of the pope. The queen's supporters were not so much intimidated as bewildered by the speed with which the stakes had been raised. By the end of the session on 7 April the Act in Restraint of Appeals was law, and although it was not (and is not) clear that the act covered Catherine's long-running case, the convocation had also ruled against her, and the outcome of Cranmer's hearing was a pure formality. From Catherine's point of view all this was just so much banditry, without legal or moral force, and Chapuys agreed with her, but her English supporters and sympathizers could not afford to take so simple a view. However much they might abhor what had been done, it was unquestionably the will of their lawful sovereign, and the recognized legislative bodies of parliament and convocation had played their proper parts in enacting it. The emperor was equally wrong-footed, and his servants were divided. On 6 May Martin Perez wrote that, considering 'the mad conduct of the king of England', Charles should get into communication with the great lords of the kingdom, arrange a suitable marriage for Mary, and make war with the people's assistance. However, on 31 May he received a more sober and realistic *consulta* from his council:

> It must be considered that although the king has married the said Anna Bulans, he has not proceeded against the queen by force or violence, and has committed no act against the Emperor which (he) could allege to be an infraction of the treaty of Cambrai, which was made after the divorce was commenced, during the proceedings in Rome. Although the Emperor is bound to the queen this is a private matter, and public considerations must be taken into account.[45]

[44] *L&P*, v, 100; Mattingly, *Catherine of Aragon*, 255.
[45] *L&P*, vi, 446, 568.

Catherine would not have been encouraged, had she known of this document, but equally she had no sympathy with the bellicose noises emanating from Perez and Chapuys. In February she had told the ambassador in no uncertain terms that, whatever became of her, she would be no party to bloodshed; nor would she attempt to leave the realm.[46]

Such views probably came as a relief to Charles, but it is unlikely that they influenced his policy. He trusted Chapuys, and regarded him as an excellent diplomat, but was obliged to take a more detached view of the English situation. Henry also seems to have accepted that the political game which he was playing, although in deadly earnest, was to be conducted within certain rules. Anne's coronation, carried out on 1 June, must have given him a very good idea both of his strength and of its limitations. He could command the overwhelming majority of his peers (but not all) to attend, and as many bishops as he thought necessary. He could also persuade the City of London to spend money on lavish pageantry, but he could not enforce the enthusiasm of the citizens. Thereafter he approached Catherine unsympathetically, but with restraint. In July a powerful delegation of councillors, headed by her own steward, Lord Mountjoy, waited upon her at Ampthill, and required her upon her allegiance to surrender the title of queen, and accept the designation 'Princess Dowager'. She refused, declaring that, although she had no wish to disobey the king, her own conscience took priority. The councillors threatened her with prosecution for treason, but she was, as ever, immovable.[47] This time, Henry did reduce her household, but was scrupulous to allow her the provision suitable to her estate as he saw it. She retained some eight or ten ladies, and a similar number of Spanish 'specialists' – physician, apothecary, chaplains etc., in addition to a modest chamber and household staff. The residence allocated to her was a former palace of the bishops of Lincoln at Buckden in Huntingdonshire, remote, but commodious and in good repair. In a sense she was under house arrest, because she could not leave Buckden without the king's permission, and Cromwell's agents kept a wary eye on her household for fear of conspiracy. On the other hand ordinary visitors came and went with normal

[46] Mattingly, *Catherine of Aragon*, 261.
[47] Ibid., 264.

freedom, and correspondence passed without interference. The only visitor who was not permitted was the one she most wanted to see, her daughter Mary.

Whatever mental or emotional suffering Catherine's defeat in the spring of 1533 may have inflicted upon her, the even tenor of Mary's life since her return from the Marches of Wales had not so far been disturbed. There had been some comings and goings in her household. Lord Hussey had replaced Sir Philip Calthorpe as chamberlain at some point before the autumn of 1530. By January 1532 the long-serving Richard Sydnor had retired to Canterbury, as prior of Christ Church, and Richard Wollman, recently the king's almoner, had become the princess's 'schoolmaster', although whether in addition to Fetherstone or in place of him is not clear. It is also possible that Lady Margaret Douglas had replaced Catherine Gordon as the head of her privy chamber, but there seems to have been no major change since the reduction of 1528. Concerning her marriage there had been many rumours, but no actual negotiations since the failure of the Cleves initiative. In April 1532 there was a rumour in Rome that she was to be betrothed to the prince of Transylvania, as part of a great anti-Habsburg coalition. In June Chapuys reported more soberly that she was still being earnestly sought by the king of Scots, and in October her name was linked again with that of the dauphin. The Scottish rumour was still circulating in March 1533, and by then it was being linked to sinister speculations about the possible use of Mary against her father. Marian Giustinian, the Venetian envoy in France, believed that the Scots had actually invaded England with the support of the emperor and the Danes, and that the English people would welcome them because they held the princess in such high esteem.[48] In July reports were circulating in Flanders of rebellion in England, supported by the Scots and an Imperial fleet commanded by Andrea Doria; only this time it was the brother of the king of Portugal who was cast as the knight errant. Such speculation indicates that Mary was becoming more important than her mother in the eyes of hostile observers, and Henry must have been aware of this threat. Yet he moved very softly in applying pressure on her to accept the new order.

[48] Giustinian to the signory, 13 March 1533; *Cal. Ven.*, IV, 863.

Such gentleness probably did not please his new queen, who had every reason to regard the princess as a menace. Once Anne was safely married to Henry, Catherine did not present a serious threat to her position, and could even be seen as a protection, but Mary was a different proposition. Anne might, or might not, be carrying Henry's son, but Mary was undoubtedly Henry's daughter, and a political card which he still had many ways of playing. Chapuys reported a curious encounter between the king and the princess 'walking in the fields' at the beginning of October 1532. This could hardly have happened by chance, and the report suggests (without actually saying so) that it was arranged to avoid the intrusive presence of Anne, which would have been unavoidable if Mary had visited the court. Nothing of great significance passed at this interview, beyond general expressions of goodwill, but in the circumstances such commonplaces possessed additional meaning. Mary seems not to have been at court that Christmas, but to have received her gifts and allowances in the usual way. In March 1533 she was sufficiently unwell to cost the privy purse £26 13s. 4d. in extra physician's fees, but this illness does not seem to have been connected with any particular emotional crisis.[49] On 10 April Chapuys wrote that Anne was openly boasting 'that she would have the princess for her lady's maid ... or marry her to some varlet'; empty threats in view of her continued usefulness to her father. The queen does seem to have achieved a temporary ban on correspondence between Catherine and Mary, against which the latter protested at the end of April, but it was a ban easily evaded and of short duration. When Mary fell ill again in June, she asked for her mother's physician and apothecary 'which the king was very well pleased to grant', and Chapuys added that Catherine 'has sent to her as often as she pleases, and I think will not be forbidden to do so'.[50] The situation was, however, delicate, and much was bound to depend upon Mary herself. She was discreet enough not to make any protest when the official news of her father's second marriage reached her, but it was bound to have more than emotional consequences. At the end of June Marian Giustinian informed the signory that it was believed in the French court that the princess would be styled 'Madame Mary',

[49] Nicholas, *Privy Purse*, 202.
[50] Chapuys to the emperor, 28 June 1533; *L&P*, VI, 720.

and that the king would make her reside in the household of his new queen. He would not give her in marriage outside the realm, 'and some say that he intends to make her a nun'.[51]

As it turned out, Giustinian was to be right on two counts, but his information can have been little more than guesswork at the time he wrote. Once Cranmer had delivered his sentence, Mary ceased to be legitimate by the laws of England, but it was September before Henry made up his mind what to do about it. In the meanwhile, he used a warning signal which he had earlier used with Catherine. In the middle of July Cromwell wrote to Lord Hussey instructing him to inventory the princess's jewels and plate, and to place the former in the custody of Frances Elmer, one of the ladies of her privy chamber. Hussey, thoroughly embarrassed by the order, got a sharp dressing down from the countess of Salisbury, and reported unhappily at the end of August that the only inventory he could get was a handlist prepared by the countess, and that the jewels would not be delivered to Mrs Elmer without written instructions from the king himself. The warning shot had been returned. It was the birth of Elizabeth, on 7 September, which focused the king's mind upon Mary's future status. Had Anne's child been the longed-for son, a daughter's position might have been less important, but in the circumstances the distinction between the legitimate and the illegitimate had to be emphasized. Within a week Mary's servants were instructed to remove her badges from their liveries, and replace them with the king's. The distinction was a purely symbolic one, since the king had paid the old wage bill no less than the new one – but it was none the less important for that. At the same time she was informed that her household was to be reduced because she was no longer Princess of Wales. As before, she would receive no such unwelcome information, except in writing from the king, and Chapuys prepared to protest in the strongest terms against 'this monstrous injury'.

In so far as his protest may have referred to the reduction of Mary's household, it was misplaced. The checkroll drawn up on 1 October contained 162 names, and was probably not much smaller than the revised list of 1528. The countess of Salisbury remained as governess, Lord Hussey as chamberlain, and Richard Fetherstone as schoolmaster.[52] The new chamber estab-

[51] *Cal. Ven.*, IV, 928.
[52] BL Harleian MS 6807 f.7.

lishment numbered about fifty, including ten ladies and gentlewomen, headed by Margaret Douglas, Mary's cousin. Both the chaplains and about a third of the other chamber servants had served since 1525; some from before that. The domestic household was less generously treated. Of the senior officers, only the cofferer, William Cholmeley, remained, and most of the departments were reduced by between a third and a half. In the year ending 30 September 1533 Cholmeley had accounted for £2901 14s. 4d., so the charges of the new establishment (which were never costed) would presumably have been between £2000 and £2500.[53] There was nothing dishonourable about either the scale or the composition of this household, and it contained a number of Mary's friends and familiars. On the other hand, it soon became apparent that the implementation of this plan depended upon her own compliance. On the last day of September she was visited at Newhall by a group of commissioners headed by the earl of Oxford, just as her mother had frequently been visited by similar groups. According to their instructions, they declared to her that the king was surprised to be informed 'both by Lord Hussey's letters and by his said daughter's own delivered by one of her servants that she, forgetting her filial duty and obedience, attempts . . . arrogantly to usurp the title of Princess, pretending to be heir apparent, and encourages [others] to do the like'.[54] In order to prevent this pernicious example from spreading, they were commanded to declare to her the folly and danger of her conduct, informing her that she had worthily deserved 'the king's high displeasure and punishment in law'. If she conformed to his wishes, and ceased to lay claim to the title of princess 'he may incline of his fatherly pity to promote her welfare.'

Given her mother's example, and the nature of her own upbringing, Mary could make only one response to this ultimatum. Not only did she reject it, in a letter of 2 October, but she struck exactly the same note of righteous incredulity which Catherine had so often used. Nothing could have been better calculated to infuriate Henry than this conclusive evidence that he now had to deal with another intransigent female conscience.

[53] *L&P*, VI, 1185.
[54] Ibid., 1186.

By the end of October he had decided to dissolve her newly created household, and to place her – to Chapuys's speechless indignation – in the establishment then being prepared for the infant princess Elizabeth. In theory it was to be a joint household for the king's two daughters, but of course the legitimate princess was to take precedence in everything, and Mary, like her mother, was to be under a form of house arrest until she should think better of her defiance.

3

Disgrace and Rehabilitation

(1533–1547)

The winter of 1533–4 was an extremely miserable and traumatic season for Mary who, at seventeen, possessed none of the life-skills necessary for survival. She received her father's commissioners in public, and baldly informed them that the title of princess was hers by right, and that she could not in conscience relinquish it. Chapuys applauded vigorously from the sidelines, but he could see perfectly well what a dangerous course his protégée had embarked upon.[1] No king, however forbearing, could have ignored or condoned such a rebuff. By the middle of October, Mary had moved to the centre of the political stage, and was both more important and more vulnerable than her mother. During September Thomas Cromwell, in one of his cryptic 'remembrances' had noted 'the ballad made of the Princess [concerning] the Lady Mary', and at about the same time a girl called Mary Baynton appeared at Boston in Lincolnshire, impersonating Mary in what must have been a calculated demonstration. According to the articles later proffered against her, she said 'that upon displeasure she was put forth into the broad world to shift for a living', and that she intended 'to go beyond the sea to my uncle the Emperor as soon as I may get shipping'.[2] In the circumstances, these were shrewd gibes, and do not suggest spontaneous adolescent fantasy, especially as the real Mary could so easily be displayed elsewhere. Catherine,

[1] *L&P*, VI, 1186, 1249.

[2] Examination of Mary Baynton before Nicholas Robson, Robert Browne and Thomas Pulvertoft, September 1533; *L&P*, VI, 1193.

as Chapuys recognized and acknowledged in his dispatch of 10 October, had consistently refused to countenance plans for active resistance on her behalf. However, 'the good and holy bishop [John Fisher]', he informed the emperor, 'would like you to take active measures immediately', and the majority of Englishmen were of the same opinion. Chapuys was always over-optimistic about potential opposition to Henry, but if Mary should be willing, deliberately or otherwise, to be used against her father, she might become a serious threat. 'It is impossible to describe the love these people have for the Princess,' he reported the following week, and Cromwell recognized the same danger in his own way, when he added to a series of notes about Mary's position that it might be better to leave her in 'the estate that she now is in, and to avoid war, than to diminish anything' – a passage which he then crossed out.[3]

In early November, about a month after her first act of public defiance, the decision was finally taken to dissolve Mary's household. Henry claimed, and may even have believed, that her servants were really responsible for her disobedience. In any case, the removal of her trusted familiars, and her exposure to a hostile environment was certainly intended to bring home to her the reality of the king's indignation, which was now turned full upon her for the first time. The times were exceedingly dangerous. Anne Boleyn had failed to produce the longed-for son, upon whom so much depended. Not only did this mean that Mary had to be positively dislodged from the position of heir apparent, it also guaranteed that the queen's many enemies would continue to insinuate that her marriage had provoked the wrath of God. In insisting upon an immediate and unequivocal submission from Mary, Henry had in one sense sprung a trap upon himself, because her refusal forced him to act more ruthlessly than he may have wished. Perhaps Anne, keenly aware of her own vulnerability, had persuaded him; if so, it was not an act of gratuitous malice, but a sensible step to protect her own interests and those of her daughter.[4] Catherine, well informed by numerous friendly but surreptitious messages, looked on with a kind of painful exaltation: 'the time has come', she wrote to

[3] Chapuys to the emperor, 16 October 1533; *L&P*, VI, 1296. Cromwell's memoranda, ibid., 1382.

[4] Ives, *Anne Boleyn*, 245–9.

Mary, 'that Almighty God will prove you, and I am very glad of it, for I trust he doth handle you with a good love.'[5] Neither of them seems to have shown any awareness of the political implications of their stand, regarding the king's inevitable severity as a martyrdom for the purity of their faith. Catherine probably wrote many times during this painful winter, sometimes by the hand of Anthony Roke, one of her servants who later confessed to years of such activity, sometimes by Miguel Soa, her physician; sometimes in English, sometimes in Spanish, 'seeing her daughter could read it perfectly'. The letters which survive are a mixture of pious exhortation and practical advice: obey the king in everything which does not offend your conscience; read Godly works; keep up your music; and above all, avoid dubious male company. This last was an insistent and understandable anxiety. Not only had Mary lived a very sheltered life under the protection of her lady governess, but the compromising of her reputation would have been an effective means to destroy the whole credibility of her position. On 16 December the infant Princess Elizabeth was sent, with her newly constituted household, to reside at the old palace at Hatfield. On the following day the duke of Norfolk went to Newhall, and peremptorily ordered Mary, in the king's name, to join her, accompanied by two of her own women. The remainder of her establishment was dismissed. Such a blow can hardly have been unexpected, and the protests of Mary herself, and of the countess of Salisbury, as reported by Chapuys, have a distinctly theatrical ring. The ambassador's account is more than a little disingenuous, for having described in detail the harshness of Norfolk's dealings, and the indignation of 'the people' (who seem to have been assembled to witness the distressing scene) he then returns to his insistent theme — how everyone is longing for the emperor to come and restore justice to the troubled kingdom. A few days earlier Charles had received

[5] BL Arundel MS 151, f.194; *L&P*, VI, 1126. Mattingly, *Catherine of Aragon*, 292–3 and n.5 describes this letter as misdated to September 1533, and says that the date is 'obviously' April 1534. However, it clearly relates to some major change in Mary's circumstances, which did not occur in April 1534, and it seems more reasonable to suppose that Catherine had just discovered something of the intended arrangements for Mary's future. Similarly the exhortation to 'keep your body from all ill and wanton company' fits better with her projected exposure to a hostile household than with the possibility of marriage, to which Mattingly links it.

another letter from his aunt, protesting about the tardiness of the papal *Curia* in providing her with a definitive sentence, and anticipating martyrdom for herself and her daughter at the forthcoming parliament. Embarrassed by the conflicting pressures of policy and moral indignation, his responses were muted and discouraging, which was no doubt one reason why Cromwell deleted the risk of war from his pressing concerns over Mary's future.

Early in December, the council appointed the duke of Suffolk and the earl of Sussex to carry out another pruning of Catherine's household at Buckden, and they duly visited her just after Christmas. How many servants were removed at this time, and how many remained, is nowhere clearly stated. As queen, even after her rejection by Henry, she had continued to keep a considerable estate, and although this had been reduced when her title had been altered, it remained a large establishment. A view of her expenses from 19 December 1533 to 30 September 1534, that is after the second reduction, lists an income of £3000, and expenditure of £2950.[6] This is approximately equal to that of Mary as princess, and suggests that the king was a stickler for propriety. It also casts an interesting light upon Chapuys's constant protests against the dishonourable penury in which she was being held. A variety of sources reveal that she retained the services of her own chaplain, physician and apothecary (all of whom were Spaniards) as well as of an indeterminate number of ladies and gentlemen who formed her chamber. Such a level of expenditure also suggests a full set of service departments, and a generous standard of housekeeping. When Chapuys later reported that Catherine was virtually confined to her room, and that her women were preparing her food over a fire in the same room, he was describing her neurotic fear of poison, and her desire to escape from unwelcome pressure and interference, rather than the lack of normal household provision. Moreover, in spite of repeated threats and visitations, most of her servants remained conspicuously loyal, and carried her messages and letters to Mary, to Chapuys, and even to the emperor, at considerable risk to themselves. Mary was less fortunate. Having no title, and an indeterminate status, she was unable to retain

[6] *L&P*, VII, 1208, wherein she is described as 'Princess Catherine, dowager of Arthur, Prince of Wales'.

any independence, however circumscribed. Even so, Chapuys's repeated descriptions of her plight contained an element of deliberate exaggeration. The two women who were allowed to accompany her to Hatfield were not her only servants. Randall Dodd, formerly a groom of her chamber, certainly remained with her, and seems to have been a loyal and resourceful messenger.[7] There may well have been a few others, because Fitzwilliam reported to Cromwell on 28 March 1534 from Hatfield that he had, upon suspicion, caused the Lady Mary's servants to be searched. What Mary did not have, and never had had, was any independent income, however small. For accounting purposes the Hatfield household was that of 'the king's daughters', and her diets, her clothing and her personal expenses were paid out of the single budget, as were those of Elizabeth. After the lavish provision of her earlier years, it is not surprising that she found her situation 'a purgatory', but of genuine physical hardship or deprivation, there was none.

In March 1535, when the expenses of the household were surveyed, and when Mary was recovering from an attack of 'her usual ailment', it was reported that 'the Lady Mary, the king's daughter, after she was restored to health of her late infirmity, being in her own house, was much desireous to have her meat immediately after she was ready in the morning, or else she should be in danger eftsoons to return to her said infirmity', and consequently, upon her physician's advice, she had been accustomed to dine between nine and ten o'clock in the morning, and to dispense with breakfast. The normal regiment of Elizabeth's house, on the other hand, did not provide for the service of dinner before eleven; 'therefore, the said Lady Mary, whose appetite was to have meat in the morning, according to her accustomed diet, desired to have her breakfast somewhat the larger, to the intent that she would eat little more meat unto supper to the continuance and preservation of her health.'[8] This was done, and together with the occasional service of supper in

[7] Lady Anne Shelton, writing to Cromwell in September 1534 about Mary's communication with the Carews, described her letters as having been carried 'by her servant Randall Dodd'; *L&P*, VII, 1172. There is also a reference in December 1533 to 'John Barre, servant to our daughter the Lady Mary'; *L&P*, VI, 1508.

[8] Expenses of the Princess Elizabeth's household, 25 March 1535; *L&P*, VIII, 440.

her chamber, was alleged to have added £26 13s. 4d. to the annual 'diet'. Not only does reasonable consideration seem to have been given to her wishes, but she was able to take her meals in company, or in her own room, as she preferred. Mary's health was a subject of constant concern. Her menstrual problem was certainly aggravated by the stress of her general circumstances, and she seems to have picked up infections with the facility typical of people whose resilience is reduced. In September 1534, during a protracted bout of illness, not only did the king send his own physician to attend her, but also allowed her to be moved nearer to her mother, so that Catherine and her apothecary were able to visit her, albeit under careful supervision.[9] The following year at the same time, she suffered from a heavy 'rheum', or cold, which again required the attention of the royal physician, and Chapuys reported that she was dreading the return of her 'ordinary malady' during the forthcoming winter. The problem was aggravated by the fact that Mary detested 'all medecines', and craved physical exercise of an unrestricted kind which Henry could not run the risk of allowing. Constraint upon her recreational activity seems to have varied with time and circumstances. At times of crisis, or when her father was particularly annoyed with her, she was virtually imprisoned in her rooms, but such periods were of short duration, and a limited amount of riding or walking was usually permitted. Mary's security was a nightmare to those who were responsible for it. Not only were there constant alarms about conspiracies to whisk her out of the country, but she shared her mother's persistent dread of poison. Anne Shelton, Elizabeth's lady governess, was reduced to helpless tears at the thought of being blamed for the possible conse-

[9] There is some mystery about this visit. On 1 September Catherine wrote to Cromwell, thanking him for arranging for Mary to be closer to her, and assuring him 'you shall certify, that if she were within one mile of me, I would not see her.' However, later in the same letter she added that 'a little comfort and mirth, which she should take with me, should undoubtedly be half a health to her', which was clearly an implicit plea; Hearne, *Sylloge Epistolarum*, 107. On 27 September, in a report to Charles V, Chapuys declared that the king had sent his own physician, and allowed the queen and her apothecary to visit her, under certain restrictions; *L&P*, VII, 1193. Why Henry should have relented on this one occasion is not clear, and the incident seems to have been ignored in the numerous denunciations of Henry's callousness to his wife and daughter.

quences of any lack of vigilance on her part,[10] and Chapuys took ironic comfort from the thought that her unsympathetic supervision was the best guarantee of Mary's safety.

The fact is (and even Chapuys sometimes indirectly acknowledged it) that during the two and a half years which she spent in the semi-confinement of Elizabeth's household, Mary was an affliction to herself, and to everyone with whom she had to deal. In February 1534 'finding herself nearly destitute of clothes and other necessaries', she sent a gentleman of the household direct to the king, with orders to bring either cash or clothes, but not to receive any writing in which she was not styled princess. At the end of March, when the household made a routine move to another residence, Mary refused to budge. The exasperated Lady Shelton had her dumped bodily into a litter, and carried off, which provoked a public protest from Mary, both against the methods used and against the implied infringement of 'her right and title'. Chapuys was alarmed by this display of unnecessary intransigence, rightly fearing that it would provoke her father into further severity. In September 1535, when the bishop of Tarbes visited Elizabeth on behalf of Francis I, Mary had a furious row with Lady Shelton, and had to be physically restrained from confronting the ambassador on the grounds that she was the true princess, and his business should have been with her. Her relations with Queen Anne were naturally bad, but the offensive responses which she made to Anne's occasional attempts at reconciliation were gratuitous, and well calculated to provoke that hot-tempered lady into the threats which Chapuys so assiduously reported. Early in 1534, when on a visit to her daughter, the queen tendered her good offices to reconcile Mary with her father, provided that she would acknowledge her status. A refusal would have been entirely understandable, but what Mary actually said was that she knew no queen save her mother, and if the king's mistress was prepared to intercede for her, she would be grateful.[11] Later in the same year, when the household was at Eltham, a misunderstanding in the chapel caused Anne to believe that Mary had saluted her. She promptly sent a conciliatory message by a servant, who was publicly rebuffed on the

[10] Chapuys to the emperor, 21 February 1534; *Cal. Span.*, v, 57; *L&P*, vii, 214.

[11] Ives, *Anne Boleyn*, 247–8; *Cal.Span.*, v, 12.

grounds that he should have delivered his greeting from the Lady Anne Boleyn, as the queen was miles away. If Mary coveted the crown of a real, as opposed to a metaphorical, martyrdom, she was certainly going about it the right way.

Chapuys himself must bear a share of the responsibility for this situation. He did not invent, or even encourage, her uniquely abrasive style, but he did offer her all the support and encouragement in his power. At regular intervals over the two and half years he confronted Henry, his council and Thomas Cromwell, with reproaches and complaints about the treatment being accorded to both Mary and Catherine. He corresponded with them regularly, interceded for their specific requests, and provided Mary, in particular, with everything from 'books of consolation' to political advice. Because he represented such a powerful master, and because Henry still, on the whole, preferred an Imperial to a French orientation in his foreign policy, Chapuys was indulged and treated with remarkable forbearance. Only occasionally did the king show the impatience which he must have felt at being lectured over his parental and political responsibilities. In February 1534 he invoked the laws of England, and told the emperor's ambassador, with reasonable politeness, that he should encourage his master to mind his own business. His most specific rebuke was delivered indirectly, via his own ambassador, whose instructions, drawn up in September 1534, required him to say in respect of Mary: 'we do order and entertain [her] as we think most expedient, and also as to us seemeth pertinent, for we think it not meet that any person should prescribe unto us how we should order our own daughter, we being her natural father.'[12] Chapuys was almost certainly responsible for the formal letter of protestation, dated 7 June 1534, in which Mary objected to the withdrawal of her title as princess and the declaration of her illegitimacy. In the same letter she then went on to declare that she would not marry, or enter religion at the bidding of her father, without the full consent of her mother. The letter was duly attested, witnessed, and deposited with the emperor's representative. It was, in effect, a declaration of conditional allegiance, and could have been construed as treasonable if the author had not been a minor. A month later he reported with satisfaction that he had

[12] *L&P*, VII, 1209.

been instrumental in causing 'the Princess' to reject another overture from the council: 'I had given her notice the day before of their visit, writing to her what seemed advisable to confirm her in her good purpose, and to keep her in hope, as I do almost every day.' On 29 August he wrote that another crisis, this time a move of residence, had caused Mary to send to him three times in twenty-four hours for advice. Not surprisingly, within a few days of this hysterical anxiety, she had collapsed into a month of illness.

Had the ambassador confined himself to offering moral support to a beleaguered girl who was endeavouring to protect her conscience, his actions might have been construed by the English government as unfriendly, but inevitable in the circumstances, and within the bounds of accepted diplomatic practice. Chapuys, however, was both deeper and more devious. At times he was disarmingly frank with both Cromwell and Henry, urging them to repair their relations with the emperor by repenting of their mistaken policies. At other times, and even at the same time, he was deeply involved with the English malcontents, speculating hopefully about the potential success of the Kildare rebellion in Ireland, and endeavouring to prepare an escape for Mary to the Continent. On 30 September 1534, in a well-known dispatch, he recorded his conversations with Lord Darcy, and Lord Hussey (Mary's former chamberlain) about the practicability of an insurrection, claiming that 'all good men' desired the emperor's intervention, and that many other peers were sympathetic. A month later the emperor's council were considering the dispatch of a force to Ireland 'considering the offers made by divers princes there to remain under the emperor's authority, and hold the country of the Queen and Princess'.[13] On 12 November Charles informed his ambassador in France that he intended to encourage the Irish to rebel as a means of upholding the 'cause of our aunt and the Princess', but all mention of actual military assistance was quietly omitted. By the following January, the emphasis had shifted to escape, and Chapuys was instructed to investigate the possibilities. They were not promising. When he reported on 9 February, Mary was ill, and strictly watched. For the time being the extra vigilance had severed his lines of communication, but he believed that she

[13] Ibid., 1206, 1336.

was very anxious to co-operate, when her health permitted. In April he suggested a wild-sounding plan for her to be carried off on horseback from a recreational walk, and rowed out to a waiting ship; 'the country people would help', he added hopefully. Charles himself vacillated. In April he was encouraging 'the enterprise'; in May he instructed Chapuys to desist because of the danger. Inconclusive plots continued to be woven until they were overtaken by events in the summer of 1536, but Mary never seems to have resented the constant raising and dashing of her hopes.

Instead, the painful experiences of these months confirmed her in the view, to which she was already inclined from her mother's experience, that the emperor was her only true friend, and the upholder of justice. At Chapuys's instigation, she solemnly promised not to marry without his consent and advice, and in October 1535 wrote to his chief minister Cardinal Granvelle that 'the affairs of this kingdom will go to total ruin if his Majesty does not, for the service of God . . . take brief order and apply a remedy.'[14] In so expressing herself, Mary became technically a traitor, not by the new categories of recent legislation, but under the statute of 1352 – for 'imagining' the king's death. This was probably not quite what she intended, because her personal relations with her father had always been good. Like almost every other opponent of the king's 'proceedings', she blamed his evil advisers rather than Henry himself, and followed Catherine in laying their afflictions principally at the door of Anne Boleyn. This was a very convenient fiction, and was assiduously promoted by Chapuys. It enabled Charles to keep up a normal diplomatic relationship with Henry, which he was anxious to do because of the perpetual threats from France and the Turks. As he confessed frankly to his ambassador in France in February 1535, he needed English support, but could not do anything prejudicial to 'the Princesses'.[15] This reasoning also had the advantage of containing an element of truth. By 1534 Catherine was no longer either a threat or an obstacle to Anne, but Mary was both. As late as 1532 Henry had assured Francis I that he still regarded Mary as legitimate, and his heir, despite the invalidity of his marriage, because she was born *in bona fide*

[14] *L&P*, IX, 596.
[15] Ives, *Anne Boleyn*, 253–5; *L&P*, VIII, 273.

parentum. Anne could not afford to accept such a view, and after her marriage to the king it disappeared from public policy. According to Chapuys she endeavoured to persuade Henry to execute his daughter, and threatened to poison her; but Chapuys, like Mary, was anxious to think the worst of Anne in order to relieve pressure upon himself.

The emperor assumed a proprietary interest in Mary which Henry was fully entitled to resent. Apart from lecturing the king via his ambassador, it was Charles who encouraged the notion that she should undertake not to marry without his consent. In October 1534 he actually offered her in marriage to James V of Scotland, and it was left to James to point out that the princess was not within his power 'and could not be obtained without great difficulty'.[16] He may have acted in this way because he was himself under moral pressure from Catherine, and was anxious to make any possible gesture which demonstrated his protective concern, but did not involve the commitment of resources or a breakdown of diplomatic relations. On 8 February 1534 she wrote to him at considerable length, dilating upon the sins of the English, and of Henry in particular; explaining in detail the nature of his responsibilities; and complaining that she and her daughter were suffering the torments of purgatory. Charles's response seems to have been to assume the mantle of protector in the manner described, to encourage the English malcontents to 'remedy affairs themselves', and to instruct Chapuys to do everything in his power to deter the king from drastic action. In May 1534 the Rota at last adjudicated Catherine's appeal in her favour, and Dr Ortiz solemnly wrote from Rome to congratulate her. It was the hollowest of victories, and did nothing to relieve the emperor's mind. In freeing him from the reproach of not having goaded the pope into action, it exposed him to the even more inconvenient reproach of not doing anything about enforcing the sentence. In April 1535 Catherine wrote again, lamenting the hardness of her lot; 'I am as Job', she complained, 'waiting for the day when I must go sue for alms for the love of God.' Coming from a princess sitting at the centre of a household costing Henry almost £3000 a year, that could be described as using the truth economically. What Catherine expected her nephew to do, given her often expressed opposition to violence, is

[16] James V to the Imperial ambassador, 4 November 1534; *L&P*, VII, 1391.

not very clear. In October 1535 she sent to both the pope and the emperor, imploring the application of unspecified remedies to 'this kingdom', and on 13 December, about three weeks before her death, declared again that she and her daughter expected to be martyred by the forthcoming parliament, and looked to follow the example of 'the holy victims' – presumably Fisher and More. It may have been that the executions of the summer had changed her mind, and that in the last months of her life she was seeking a military solution as the only option left, but this seems unlikely. Probably she was not urging any more than the publication of the papal Bull of Excommunication against Henry, which had already been drawn up.

Half a century ago, Garrett Mattingly believed that if Catherine had chosen to lead a rebellion in her daughter's name in 1535, she could have overthrown Henry, and he quoted the king's alleged statement to his council:

> The lady Catherine is a proud, stubborn woman, of very high courage. If she took it into her head to take her daughter's part, she could quite easily take the field, muster a great array, and wage against me a war as fierce as any her mother Isabella ever waged in Spain.[17]

Whether Henry ever expressed such an opinion or not, more recent research has not tended to confirm Mattingly's thesis. That there was indignation and distress at the king's treatment of his first wife, and widespread hatred of Anne Boleyn, is clear enough. But so much of the evidence of conspiracy comes through the single source of Chapuys's letters, and so little actually happened, that it has to be treated sceptically. Six years later, in 1541, the French ambassador, Charles de Marillac, reported to Francis that many in England regretted the discarding of Anne of Cleves, 'who has conducted herself wisely in her affliction . . . and [is] more regretted and commiserated than Queen Catherine in like case'.[18] This must be classed as an interested exaggeration, but Marillac was not a fool. Like Chapuys, he was inclined to believe what he was told, particularly when he wanted to believe it, but he did not invent such sentiments. It is intrinsically improbable, given the amply

[17] *Cal.Span.*, v, 430; Mattingly, *Catherine of Aragon*, 291.
[18] Marillac to Francis I, 11 November 1541; *L&P*, xvi, 1332.

attested fears which attended the possible advent of a female ruler, that the English aristocracy would actually have deposed Henry (a formidable king who was still in his prime) in favour of his eighteen-year-old daughter. When rebellion did come, in the following year, the removal of the king was never canvassed. That may have been one of the reasons why the Pilgrimage failed, but it was also one of the reasons why it was able to start in the first place.[19] Quite apart from her genuine and conscientious objection to the use of force, Catherine was wise not to be seduced by the evidence of her popularity into supposing that a remedy lay that way. Whatever Chapuys may have been told, a large influx of Imperial mercenaries would have been no more welcome in England than they were in Italy, and the will to insurrection within the country was much less strong than he supposed. In the event, both Catherine and Mary were able to flirt with treason, and escape. A failed rebellion in their names would have spelled the end for both of them.

Whether out of prudence, forbearance, or fear of the emperor, Henry did not enforce the Succession Act of 1534 upon either of them personally. The relevant portion of the Act, which received the royal assent on 30 March, ran:

> And if any person or persons, of what estate, dignity or condition soever they be, subject or resiant within this realm ... after the said first day of May ... do, or cause to be procured or done, any thing or things to the prejudice, slander, disturbance or derogation of the said lawful matrimony solemnised between your Majesty and the said queen Anne, or to the peril, slander or disherison of any the issues and heirs of your highness being limited to this Act ... then every such person and persons ... their aiders, counsellors, maintainers and abettors, and every of them for every such offence shall be adjudged high traitors.[20]

[19] There is still much controversy over the motives and origins of the Pilgrimage, but the Pilgrims consistently denied that they were rebels, and claimed to be seeking the redemption of the king's honour from the hands of his 'evil councillors'. This was one of the reasons why the leaders were willing to trust the king's promises of pardon. On this see particularly G. R. Elton, 'Politics and the Pilgrimage of Grace' in *After the Reformation: Essays in Honor of J. H. Hexter,* ed. B. C. Malament, and M. E. James, 'Obedience and dissent in Henrician England: the Lincolnshire rising of 1536, *Past and Present*, XLVIII (1970); also James, *English Politics and the Concept of Honour, Past and Present* Supplement 3.

[20] Statute 25 Henry VIII c.22; *Statutes of the Realm*, III, 471–4.

At the same time, Thomas Cromwell noted 'To send a copy of the Act of the king's succession to the Princess Dowager and the Lady Mary, with special commandment that it may be read in their presence, and their answer taken'. There then followed a protracted game of cat and mouse. On 21 April the earl of Wiltshire and Sir William Paulet visited Mary, but did not, apparently, attempt to extract any oath from her. The following day Chapuys reported in alarm that the king was threatening to put his daughter to death now that her disobedience had become treasonable. John Fisher and Thomas More were not protected by royal blood, and were well known as leading opponents of the Boleyn marriage. In early April both were summoned to swear to the Act, and both refused. Logically, but rather surprisingly, they were prepared to accept the Act itself, which asserted the lawfulness of the marriage, and settled the succession on its issue, but not the oath as tendered with its derogatory implications for the bishop of Rome and his 'usurped authority'.[21] From their point of view the succession was a secular matter, and within the scope of positive law, while the jurisdiction of the papacy was a matter of divine law. Cranmer, writing to Cromwell on 17 April, urged that their partial oaths should be accepted, because 'this will be a great occasion to satisfy the Princess Dowager and the Lady Mary, who think that they would damn their souls if they relinquished their estates.' He was probably over-optimistic, but the matter was not tested because his advice was rejected, and both Fisher and More went to the Tower. By the middle of May Catherine's household and Mary's remaining servants had been compelled to swear. This does not seem to have affected either their behaviour or their loyalties, and most of them continued to serve as before, with increased discretion and flexible consciences. Catherine's later description of them as 'guards and gaolers rather than servants', because they had taken the oath, seems to have been less than just. At the end of May, Henry had still not proceeded beyond threats, and in spite of Chapuys's fears, never did so. Several attempts were made to persuade both Catherine and Mary to

[21] Cranmer believed that they were willing to accept the Act itself, but not the preamble. In fact More's objection was much more subtle, because he interpreted the oath to cover all the anti-papal legislation passed during the session. For a full discussion see G. R. Elton, *Policy and Police*, 223–5.

swear to the Act, but without success, and it was never formally administered to them. Henry behaved rather as Elizabeth was to behave with her catholic bishops at the beginning of her reign; to refuse the oath of supremacy twice was treasonable, so she made sure that it was administered only once.[22]

Contrary to what is sometimes alleged, and was believed in Imperialist circles at the time, the king had no desire to make a martyr out of Catherine, however determined she may have been to become one. And Mary was far too useful to be cast away in such a fashion, unless she should so act as to leave him no alternative. His fury at her disobedience was partly that of frustrated affection. He still wanted her, but upon his own terms and for his own purposes, as he wanted everything else. This affection was shown in a number of ways. He was always solicitous during her frequent illnesses, and on one occasion, in February 1535, asked Chapuys to provide physicians to attend her, in case his own should be suspect. From time to time he sent her small gifts of money, and in April 1535 allowed her to remain at Greenwich for ten days on her own after Elizabeth and the majority of the household had left. In one respect only was he unremittingly harsh. On only one brief occasion in five years was she allowed to see her mother, and that ban was not relaxed during Catherine's last illness in January 1536, to the great distress of both of them. The reason for this seems to have been just as much personal as political. To Chapuys Henry claimed, not unreasonably, that Catherine encouraged her daughter in her obstinacy, and received from her the obedience which was due to himself. But the real cause seems rather to have been that the king was jealous of the deep and spontaneous love which bound them together; and having the power to be malicious in this respect, exercised it. Whatever positive qualities she may have had, Anne Boleyn was not a gentle and loving spouse, and Henry found himself shut out of his daughter's affections by his quarrel with her mother. He could not compel Mary to love him, any more than he could command her to obey him against her conscience, so he was determined that she was not going to enjoy the warmth of a relationship which was denied to him, and acted

[22] Chapuys to the emperor, 29 May 1534; *L&P*, VII, 726. The situation was made more dangerous by the Treason Act of the same year, which made the 'malicious' refusal to swear high treason.

in this respect in a far meaner spirit than the political circumstances actually required.

It seems likely that this prolonged period of psychological stress did Mary lasting damage. At a stage in her life when she could reasonably have expected to marry, or at least to have played a leading role in the ceremonies and entertainments of the court, she was kept in semi-seclusion, with no public function at all. Her formal education also seems to have ceased. There is a single mention of 'my Lady Mary, her schoolmaster', at the end of May 1534, but the reference is to a benefice holder who had not taken the oath of succession, and could well refer to her former teacher, Richard Fetherstone. In 1541, when Marillac was conducting some enquiries in connection with a further marriage proposal, he talked to a woman who had 'served in her Chamber from her infancy', and who was married to a Frenchman. This lady, who may have been Mrs de Bruxia, professed to know a lot about how Mary had coped with adversity, and described her enjoyment of books of *literae humaniores* 'which were her solace in sleepless nights when she was molested'.[23] She did not, however, refer to any continuing education. There is also some suspicion that Marillac's informant told him what she thought he wanted to know, because although she admitted that when her mother's trouble had first begun, Mary had been sick with 'ennuy', she also claimed that after she had been visited and comforted by the king, her sickness had gone and had not returned – a statement which is contradicted by evidence from every year after 1532. Since Marillac was interested in her capacity to bear children, both the question and the response are understandable. Apart from stress, boredom was probably her main problem during these years. Even the most innocent attempts to keep in touch with friends aroused suspicion of intrigue. In September 1534 Mary wrote to Sir Nicholas Carew, a strong supporter of her mother. The reply, from Lady Carew, contained an urgent exhortation to obey the king in everything – which can hardly have been a welcome response – but Lady Shelton was instructed to report every detail of the episode.[24] The marchioness of Exeter, who had been a regular visitor to her house in happier times, was also an occasional correspondent, as

[23] Marillac to Francis I, 12 October 1541; *L&P*, XVI, 1253.
[24] *L&P*, VII, 1172; Anne Shelton to Cromwell.

were her husband the marquis, William Wriothesley, and the emperor's sister, Mary of Hungary. Catherine wrote regularly, and her surviving letters are full of affection and encouragement; but Mary's most consistent and accessible supporter was undoubtedly Chapuys. His activities were tolerated, for reasons already noted, but he was the most important single factor in thwarting Henry's attempts to put pressure on his daughter at this stage. Chapuys's letters and messages, usually delivered by his own servants, arrived almost daily, and sometimes more than once a day. Every so often Cromwell became exasperated by his interference, and ordered that these visits should stop, but the bans were never of long duration. Either Chapuys's own representations, or the onset of another bout of sickness, soon restored the status quo.

The conventional picture of these years is that of innocent women persecuted by a small-minded bully, but the reality was much more complex and ambivalent. When was a conspiracy not a conspiracy? Chapuys's intrigues with discontented noblemen anxious to oust the Boleyns and restore Catherine and Mary to their former status, undoubtedly had that hostile nature; as did his attempts to get Mary out of the country. Either would have justified his expulsion. Imperial interference in Ireland could be placed in the same category. Refusal to swear to the Act of Succession was high treason, and encouraging another person to refuse was misprision. At the same time Charles and Henry needed each other, and each in his own way turned a blind eye to the improprieties and unfriendly actions of the other. Hardened politicians as they were, neither of them suffered any real damage from these months of skirmishing. Catherine, too, behind her histrionic displays of lamentation, was extremely tough. The principal sufferer was Mary, who bore the emotional scars of this period to her grave, with painful consequences for herself and others. Strategically, Henry had little option but to be severe. He was playing for high stakes, the future of his dynasty and the power of his Crown. He could not afford to appear dictated to, by either pope or emperor; and in the last analysis he could not allow his daughter to get away with flagrant defiance of his laws. Why should Fisher and More be executed, while Catherine and Mary survived? He had, of course, got himself into that situation, but he had done so for reasons which were at least partly legitimate; and having chosen his policy, the only route to a secure future lay through successful enforcement. With Chapuys doing his best to persuade his master to invade, and malcontents like John Snappe of Horsington muttering in every alehouse that they would 'bestow [their lives] and all that [they] had upon my Lady Mary's title against the issue that should come of the Queen',[25] Henry could not afford to be squeamish, and at the end of 1535 he seemed to be no nearer to a solution.

Within a few days, however, the situation had been significantly changed by the death of Catherine. She had been ill before Christmas, and had appeared to recover, but on 6 January she relapsed, and her condition deteriorated rapidly. On the morning of the 7th in the company of a small group of her loyal familiars, she received the last rites, and died at about two in the afternoon. Chapuys at once suspected poison, and quoted de Soa as saying 'after she had drunk some Welsh beer, she had been worse, and that it must have been a slow and subtle poison'. That was less than fair to Welsh beer, and the evidence, both of the progress of the illness and of the autopsy, points to a coronary thrombosis.[26] When the news of her death spread abroad, it was believed as far apart as Rome and Wittenberg that Mary was *in extremis* also, and even the emperor declared that she was 'given up for lost'. However, these reports were based upon the assumption that Catherine had been poisoned, and in fact the pressure upon Mary was relaxed rather than increased in the period immediately after her mother's death. This was due less to humanitarian considerations on Henry's part than to the conviction that Catherine had been the main cause and inspirer of her daughter's obstinacy. He decided to try a different tactic. On 10 February Chapuys reported with some surprise that there had been no further mention of the oath, that Mary was being better treated, and that the king had given her 100,000 crowns (about £17,500). The sum was probably mistaken, because that amount of money would have supported a

[25] SP 1/83 f.96; *L&P*, VII, 497.

[26] Ives, *Anne Boleyn* (341) says unequivocally 'Katherine of Aragon died of cancer', without supporting the assertion. Her illness in early December, subsequent apparent recovery, and sudden death on 7 January, would be equally consistent with two (or possibly three) heart attacks, and the descriptions of her heart as 'blackened' when the body was opened, seems to support the diagnosis offered here. Chapuys to the emperor, 9 and 21 January 1536; *L&P*, x, 59, 141.

full household for five or six years, but there was no mistake about the change of attitude. Even Anne Boleyn wrote to Lady Shelton, her aunt, not to press further on the question of Mary's submission. Mary, absorbed by grief, hardly seems to have noticed, and continued to press Chapuys to find her a means of escape, or to persuade the emperor to remedy her situation in some other way. Charles was willing to oblige, but Catherine's death had altered the position significantly as far as he was concerned. He was not bound to Mary, as he had been to her mother, by his own sense of family honour, and could afford to treat England more objectively as a political problem. At the end of February he wrote to Chapuys that it was now necessary and possible to negotiate a fresh agreement with Henry against the French, and that such an agreement would also afford the best opportunity to improve his cousin's lot.[27]

There was a spirit of cautious optimism in the Imperial camp during the early weeks of 1536, because Catherine's death enabled the political waters to thaw and flow again after nearly three years of hard frost. Ironically, the first and most important victim of this thaw was Anne Boleyn. Her marriage to the king had been in difficulties since the unwelcome birth of Elizabeth, although she had demonstrated her fertility, and could reasonably hope for a son next time. The main problem seems to have been that her strength of character, independence and outspokenness, which had captivated Henry during their prolonged courtship, had pleased him much less in wedlock. This was not entirely the result of the king's inconsistency. Tudor wives were expected to conform to a somewhat different model from their unmarried sisters, and Henry was extremely conventional. Catherine had been astute enough to realize this, and had acted the patient Griselde with some conviction until he tried to discard her. Not so Anne, who continued after marriage with the storms, scenes and reconciliations which had preceded it.[28] Henry had not entirely lost his roving eye, and played the game of courtly love with continued enthusiasm. Whether any of his rumoured amours between 1533 and 1535 were real as opposed to purely conventional cannot now be determined, but Anne's reactions were neither wise nor temperate. In the autumn of

[27] *L&P*, x, 373.
[28] Ives, *Anne Boleyn*, 244–5.

1534 and again in the summer of 1535, rumours were being spread by her many enemies that she had been supplanted in the king's affections. Much of this was wishful thinking. Nor did it matter very much whether Margaret Shelton was Henry's mistress; as long as the old queen was still alive, he could not discard Anne without coming under enormous pressure, both at home and abroad, to take Catherine back. Consequently, when the latter died, the king's pleasure, so tastelessly displayed, had more than one face; while the queen's, as some astute observers noticed, was less real than she pretended. On 29 January Anne miscarried of a son, and her fortunes took another downward step. She claimed that it was the result of an accident which Henry had suffered in the tiltyard, but the general stress of her increasing insecurity is more likely to have been responsible. On the same day Chapuys reported that the king 'believes himself to have been led into this marriage by witchcraft [and] that God has punished him by withholding a male heir'. As the sworn enemy of Anne, Chapuys is a suspect source, but these sentiments have an authentic ring, and Henry certainly voiced them later. By this time, although she may not have known it, Anne's opponents had succeeded in finding the right lever to topple her from favour.

The young lady concerned was Jane Seymour, daughter of Sir Thomas Seymour of Wulf Hall near Marlborough, sister of the rising soldier, Sir Edward Seymour and a former member of Catherine's chamber. The king and queen had stopped at Wulf Hall during the summer progress of 1535, but the Seymours were a courtly family, and Jane had been known to Henry for several years before that. Why his casual interest in an attractive girl turned into a serious pursuit during these critical weeks is not clear. Probably it had less to do with the charms of Jane than with the increasing attractiveness of a third marriage, unencumbered by doubts or legacies of the past. Anne was becoming a liability, not so much because of her sharp tongue as because of the long train of political opposition which she drew behind her. To repudiate her now would no longer look like yielding to papal or Imperial pressure, and offered the best opportunity to reconcile the factions which had developed over the previous six or seven years. A new marriage might also solve the intractable problem of Mary. As the king had once intended to declare, she could be recognized as legitimate through her parents' good faith, and included in the succession. Only the Boleyn marriage had blocked that solution. Without it, there was no reason to prefer Elizabeth to Mary in default of a male heir, and every reason not to. Typically, however, Henry had to work himself up into a state of righteous indignation before he could take such a step – or to put it more charitably, had to be convinced that there were legal and moral grounds for the course he wished to pursue. From January to April the battle raged at court, and particularly in the privy chamber.[29] Against the Boleyns, who were still scoring notable successes as late as the middle of March, were the Seymours, and Mary's friends – the marquis and marchioness of Exeter, Lord Montague, Sir Thomas Elyot, Sir Nicholas Carew, and of course Eustace Chapuys. Chapuys's role, however, was less straightforward than he would have liked, because the emperor's desire to reach an accommodation with Henry obscured the black and white terms in which he saw the struggle. Charles had never recognized the Boleyn marriage, but was extremely anxious to ensure that the king did not seek a new bride in France. He therefore instructed Chapuys to make some overtures to the Boleyns, with a view to promoting a package which would restore limited links between England and Rome, recognize Mary's position, and provide him with some military support in Italy. The Boleyns responded favourably, and so did Cromwell. Briefly it seemed to some alarmed observers as though the emperor was going to change sides.

In the event, however, the deal came to nothing, largely because Henry would accept nothing less from Charles than a full acknowledgement of the propriety of all that he had done since 1527 – and no amount of English aid could induce the emperor to climb down so far. The failure of this negotiation had critical consequences, because it convinced Thomas Cromwell, who had hitherto supported the Boleyns, that the king's second marriage was an impediment to diplomatic progress which would have to be removed.[30] Cromwell knew exactly the right note to strike with Henry. He made his decision about 20 April, and on 2 May the queen was arrested on a charge of treasonable adultery, and lodged in the Tower. How this trick was worked is still a considerable mystery. As Professor Ives recently expressed it, Henry was 'bounced' into a decision, because in spite of all

[29] Ibid., 346–56.
[30] Ibid., 354–6.

the telling arguments against Anne, as late as 25 April he was still referring to her in official correspondence as 'our dear and most entirely beloved wife'. Between that date and 30 April when Mark Smeaton, a court musician, was arrested on a charge of having 'had to do' with the queen, Henry became convinced of a guilt which he had hitherto not suspected. Perhaps Anne's public and incredibly foolish quarrel with Henry Norris on 30 April provided the crucial spur, but it seems a weak cause to have such momentous consequences, even if reinforced by reports of her indiscreet conversation with Smeaton a day or two before.[31] A more probable explanation, recently canvassed by Dr Retha Warnicke, is that the foetus of which Anne had miscarried on 29 January had been deformed, or in some sense abnormal. A deformed or monstrous birth was held to be a judgement of God upon both parties to the conception, and it would not therefore have been difficult to persuade Henry that he could not possibly have begotten such a child.[32] The evidence supporting such a thesis is entirely circumstantial, but if Thomas Cromwell had come upon such information soon after deciding to devote his prodigious energy and ingenuity to removing Anne, it would explain a number of features of the case which are otherwise hard to account for. One of these is the speed with which the eventual decision was made. In spite of his deteriorating relationship with Anne, and the attractions of regaining his freedom, at Easter 1536 the king was still, on balance, more favourable to the Boleyns than hostile. By 30 April he was not only convinced of his wife's guilt, but also of its particularly heinous and unnatural nature. Another is the mysterious statement later made that much relevant evidence did not come out at the trial. If the foetus was, as it was described, male and of about three and a half months, it must have been very carefully examined. But whoever examined it (presumably the midwife) must also have concealed her knowledge for nearly three months, and would therefore have needed a special immunity to avoid prosecution for misprision. The involvement of Lord Rochford may also be partly explained by this theory, since the first two men suspected were Norris and Smeaton, and Smeaton's confession alone

[31] BL Cotton MS Otho C x ff. 209v, 222, 223, 224v, 225; Harleian MS 283 f.134; SP 1/103 ff. 313–14; Ives, *Anne Boleyn*, 365 and n.

[32] R. Warnike, 'Sexual heresy at the court of Henry VIII', *Historical Journal*, xxx, 247–68.

would have been sufficient to condemn Anne. Incest was held to be an unnatural vice, and therefore much more likely to produce a monstrous birth than straightforward adultery. Since Rochford was much in Anne's company, and a formidable political opponent, it was both easier and more necessary to destroy him by means of such arguments. The idea that Rochford may have had a genuine homosexual relationship with Smeaton, and that the behaviour of each in this crisis may be explained in those terms, is interesting, but even harder to substantiate.[33]

As with Wolsey, so with Anne Boleyn. Once her spell upon the king was broken, the malice of her many enemies was given full rein. The slanderous tales that she had poisoned Catherine, and plotted to poison Mary, gained new currency, promoted particularly by the Seymours. Even her enemy Chapuys commented that the Londoners 'spoke strangely' of the manner of her trial on 15 May, and the speed with which her execution followed four days later. 'Stone dead hath no fellow' was later to be said of another powerful political figure hustled to the scaffold.[34] Two days before she died, her marriage to the king was annulled; not, of course, on the grounds of her subsequent adultery, but because of Henry's earlier liaison with her sister! Having come to his decision, the king immediately began to act as though Anne no longer existed, and his relationship with Jane Seymour developed daily, with a strange mixture of courtly propriety and indecent haste.[35] The queen had been the victim of a political coup of great skill and ruthlessness, which also destroyed the family-based faction which she had led. Mary and her friends at court, particularly Carew, the Poles and the Courtenays, believed themselves to be the victors, and looked for Mary's speedy restoration to grace. The experienced Chapuys was less sure, and his doubts were fully justified. A few days before the crisis broke, the king had told him:

> As to the legitimation of our daughter Mary . . . if she would submit to our Grace, without wrestling against the determination of our laws, we

[33] Ibid.

[34] Thomas Wentworth, earl of Strafford.

[35] Even before Anne was tried, Henry brought Jane to a convenient house near Whitehall, where he also arranged for her to be closely chaperoned. They were betrothed on 20 May, the day after Anne's execution, and married on the 30th. *L&P*, x, 926.

would acknowledge her and use her as our daughter; but we would not be directed or pressed herein.

By the time that Anne was executed on 19 May, he had received no word of any change of heart. The common people, he wrote, the council, and Jane Seymour herself, were all urging Mary's unconditional restoration, but he had seen no sign that the king was inclined to it. Instead, all the indications pointed to his insistence that she should swear to the statutes decreeing her own bastardy and the abolition of the papal jurisdiction. Instead of transforming her situation, as far as Mary was concerned, Anne's fall changed very little. Cromwell knew the king better than his courtier allies, and realized how strongly he was committed to the ecclesiastical supremacy. Logically the deaths of Catherine and Anne in rapid succession should have restored the status quo ante in England. The pope suspended his process of excommunication in the hope of a new negotiation, and the emperor suggested a marriage between Henry and the infanta of Portugal; but both were making premature assumptions.

Under a similar misapprehension, several of Mary's former servants turned up at Hunsdon, expecting to be reinstated. But Elizabeth's status was now as indeterminate as her sister's, and Chapuys wisely advised Lady Shelton to entertain no one without the king's express orders. For the time being, at least, the king had two illegitimate daughters, and the household which supported them had no particular designation. The events of May and June 1536 were a cruel torment to Mary, whose sophisticated education paradoxically seems to have given her a naïve view of the world around her. During May she was receiving felicitations from everyone, except the person who really mattered. No word came from Henry. Realizing at last that she was expected to make the first move, on the 26th she wrote to Cromwell asking for his intercession now that 'that woman' had gone who had alienated her father from her.[36] The secretary replied promptly, and obviously informed her that obedience was looked for as a condition of reinstatement. Totally deceived by her own convictions, Mary did not read the signal. On the 30th she wrote again, requesting leave to see her father,

[36] *L&P*, x, 968. BL Cotton MS Otho C x, f.283; Thomas Hearne, *Sylloge Epistolarum* (Oxford, 1716), 140.

and offering to be 'as obedient to the king's Grace as you can reasonably require of me'. Without waiting for a response to this piece of alarming innocence, on the following day she addressed her first letter to Henry. In tone it was entirely disarming, acknowledging her offences, and begging his blessing and forgiveness 'in as humble and lowly a manner as is possible'. She congratulated him upon his recent marriage to Jane Seymour, and asked leave to wait upon the new queen. Unfortunately, she also made it perfectly clear that there were limits to her submissiveness. She would obey her father in all things 'next to God', 'humbly beseeching your Highness to consider that I am but a woman and your child, who hath committed her soul only to God, and her body to be ordered in this world as it shall stand with your pleasure'.[37] Since the two points upon which he had required her obedience, the ecclesiastical supremacy and her mother's marriage, were both reserved by this form of words, she was offering nothing, and received no reply. Instead, the king went ahead and drew up a series of articles to be presented to her, which would leave no room for equivocation or evasion.

Chapuys was on tenterhooks. Ostensibly, Cromwell took him into his confidence, showing him a draft of the letter of submission which was to be presented to her. He thought it 'very dishonourable', but feigned a willingness to co-operate, realizing that Henry was extremely angry, and Mary's position consequently dangerous. Confident of his own influence with both sides, he reported on 6 June that he believed he could see an honourable way out. He was deceived, although whether by Cromwell or himself is not clear. Perhaps he communicated his mistaken optimism to Mary, because on the 7th she wrote to Cromwell asking for some token from the king before she paid her anticipated visit to the court, and on the following day to Henry himself, expressing her joy at the news that he had 'withdrawn his displeasure'. Again there was no response. Anxious, but not yet disillusioned, she tried again on 10 June, asking for her father's blessing, and sending a copy of her letter to Cromwell with a covering note begging not to be pressed in submission further than her conscience would bear. It may be that Mary was less naïve than these communications make her appear, that she had some secretly communicated hope that her

37 *L&P*, x, 1022. BL Cotton MS Otho C x, f.278.

friends in the council and court would succeed in changing the king's mind, and that time was on her side. In either case she was in for a rude awakening. Within a day or two, probably on the 15th,[38] the duke of Norfolk, the earl of Sussex and the bishop of Chichester visited her at Hunsdon, bearing the king's commission, and demanding an answer to two unequivocal questions. Would she accept her father's ecclesiastical supremacy, repudiating the 'bishop of Rome'? And would she accept the nullity of her mother's marriage? In a stormy and emotional confrontation, she rejected both demands. The crisis which Chapuys had long dreaded had finally arrived.

Mary was now a traitor to the king's laws and estate, and the judges confirmed that she should be proceeded against. The council held a series of emergency meetings, from which her supporters, Exeter and Fitzwilliam, were excluded. At the same time, two of her friends in the privy chamber, Sir Anthony Browne and Sir Francis Bryan were arrested and examined 'concerning talk had of the estate of the Lady Mary'. What emerged was hardly treasonable even by the standards of 1536, but reveals how extremely sensitive the situation had become. Some in the inner circle of the court had expressed the perfectly reasonable view that Mary would make a very satisfactory heir, if she would submit to her father, and if the present queen had no issue. Others had doubted the prospect of her submission. The phrase *in bona fide parentum* had again been canvassed, although both the examinees professed their ignorance of such discussions. The exact chronology of events during these tense days is not very clear. As late as 12 June Cromwell still seems to have been endeavouring to extract a satisfactory general letter of submission from her, because on the 13th she wrote to him in considerable distress, to say that she could think of nothing better to do than copy out the draft which he had sent to her. Perhaps this was still unsatisfactory, or perhaps the secretary's painstaking efforts were overtaken by the king's decision to send the commission. On the 14th she was still wondering innocently why she had received no token of forgiveness. When Cromwell received the news of her disastrous interview with Norfolk and

[38] None of the documents immediately connected with this crisis is dated, but Mary was still enquiring hopefully about her general submission on the 14th. On the 26th, she received her first message of forgiveness, so the Thursday when she signed her submission must have been the 22nd. BL Cotton MS Otho C x, f.289, *L&P*, x, 1136; for a discussion of this dating see *Reign of Mary*, 20–1 and ns.

his colleagues, he drafted a fierce letter of rebuke, lamenting his own foolishness in having endeavoured to help her: 'I think you are the most obstinate woman that ever was.' The letter was probably never sent, but it was an understandable expression of his exasperation. As long as she remained intransigent, she was the figurehead of a powerful political faction, and a focus for opposition to the regime. On the other hand, Mary's execution for high treason played no part in the secretary's plans. Potentially she was a valuable stabilizing force in domestic politics, and a means of rebuilding the Imperial alliance which he believed to be so important. This could only be achieved, however, and her supporters neutralized, if she submitted and was reconciled to the king. According to Chapuys, the crisis which followed the commissioners' visit to Hunsdon lasted about a week, and during that time, Cromwell used all his ingenuity to find a constructive solution to the deadlock.

This he seems to have achieved eventually by indirect means. Mary still had confidence in his powers of intercession, but he succeeded in convincing both her and Chapuys that the immediate alternative was submission or death. In view of Henry's long record of hesitation and uncertainty in his dealings with both Catherine and Mary, it is by no means certain that she was within days of arrest and trial at this juncture, but the atmosphere of panic achieved its desired end. When it came to the point, Mary did not share her mother's appetite for martyrdom. With Catherine's moral stiffening removed, and Chapuys urging surrender to save her life, her conscience could find no support. The psychological pressure was cruel, and gave her insomnia, toothache and neuralgia. Her old friend Lady Hussey, the wife of her former chamberlain, was sent to the Tower for speaking in her support. According to his own account, Chapuys then argued that she could 'do great good' if she were restored to favour, and that in any case a concession made under such constraint could never be binding in conscience.[39] Cromwell himself could not have put it better, and perhaps had put it so to the ambassador. Finally, on Thursday, 22 June, she gave way. According to Chapuys, she signed a further set of articles from her father without reading them, but she also wrote a covering letter, remitting her whole life and estate to his discretion,

[39] Chapuys to the emperor, 1 July 1536; *L&P*, XI, 7.

and professing unconditional surrender. Perhaps that was also copied from a draft which the secretary had sent her; the tone of effusive thanks in which she wrote to him a few days later indicates that she believed his help to have been crucial, and it is difficult to see what else he could have done during those final hours of crisis which would have so impressed her. As soon as the news of Mary's submission was known, relief and rejoicing were almost unanimous. Within a few days she had received gracious messages both from her father and Jane Seymour, and was taking a lively interest in the prospective reconstitution of her household. Her state of mind at the end of June is hard to gauge. She had just passed through the most shattering experience of her life, and Chapuys reported her to be prostrate with grief and remorse, begging him to obtain a special dispensation from Rome to ease her conscience.[40] At the same time her surviving letters to Cromwell and the king suggest a newly discovered talent for the soft answer, and an appetite to recover the fruits of favour. She was young, and there may well have been an element of truth in both those impressions, but we must remember that the ambassador had his own conscience to salve, as well as Mary's reputation to defend in the face of catholic Europe.

On 6 July the king and queen visited Hunsdon, and stayed two days. It was said that Mary's household would be re-established within a matter of days, and that she would then return to court. The news of her rehabilitation had spread rapidly, and gained in the transmission. In Rome it was believed that she would immediately be recognized as heir, and that the king would return to the Church. A great crowd had greeted the return of the countess of Salisbury to the court, it was reported, because it was thought that the princess was with her. In fact events were not moving so fast. Nothing was said about the succession, and the rumour that Mary would be created duchess of York turned out to be groundless. One reason for this was probably the serious illness of the duke of Richmond. Although nothing had been said about his position for a number of years, if all the king's children were illegitimate, then the only son was in a very strong position. If Richmond died, however, Mary would again become the heir apparent, irrespective of any formal

[40] Ibid.

declaration to that effect. On 23 July Chapuys reported that the young duke's life was despaired of, and that Henry had 'certainly intended' to name him as heir. He died later the same day, at the age of eighteen, and the king once again left without any semblance of a male heir. Meanwhile, Mary's rehabilitation was steadily put in hand. The first sign of this was renewed talk of her marriage, a subject which had been canvassed warily during the previous three years, but not negotiated. Within a few days of her submission, however, Diego de Mendoza arrived in London with powers from the emperor to suggest a match with Dom Luis, the younger brother of the king of Portugal.[41] At first, Chapuys was sceptical, believing that Henry would never allow her to marry out of the realm, and was likely to force her into a domestic marriage in order to keep her under effective control. At the beginning of August she renewed her pledge to him not to wed without the emperor's consent, and declared that 'save for some great advantage to the peace of Christendom', she would prefer not to marry at all. Nevertheless, by early September the prospect seemed brighter, and he declared that the king favoured such a negotiation. Henry was picking up some of the diplomatic threads which he had been forced to drop in 1533, because the young duke of Angoulême was again a serious suitor by mid-September. On the 12th the king wrote to his agents in France, instructing them to offer Mary's legitimation and succession in default of male heirs, in return for an undertaking that Angoulême would live for a time in England.[42] How serious he

[41] Dom Luis of Portugal. Born at Abrantes, 3 March 1506, the second son of King Emmanuel 'the Fortunate', and younger brother of John III. His mother, Mary of Castile, was the second daughter of the Catholic kings, and elder sister of Catherine of Aragon. He was consequently cousin to Charles V, and became his brother-in-law when Charles married his sister Isabella in 1526. He is best known as patron of letters and the arts. None of his various marriage projects succeeded, and he died unmarried in 1555, leaving a son by his mistress, Violante Gomes. This boy was Dom Antonio, later Prior of Crato, and pretender to the Portuguese throne after the death of Sebastian. Robert Ricard, 'Pour une monographie de l'enfant D.Luis de Portugal', *Charles Quint et son temps*, Colloques Internationaux de Centre National de la Recherche Scientifique, Paris, 167–75.

[42] Henry VIII to Gardiner and Wallop; *L&P*, XI, 445. This refers to Charles, Francis's third son. Following the death of the dauphin, Francis, on 10 August 1536, Henry, the second son, became dauphin, and Charles duke of Orleans.

was about either of these plans is hard to gauge, and Mary's defensive remarks to Chapuys suggests that she did not believe in his sincerity, but by the autumn of 1536 she had recovered her status in the European marriage market.

The other sign of returning favour was the re-creation of her household, or, more accurately, her chamber. This was being discussed before the end of June, when Mary responded to a request for suggestions by naming Susan Clarencius, Margery Baynton and Mary Browne. From the wording of her letter it seems likely that Clarencius and Baynton were already with her, having been appointed since the dispersal of her earlier household;[43] while Mary Browne, who had been named in October 1533, may have been the 'confidential maid' who had been dismissed early in 1534. In the event, Clarencius and Baynton were appointed, but Browne was not. On 3 August Chapuys reported that the expected arrangements had still not been made, but they must have been completed by the 16th, when Sir John Shelton, the controller, wrote to Cromwell describing the household as being 'served on two sides'. The whole new provision was for twenty-nine servants; four gentlewomen, two chamberers; five gentlemen; five yeomen; four grooms; four grooms of the stable; a physician; a chaplain; a footman; a woodbearer; and the long-serving laundress, Beatrice ap Rice.[44] Of these, twenty-four could be described as chamber servants in the proper sense – less than half the size of her previous establishment, but Mary was not disposed to complain after the restricted existence of recent months. Nor was Chapuys, who, rather surprisingly, described it as 'very honourable'. Of the twenty-four, thirteen had appeared on the list of October 1533, and eight had served before that, going back to 1525. Randall Dodd, now a gentleman of the chamber, had been with Mary throughout her period of disfavour, and so, probably, had Beatrice ap Rice. Such a team made up in loyalty anything it may have lacked in numbers, and its composition indicates that both Henry and Cromwell were willing to accept Mary's desire for the support of old friends. It was, however, a comparatively

[43] Mary to Cromwell, probably 30 June 1536; *L&P*, x, 1186.

[44] BL Cotton Vespasian C XIV, f.246; *L&P*, x, 1187. The number forty-two, which is quoted for the size of this household, arises from the conflation of two lists, which were clearly alternatives.

humble team – there was no lady governess, and no lord chamberlain. At the same time Elizabeth's establishment was drastically reduced, and a new chamber staff of seventeen servants appointed.[45] The existing domestic household seems to have continued substantially unchanged, but instead of Elizabeth being magnificently attended, and Mary having only a handful of servants, by August 1536 the latter was the dominant partner. In fact the size and composition of the two chambers exactly reflected the legal status and precedence of the two girls. Lady Margaret Bryan, whose services to Elizabeth probably ended at this time, wrote to Cromwell at the end of July to complain that her charge was in great want, and to protest against 'Mr Shenton's' assumption of responsibility for the whole household. But Shelton was certainly acting on Cromwell's orders, and if there was a shortage of money at Hunsdon, there is no reason to suppose that it was deliberate. The controllers' own estimate for the future cost of this rather curious ménage was £4000 a year, so economy does not appear to have been a major consideration.

By September Mary was enjoying some of the fruits of renewed favour. The queen sent her kind messages; she wrote to her father, commending her 'sister Elizabeth' ('such a child toward as I doubt not but your Highness shall have cause to rejoice of in time coming'); Henry sent her £20, Cromwell the gift of a horse.[46] Meanwhile, Chapuys's representations on her behalf in Rome were meeting with an unsympathetic reception, and the ambassador himself was rebuked by count Cifuentes for having led her astray. It was impossible, Cifuentes argued, to issue a secret dispensation, even if it could be justified. In the first place, Mary's protestation should have been made before witnesses, and in the second place, the French would be bound to find out and tell Henry. The best he could suggest was a 'vivae vocis oraculo in genere', empowering confessors to absolve all those who had fallen into 'these new English errors'.[47] Chapuys grumbled at such a legalistic attitude, and defended his own role, but Mary presumably had to make do with such vague and informal reassurances. Cifuentes was right, however, in

[45] BL Cotton Vesp. C XIV, f.246.
[46] *L&P*, XI, 132; 334; 381.
[47] Count Cifuentes to the emperor, 8 October 1536; *Cal.Span.*, V, 106.

believing that she would have been in great danger if Henry was given any cause to believe that he had been deceived. At the beginning of October he caused her to write highly specific letters, both to the emperor and to Mary of Hungary, explaining that she had now been enlightened by the Holy Spirit, and realized both that her mother's marriage had been unlawful, and that the pope's authority was usurped. To Charles she also added the request that he should not act against her father's interests in the general council which was under discussion, lest she should be made to suffer for it. Chapuys, who is the only authority for the existence of these letters, does not suggest any further conscientious scruples on Mary's part, which may mean that she was numbly acquiescing in everything that Henry required. On the other hand, it may equally mean that she had learned to dissemble, or even that she had come round to agree with the viewpoint which had initially been forced upon her. The human mind is capable of far more subtle reactions than are normally attributed to Mary at this time. There are certainly no other signs that Henry distrusted the sincerity of her conversion. During the dangerous months from October to December, when first Lincolnshire and then the north was in rebellion, and Mary's name was often on the lips of the rebel leaders, she was at Hunsdon or Richmond, writing friendly notes to the king, Cromwell and Wriothesley for small favours received, apparently well in health and spirits. At the end of October she visited the court, and Cardinal du Bellay reported 'Madame Marie is now first after the queen, and sits at table opposite her.' The French and the Imperialists were still vying for her marriage, and she spent Christmas with the court at Greenwich, having felt sufficiently sure of herself on 8 December to request an increase of the £40 a quarter 'pocket money' which Henry was allowing her.[48]

From Mary's point of view, the year 1536, which had been so stormy and traumatic, ended quietly. For the first time since her childhood, she was often in her father's company, and had many long private conversations with him. As to what passed between them, we have only Chapuys's somewhat jaundiced guesses, but it seems likely that she may have come to understand something

[48] Mary to Cromwell, *L&P*, XI, 1269. *The Privy Purse Expenses of the Princess Mary*, ed. F. Madden, 1.

of the pressures which operated upon his complex personality. Her relations with Jane Seymour were consistently good, and this undoubtedly helped to bring her closer to the king. The interrogations and trials of the leaders of the Pilgrimage, which took place in April and May, did not touch her directly; and although her former steward, Lord Hussey, was one of those executed, there was no suggestion that she had in any way consented to their actions. Fortunately, those of them who were her friends did not know of her approach to the emperor in the autumn of 1535. In March 1537 she wrote again to Charles, this time via Henry's new ambassador, Sir Thomas Wyatt, and the content of her letters seems to have been very different. Don Diego de Mendoza, in conversation with Mary some two months later, expressed polite doubt about the letters' authenticity, and received the reply, 'They were undoubtedly mine, and in the same I wrote the truth, as I thought and think.' Mendoza commended her somewhat formally upon her wisdom and good learning, and took his leave.[49] Whatever she had written had not been much to Charles's taste, and had presumably echoed the sentiments of the previous October. Later in the year she wrote again via Wyatt, but there is no evidence that she received any direct reply. Although in one sense the emperor was relieved by Mary's restoration to favour, he could not bring himself to believe that her change of heart was genuine. In her new frame of mind, she was no use at all as a means of bringing pressure to bear upon her father. Mendoza's instructions on his arrival in England in March 1537 included an attempt to resurrect domestic opposition, linking Mary with Reginald Pole, so his frustration is understandable. Like him, we do not know whether she was being honest, or merely intimidated, but in the circumstances a genuine (if temporary) conversion is entirely possible.

As in earlier years, negotiations for her marriage focused upon the question of the succession. In February 1537 the emperor, now uncertain about his protégée's attitude, as well as about her status, was pressing the Portuguese hard to make a decisive bid on behalf of Dom Luis. John III was not enthusiastic, but was willing to oblige his powerful kinsman, and gave his ambassador in London full powers to negotiate at the beginning of March. The negative advantages of such a match would have been

[49] *L&P*, XII, 637, 1314.

greater than the positive, from Charles's point of view. It would have kept her out of the hands of the French – always a prime objective of his policy – and would have protected her against domestic disparagement. For these reasons he was willing to allow the succession to be passed over in silence in any Anglo-Portuguese treaty. However, for his own honour, and for that of Portugal, he could not allow Dom Luis to take her as explicitly illegitimate and incapable of succeeding. Chapuys had earlier believed that Henry would not father any more children, and that thought may have been behind the emperor's comparatively relaxed attitude in February. In view of his earlier attitude to the French negotiation, Henry might even have been willing to accept such a concession, but by the middle of March he knew that his queen was pregnant, and began again to insist upon a public recognition of Mary's illegitimacy.[50] In what seems to have been a new theoretical departure, he instructed Wyatt to inform the emperor that, although she had been born *in bona fide parentum*, such *bona fides* could not be alleged when the prohibition arose from the law of God. In spite of this, the negotiation dragged on until June, when Henry finally killed it off by introducing another new consideration – that both monarchs should have any treaty ratified by their respective estates. It may have been the French who had alerted him to the potentialities of parliament in this connection, or he may have been already aware of the implications of the Succession Acts of 1534 and 1536. The second Act, in not only repealing but directly contradicting the first, had in effect allowed parliament to assume the right to determine the succession. This not only made it important to have a treaty which affected the succession ratified – something which had never been sought in the past – but also meant that it became feasible to include Mary, or Elizabeth, or any other child, irrespective of its legitimacy; a point which was to be made fully explicit in the final Henrician Act of 1543.[51]

Henry had disentangled these issues in his own mind by February 1537: at the same moment that he was insisting upon Mary's bastard status to Wyatt, he was also writing to Gardiner

[50] *L&P*, XII, 212. Bishop of Tarbes to Francis I, 4 July 1537, discussing the breakdown of the Anglo-Portuguese negotiations in the previous month.

[51] Henry VIII to Gardiner, 17 February 1537; *L&P*, XII, 445; *L&P*, XII, 212; Statute 35 Henry VIII c.1; *Statutes of the Realm*, III, 955–8.

(in France) in terms which make it clear that the parliamentary determination of the succession had already been explained in that quarter. The French might object, the king recognized apropos of his negotiation concerning the duke of Orleans (formerly Angoulême), that if Mary's title depended only upon parliament, then Henry's son, if he had one, could cause her to be excluded again by the same means, leaving Orleans no certain prospect. They might have added that Henry himself could have done the same thing. The prospect of a 'constitutional' succession was a new one in dynastic politics, and it is not surprising that no one knew quite how to deal with it. Henry could only declare, rather lamely:

> it is not to be supposed that the nobles and commons of this realm could be so light and inconstant as to disinherit her without cause . . . and though not legitimate, of such noble parentage on both sides.[52]

Aware of the weakness of this argument, he added that if Francis found the situation strange, he should remember that he held his own crown, not by indefeasible heredity, but by the Salic law. Gardiner was probably too wise to say any such thing, because although in a certain technical sense Henry was right, the cases were in no way similar.[53] There the matter rested until October, when Francis made a bid to invoke Henry's military aid 'according to the treaties', and offered further marriage negotiations as an inducement. Henry did not respond, and it seems unlikely that he was seriously interested in any marriage for Mary at this stage. Reginald Pole, believed by Chapuys to be the only man in whom Mary herself was interested, and whose prospects were hopefully discussed in Rome, was by this time Henry's 'arrant traitor', and when he put in a belated appearance in northern

[52] *L&P*, XII, 445.

[53] Francis was the heir of the cadet Valois branch of Angoulême, and proclaimed himself king when Louis XII died without heirs male, irrespective of the fact that Mary Tudor might have been carrying Louis's son. R. J. Knecht, quoting the contemporary jurist de Moulin, writes 'The crown is not hereditary, for the new king is not the heir of his predecessor, and does not succeed him in the possession of his goods or in the heritage abandoned by the deceased, but he succeeds to the crown by right of blood in accordance with the Salic Law'. It was upon the basis of this principle that Francis secured the throne. *Francis I*, 13.

Europe in March, the king did his level best to have him extradited, kidnapped or murdered.

Mary's domestic routine during these months is elusive. Her privy purse expenses survive from December 1536, and provide a lot of circumstantial detail,[54] but no direct information about the household, because she was not paying the bills. After spending most of her time at Hunsdon over the previous three years, she obviously enjoyed the opportunity to move more freely. Having spent Christmas with the court at Greenwich, she paid brief visits to Hatfield and Newhall in January, returning to Greenwich by the middle of the month. At the end of February she went to Westminster, to Hatfield again, and then Chelmsford and Hunsdon before Easter. Most of the early summer was spent at Greenwich, but during July and August she visited Hampton Court, Guildford, Easthampsted, in Berkshire, and Windsor. September and October were passed mainly at Richmond, and November at Hampton Court. This degree of mobility, which does not seem to have been shared by the infant Elizabeth, raises the question of whether Mary had recovered a fully autonomous establishment. A reference to one Spencer 'one of the yeomen cooks of the Lady Mary', in March 1537, suggests that she had her own service departments. On the other hand the financial arrangements laid down in the king's warrant to Sir Brian Tuke on 28 August 1536, made no such provision.

> 'We woll and command you', the warrant ran, 'that ye incontynent upon the sight hereof do of our money which shall come to your keeping, pay or cause to be paid unto our trusty and wellbeloved servant Sir John Shelton knight, steward of the household of our children, the sum of foure thousand pounds in advancement of the charge of the said household for one hole yere.'[55]

This was the sum which Shelton himself had named, and was to be paid at the rate of £1000 a quarter. Tuke was most unhappy with this arrangement, claiming that he could not sustain the charge, but his protest seems to have been overruled. In April 1537 the council recommended that both Mary and Elizabeth be 'advanced to some certain decent living' on the grounds that

[54] BL Royal MS 17 B xxviii; printed by Frederick Madden as *The Privy Purse Expenses of the Princess Mary*.

[55] BL Additional Charter 67534.

they would be 'held in greater estimation', and would become more acceptable as brides 'to provide the king with friends in his present need'.[56] As a statement of the political value of royal daughters, this could hardly be neater, but the advice was not taken. At the end of May Sir Brian Tuke was again complaining to Cromwell about his inability to meet Shelton's warrant 'for the household of the ladies Mary and Elizabeth', so that instead of assigning the revenues of particular estates, it appears that Henry continued to support his daughters out of his own household. Since they did not spend very much time together, what this probably meant in practice was two households financed through a single officer, like the king's side and the queen's side of the court.

The money which Mary controlled personally came not from Sir Brian Tuke but from Thomas Henneage, a gentleman of the king's privy chamber who was knighted and appointed chief gentleman at about this time. It thus came from the privy purse, and not through the usual accounting procedures of the chamber. Between December 1536 and December 1537, £430 was received from this source, and from January to December of 1538 a further £260.[57] This money was disbursed in a great variety of ways which cast light on Mary's tastes and habits at this time. Rewards to her own chamber servants, and liveries for them, are regular items, as are the rewards to those who brought her innumerable gifts – from the servants of nobles and prelates who delivered their masters' New Year offerings, to 'one that brought pheasants and Chese to my ladies grace'. The king's watermen received tips for ferrying her about, and the keepers of the various royal residences which she visited in her peripatetic existence. In February 1537 she paid 10s. rent for a chamber at Greenwich in which to store her robes. When she spent a period at court, the various departments of the royal household received small rewards; 40s. to the king's cooks at Easter 1537, and 10s. each to the pantry and the scullery at the same time. She was generous to her godchildren, who seem to have been numerous,

[56] 'Things treated of in Council, April 1537'; *L&P*, XII, 815.

[57] Madden, *Privy Purse Expenses*, 1. This money was paid for the most part in sums of £40 or £100, but not on a fixed regular pattern. In June 1537 Mary received £40 from Henneage, and £50 from the queen, for some unexplained reason.

and mostly of humble status, and to the dependants of her servants. In August 1537 Beatrice ap Rice received 5s. for 'her sons table at Windsor', and her daughter 8s. for her board in London at the same time.[58] A band of minstrels was retained in her name, and 'Jane the fool' makes her first appearance at this time, although not mentioned in any surviving household list. Mary purchased goldsmiths' work, jewellery and special cloth in modest quantities, and spent regularly and heavily on card games. On the whole, an attractive impression of her personality emerges, but there are some surprises. Given her known enthusiasm for hunting, there are few references to matters connected with the chase, apart from 4s. compensation paid to William Alan of Richmond, for two sheep killed by her greyhounds. Probably most of those bills were paid through the main account. Charitable gifts are frequent, but religious offerings appear only at Easter and Candlemas. Above all, considering her reputation for musical skill and learning, there are remarkably few references to either instruments or books. The latter do not feature at all, except as New Year gifts received, and there is no suggestion that she either collected books or maintained a library.

Throughout the period covered by these accounts, Mary's health appears to have been good.[59] There is only one clear reference to her 'being sicke' in June 1537, an improvement which must have been related to her changed circumstances. Miguel de la Soa and Juan de Soto, both Spaniards formerly in Catherine's service, were retained as her physician and apothecary, with annuities of 100 marks and 40 marks respectively. But they do not seem to have lived in her household, as there are occasional references to one or the other being sent for – sometimes to attend the resident servants, rather than Mary herself. There are several suggestions that Mary's service was attractive, and that places in her household were eagerly sought after. However, she was not a magnate in her own right, and

[58] Madden, *Privy Purse Expenses*, 38, 40.

[59] This impression may be misleading, because there are external references to illness which are not reflected in the accounts. For example, Lady Kingston wrote to Wriothesley in January 1538 that 'on New Years day she could neither sit nor stand but was fain to lie on her bed for faintness' and was asking for Cromwell to arrange for Dr Buttes to visit her 'because he hath been with her in such cases in time past'. However, such episodes do not appear to have been frequent. *L&P*, Addenda, 1294.

Thomas Cromwell kept a sharp eye on the situation. In October 1537 the countess of Sussex, who was a close friend to both parties, attempted to place Katherine Basset, Lady Lisle's daughter, in Mary's chamber, only to receive the 'plain answer' that 'her grace shall have no more than her number'.[60] In spite of her importance, and her new found favour with the king, there are no indications that Mary acquired a clientage, or exercised the slightest political influence. If anything, she was herself a client, and her patron was Thomas Cromwell. Her occasional letters to him were always of gratitude for his guidance and support, for his generosity to her servants, or for small gifts. In June 1537, when the duchess of Norfolk appealed to him in dramatic and touching terms against her husband's maltreatment, she declared that she was prompted to approach him because she had heard how good he had been to 'the Lady Mary, the king's daughter' in her trouble.[61] She might, of course, have added that she knew there was no love lost between Cromwell and the duke; but his friendship for Mary, although politic, was none the less genuine. It was to stand her in good stead in 1538, when he made no attempt to implicate her in the destruction of her other and older friends, the Courtenays and Poles.

In October 1537 her fortunes were altered again, although more subtly, by the birth of the longed-for prince. God, Hugh Latimer roundly proclaimed, was English, and had recognized, albeit belatedly, the righteousness of the king's proceedings over the previous decade. Although it might be declared in Rome that Edward was illegitimate, because he had been born, and his parents married, during a period of schism from the Church, no one in England took this objection seriously. Mary was no longer the immediate heir, even in the eyes of her most fervent admirers, and even Eustace Chapuys began to lose interest in her. On 15 October she stood godmother to her half-brother, amid the universal and noisy rejoicings of London, and a fortnight later was named as the chief mourner for the queen: the child had been delivered naturally, but Jane's constitution was not equal to the strain; she developed puerperal fever and died on 25 October. Thus Mary lost a good friend, and was too 'accrased' to attend the first stage of the obsequies, celebrated on

[60] *The Lisle Letters*, ed. M. St Clare Byrne, IV, 167, 192.

[61] Elizabeth, duchess of Norfolk to Cromwell, 26 June 1537; *L&P*, XII, 143.

30 October, when her place was taken by the marchioness of Exeter.[62] By the time of the actual interment on 12 November, she was able to take her place behind the bier, and was later to receive a generous proportion of the queen's jewels, but her ceremonial precedence did not conceal the fact that she was now a long step further from the centre of events. Until her father remarried, Mary was in a sense the first lady of the kingdom, but there are few signs of this in the surviving evidence. The court passed Christmas 1537 in mourning, and the usual festivities were much curtailed, so although Mary seems to have been present at Greenwich, there was little opportunity for her to preside at her father's side, even if he had been disposed to allow her to do so. In March 1538 she stood godmother to the infant son of the earl and countess of Sussex, a ceremony at which the king, Cromwell and Sir John Dudley were the godfathers. Henry dined with her at Richmond in May, one of the few occasions on which she was able to play the hostess, and she was often at court – so often that her visits were no longer specifically commented upon. She continued to share a joint household with Elizabeth, which by March 1538 was presided over by Lady Mary Kingston, the wife of Sir William, the controller of the king's household. The servants who feature from time to time in the royal accounts as receiving specific rewards or other payments are for the most part familiar names: Miguel de la Soa, John 'Poticary', Richard Baldwin (her long-serving chaplain), Randall Dodd and Beatrice ap Rice. Once reconstituted in 1536, Mary's chamber seems to have retained a remarkable stability to the end of the reign, although the management of the household itself changed from time to time. In April 1539 Lady Kingston was replaced by Sir Edward and Lady Baynton, although it seems unlikely that this in itself made any difference to the domestic arrangements.[63]

Although he was never created prince of Wales, Edward was recognized as heir to the throne from the moment of his birth, and given an establishment of suitable size and dignity – very similar to that which Mary had enjoyed between 1519 and

[62] *L&P*, XII, 1060.

[63] *L&P*, XIV, 655. This was Sir Edward Baynton of Bromham, Wiltshire, and his second wife, Isobel. Both are referred to in the privy purse accounts, but only in terms which suggest acquaintance, rather than close association.

1525.[64] The relationship between the court, the prince's household and the joint household is very hard to determine, and varied with the king's own marital status. While Henry was unmarried, there seems to have been considerable flexibility. For example, in March 1538, when Chapuys was doing a 'social round', the king was at Hampton Court, Edward and Elizabeth together 'about three miles off', and Mary at Richmond. Whether Elizabeth was visiting her brother, or the households had been temporarily reorganized, is not clear. The brief Cleves marriage, from January to July 1540, did not establish a pattern, but after Henry had married his fifth wife, Catherine Howard, at the end of July, Mary seems to have resided at court for long periods. This may have been more on Henry's initiative than Catherine's because relations between the two women were not cordial; they were too near in age and too different in temperament. Nevertheless in November 1541, when Catherine was arrested, and her household dismissed, it was noted that 'Sir John Dudley shall conduct my Lady Mary to my Lord Prince's with a convenient number of the queen's servants', while Lady Margaret Douglas was sent to Kenninghall, to the duchess of Richmond. Elizabeth was not mentioned. Presumably Mary had been living on the 'queen's side' at court for some time, and either could not, or did not wish to, rejoin her sister. Throughout the spring and summer of 1542 Henry was depressed and morose, and did not keep company with any of his children. Mary was certainly not with him at the end of March, when she fell seriously ill of what was variously described as 'a strange fever' and palpitations of the heart. The king sent to enquire after her health and put his physicians at her disposal, but he did not visit her, perhaps because of his morbid fear of infection. It was only in November, with the news of victory at Solway Moss, that Henry's spirits began to revive. On 17 December Chapuys reported that the princess was summoned for the Christmas festivities 'with a great number of ladies', and there was speculation that the king might marry again.[65] On the 21st Mary arrived, 'accompanied and met in triumphal manner', and remained with the court for several months. Henry's policy was

[64] For a discussion of this early household, see W. K. Jordan, *Edward VI: The Young King*, 38–9.

[65] Chapuys to the queen of Hungary, 17 December 1542; *L&P*, XVII, 1212.

moving decisively towards an Imperial alliance, and in an ironic reversal of their earlier roles, for a few days in the middle of January, Chapuys found himself dependent upon her for information about the king's current state of mind. She was able to reassure him that the French ambassador's intrigues would not be allowed to harm the emperor's interests. This was an unaccustomed role for Mary, but she was now in high favour, and after the signing of the new Anglo-Imperial treaty on 11 February, the king was calling at her apartment two or three times a day. In March she was even allowed to invite Anne of Cleves for a three-day visit; a rare treat for the latter, who was normally kept away from the court during Henry's later intervals of celibacy, because of persistent rumours that he would take her back. In July 1543 she attended her father's last wedding, to Catherine Parr, one of only eighteen people to be so honoured, but her own favour was not abated by this change. She was 'retained to be with the queen', while Elizabeth was sent to share a household with Prince Edward.[66] Although she continued to move about with the restlessness which always characterized her periods of freedom, for the rest of her father's life – about three and a half years – Mary appears to have been based in the court. Her chamber servants remained with her, but her joint household with Elizabeth, which had existed in one form or another since the autumn of 1533, had certainly disappeared by December 1542, and possibly as much as two years earlier.

Mary's relationship with Catherine was affectionate and close. They exchanged gifts, and spent a considerable amount of time together. It may even have been Mary who stimulated Catherine's latent interest in learning and education, because the latter had not enjoyed a humanist upbringing, and only began to learn Latin after her marriage to the king.[67] Catherine approached her own education with all the enthusiasm of the convert. It was she who commissioned a new translation of Erasmus's *Paraphrases*, but she was not competent to undertake any of the work, whereas Mary did make a contribution until a further attack of illness caused her to relinquish the task. Nicholas Udall, the general editor, specifically praised her in his

[66] 12 July 1543; *L&P*, XVIII, 873; Chapuys to Charles V, 13 August 1543; *L&P*, XVIII, 39.

[67] Dowling, *Humanism in the Age of Henry VIII*, 236.

introduction as 'a peerless flower of virginity' who 'doth now also confer unto [us] the inestimable benefit of furthering both us and our posterity in the knowledge of God's word, and to the more clear understanding of Christ's gospel'.[68] Ironic words, in the light of her subsequent reputation. There are a number of other tributes to Mary's learned accomplishments as an adult, including the dedications which Henry Parker, Lord Morley addressed to her, but there is no first hand evidence. No works survive from her pen to match Catherine's *Prayers or meditacions*, or her *The lamentacion of a sinner*. Three of Elizabeth's translation exercises are extant from the same period; an English version of Margaret de Valois's *A godly medytacyon of the christen sowle*, a French translation of Erasmus's *Dialogus Fidei*, and a polyglot rendering of Catherine's *Prayers or meditacions* into French, Latin and Italian. But from Mary we have nothing which can be readily identified, and taken in conjunction with the negative evidence of her household expenses, this suggests at best passive rather than active scholarship. The continuing uncertainty of her health may have been one reason for this. In September 1543 she was reported to be 'very ill of a colic', and in June 1544 acknowledged to Lady Hertford that she had 'byn nothing well as yet these holydayes'.[69] She ran up considerable bills with her apothecary, and was often let blood. The optimistic Marillac in 1541 described her as not looking more than eighteen or twenty, in spite of being twenty-four, of mediocre beauty, and with a masculine voice. According to him, there was nothing wrong with her health, but more direct evidence says otherwise, and there is no reason to suppose that the symptoms of this period were psychosomatic.

Catherine's piety was distinctly inclined to the new learning. *The lamentacion of a sinner* has been described as 'explicitly Lutheran', but that was not published until after Henry's death.[70] While he lived she patronized reformers, and encouraged Bible-reading, but was wise enough to defer to the king as soon as their opinions began to diverge. This does not appear to

[68] Udall, *Paraphrases of Erasmus* (STC 2854), preface to Luke.

[69] Chapuys to Charles V, 9 September 1543; *L&P*, XVIII, 156; Mary to Lady Hertford, 3 June 1544; *L&P*, XIX, 620.

[70] Dowling, *Humanism in the Age of Henry VIII*, 236; the *Lamentation* was published in 1548.

have put any strain upon her relationship with Mary, not because the princess had (as she once claimed to her father) abdicated all her former views, but rather because Mary was herself strongly influenced by the new learning. Her opinions on the papal authority she prudently kept to herself, and her devotion to the mass was no stronger than Henry's, who was to decree that daily celebrations were to be made for his soul 'while the world shall endure'. Like many other catholic humanists, she approved of Bible-reading and sermons, and had no particular yearning for the shrines and pilgrimages which had come under official attack after 1535. Her accounts show dozens of examples of almsgiving between 1536 and 1544, but only a handful of sums paid 'for the maintenance of God's service', and none for the traditional pieties of the local altar or saint. Her virtue and godliness were praised by conservatives and reformers alike during this curious period of precarious ecclesiastical balance, and her position seems to have been very close to that which her kinsman Reginald Pole was soon to defend, and lose, at the council of Trent.[71] With her deeply rooted academic training Mary was probably more intellectual in her approach to the faith than Catherine, but the evidence is too flimsy for any firm conclusions. The more puritanical reformers did not approve of her, not on account of her conservatism but on account of her frivolity. She loved jewels and fine clothes, gambled compulsively, and continued to develop her musical talents, employing Philip Van Wilder to teach her the lute. She also hunted enthusiastically, on one occasion receiving a present of arrows from her father, and walked 'often two or three miles'. But it was her zeal for dancing which aroused their particular ire, and one of Edward's tutors caused the nine-year-old prince to send a Latin admonition to Catherine in May 1546, praying her to beg his dear sister Mary 'to attend no longer to foreign dances and merriments, which do not become a most Christian princess'.[72] It is to be hoped that the queen did not transmit so unsympathetic a message, and was in a position to identify its source.

[71] D. B. Fenlon, *Heresy and Obedience in Tridentine Italy*, discusses Pole's attempts to defend humanist priorities, particularly over vernacular scriptures.

[72] Edward to Catherine Parr, 12 May 1546; *L&P*, XXI, 802; *Literary Remains of King Edward VI*, ed. J. G. Nichols (Roxburgh Club, 1857), I, 9.

The records of Mary's domestic life during the last decade of her father's reign suggest a relatively tranquil routine, apart from a brush with Catherine Howard, which resulted in the dismissal of one of her favourite attendants.[73] But she was still close to the centre of political events, particularly as the king's failing health made it increasingly likely that Edward would succeed as a minor. The debate over her place in the succession continued until it was resolved by statute in 1543, when she took her place behind Edward, the heirs of his body, and any son who might be born to Catherine Parr.[74] Henry would never admit that either she or Elizabeth was legitimate, but treated them both in practice as though they were, and accorded them precedence over the undoubtedly legitimate daughters of his sister Mary. This was a painfully ironic conclusion in view of the number of lives which the issue had cost, most recently those of Mary's old friends, the marquis of Exeter and the countess of Salisbury. The so-called 'Exeter conspiracy' of 1538 was partly the result of the king's paranoid reaction to Reginald Pole's *Pro ecclesiasticae unitatis defensione*, partly of his fear of the last branch of the house of York, and partly of Cromwell's determination to remove a potentially powerful faction.[75] The Courtenays and the Poles had been high in favour, and close in friendship with the king, until they had taken Catherine's side in the marriage dispute. The fall of Anne Boleyn, and Mary's subsequent submission, had appeared to restore them to a position of strength, but the appearance was deceptive. In May 1538, when the possibility of a serious catholic initiative against England began to be considered, Cromwell sent a significant letter to Mary, warning her not to give her father grounds for suspicion, particularly by entertaining 'strangers' in her house. Who these 'strangers' were is not apparent, but she did not deny their existence, merely protesting that their presence had been reported 'to the worst'.[76] At the same time an informer reported from Genoa that it had been openly declared by an Englishman in that city that: 'If anything should fortune to the king . . . then Lady Mary, the king's daughter, might marry with the Marquis of

[73] Chapuys to Mary of Hungary, 5 December 1540 and 6 February 1541; *L&P*, xvi, 314, 523; *Cal.Span.*, vi, 143, 151.

[74] 35 Henry VIII c.1.

[75] *L&P*, xiii, 802, 961; Scarisbrick, *Henry VIII*, 364–5.

[76] Mary to Cromwell, 27 May 1538; *L&P*, xiii, 1082.

Exeter's son, and so they to enjoy the realm.' By August Cromwell was ready to strike. Geoffrey Pole, Reginald's younger brother, was arrested and taken to the Tower. In fear of his life, he revealed all manner of inconsequential conversations among his family and friends that determined construction could put to sinister use: the old proposal that Reginald should marry Mary; harmless statements about Mary's title to the Crown, and her reconciliation with her father. Upon this sort of evidence the marquis, his wife and son, Geoffrey's eldest brother, Henry, lord Montague and Sir Edward Neville were arrested. In November the three men were brought to trial and convicted. On 9 December they were executed.

The evidence of treasonable intent was negligible. The substance was that Reginald Pole, a cardinal since 1536, was the king's enemy, having twice been entrusted by the pope with missions designed to overthrow the English government. Mary may have been perfectly sincere in her professions to Cromwell that she would 'rather suffer bodily pain than lose any jot of the king's favour', and he may have been sincere in his friendship, but they both knew that she was a weapon which could easily be turned against her father, and that any idle talk of her marriage could assume an aspect of conspiracy. It is not surprising that she begged the powerful minister to continue as her guide and protector. Once the victims were safely dead, fresh evidence was conveniently discovered – copies of letters from the marquis to the cardinal – in 'a little coffer' belonging to the marchioness. On 9 January Cromwell informed Chapuys that it was clear 'the Marquis had designed to usurp the kingdom by marrying his son to the princess and destroying the prince.'[77] A month later the story had been embroidered still further. By then the treaty of Toledo had been signed, whereby Francis and Charles had pledged themselves not to make any fresh agreements with England, and Pole was again journeying north to press the papal arguments for a crusade. In acute alarm, Henry sought to invoke the treaty of Cambrai, and required the expulsion of 'his traitor'. A long denunciation of Pole accused him of counselling his brother and the marquis to destroy, not only the king and prince,

[77] Chapuys to Charles V, 9 January 1539; *L&P*, XIV, 37. For a full discussion of the case against the marquis and his associates, see M. H. and R. Dodds, *The Pilgrimage of Grace and the Exeter Conspiracy*.

but Mary and Elizabeth as well 'to usurp the whole realm', a plot he was alleged to have nurtured for ten years.[78] The early months of 1539 were months of acute political crisis, when England mustered and prepared to resist the expected invasion. The king's extravagant language was one reflection of this; another was the arrests of Sir Nicholas Carew and the countess of Salisbury, Pole's mother and Mary's former governess. Both were interrogated about their connection with the alleged conspiracy, and Carew was accused of betraying the secrets of the council. Both were convicted of treason, and Carew was beheaded on 3 March. The countess remained in prison until 1541, when a minor insurrection in Yorkshire brought her to the block also. As Chapuys observed, all those who suffered as a result of Pole's crusading zeal were good friends to Mary, and he added, 'It would seem that they want to leave her as few friends as possible.' In February 1539 the cardinal responded by addressing to the emperor a long and extremely bitter denunciation of Henry, urging all Christian princes to turn their swords against him as an infidel and tyrant. Mary cannot have been unaware of these tragic events, but we have no evidence at all of her reactions to them. She may have been deeply distressed by the fate of so many men and women to whom she had been close, and who, in a sense, had suffered for her sake. On the other hand her letters to Cromwell suggest that she had become so dependent upon him as a mediator with her father that she may even have come to share some of his perceptions of events. Her later actions as queen suggest that she nursed a grudge against her father for the sake of these friends, but at the time she was discreetly silent, and there is no suggestion of the kind of emotional crisis which had followed her mother's death.

If Mary had in any sense been converted by Cromwell's assiduous attention and numerous small services, and if she was as dependent upon his advice as she claimed, then his fall in June 1540 must have come as another disturbing shock. Again, we have no indication of her personal feelings, but one of the more implausible charges reported to have been made against the disgraced minister was that he had conspired to marry her.

[78] Henry VIII to Wyatt, 13 February 1539; *L&P*, XIV, 280. Interrogation of Carew, ibid., 189.

No such accusation was formally entered, but the rumour is significant. It suggests that his cultivation of her goodwill was well known, and also that there was much speculation about the repeated failure of negotiations for her marriage. On 6 July Henry's envoys in France reported that it had been generally believed in Francis's court that Cromwell would be created either earl or duke, and that Henry would then bestow Mary upon him 'as he had given his sister to the Duke of Suffolk'.[79] For that reason the ambitious minister had sabotaged every other attempt to secure her hand. Like Wolsey before him, Cromwell had become a scapegoat for the frustrating, and often contradictory, twists and turns of the king's own policy. In details the story of Mary's abortive marriage negotiations is Byzantine in its complexity, but in outline relatively straightforward. In January 1538 Charles V revived the idea of the Portuguese match which had been dropped the previous summer. His main objective was to involve Henry in a league against France, and he was willing to invest Dom Luis with the duchy of Milan in order to secure such an agreement. The king responded favourably, but also indicated his own interest in the dowager duchess of Milan, and pressed the emperor to take his part in the threatened general council of the Church. By the end of February a partial agreement seemed to be in sight, and Henry believed that he had persuaded the Imperial ambassadors to accept Mary 'as to succeed only in default of all other lawful issue, male or female', and with 100,000 crowns in *dot*. At the end of March it was believed in Rome that the deal was complete, and that Dom Luis would receive Milan. But at that point Henry was drawing back and haggling over the *dot*, because the French had also revived their earlier offer of the duke of Orleans. It soon transpired that Francis was doing this, not only to check the emperor, but also in the expectation that Henry would marry the dowager duchess, and receive Milan as her dowry. By offering to take Mary unconditionally for his son, he was hoping to persuade the English to pass on the Italian duchy, which Henry could not hope to

[79] John Wallop and Edward Carne to Henry VIII, 6 July 1540; *L&P*, xv, 842. See also ibid., 792, a report of rumours concerning Cromwell's fall, 16 June.

defend, and thus fulfil a major policy objective without the expense of war.[80]

In early May, Henry was stalling on the Portuguese negotiation, and encouraging the French, but he was making no progress in securing the duchess of Milan, and consequently was heading for an impasse on both fronts. There were three reasons for this. In the first place the king was still trying to attach conditions about the general council; secondly, he already had a degree of affinity with the duchess, which in Imperial eyes required a dispensation; and thirdly, the duchess herself was distinctly averse to such a match. At this point the French altered their tactics, and began to offer a variety of French brides for Henry, perhaps hoping by a double marriage alliance to obtain an advantage for which it would be worth abandoning the attempt on Milan. Impressed by these overtures, Henry then endeavoured to enlist Francis's aid against the pope, at which point the French beat a cautious retreat. In June the whole English strategy received a setback when Francis and Charles met at Nice upon the pope's initiative, and signed a ten-year truce. At the beginning of August the French believed that the emperor had given up any intention of conferring Milan upon either Henry or his daughter. In fact they were mistaken, because Charles had just issued powers to Mary of Hungary to conclude both marriages, and the negotiations continued inconclusively. Ostensibly Henry was more interested in the French offers, particularly for himself. Hans Holbein shuttled back and forth across the Channel with portraits of selected royal beauties, and at one point he even had the temerity to suggest a parade at Calais for his benefit.[81] Francis no doubt sympathized, but propriety required the rejection of such a notion out of hand. Behind the scenes the Imperial envoys were making more progress. On 26 August Chapuys and Mendoza visited Mary herself

[80] Charles V to Granvelle, 19 January 1538; *L&P*, XIII, 110. Same to Chapuys and Mendoza; ibid., 207. Chapuys and Mendoza to Charles V; ibid., 241. Henry VIII to Wyatt, 22 February; ibid., 329. Council to Stephen Gardiner, 31 March; ibid., 628. Francis I to Chastillon, 9 April; ibid., 723. In the midst of these negotiations, Henry tried to raise the stakes by offering Elizabeth for one of the emperor's nephews, and Edward for his daughter, Mary; Cromwell to Wyatt, 11 February; ibid., 255.

[81] Montmorency to Chastillon, 2 August 1538; *L&P*, XIII, 23. Commission (undated), ibid., 1470. Gardiner's instructions for Bonner, 20 August, ibid., 143. Scarisbrick, *Henry VIII*, 359–60.

at Havering. They were disappointed by her attitude, which they correctly believed had been dictated by Cromwell. She reproached them for their unwillingness to meet her father's wishes, and expressed her disappointment at the meagreness of the settlement offered. They in return commended her wisdom in being so well informed about the negotiation, and politely rejected the notion that their master was responsible for the difficulties. Their attempts to depart from the text met with only partial success. Mary was willing to express her continued devotion to the emperor, but did not respond to the suggestion that she might still like to leave the realm in secret. In reporting the conversations to Cromwell afterwards, she naturally gave them a different twist, emphasizing that the ambassadors had reiterated the emperor's goodwill to her, and had urged her to remain 'in the obedience and goodwill of my father', but saying nothing about their surreptitious overture.[82] She had learned a good lesson in discretion over the previous two years, and it is hard to tell what she really felt.

Throughout September and October, as the French negotiations languished, an Imperial settlement seemed likely, with Dom Luis receiving Milan, and agreeing to abide by the laws of England in the event of his inheriting the realm in Mary's right. However as Henry, threatened with diplomatic isolation, grew keener, the emperor retreated. In early November Wyatt advised the king that Milan would not be conceded – 'the occasion is past' – and by the end of the month Charles's 'coldness' towards the whole proposal was evident to all involved. By one of those sudden twists so characteristic of renaissance diplomacy, Francis and Charles were rapidly approaching an agreement, and by the end of December their envoys were contemplating Henry's mounting alarm with ill concealed amusement. The pope's persistent pressure was at last achieving some success. On 17 December the Bull of Excommunication, prepared in 1535, was given another airing, and there was talk of a joint embargo on English trade. 'The abominable cruelty of the king of England towards the church and the chief persons of his realm' was belatedly discovered to be a compelling cause for political action,

[82] Mary to Cromwell, 24 August 1538; *L&P*, XIII, 174; and 27 August, *L&P*, Addenda, 1348. Chapuys and Mendoza to Charles V (after 27 August); *L&P*, XIII, 232.

and on 12 January 1539 the treaty of Toledo was signed, whereby both rulers agreed to withdraw from all negotiations with the schismatic islanders.

For three or four months war was generally expected. The 'enterprise of England' was spoken of hopefully in Rome. Henry was to be deposed, Edward ignored as illegitimate, and Mary married to the duke of Orleans, who would be invested with the kingdom.[83] It was an unrealistic dream. The warlike preparations were all in England, and by April it was clear that no attack would come. Mutual suspicion between Charles and Francis began to revive, and at the end of May the pope was reported to be 'in great dread' because of a rumour that the emperor, whose wife, Isabella, had recently died, was about to marry the princess of England. In July, Philip Melachthon reported hearing the same rumour, but there was no substance in it at all. Instead, the emperor paid a state visit to France in November, and the *entente cordiale* survived well into 1540. The main consequence of this for England was not war, but a somewhat desperate search for alternative allies. As early as June 1538 the possibility of an anti-papal front with the German Lutherans had been canvassed, and Chapuys believed that a double marriage alliance with the duchy of Cleves was in the air. An anti-papal league was sought with some energy in the early months of 1539, involving Denmark, Saxony and Hesse, but the negotiations came to nothing, partly because the danger to England receded, and partly because the Lutherans attempted to insist on Henry's acceptance of the Confession of Augsburg.[84] Discussions with Cleves, on the other hand, prospered after a slow start. In January 1539 Chapuys believed that the main emphasis would be upon a marriage between William, the

[83] Aguilar to Charles V, 26 December 1538; *L&P*, XIII, 1148; Don Lope de Saria to Charles V; *L&P*, XIV, 372; memorandum by Cardinal Carpi (misdated January 1540); *L&P*, XV, 134. Pole, on the other hand, who was doing his best to stimulate joint action, formed the correct impression that nothing would be done, and withdrew to the papal city of Carpentras to await fresh instructions. Scarisbrick, *Henry VIII*, 362–3.

[84] Instructions from Cromwell to Christopher Mont, 20 January 1539; *L&P*, XIV, 103; Henry VIII to Carne, Wotton and Birde, 10 March; ibid., 489; report of John Parker from Brussels, 14 April; ibid., 768. These negotiations were going on at the same time as the conservative Act of Six Articles was proceeding through parliament. Scarisbrick, *Henry VIII*, 366–7.

duke's heir, and Mary, and Cromwell's instructions to Christopher Mont in the same month support that view:

> Although she is only the king's natural daughter, she is endued, as all the world knows, with such beauty, learning and virtue, that when the rest is agreed, no man could stick.

However, William succeeded his father in February, and the balance of the negotiation changed. Neither William nor his family were Lutherans, but rather reforming catholics, at odds with the pope and the emperor, and consequently very much to Henry's taste. The duke's sister, Anne, was also very much to his taste, or so he thought after seeing Holbein's portrait. Although there were widespread rumours during the spring and summer that William would marry Mary, Henry eventually gave priority to his own affairs, and the treaty which was concluded on 6 October made no mention of his daughter.

In view of the outcome of the king's fourth marriage, it is sadly ironic that it seems to have been pressed at the expense of a promising opportunity for Mary, but William showed little interest in her, and it is quite possible that Henry once again preferred to retain her as a diplomatic card. In November she headed the list of ladies appointed to receive the new queen, but she was now twenty-three and her unmarried state was beginning to appear anomalous. As Marillac, the French ambassador, remarked in December, the old problem was still unresolved: whatever conditions her father might attach to her union, a powerful prince could still take advantage of her birthright to challenge the English succession. But as he also noted, it was precisely that consideration which favoured the next challenger for her hand, and the only suitor, in the proper sense, who ever appeared. This was duke Philip of Bavaria, the son of the elector palatine, who had come to England, apparently on his own initiative, just before Christmas, to offer his military service to Henry and to ask for Mary in marriage.[85] Whether the king was wrong-footed by his effrontery, or touched by his knight errantry, at first he seemed to carry all before him. Cromwell sent Thomas Wriothesley to Hertford, where Mary was then living, to sound

[85] Philip, duke of Bavaria, to Henry VIII; *L&P*, XIV, 658; Marillac to Montmorency, 24 December 1539; ibid., 732.

her out. Unlike the duke of Cleves, Philip was a Lutheran, and Mary admitted frankly 'that she would prefer never to enter that kind of religion' – but she committed herself entirely to her father's will. On 26 December they met. It must have been a somewhat chilly tryst on such a day in the gardens of the abbot of Westminster, but Philip did his best to warm it up. He actually kissed her, reported the well-informed Marillac, as though he had been hidden behind one of the bushes, 'which is an argument either of marriage or of near relationship, seeing that since the death of the late Marquis [of Exeter] no lord of this kingdom has dared to go so far'.[86] They had conversed, partly in German through an interpreter, and partly in Latin, and at the end of the interview he had declared his resolution, with the king's agreement, to have her as his wife. Mary, who may well have been unnerved by such unusual and direct tactics, merely repeated that she would obey her father. Marillac expected the wedding to take place 'within ten to fifteen days', and indeed a treaty was drawn up, whereby Philip agreed to take his bride 'by the laws and statutes of the realm incapable of succeeding to the crown' with a *dot* of 40,000 golden florins (about £7000).[87]

The Imperialists were taken completely by surprise. Early in January word reached Rome that Mary was married 'without the advice or knowledge of the emperor', and on the 15th Chapuys was reduced to asking around the English court to find out if the news was true. In fact it was not. Although the emperor's council decided it would have to accept the *fait accompli*, by the time the news reached them, Philip had already left England, a disappointed man. Either he had found some aspect of the draft treaty unacceptable, or, more likely, Henry had attempted to impose some additional condition at the last minute. It would have been entirely consistent with the king's whole attitude to his daughter's marriage if he had found some pretext to withdraw, fearing both to lose his control over her,

[86] Mary to Cromwell, 17 December 1539; *L&P*, XIV, 696; Thomas Wriothesley to Cromwell, 17 December; ibid., 697; Marillac to Francis I, 27 December; ibid., 744. It was during this visit that he gave her the cross of diamonds, which Henry subsequently required her to surrender. Madden, *Privy Purse Expenses*, 176.

[87] Draft treaty; *L&P*, XIV, 733. For a fuller account of the negotiations, see *L&P*, Addenda, 1425–7 (9–27 December 1539).

and to present an opportunity to someone else. Briefly, there had been a real chance that Mary would marry, and leave England for a new life with her father's consent and blessing. Whether she was at all attracted to Philip, we do not know, but in spite of her professions to the contrary, it may well be that she desperately needed a husband by 1540, and his wooing, perfunctory though it was, was the only episode of its kind that she was ever to enjoy. In spite of his disappointment, the duke did not give up easily. Encouraged, perhaps, by his creation as a knight of the Garter, and a reward of 2000 marks, in April he tried again. Marillac expected him to return to England, but instead he wrote to Cromwell with a new set of proposals. Because of Cromwell's arrest, the letter went astray, and when he tried again in August, the circumstances had changed. In May 1543 he was back, again offering Henry his sword, and raising 'the old question' of marriage. Again he departed with a gift, but no other satisfaction. When Henry was negotiating with Duke Maurice of Saxony in January 1545, his envoys were specifically instructed to reject any further overtures on Philip's behalf, but in March 1546 he was again in England, 'honourably received'. On that occasion he obtained a contract for 10,000 foot and 1000 horse, but still no marriage. He did, however, see Mary for a second time during his visit, and provoked renewed speculation.[88] On that occasion he was also an emissary for his father, but the large negotiation for a treaty of alliance broke down over the question of religion. In September of the same year, Henry seems to have re-opened the matter himself, and Philip came for a third time. The French envoy, de Selve, misunderstanding the situation, believed that his persistence had a financial motive, and that his real objective was to be bought off. The king had no cause to be generous for that reason, but it was finally a pension and not his long-sought bride that Philip took back to Germany.

Apart from these occasional appearances by the duke of Bavaria, the diplomacy of Mary's marriage, from October 1540 to Henry's death in January 1547 returned to the old see-saw of

[88] Scepperus to Schore, 28 March 1546; *L&P*, XXI, 479; Scepperus and Van der Delft to Charles V, 12 April 1546; ibid., 588; John Mason to Henry VIII, 11 May 1546; ibid., 796. Mason wrote of a 'bruit' 'which might well be sprung from some of the Duke's servants who saw conference once or twice between Lady Mary and him'.

the emperor versus a French prince. It is hard to take any of these negotiations seriously. In October 1540, Henry made advances to Charles, to which the latter appeared to respond, despite the fact that, as Marillac observed, there was no chance that Henry would risk having the emperor succeed him as his son-in-law, and no chance that Charles would take her on any other terms. In February 1541 Francis heard a rumour that an Imperial marriage had been concluded, but Marillac was able to scotch it immediately. In June of the same year the French ambassador reported optimistically that Mary was deliberately avoiding private conversations with Chapuys for fear of offending her father, and, taking advantage of this apparent estrangement, re-opened the suit of the duke of Orleans. It was in connection with this overture that Marillac 'appraised' the princess, as we have already seen. But the objection to Orleans was ultimately the same as the objection to the emperor – the prospect of a foreign king – and several observers thought that the French were dissimulating, mainly to head off a threatened Anglo-Imperial alliance. The treaty of Toledo was occasionally alluded to, but ignored in practice by both parties to it. Francis was sufficiently serious by November 1541 to be discussing financial terms, whereupon Henry promptly began to claim the arrears of several pensions agreed by the French in treaties going back to 1515, thereby ensuring a further protracted round of discussions.[89] He was, in a sense, double-crossing the others. At the end of December, Chapuys revealed to Henry that the French were also negotiating with the Portuguese, and the Anglo-French discussion stalled. Although he was still extremely sceptical of the Imperial marriage, in January 1542 Marillac sensed that he was losing the diplomatic duel, and revived his earlier proposals, obtaining full powers from Francis on 10 February.

Later in the same month William Paget, Henry's envoy in France, injected a touch of much-needed romance into the bargaining, by reporting that Orleans was 'far in love' with Mary (whom he had never seen), and would give one of his hands to have her. The English pushed up their financial

[89] Francis I to Marillac, 17 September 1541; *L&P*, XVI, 1186; Chapuys to the queen of Hungary, 26 October 1541; ibid., 1292; Francis I to Marillac, 15 November 1541; ibid., 1351; Chapuys's 'intelligences', November 1541; ibid., 1390.

demands, and found fault with Marillac's powers. They justified this by pointing out that Orleans could well become king of England, but the real reason for Henry's aggressiveness seems to have been that he was angling for a general alliance with the emperor, and putting pressure on the Scots to make amends for the incursions of their undisciplined borderers. In April 1542, in a moment of rare candour, Henry admitted that 'he loved his daughter well, but himself and his own honour better'.[90] Although there was no more talk of an Imperial marriage, the French negotiations were no nearer a conclusion by the middle of May, when Francis broke up the conference in some disgust. Immediately the rumours of an Imperial alliance revived, complete with financial details, only this time the bridegroom was to be a son of the king of the Romans, the emperor's brother Ferdinand, who was to come to England and be created duke of Bedford. In July 1542 the treaty of Toledo was finally laid to rest by a resumption of the Franco-Habsburg war, and although Marillac again raised the Orleans marriage in October, Henry was by that time set on joining the emperor in an invasion of France. The relevant treaty was concluded on 11 February, without any reference to marriage, and Mary's matrimonial fate dropped out of political consideration for almost two years.

This was a period of war, both with Scotland and with France, the details of which do not concern us in this context. The English victory at Solway Moss on 23 November 1542 raised Henry's spirits, and may have pointed him towards his sixth and final marriage. It certainly brought Mary back to court, but did nothing for her matrimonial prospects. In January 1545 a touch of novelty was briefly added by the suggestion of Adolph of Holstein, the twenty-four-year-old brother of the king of Denmark. But beyond his age he had nothing to commend him, and no negotiation resulted, although there was another rumour in January 1547 that the English were interested in such a marriage. By the summer of 1544, Francis had lost interest, after a final brief flirtation with the Orleans match as a means of ending the war. Instead, he used Orleans as a means to bring his war with the emperor to an end at the peace of Crêpy on 18 September 1544, betrothing him to Charles's daughter Mary.

[90] Paget to Henry VIII, 26 February 1542; *L&P*, XVII, 128; council to Paget, 12 April; ibid., 246.

The marriage never took place, because Orleans died in September 1545. After Orleans's death there was talk of an approach on behalf of Anthony of Bourbon, duke of Vendôme, but it came to nothing, and when peace was eventually agreed between France and England in June 1546, there was no mention of a marriage alliance. The Imperial negotiation appeared again for the last time in the autumn of 1545, as Henry tried to recover the ground he had lost at Crêpy. On 23 October Stephen Gardiner and Thomas Thirlby were commissioned to present a tripartite plan, whereby the emperor would marry Mary, Edward would marry the emperor's daughter, and Elizabeth his son Philip, whose first wife had died in July. Charles responded politely, but negatively. He was not inclined to re-marry now, and his son was too distressed to consider such a proposition. The rebuff was clear, and although Henry was reluctant to accept it, he had no option. Rumours persisted, but it was Mary herself who had made the shrewdest appraisal of the situation, as far back as June 1542, declaring,

> that it was folly to think that they would marry her out of England, or even in England, as long as her father lived; adding that she knew what had been said of it, both on Francis's part and on the Emperor's . . . but it was certain that nothing would be got from them but fine words, for she would be, while her father lived, only Lady Mary, the most unhappy lady in Christendom.[91]

Apart from her unmarried state, which frustrated so many of the ideas of a Christian princess which her education had instilled into her, she had no particular reasons for unhappiness as her father's life drew to a close. She had lost another old friend with the departure of Eustace Chapuys in March 1545, but she had lived to fight another day, and that was no mean achievement when it was being said, as late as May 1538, that if the king died there would be two parties contending for the succession 'one for the young prince and the other for madame Marie'. She was, as all reports agree, 'universally adored' by the English, and the subject of all sorts of flattering encomia from abroad, including an approach from the princess of Portugal in November 1545, who, having heard 'the fame of her virtue and learning',

[91] Marillac to Francis I, 3 June 1542; *L&P*, XVII, 371.

solicited an exchange of correspondence.[92] When Henry died on 28 January 1547 his will, making no mention of her legitimacy, confirmed her place in the succession after Edward, and stipulated that she should not marry without the written and sealed consent of a majority of Edward's council. The problem which had dogged her from her birth had still not been resolved, and might not ever be resolved, because by the time Edward had reached manhood and produced heirs of his own, she would be past the years of childbearing. The prospect of £10,000 in cash as a marriage portion must have seemed a small consolation, because in spite of what she had said, her frustration did not depend entirely upon her father's life. However, if her marriage prospect still seemed cloudy, in one respect her father's will clearly presaged better things. For a princess who had lived all her life under the direct financial control of the royal household, and the last three and a half years without any household of her own, beyond her chamber servants, the prospect of a guaranteed independent income of £3000 a year must have been appealing. For the first time in her life, she was about to acquire a measure of independence, and the responsibility, at least to some extent, for managing her own affairs. She might be 'only the Lady Mary', but with an income equal to that of a major peer, she could at last look forward to being something more than a symbol and a figurehead.[93]

[92] Chastillon to Montmorency, 14 May 1538; *L&P*, XIII, 995; memorandum of the duke of Nayera's visit to England, 5 April 1544; *L&P*, XIX, 296; Mary of Portugal to Mary, 5 November 1546; *L&P*, XXI, 355.

[93] Henry's will is among the Royal Wills in the Public Record Office, E.23, IV pt.i ff. 1–17; *L&P*, XXI, 634. The protracted controversy surrounding its authenticity, and the king's exact intentions, do not affect the provision made for Mary and Elizabeth. Both were living at court in the closing months of the reign. An 'Ordinary' of the king's household from the summer of 1546 shows them heading the 'Queen's Ordinary accustomed to be lodged'. BL Cotton Vespasian C XIV, f.92: *L&P*, XXI, 969.

4

The Conservative Magnate

(1547–1553)

Henry VIII was buried with elaborate and protracted ceremonial 'as to the dignity of such a mighty prince it appertaineth'. His body lay in state in the chapel at Westminster until 14 February, when it was conveyed with great solemnity to Syon. The following day the cortege passed by way of Eton to Windsor, and on the 16th the king was finally laid to rest in the chapel of the Order of the Garter, with a magnificent requiem mass, and a sermon from Stephen Gardiner on the question-begging text *Beati mortui qui in Domino moriuntur.* Apart from the ritual proclamation of Edward VI over his father's grave, no one reading the lengthy and detailed account published by John Strype would gain any impression of the political or personal realities of the situation which had been created by Henry's death.[1] The chief mourner was Henry Grey, marquis of Dorset, no blood relation but, as the husband of the king's elder niece, Frances Brandon, the nearest thing to a male kinsman after Edward. The powerful men in the government which was then being formed – Edward Seymour, earl of Hertford, Sir William Paget, John Dudley, Viscount Lisle, Thomas Cranmer, archbishop of Canterbury – played no significant part. The contrast between form and substance could hardly have been more marked. Their bodies were present in the chapel at Windsor, but their minds may well have been elsewhere, since the protectorate was newly established, and on the following day, 17 February, Hertford was to be created duke of Somerset and Lisle, earl of

[1] J. Strype, *Ecclesiastical Memorials*, II, 2, 289–311.

Warwick.[2] If political convenience reduced the role of many leading councillors, custom excluded others close to Henry from his formal obsequies. Edward remained in London. The widowed queen watched the interment and requiem mass from 'the Queen's closet above', an enclosed part of the chapel gallery, and if Mary and Elizabeth were with her, there is no explicit mention of the fact. The Imperial ambassador, Van der Delft, subsequently wrote that Mary had been very displeased with Hertford at this time, because 'he did not visit her nor send to her for several days after her father's death'. But she would have been naïve indeed if she could not have perceived the reason for such an oversight. The first two weeks of February 1547, while the old king lay unburied, was a period of great political delicacy. Not only were the ascendant councillors manœuvring urgently to secure themselves in power, but even the security of Edward's succession itself could not be taken for granted. In the eyes of catholic Europe the prince was illegitimate, and the authority of statute unacknowledged. Mary was her father's lawful heir. The earl of Hertford knew this perfectly well, and the longer she could be kept in ignorance or uncertainty of what was afoot, the less chance she would have of making a disruptive move.

In fact no such thought seems to have crossed her mind, or to have been suggested by the defeated conservative faction at court. However Mary may have been regarded at the papal *Curia* or the Imperial court, she herself accepted her father's will, and there does not appear to have been any significant body of opinion in England which took a different view. Deep divisions were already beginning to appear upon religious issues, but the papal verdict on Edward's legitimacy was universally ignored by all parties. In his last great battle on the issue of the succession, Henry's victory had been total. It took some weeks for this to be appreciated outside England. When Edward was first proclaimed on 31 January, Van der Delft expressed surprise that the princess was not mentioned, and on 6 February Mary of Hungary wrote carefully to the ambassador:

[2] These dignities, and others, had been resolved in council on 15 February, and conferred on the 17th, so Henry's obsequies in fact delayed the creations by one day. *Acts of the Privy Council*, ed. J. R. Dasent, II, 34–5; *The Chronicle and Political Papers of King Edward VI*, ed. W. K. Jordan, 5; BL Hargrave MS 497, f.35.

> We make no mention at present of the young prince, as we are ignorant as yet whether or not he will be recognised as king ... We likewise refrain from sending you any letters for our cousin Mary, as we do not know yet how she will be treated.[3]

A fortnight later, the emperor was equally cautious, although a shade more revealing about his hopes. As he informed Van der Delft, he had returned the greetings sent to him in Edward's name, without acknowledging the latter's title:

> We went no further than this with regard to the young king, in order to avoid saying anything which might prejudice the right that our cousin the Princess might advance to the throne.[4]

Charles had obvious reasons for preferring his biddable cousin to the highly suspect regime which was beginning to take shape in London, just as he had attempted to use her to bring pressure to bear on her father ten years earlier. The newly installed protector understood this, but he also realized that the emperor would make no move unless he was convinced that the political situation in England was already going decisively in the desired direction. Consequently the English council maintained a bland confidence, and by the end of April the king was fully recognized in every court save that of Rome.

Meanwhile Mary continued to live quietly in the queen dowager's household.[5] We have no idea of her personal reactions to the death of her overbearing parent. In later years she consistently referred to him with every mark of formal respect, but with no trace of affection or admiration. His tomb was never completed, but the story that, after her accession, she had his body exhumed and burned, is based on no contemporary evidence. Her predominant emotion at this time was probably one of relief – a feeling which she may well have shared with Catherine, and which would have helped to keep them together.

[3] *Cal. Span.*, IX, 7, 15.

[4] Ibid., 38.

[5] This arrangement, which had commenced long before Henry's death, seems to have continued until about 14 April. Robert Rochester's assumption of responsibility for her finances probably coincided with the date of separation. The story of Henry's exhumation was retailed many years later by Sir Francis Englefield. Scarisbrick, *Henry VIII*, 497.

However, the queen was already being besieged by her old flame Thomas Seymour, recently created Lord Seymour of Sudely,[6] and by the middle of April this developing relationship made the princess's presence inconvenient. By the end of April Mary had been allocated the patrimony decreed in her father's will. It appears that she never saw the will itself, nor was informed of its exact terms, because later in the summer, when the emperor complained that he was being kept in ignorance, and instructed Van der Delft to ask her what marriage portion she was to be allowed, Mary declared that she did not know that, or any other particulars. She had no idea, she added, whether the will which had been acted upon was genuine or not, but in respect of her own position, it was very similar to that which had been made in 1544.[7] Like Chapuys, the ambassador saw disparagement of the princess at every turn, complained constantly about how little honour and respect was shown to her, and informed her in July that he considered her landed revenues of 12,000 ducats (£4000) 'a most miserable allowance' and far short of what Henry had actually left her. In fact her estates were valued at £3819 18s. 6d., which was about 20 per cent more than the will had required, and made her the fifth or sixth wealthiest peer in England.[8] The lands, advowsons and other perquisites which made up this endowment were situated for the most part in Norfolk, Suffolk and Essex. A number of them were former Howard properties, including the lordship and manor of Kenninghall, which had only been in the hands of the Crown for a matter of weeks, following the attainder of the third duke of Norfolk. Also included in the grant were the royal manor and

[6] Thomas Seymour, the younger brother of the earl of Hertford, had aspired to marry Catherine, then the widow of Lord Latimer, before she had been taken up by Henry. He seems to have resumed his suit within a few weeks of the king's death, much to the annoyance of his brother. By May they were exchanging letters in terms of warm affection. In early June, aware of the obstacles in his path, he tried unsuccessfully to enlist the support of Mary for his suit. The couple eventually married in obscure circumstances in early July. PRO SP10/1/99, 43; J. Maclean, *The Life of Sir Thomas Seymour*, 44–7.

[7] Van der Delft to the emperor, 10 July; *Cal.Span.*, IX, 123.

[8] *Calendar of the Patent Rolls*, Edward VI, II, 20. In 1559 there were five peers with gross rentals over £4000 a year – Norfolk, Shrewsbury, Pembroke, Northumberland and Derby. Of those, Norfolk and Northumberland were Marian restorations. In 1547 their places would probably have been filled by Somerset and Warwick. Stone, *Crisis of the Aristocracy*, appendix VIII.

residence of Hunsdon, where Mary had spent much time in earlier years, and another of her favourite houses, Newhall (also called Beaulieu) in Essex. The rebuilding of Newhall had been one of Henry's major building projects in the earlier part of his reign, £17,000 having been spent on it between 1517 and 1521. In 1547 it was a substantial and dignified mansion, in good repair, and it was to be Mary's principal home over the next six years.

It is not clear whether she was consulted before these allocations were made, but if not, some knowledgeable and sympathetic person must have selected them. Hunsdon and Ware in Hertfordshire; Stansted Abbot, Roydon, Epping, Copped Hall, Newhall and Writtle in Essex, formed a convenient block of manors only some twelve to fifteen miles from London, and well provided with good houses. A second coherent group of estates lay in East Essex, near the coast, and centred on Great Clacton and Chiche St Osyths. The rest were more scattered, from Olney and Great Marlowe in Buckinghamshire to Wells and Sheringham on the north Norfolk coast. Only Shotwick, in Cheshire, lay outside the Home Counties and East Anglia. Van der Delft was prone to refer misleadingly to Kenninghall as 'the north parts', as though it had been situated in Yorkshire, but there was no question of Mary having been banished from the vicinity of the capital. Indeed, given her rank and past history, it would have been foolish for the council to have done any such thing. It suited the protector to have her under observation, and it consorted with her honour to be close to the court. The formal grant of these lands is dated 17 May 1548, with issues from the preceding Michaelmas,[9] but most of them had at least been identified by April 1547, when Van der Delft reported that Mary had left the queen dowager's household, and was shortly going into Norfolk 'to the possessions formerly held by the duke of Norfolk'. By 16 June he knew that her 'allowance' was to be 12,000 ducats, derived from lands in Norfolk and Suffolk, but at that time she was still at Havering in Essex (not a part of her own estate), and she did not travel into Norfolk until July. Probably some interim arrangement was made for her financial support, because between 12 April and 24 July warrants were authorized by the council for £1700 to be paid to her servants Richard Wilbraham

[9] *Cal. Pat.*, Edward VI, II, 20.

and Robert Rochester, towards her 'pension' or 'assignment'. During the same period the cofferer of the king's household was still paying some of her bills; £27 12s. 6d. on 14 April; £178 9s. 6d. on 24 August; and £100 on 4 September 'for provision of horses for my Lady Mary's grace and her ordinary gentle-women'.[10] The implication is that Mary created her independent establishment, not suddenly, but over a period of months from mid-April to mid-September, and that her pension was a temporary expedient until she began to receive the revenues of her own lands, on and after 15 August. Such an interpretation can also be supported by the fact that a warrant for £200 on 12 April was authorized to her long-standing servant Richard Wilbraham, while another for £400 two days later was to be paid to Robert Rochester. Rochester, who can be identified as controller of her household by 1549, presumably took up his duties at this point.

Mary's estates were granted for life, or until the council made a suitable marriage for her in accordance with the terms of her father's will; and in the event she was to hold the bulk of them undisturbed, until they returned to the Crown on her accession. The only exceptions were the manors of St Osyth, Little and Great Clopton, and Willeigh. On 3 December 1552 Mary agreed to exchange these properties with the king, and regranted them to the Crown on 17 April following. In return she received the lordships and manors of Eye, Framlingham and Bungay, all in Suffolk, to an annual value of £604 17s. 1d.[11] This was probably an advantageous bargain, but it seems to have been forced upon her. In April 1551, when Sir Thomas Darcy was created Lord Darcy of Chiche, he was granted the reversion of these lands. They were appropriate to his title, but it may also have been part of the council's intention to reduce Mary's access to the sea, as they were aware by that time of her desire to leave the country. Having persuaded her at length to surrender them, they were finally granted to Lord Darcy in possession on 22 May 1553, about six weeks before Edward's death. The strength of Mary's following in East Anglia during the succession crisis of July and August 1553 has often been commented upon, but it is worth

[10] *Acts of the Privy Council*, II, 84, 86, 92, 100, 120, 122, 141. Household 'stuff' was delivered to Kenninghall for her on 2 May 1547. SP 46/1/19; Harleian MS 1419 (2), f.136.

[11] *Cal. Pat.*, Edward VI, v, 176.

remembering that she was to a very large extent the heir to the dominant Howard interest, which had been destroyed in 1546, and throughout Edward's reign the most powerful peer in the region. Her household also showed strong East Anglian roots. No list survives earlier than that for 1549, and that is very incomplete because it is a subsidy assessment.[12] Only three gentlewomen appear, because they were widows of some substance, and consequently liable for taxation in their own right. Two of them, Eleanor Kempe and Susan Clarencius, had been with Mary for several years. The remainder of the group can be partially reconstructed. Cecily Barnes, who first appeared in 1536, was still a member of the privy chamber in 1558, and probably served continuously. Frideswide Knight, also appointed in 1536, married Robert Strelly, a gentleman of the same household, in 1548, and was still in post when Mary died.[13] Frances Baynham, another 1536 appointee, featured in a set of verses written about the queen's ladies in about 1555, and it is probable that Jane Dormer was also in Mary's service before she came to the throne. Barbara Hawke certainly, and Frances Jerningham probably, were also members of the establishment at this time.[14]

Of the men listed in 1549, by far the most substantial in terms of wealth was Sir Francis Englefield, assessed at £200. Although he appears frequently in the records, Englefield's office is not specified. He could not have been an ordinary gentleman servant, and was probably chamberlain, since it was clearly the three 'head officers' – Englefield, Edward Waldegrave and Robert Rochester, who were summoned before the council in 1551. By a similar logic, it is possible to identify Waldegrave as steward.[15] Both Rochester and Waldegrave were assessed at £40, and may fairly be classified as 'minor gentry' at this stage. The former came from Essex and the latter from Suffolk, but neither sat on the commission of the peace until after Mary's accession.

[12] PRO E179 69/65. See also appendix.

[13] *Cal. Pat.*, Edward VI, II, 126; grant of a messuage called Oxehedd, and other lands, to Robert and Frideswide jointly, in return for the surrender of her annuity of £10. PRO LC2/4.

[14] Both can be shown to have been in Mary's service before 1547, and after 1553. The verses are in BL Cotton MS, Titus A xiv, f.83v; see also D. M. Loades, *The Tudor Court*, 213.

[15] E179 69/65.

Other East Anglian gentlemen in Mary's service in 1549 were Henry Jerningham and the lawyer William Cordell. Altogether thirty-two men are named, twenty-three of them gentlemen, and of these only two, Richard Wilbraham and Randall Dodd, had been with her for any length of time. Her apothecary, John de Soda, survived from earlier days, but the physician Dr Howes, was new to her service, and so were the other yeomen, apart from Thomas Gent, in charge of the stables. The list for the second payment of the subsidy in 1550 contains only twenty-five names, but whether this was on account of reductions in the household, or variations in the requirement to pay, is not clear.[16] The final list, of 10 March 1552, reflects the crisis which had overtaken Mary in the course of the previous year. Englefield, Waldegrave and Rochester were in prison, and did not return to duty until 14 April; Jerningham has also temporarily vanished, and the whole list numbers only seventeen.[17] Of course Mary had other servants who did not appear on these lists, either because they lacked sufficient substance or because they were taxed elsewhere; four 'ordinary chaplains', Mallet, Hopton, Baker and Richardes, are mentioned in connection with her religious demonstrations; Henry Shoemaker, identified in the same connection, and John Tyrell. A household containing at least six ladies and twenty-three gentlemen would probably have numbered a hundred or more in total – appropriate to her rank and level of income. Van der Delft's lament of June 1547, that Mary was 'less and less regarded', and was being packed off to some remote dwelling in 'the north' was very far from the truth. She was a person of great importance in East Anglia, and a major factor in whatever political plans her brother's councillors might have been contemplating.

As her father's daughter, and second in line to the throne since 1543, Mary was not short of 'well willers', in addition to her own servants and officers. How far she could be said to have had an 'affinity' in the traditional sense is harder to determine. The Courtenay/Pole group, which had had something of that nature between 1536 and 1538, had long since been destroyed, and Mary's contacts with the conservative Howard/Gardiner group in the 1540s were not particularly close. Her personal friendships

[16] E179 69/66.
[17] E179 69/67.

during that period, as we have seen, had tended to be with Catherine Parr and her circle. However, after 1547, when the mass itself began to be an issue of public religious policy, her position changed and began to develop rapidly. As long as Henry VIII lived, the mass as the central act of worship had not needed defending. Controversy and factional strife had raged over preaching, pilgrimages, saints' days, shrines and relics, but sacramentaries were heretics, just as those who still hankered after the old unity of the church were papists – and both were unacceptable to the king. By 1549 the mass was in the front line of controversy, and Mary had made her opposition to the council's policy abundantly clear. In so doing, she became the acknowledged leader of the 'catholic party', and an affinity developed on that basis. As Henry Clifford wrote in 1643, 'In those days the house of this princess was the only harbour for honourable young gentlewomen, given any way to piety and devotion. It was the true school of virtuous demeanour, befitting the education which ought to be in noble damsels. And the greatest lords in the kingdom were suitors to her to receive their daughters into her service.'[18] Names, however, are hard to find, with the exception of Jane Dormer, the subject of Clifford's work, whose connection with Mary appears to have begun in this way. In all probability, it was not the daughters of Edward's peers, even those out of favour like the earls of Arundel and Southampton, who were placed in Mary's household, but those of substantial East Anglian gentry, such as Coke, Cornwallis and Jerningham. Had these dependants been of very high rank, or particularly numerous, it is unlikely that the assiduous Van der Delft would have failed to comment on the fact. When it was necessary to put on a show of a traditional feudal kind, these were the men who rode with her, and formed her 'manred'. For example, when a major crisis was brewing in March 1551, and Mary was summoned to court, she arrived at her London residence, the former hospital of St John, Clerkenwell 'with fifty knights and gentlemen in velvet coats and chains of gold afore her and after her iiii score gentlemen and ladies, every one havyng a peyre of bedes of black.'[19] Similarly in February 1553,

[18] Henry Clifford, *The Life of Jane Dormer, Duchess of Feria*, ed. J. Stevenson, 63.

[19] Henry Machyn, *The Diary of Henry Machyn*, ed. J. G. Nichols, 4–5.

when rumours of the king's health had begun to be alarming, and another show of strength was deemed to be necessary, 'cam to London and rod thrughe London my lade Mare's grasse, the kynges syster, with a grett nomber of lordes and knightes, and her grace a grett number of lades and jenttyll women and jentyll men to the number of ii hondred horsse, and thrug Chepe unto Saynt Johns.' A few days later the earl of Pembroke arrived with three hundred horsemen, for the same reason, and that is the context in which Mary's style of living during this period has to be seen. Pembroke's followers wore his wyvern badge upon their sleeves; Mary's carried rosaries; the purpose was the same, each was the symbol of their respective affinities. And if Mary's consisted of supporters rather than retainers, it was no less formidable for that.

Mary's piety had often been commented upon by sympathetic observers in the past, but only in the same sense as her learning or virtue – an admirable quality to enhance her honour, but not something distinct and significant in itself. As we have seen, her household expenses between 1536 and 1542 do not suggest any unusual or intensive level of religious observance. However, in the summer of 1547, when the traditional practices were coming under attack, and the protestant minority was being encouraged and patronized, Van der Delft commented specifically upon Mary's firmness in the ancient faith, and reported that she was hearing as many as four masses a day.[20] By the end of 1548 the council was becoming concerned about the ostentatious nature of her devotions, perhaps suspecting that she was deliberately seeking a political confrontation. Jehan Dubois, Van der Delft's secretary, wrote in December, just after Mary had returned to Newhall out of Norfolk, 'I understand that she was much welcomed in the north, and wherever she had power she caused the mass to be celebrated, and the services of the church performed in the ancient manner.' A delegation from the council awaited her upon her return, but if they endeavoured to dissuade her from her chosen course of action, they certainly did not succeed. As the Bill of Uniformity made its way through parliament, it must have become clear that there was no way of avoiding a head-on collision with the heir to the throne. Such a collision presented two distinct but related threats to the pro-

[20] Van der Delft to the Emperor, 16 June 1547; *Cal.Span.*, IX, 100.

tector's government. The first arose from Mary's status itself, and her apparent decision to appeal to the popularity of traditional religion to build up her following. The second was a consequence of her special relationship with the emperor. At some point during the first year of the reign, probably in the autumn of 1547 and in response to the royal injunctions, the princess had written to Protector Somerset (with whom her personal relations had always been good) what appears to have been a formal letter of protest against the direction of his religious policy. In reply, the protector professed astonishment at her attitude, either seeing, or pretending to see, the promptings of conservative clerics such as Stephen Gardiner.[21] In so far as her letter can be reconstructed from Somerset's response, it does indeed seem to have borne a striking resemblance to the representations which Gardiner had made earlier in the year. He had argued vigorously against any change being made to the religious settlement imposed by the Act of Six Articles, until the king came of age. The protector, he claimed, had undertaken 'to deliver this realm to the king at eighteen years of age, as the king his father, whose soul God assolye, left it'.[22] Moreover, innovation would create a number of dangers, stirring discord in the country, and presenting the papacy with the telling argument 'that where his authority is abolished, there at every change of governors shall be change of religion.' According to Somerset, Mary accused him and his fellow councillors of neglecting her father's will, so 'that the more part of the realm through a naughty Liberty and presumption are now brought into such a division, as if we executors go not about to bring them to that stay that our late master left them, they will forsake all Obedience'. Henry, she claimed, had left the country 'in Godly order and Quietness', which they were disrupting with their new-fangled ways. The protector denied negligence, and claimed, with more conviction than justice, that most people approved the young king's 'Godly proceedings', and that it was the objectors, like herself, who were stirring up discord and resent-

[21] G. Burnet, *History of the Reformation*, II, 115, reproduces the text of the Protector's letter. For Gardiner's views on the same subject, see his letters to Somerset, written from the Fleet between 14 October and 4 December 1547; Stephen Gardiner, *The Letters of Stephen Gardiner*, ed. J. A. Muller, 379–428.

[22] Gardiner to Somerset, 21 May 1547; Gardiner, *Letters*, 276.

ment. More tellingly, he argued that Henry had not left a peaceful and stable situation, but an uncompleted reformation. There was only one way to consolidate the abolition of papal authority, and that was by the abolition of 'popish doctrine' also. 'It may please your Grace', he went on, 'to call to your remembrance what great Labours, Travels and Pains his Grace had before he could reform some of those stiff necked Romanists or Papists; yea, and did they not cause his Subjects to rise and rebel against him?'

Mary's position, both at this time and during the subsequent crises in 1549 and 1551, was self-consistent if not particularly logical. Unlike Gardiner, she placed no emphasis upon the Act of Six Articles, and her arguments were consequently unaffected by its repeal in December 1547. In her eyes the mass and other traditional rites of the church simply represented true religion, which no one had any power to interfere with. In the letter quoted, Somerset could not resist indirectly reminding her that she had taken the same view over papal authority, until more 'godly instructed' by her late father. No doubt, he added, perhaps with genuine optimism, she would be similarly converted to the new liturgy when it had been properly explained to her. If Mary was at all abashed by such a response, she did not allow anyone the satisfaction of seeing it. Edward, as she constantly reminded him and everyone else, was still a minor. This meant that he could be deemed incapable of making mature judgements in matters of religion, that he could be represented as abused and misled by his evil regents, or even that his power could be seen as insufficient to wield so personal an authority as the royal supremacy. Gardiner, who was an experienced statesman, accepted that during a minority the regent (in this case the council) had to have adequate powers to govern, and that consequently imperfections in the king's authority were exceedingly dangerous to urge. Whatever his private feelings, his public position was simply that it was unwise and inexpedient to make major innovations at such a time. He did not challenge either the king's authority or the validity of his laws. Mary did both. When the Act of Uniformity came into force on Whit Sunday, 1549, she had mass celebrated with especial pomp in her chapel at Kenninghall. Quickly apprised of this deliberate defiance, on 16 June the council wrote, with some restraint, 'giving her advice to be conformable and obedient to the observation of his Majesty's laws, to give order that Mass should be no more used in her house [and] that she should embrace and cause to be celebrated the Communion'.[23] On the 22nd she responded, in a letter which reveals clearly what a serious political threat she had become. 'I have offended no law', she declared, 'unless it be a late law of your own making for the altering of matters in religion, which, in my conscience, is not worthy to have the name of law.' When the king came of age, he would find her his good and obedient subject in this, as in every other matter, but until then she had no intention of changing the practices dictated by her conscience. The reason which Mary advanced for this conduct (apart from pleading indulgence on the grounds of ill health and short life expectancy), reads very curiously in the light of her previous and future conduct. She was obeying her father's laws, which 'were all allowed and consented to without compulsion by the whole realm, both spiritual and temporal . . . so that it was an authorised law'.[24] Consequently, it was the council and not herself which was breaking a settlement which rested at one moment on conscience, and at another on some process of consent which she presumably regarded as different from that which had produced the Act of Uniformity. The council, not surprisingly, was profoundly disturbed by this letter, and summoned Rochester, Englefield and Hopton, her senior chaplain, to appear before them, in the hope of being able to bring pressure to bear upon her through her servants. This provoked a further letter from Mary on 27 June, in which she accused the council of unfriendly conduct, and added, 'I thought verily that my former letters should have discharged this matter . . . not doubting but you do consider that none of you all would have been contented to have been thus used at your inferiors' hands.' Given Mary's consciousness of her status, she cannot have been unaware of the importance of her household and developing affinity. Nor, in the dangerous summer of 1549, can she have failed to appreciate the impact which her example of disobedience would have. So her professions of surprise at the council's unsympathetic attitude to her well-intentioned representations have a distinctly disingenuous appearance.

Whether the confusion of her arguments was genuine or contrived, in June 1549 Mary was endeavouring to reserve her

[23] *APC*, II, 291.

[24] Mary to the council, 22 June 1549; J. Foxe, *Acts and Monuments*, VI, 7.

1 Mary: a late sixteenth-century Italian bust, which, although not executed from life, captures the essential pathos of the queen's character.

2 Edward: from the same set, which brings out a physical resemblance to his father, much less apparent in most other portraits.

3 Mary at the age of about seventeen, by Hans Holbein. In spite of the contemporary title, the identity of the sitter is in dispute.

5 Henry VIII: a magnificent king at the height of his powers, by Hans Holbein.

4 A young woman, thought to be Catherine of Aragon, by Michel Sittow.

6 Henry VIII in later life, decayed and increasingly capricious. From a contemporary engraving.

7 Margaret Pole, countess of Salisbury. Mary's Lady Governess for most of her childhood and adolescence.

8 Elizabeth as princess. A clever and attractive girl who aroused Mary's intense dislike and distrust.

9 Philip II, by an unknown artist. It was a smaller version of this portrait which caused Mary to be 'half in love' with the Prince of Spain.

10 Lady Jane Grey, by an unknown artist. Edward's choice as his successor, her supporters quickly revealed a lack of commitment.

11 Henry Fitzalan, earl of Arundel, attributed to Stephen van der Meulen. A political survivor who was never as close to Mary as his offices would seem to indicate.

12 Simon Renard by an unknown artist. His skill and his position as the Emperor's ambassador made him Mary's chief *confidant* in the first year of her reign.

13 Anne Boleyn, by an unknown artist. An intelligent and forceful woman, upon whom Mary blamed all the unhappiness of her early adult life.

14 Edward Courtenay, earl of Devon, by an unknown artist. Having grown up in prison, he emerged to a life of self indulgence and irresponsibility.

15 Sir Nicholas Carew, by Hans Holbein. Having started his career as a jousting companion of the king, he fell out of favour when he supported Mary's reinstatement.

16 'Dormer is a darling.' Although the identity of this young lady is not certain, it is reputed to be Jane Dormer, later duchess of Feria, and Mary's youngest familiar. Portrait by Antonis Mor.

conscience over an issue of allegiance, just as she had attempted to do with her father thirteen years before. In 1536 Henry had broken her ruthlessly, before she could become a major threat; but Somerset was not the king, and his position was becoming increasingly insecure. Moreover, Mary at thirty-three was a tougher proposition than Mary at twenty, and knew better how to play to her strength. The emperor, as always, was her strongest card, and Henry's death had restored her value to him as a means of exercising influence in England. In January 1549 he appears to have taken the initiative, as soon as he heard of the passage of the Act of Uniformity, and instructed Van der Delft to inform the English council that he would not tolerate any pressure being put upon his cousin to conform to its terms.[25] While the ambassador sought an opportunity to deliver his statement, Mary began to send messengers, looking for reassurance from him as she had earlier done from Chapuys. In March he visited her, handing over an official letter from his master, and informally speaking the words of comfort which she constantly craved. In response she complained bitterly of the changes which were taking place in the kingdom, and reiterated that Charles was her only solace and support. 'Her life and her salvation are in your Majesty's keeping', he reported. Shortly after, she replied to the emperor's letter in similar terms. Charles pressed the council hard. Regarding them as a weak and unfriendly government, he took a dictatorial tone, perhaps hoping to bring about their overthrow by public humiliation and discredit. On 10 May he instructed Van der Delft to demand 'a written assurance, in definite, suitable and permanent form, that notwithstanding all new laws and ordinances made upon religion, she may live in the observance of our ancient religion as she has done up to the present, so that neither king nor parliament may ever molest her, directly or indirectly by any means whatsoever.'[26] No self-respecting government could afford to submit to such explicit bullying, and Somerset did not do so. He pointed out that Mary's religious observances were not a matter of her private conscience, but of the public order of the realm. If

[25] Emperor to Van der Delft, 25 January 1549; *Cal.Span.*, IX, 330.

[26] Van der Delft to the Emperor, 30 March 1549; *Cal. Span.*, IX, 350. Emperor to Van der Delft, 10 May 1549; ibid., 375. Jordan, *Edward VI: The Young King*, 206–9.

her demonstrations of defiance were not curbed, the result would be open and large-scale sedition. In a case like this, formal dispensation to ignore an Act of parliament was out of the question. He was, however, prepared to suggest a compromise. Because of her status, and the apparent tenderness of her conscience, she might continue to enjoy her mass until the king came of age, but privately, in her own chamber. Van der Delft was not impressed; indeed, in his indignation he was tempted into an indiscretion. Even if Mary wanted to change her religion, he declared, the emperor would not allow it. He can hardly have made such a bizarre statement out of his own imagination. Solicitous as Charles may have been for his cousin's soul, her usefulness to him depended upon her successful resistance; there must be no repetition of the backsliding of 1536, and the ambassador knew his master's mind. The emperor was indignant at the very thought of his cousin being treated like an ordinary subject, and instructed Van der Delft to keep up the pressure, but his bluff had been called, and there was little more that he could do for the time being.

Inconclusive skirmishing continued throughout the summer. Mary constantly looked to Van der Delft for advice, and he offered the services of his own priests if hers should yield to official threats. The council harried her servants, and endeavoured to find incriminating links between her household and the rebellions in Devon and Norfolk. One of her receivers, Thomas Poley of Ipswich, was denounced as a leader of 'the worst sort of rebels',[27] but the mass was not an issue in Kett's camp, and attempts to identify one of Mary's chaplains as an instigator of revolt in Devon appear to have come to nothing. She gave Van der Delft a detailed account of her struggles, which he passed on to the emperor, along with reports of his own dealings with the council. Somerset tried as hard as possible to maintain the distinction which he had made between private and public worship, while Mary did her best to ignore it. Her chaplains conformed when they were in their own benefices, but celebrated mass when they were in her household. At length, in September the ambassador was visited by Paget and St John, who offered a

[27] PRO SP10/8 f.30. In spite of this, Poley seems to have continued unmolested in Mary's service; E179/69/66, 67. Mary briskly denied all involvement, and no attempt was made to follow up the charges.

slightly clearer formula, whereby 'private' should be deemed to embrace the members of Mary's household, but not outsiders, and that her chaplains should be exempt in respect of all services performed in camera. This verbal assurance seems to have satisfied the princess herself, who preferred it to a formal dispensation in writing, on the grounds that 'if letters were accepted . . . they might amount to a recognition of the laws against religion, which she would always deny, for these innovations were no laws, nor had they the force of laws, for they were not duly given, but contrary to God, to her father's will and to the welfare of the realm.'[28] Nevertheless, she remitted everything to the emperor's discretion. Mary's grasp of the nature of law had not improved over the previous three months, and Charles was no more impressed by verbal concessions than he had been earlier. He instructed Van der Delft to continue his attempts to obtain Letters Patent, irrespective of his cousin's views, on the grounds that the English never kept their word.

If part of the emperor's purpose had been to de-stabilize an unsatisfactory regime, then he succeeded, because in October the protector was overthrown in a palace revolution.[29] In this process Mary played no more part than she had done in the rebellions of the summer, although she was well aware of what was intended. In September she informed Van der Delft that she had been approached by Lord St John, and by the earls of Warwick, Southampton and Arundel, to lend her support to a process of impeachment. She refused to become involved, but the invitation was significant. At that stage Warwick, who was the prime mover in the conspiracy, was working mainly with the support of the religious conservatives, and Somerset's protestant policies appeared to be one of the main grounds of the attack. When the crisis finally came, in early October, the protector believed that one of his opponents' objectives was to make Mary regent, thereby undoing his religious settlement. In November Van der Delft was persuaded that Stephen Gardiner, and

[28] Summary of Van der Delft's instructions to Jehan Dubois, September 1549; *Cal.Span.*, IX, 444. The ambassador himself admitted that Mary had been 'increasingly making a public spectacle' of her private mass; ibid., 405.

[29] There are numerous accounts of the events leading up to Somerset's overthrow, which do not need repetition in this context. See particularly, Jordan, *Edward VI: The Young King*; M. L. Bush, *The Government Policy of Protector Somerset;* and B. L. Beer, *Northumberland.*

Edmund Bonner, the imprisoned bishop of London, were about to be released. Southampton and Arundel were among the peers entrusted with the care of the king's person, and the protestant John Hooper wrote gloomily to his friend Heinrich Bullinger in Zurich: 'We are greatly apprehensive of a change in religion . . . The papists are hoping and earnestly struggling for their kingdom.'[30] But neither the emperor nor Mary was much impressed by these indications. Mass began to be celebrated here and there, and an embargo was placed upon preaching, but it lasted only a week, and no official steps were taken to modify the Act of Uniformity. The princess, Van der Delft reported on 7 November, 'is unable to believe that religion is to be restored while the common people are so infected'. Her doubts were fully justified. By the end of November Warwick had achieved ascendancy in the council, and again excluded the conservatives from positions of influence. Southampton, the most powerful of them, did not attend the council after 18 October, and on Christmas day a statement was delivered to the bishops in the king's name which revealed unequivocally the outcome of the power struggle. 'divers evil disposed persons, since the apprehension of the duke of Somerset, have bruited abroad that they should have again their old Latin services, their conjured bread and water, with such like vain and superstitious ceremonies, as if the setting forth of the said book [of Common Prayer] had been only the Duke's act.'[31] Mary likened this outcome to the hardening of Pharaoh's heart, and believed that God was preparing to exact a terrible revenge upon the apostate kingdom. While Elizabeth was fêted and made much of at court during the holiday season, her elder sister remained at Newhall, surrounded by her loyal servants, but acutely apprehensive of fresh attacks upon her position. She longed, she told Van der Delft, to escape from the wrath to come, and the ambassador advised his master to take such a possibility seriously.

At this point Charles must have had a powerful sense of *déjà vu*. The options were the same as they had been fifteen years before – marriage or flight. Marriage was the more orthodox

[30] John Hooper to Heinrich Bullinger, 7 November 1549; *Original Letters, relative to the English Reformation*, ed. H. Robinson, 69.

[31] PRO SP10/9 f.57. W. K. Jordan, *Edward VI: The Threshold of Power*, 29–30.

option, but required the co-operation of several different parties with incompatible views and interests. Dom Luis, that most persistent of suitors, had raised the matter with the emperor a few weeks after Henry's death, perhaps thinking that the old king had been the main obstacle to a settlement. Van der Delft was instructed to find out about her dowry provision, but the matter was not pursued with any energy. In June 1547 there was a rumour that the duke of Ferrara was angling for a match; in July it was an unnamed French duke, probably Vendôme. At first, Henry II was convinced that the emperor was about to attack England, in order to put Mary on the throne, and he considered offering a marriage with Vendôme, both as a means of preventing that, and also as a means of forestalling any insurrection on her behalf, which he rightly judged would receive Imperial support.[32] By May 1549 Charles was convinced that there could be no serious negotiations with the Portuguese 'unless the present innovations cease', but by then relations with France had become very strained on account of Boulogne, and the English council was faced with the hostility of both its powerful neighbours. Consequently they suddenly discovered previously unperceived virtues in Dom Luis, and Paget went across to Brussels to talk about a possible financial arrangement. The aging but ever perceptive Chapuys had already told the emperor that he did not believe Mary would actually be allowed to marry out of the kingdom until her brother came of age, and that was probably sound judgement. At the same time only Thomas Seymour, recklessly ambitious after Catherine's death in September 1548, considered a domestic marriage a possibility. Taxed by lord Russell with seeking either Mary or Elizabeth as his wife, 'he replyed sayinge, It is convenyent for them to mary and better yt were that they were marryed within the realme than in any foraign place and without the realme.'[33] Needless to say, he made no progress with Mary, although his advances to the young Elizabeth seem to have met with a more favourable response, and to have been one of the main causes of his downfall. At the end of October 1549, after Somerset's arrest,

[32] Saint-Mauris (in France) to the emperor, 11 February 1547; *Cal.Span.*, IX, 493.

[33] PRO SP10/6 f.16; January (?) 1549; deposition by Lord Russell relative to the charges against Thomas Seymour, then being investigated.

Mary herself raised the question of the Portuguese match with Van der Delft, because Charles had not responded to the latest English offer. She would accept such a marriage, if he advised it, she declared without enthusiasm, but would really prefer some other means of escape from the country.

However, the expected assault upon her virtue did not come immediately. In January 1550 the ambassador, himself loudly lamenting the deplorable politics and theology of the English, reported that she was in a very miserable and apprehensive frame of mind. She had been invited to court for Christmas, but had excused herself on the pretext of ill health. 'They wished me to be at court so that I could not get the mass celebrated for me', she declared. 'I would not find myself in such a place for anything in the world.' Like Chapuys before him, Van der Delft had become convinced that Mary was in imminent danger, and that only if she were safely out of the realm could pressure be brought to bear upon the English government: 'as things are now', he wrote, 'they safeguard themselves against her, who is in their power.'[34] The 'righteous . . . who are still numerous, would never be content to suffer the present government if they had anyone to favour them.' The emperor did not respond to these pointed hints. He did not see Mary as a hostage, but as a means of access, a pressure point in English politics. An honourable marriage, if one could be arranged, was one thing, but mere flight was little more than desertion, and direct military intervention was no more feasible than it had been in the time of his late aunt. So the inconclusive negotiation with the Portuguese continued through the early spring, and Mary continued to celebrate her mass in the very public privacy of her substantial household. Each side accused the other of diplomatic delays, and in March Van der Delft reported that the English did not even seem to be clear whether the intended bridegroom was Dom Luis or his nephew Sebastian, the heir to the Portuguese throne. The earl of Warwick, he declared with a sour touch, was opposed to the marriage because he would have to find the dowry. At the same time the emperor continued to press for written guarantees of religious privilege for Mary, a campaign which provoked some members of the council to murmur audibly that he had no right to interfere in the domestic affairs of

[34] Van der Delft to the emperor, 14 January 1550; *Cal.Span.*, x, 6.

the kingdom. Mary might be Charles's niece, but she was also Edward's sister, and that was a much closer relationship.[35]

By the beginning of May a fresh crisis was brewing. Mary believed that it was her duty to provide mass for anyone who came to her house seeking it, and maintained a high profile of non-conformity. The council claimed, with considerable justice, that the indulgence which had been extended to her was being abused. By the middle of April they were considering further measures to make sure that her celebrations were genuinely private by excluding the household at large, and restricting permission to her chamber servants only. Both Mary and Van der Delft then protested loudly that the council was going back on the promises which Somerset, St John and Paget had made in the previous autumn. At the very end of April, probably on the 30th, the ambassador visited Mary at her own request at one of her minor residences, Woodham Walter, near Maldon in Essex. There he found her in a state of high agitation. The marquis of Brandenburg was seeking her hand in marriage, and she had informed the council that she considered the emperor to be her father, and would not marry without his consent. What should she do? Somewhat thrown by this demand, Van der Delft advised delay for mature consideration, and was treated to another tirade upon the godlessness of the English government, and upon their plans to martyr her as her father had once done: 'it is evident to all, and the whole world may see that such people fear no God, and respect no persons, but follow their own fancy; and my cause is so righteous in God's sight, that if his Majesty favours me . . . I need take no further justification by delaying until I am past all help.'[36] The ambassador smoothly professed to find her answers 'wise and prudent', but she had clearly become a major problem. If the emperor would agree to expedite the Portuguese marriage, and not quibble over details, that would be the best solution. But failing that, she had better be 'evacuated' as swiftly and secretly as possible. Once she was in safety, 'the righteous' might then be encouraged to rise in revolt and destroy this iniquitous regime. Van der Delft already had one scheme of escape prepared, and Mary herself another. The

[35] Van der Delft to the emperor, 18 March 1550; *Cal.Span.*, x, 40; same to same 2 May 1550; ibid., 86.

[36] Van der Delft to the emperor, 2 May 1550; *Cal. Span.*, x, 80.

ambassador was about to be recalled on the (genuine) grounds of ill health; if he chose his time and route correctly, the princess could join his ship in disguise. Alternatively, a boat could be sent into Maldon on the pretext of trading grain, and she could slip down from Woodham Walter, only three miles away, and be taken out to an Imperial ship waiting off the coast.[37] At length Charles allowed himself to be persuaded, or possibly he remitted the whole matter to his sister, Mary of Hungary, who had a more incisive way of resolving doubts and exercised a major influence over Imperial policy. The second plan was approved, because if anything went wrong, no Imperial diplomat would be directly involved. In mid-May Van der Delft was recalled. He departed at the beginning of June, and his replacement, Jehan Scheyfve, was carefully told nothing, so that his subsequent protestations of ignorance could be perfectly genuine. On 30 June the attempt was made.

The agent was Jehan Dubois, secretary successively to Van der Delft and Scheyfve, and his report, written in mid-July, contains a detailed account of the adventure.[38] The matter had become more difficult than anticipated, because in early June the council had ordered watches to be kept from village to village. Whether there was some suspicion of what was in preparation, or it was simply a precaution against the kind of summer riots which had occurred in the previous year, both Mary and Van der Delft regarded this as a major setback. Presumably neither was as convinced of the sympathy of the country people as they claimed to be, and their doubts were amply justified. Two Imperial warships, commanded by Cornille Scepperus, arrived off Maldon late on Monday, 30 June, and

[37] There seem to have been at least three plans prepared for Mary's escape. Mary's own original plan was much more complicated than either of the two mentioned here, and involved bringing several of her women with her. The plan eventually adopted may have been a modified version of that, or it may have been a new scheme prepared by Mary of Hungary, who was deeply involved in the plot. Van der Delft to the emperor, 6 June 1550; *Cal.Span.*, x, 94; Dubois's report to Mary of Hungary, mid-July; ibid., 124–35. H. F. M. Prescott, *Mary Tudor*, 132–43.

[38] *Cal. Span.*, X, 124–35. Van der Delft died a few weeks after returning to the Low Countries, and at first it was feared that he had betrayed the secret on his deathbed. The emperor specifically approved the chosen plan on 21 June. *Cal.Span.*, x, 111.

Dubois landed very early on the Wednesday morning. He then wrote to Rochester, explaining that Scepperus was planning to move one of his ships further up the estuary on the high tide the following night, and urging haste with the preparations. To his dismay, the controller responded by arriving in person, and summoning him to confer in a 'safe' house in Maldon. According to Dubois, he then began to make difficulties: the watches made the enterprise very hazardous; not everyone in Mary's own household was to be trusted; and, more fundamentally, there was no pressing need for escape. He was convinced that there would be no further pressure upon her until the end of the next parliament, and meanwhile, should her brother die while she was out of the country, she would forfeit all chance of the succession. Dubois concealed the annoyance which he must have felt at this turn of events, and merely replied that such doubts did not at all correspond with what Mary had said to him, just before Van der Delft's departure. The last time the ambassador had visited her, she had placed herself in his hands saying, 'I am like a little ignorant girl, and I care neither for my goods nor for the world, but only for God's service and my conscience', and the ambassador, in Rochester's presence, had urged her to go.[39] All the arguments had been rehearsed many times, and there was nothing more to be said. The controller then departed with one of Dubois's servants, promising to send for him when he knew his mistress's mind. Dubois went about his pretended business of getting customs clearance for his corn, which involved a brush with local officials, amicably resolved when they were told that he had sold his cargo to Mary's controller, because they held 'my Lady's Grace' as high as the king's person.

Eventually word came from Woodham Walter, and Dubois was escorted the short distance to the house. There he found the princess in great agitation, fussing over 'packing up some of her property in great long hop-sacks'. Summoning all his patience, he reminded her that she would lack for nothing in the emperor's dominions, but eventually Mary told him that she could not be ready until Friday, which was two days away. This presented the secretary with all kinds of difficulties. He would have to warn Scepperus not to come that night, and preferably to withdraw

[39] Dubois's report; *Cal.Span.*, x, 127.

both his ships for the time being in order to avoid arousing suspicion. Meanwhile, he himself would have to find some fresh pretext for remaining. Before he could begin to resolve these problems, however, they were interrupted by one of the controller's agents, who had ridden over from Maldon with the news that the townsmen were proposing to arrest Dubois's boat, because they had already become suspicious of Scepperus's ship lying off the town. Dubois was all for whisking Mary away at once, but Rochester would not hear of it; the watches were being doubled, and the danger was growing all the time. The princess's only contribution to this urgent debate seems to have been to repeat, over and over, 'What shall I do? What is to become of me?' At length the men agreed that Dubois should return to Maldon, stick to his guise of corn-chandler, and simply brazen it out. In ten or twelve days, time, when the alarm had died down, Rochester would send him word by a confidential servant, and he would try again. So, very late at night, Dubois and Rochester's friend returned to the town, where they did encounter the watch, but managed to bluff their way past. Dubois embarked at two o'clock on the Thursday morning, and was able to make his way out to Scepperus's ship without further molestation.

It is difficult to know quite what to make of this escapade, except that Mary was obviously not in command of the situation. Rochester's servant never turned up at the rendezvous in Antwerp which had been agreed, and it looks very much as though the controller engineered the whole panic in order to abort a move of which he strongly disapproved. He had, apparently, been consulting astrologers, and had informed Dubois that the king would not live another year.[40] He may also have been less than enthusiastic about his mistress's marked predilection for foreigners, because he was later to be a supporter of the Courtenay marriage project. A few days after Dubois's departure, Scepperus set men ashore in the same area, and believed that he had successfully deceived the local people into thinking that he was pursuing a Scots pirate named James Green. If he had, they were more gullible than the council in London, who, on 13 July, sent Sir John Gates into Essex with a

[40] Ibid. Casting royal horoscopes was a criminal offence, so it is not surprising that he spoke of it secretively.

troop of horse 'to stop the going away of the Lady Mary, because it was credibly informed that Scipperus should steal her away to Antwerp'.[41] However popular Mary may have been, there seems to have been no shortage of men in the Maldon area who were willing to do the council's bidding, or to report their suspicions. There was certainly no inclination to welcome Imperial warships as allies against a hated regime, and Dubois, who was a cool-headed man, was convinced that the prevailing atmosphere was suspicious and hostile. On 24 July the president of Flanders reported to the queen dowager that the enterprise was being widely discussed, and that some believed Mary to have arrived in Flanders. A couple of days later, the French ambassador, Bassefontaine, informed the president that 'the English believed his Imperial Majesty, once he had her in his court, would marry her to the Prince of Spain, maintain her to be the rightful Queen of England, because the present king was the schismatic son of a schismatic father ... and would then wage war against the English for her.'[42] Such a view may have overemphasized the decisiveness of which Charles was capable by this time, but with Imperial policy falling increasingly into the hands of Mary of Hungary and the bishop of Arras, it was an entirely justifiable suspicion. Realizing that Scheyfve, the ambassador in England, was bound to hear the same rumours, Mary wrote to him twice in early August. On the first occasion she informed him that the English were spreading the reports as a pretext for taking further action against the princess; and the second letter instructed him to deny that Scepperus had ever come to England to take her away, on the accurate if misleading grounds that he had never landed.

At the same time the council fired another warning shot in the form of a further instruction to the princess's chaplains to desist from saying mass. Her automatic reaction was a fresh complaint to the Imperial ambassador. There seems to have been no particular reason why Mallet and another unnamed priest should have been indicted at this time, unless to provoke Mary

[41] M. d'Eecke (Scepperus) to the queen dowager, 17 July 1550; *Cal.Span.*, x, 135. *Chronicle*, 40.

[42] Conversation between Bassefontaine and St Mauris, 28 July 1550; *Cal. Span.*, x, 145. As far as I am aware, this is the first mention of a marriage between Philip and Mary, although they had corresponded briefly six years before.

into revealing once again the extent of her dependence upon foreign intervention. Such a demonstration would have been given added significance by the reports of her intended flight, and if that was the intention, then she walked straight into the trap.[43] On 4 September Charles instructed Scheyfve to demand unconditional assurances: 'you will persist in your request at all costs', he wrote. 'Give them plainly to understand that if they decide otherwise, we will not take it in good part, or suffer it to be done.' Presumably the ambassador made his representations as instructed, but there were no immediate consequences, and his correspondence for the remainder of the autumn was mainly concerned with commercial disputes and the affairs of the Admiralty court. The council continued to monitor Mary's lines of communication, and when it was discovered that one of her servants named Kempe had gone across to Flanders, he was ordered to return without reference to his mistress. However, when Mary protested, they allowed him to remain, and nothing was ever said directly to the princess herself, either about her relations with successive Imperial ambassadors, or about her abortive attempt to escape, although the latter was by then the common gossip of Europe.

In December, the brief truce over her religious nonconformity came to an end, and a crisis began to develop which was to last throughout the following year. The origin of this struggle may have lain in a council letter of 1 December instructing Mary to allow the sheriff of Essex to serve long-outstanding writs upon her chaplains. On the other hand, the young king was beginning to show signs of an evangelical determination which was at least the equal of his sister's conservative obstinacy, and he may himself have been responsible for this latest round. Mary replied to the council's letter on 4 December, saying in effect that her chaplains were covered by her own immunity, and that neither of the accused men was currently in her household, anyway.[44]

[43] On 22 July Petre and Rich were appointed to interview Mary for some unnamed purpose, which may have been connected with this. 'After long communication' she declined to come to court, but agreed to meet them at Leighs Priory. *Chronicle*, 41–2. Jehan Scheyfve to the emperor, 26 July 1550; *Cal. Span.*, x, 140. The queen dowager, who does not seem to have had much sympathy with Mary, at the same time expressed the hope that she would have the good sense not to pester him too often with such matters.

[44] *APC*, III, 171; Foxe, *Acts and Monuments*, VI, 13–14; *APC*, III, 177.

On 25 December the council wrote again at great length, a letter which was more than half protestant sermon, but the main substance of which was to explain that the promises made on the king's behalf had never covered more than her own closet service, and had been granted as a concession to the weakness of her theological understanding. They had never conferred immunity upon her household as a whole, and certainly did not permit celebrations conducted (as in this case) in her absence. The matter might have ended there, as just another futile exchange of gestures, if the king had not then chosen to intervene. On 24 January he sent a letter, partly in his own hand, upbraiding her for her errors, and continuing, 'in our state it shall miscontent us to permit you, so great a subject, not to keep our laws. Your nearness to us in blood, your greatness in estate [and] the condition of this time, maketh your fault the greater.'[45] The threat was implied rather than explicit, but Edward's personal involvement clearly disturbed Mary greatly, since one of the main bases of her position had been that he was too young to understand such matters, and that his youth was being abused by evil councillors. Hitherto she had always undertaken to defer to his judgement when he came of age. Now, for the first time, it began to seem probable that she would find his own judgement as unpalatable as she found that of his present advisers. His letter caused her, she professed, 'more suffering than any illness, even unto death'. She was so ill that she could hardly hold up her head, let alone write. But she was not too ill to write urgently to Scheyfve, the emperor and the queen dowager, or to rehearse the familiar arguments about the previous year's undertakings and her willingness to obey the king in all matters 'saving her conscience'. If any of the council remembered her protestations of the summer of 1536, this must have had a familiar ring.

Mary's arguments during this protracted controversy were simple, and very easy to sympathize with, but they contained little logic, either political or religious. At no point did she suggest, even in her letters to the emperor, that she had retracted her submission to her father, or repudiated the authority of the English crown over the *ecclesia anglicana* as a matter of principle. Instead she stuck doggedly to the position that nothing should

[45] Foxe, *Acts and Monuments*, vi, 11–12; *Cal.Span.*, x, 209–12.

be changed during Edward's minority, clearly stating on a number of occasions that she was entirely satisfied with the situation as her father had left it. Presumably, if she had thought about it, she would have argued that the ecclesiastical supremacy was personal to the king, and not a part of his normal office, which could be exercised through parliament and the council. Consequently, during a minority it became a purely administrative function. As Gardiner had already realized, this was an extremely difficult position to sustain with any clarity and consistency.[46] At the same time Mary also declared repeatedly, and with great emotional force, that the mass and the traditional rites of the church represented 'true religion', which her conscience would not permit her to surrender, and which no one had any power to alter. It was upon this latter point that her brother took her up so sharply, urging the truth and purity of evangelical doctrine, 'To teach and instruct you, we will give order,' he concluded, 'and so procure you to do your duty willingly, that you shall perceive you are not used merely as a subject, and only commanded, but as a daughter, a scholar and a sister, taught, instructed and persuaded.' Nor was he willing to accept that she was, in fact, defending their father's settlement. 'You shall err in many points, such as our father and yours would not have suffered, whatsoever you say of the standing still of things as they were left by him.' He was the king, and he intended to be obeyed. This letter is generally regarded as representing the tough-mindedness of the earl of Warwick, rather than the thirteen-year-old Edward, but it is also consistent with all that is known about the young king's attitude to such matters during the last two years of his life. By whatever means Mary might now seek to defend her mass, there was little point in claiming a special indulgence until he came of age. Whoever was responsible for making the decision, the English government was no longer willing to regard the king's minority as a relevant consideration. Mary took refuge in the private conviction that her brother could not have so resolved his religious position at such a tender age, but abandoned her professions of willingness to be ruled by his mature judgement.

[46] For discussions of this point, see L. B. Smith, *Tudor Prelates and Politics*, 251–81; D. M. Loades, *The Oxford Martyrs*, 52–6; and R. H. Pogson, 'Stephen Gardiner and the Problem of Loyalty' in *Law and Government under the Tudors*, ed. C. Cross, D. M. Loades and J. J. Scarisbrick, 67–89.

Jehan Scheyfve quickly found himself in the thick of this new controversy. By the end of January he was commenting in detail on a draft response to the council which she had sent for his perusal. 'As for the king's majesty', he wrote, 'you consider him your sovereign lord. But I would leave the phrase "as it seems he is not" alone, for if you go so far it is to be feared that they will say that you are menacing them or calling into question the king's authority.'[47] Such advice was sensible and timely, but it is somewhat surprising that Mary should have been in need of it. She was not a green girl, but a highly educated princess, with her own council and numerous political and religious allies. The only reason why she should have called upon this not-very-bright Fleming to write her letters for her was a profound sense of dependence upon the power which he represented. On 16 February, goaded by her frequent signs of alarm, Scheyfve presented himself before the English council and repeated the emperor's standard demand that his cousin should be no more molested for her religion. He spent two long sessions with them discussing the matter, sessions which were wearisomely repetitive in terms of their content, and which ended in defeat for his efforts. Whatever Somerset or Paget may have said in 1547, or 1549, by this time the council was adamant that Mary's permission was for herself alone, with her personal chamber servants, and not for her household or friends. In the course of the interview the earl of Warwick also added meaningfully that the king was three years older than he had been when the original promise had been made. In reporting the results of his efforts to Mary of Hungary, Scheyfve added that he feared a fresh campaign of harassment, and that the princess 'commended herself in all humility to your Majesties, whose poor suppliant and humble servant she remains'. Anglo-Imperial relations were distinctly tense by the middle of March, not only because of Mary's position, but also because Warwick had found a way to make a counter-demonstration. Sir Thomas Chamberlain, the English ambassador in Brussels, acting upon the king's specific orders, petitioned Mary of Hungary for licence to use the English service at his residence – pointing out that Scheyfve

[47] Scheyfve to Mary, January/February 1551; *Cal.Span.*, x, 428; Scheyfve to the emperor, 27 January 1551; ibid., 204.

enjoyed a comparable privilege in London.[48] Both the emperor and the queen were scandalized, and denied that there was any parallel between practising the true faith in a heretic country and licensing a heretic to pollute their own dominions. Having made their point, the English council realized that they were in no position to press it, and Chamberlain overstepped the mark in attempting to preach evangelical doctrine to Charles himself.[49]

On 15 March Mary made the state entry into London which has already been mentioned, and was received in private by her brother. Later, in a session also attended by the council, she declared flatly, and without any of her earlier equivocations, that her faith would not be constrained. Edward, with equal candour, replied that he was not now concerned with her faith, but with her behaviour. As a subject she must obey, lest 'her example might breed too much inconvenience'. To emphasize the point, Sir Anthony Browne, who had twice heard mass in Mary's household over the previous few days, once at Newhall and once at Romford, was imprisoned in the Fleet.[50] A week later Robert Rochester was again before the council to answer questions about her chaplains, and in the following month a certain Benett of Ware was examined concerning rumours that 'my lady Mary would go westward to the earl of Shrewsbury'. In other words, a conspiracy of the conservative nobility was feared. Meanwhile, on 18 March, Scheyfve had returned to the charge, with a renewed representation which Edward interpreted as a threat of war. An anguished debate ensued, during which Cranmer and Ridley advised that although 'to give licence to sin was sin; to suffer and wink . . . for a time might be borne.'[51] England was in no state to wage war, and further disruption to the cloth trade would have been disastrous, so it was decided to take no further action against Mary for the time being, and to send Nicholas Wotton to the emperor with a mission of conciliation. At the

[48] *APC*, III, 215; Scheyfve to the queen dowager, 1 March 1551; *Cal.Span.*, x, 230; emperor to Scheyfve, 7 March 1551; ibid., 237. Sir Richard Morrison, accredited to the emperor (then in Augsburg), made the same request, and greatly offended the emperor by his persistence.

[49] *Cal.Span.*, x, 239–40.

[50] *APC*, III, 239; *Chronicle*, 56, 55.

[51] *APC*, III, 240; *Chronicle*, 56; *APC*, III, 264; Scheyfve to the emperor, 6 April 1551; *Cal. Span.*, x, 251.

same time, Charles wrote to Scheyfve: 'If they may be brought to consent that she may hear mass privately in her own house, without admitting any strangers, let her be satisfied with that; for her conscience cannot be hardened by submission to outside violence.' Charles was no more anxious for war than the English. Although he had an uneasy peace with France, his hands were more than full in Germany. It may be that Edward had misinterpreted Scheyfve's meaning, for the ambassador's own dispatches contain no hint of such a radical threat. Perhaps the extra menace had been injected by Mary of Hungary, to whom Scheyfve also regularly reported. Whatever had happened, the bluff worked up to a point. Mary had six months respite thereafter. But the council had also made it clear that it would not tolerate the household at Newhall becoming a focus for conservative resistance. Dr Mallet, the offending chaplain over whom this particular dispute had begun, was committed to the Tower at the end of April, and repeated representations by Mary on his behalf over the following two months were rejected: 'we are sorry to perceive your grace so ready to be a defence to one that the king's law doth condemn.'[52]

The next round began on 9 August when the council, having sworn in the conservative earls of Arundel and Derby as 'occasional councillors' the same morning, resolved to take the final step, and prohibit even the most private mass for Mary's benefit. The reason for this move can hardly have been tactical, because the constraints already applied were adequate to deal with the 'scandal' of nonconformity. The explanation commonly advanced (particularly by Mary's biographers) is that it was an act of gratuitous malice – a piece of revenge upon the princess for having been such a nuisance.[53] But that can hardly be the true explanation, particularly in view of the advice which Cranmer and Ridley had given in March. The earl of Warwick was a shrewd and responsible governor, and Mary presented the same kind of problem to him that she had presented to Henry VIII in 1536. As long as she held out, and could maintain that her conscience was inviolate, she would retain her credit, her tacit leadership of the English conservatives, and her menacing

[52] Mary to the council, 2 May, 11 May, 21 June; council to Mary, 6 May, 27 May, 24 June 1551; Foxe, *Acts and Monuments*, VI, 18–21.

[53] *APC*, III, 329; Prescott, *Mary Tudor*, 148–52.

Imperial support. In other words she had to be crushed in order to destroy her credibility as a leader of opposition, just as her father had destroyed her usefulness to the papal party fifteen years before. Fortunately the young king was easily persuaded that this was a matter which touched his conscience, and that his sister (of whom in other respects he was fond) was an affront to his own godliness. The emperor had perceived this very point when he had allowed Van der Delft to declare that he would not allow her to change her religion, even if she had wanted to. The timing of the move was more obvious than the motivation, because by August 1551 the threat of a Franco-Habsburg war was rising again, and Warwick was busy building bridges to the French. For the same reason, and on the same day, the council also returned to the question of reciprocal religious privileges, and threatened to withdraw Scheyfve's 'mass licence', because Chamberlain had again been refused a similar permission, on the grounds that the English laws were 'erroneous innovations'.

On 14 August Rochester, Englefield and Waldegrave were again summoned before the council, and instructed to convey the king's commands to the household at Newhall. The chaplains were not to say mass, and neither they, their servants nor their families were to hear it. As before, Rochester made their excuses; it was not seemly for them, as servants, to instruct their mistress how to run her house. He was brusquely informed that this was a matter of his allegiance, which no loyalty to his employer could obstruct. The outcome was predictable. On the 16th the unhappy trio presented themselves at Copthall, where Mary was then living, and were forbidden by her to deliver any part of the council's message. Instead, they were sent back to London with a personal letter to the king, repeating all the familiar arguments of the past two years, including the customary evasion that these unpalatable orders came not from Edward but from 'such as do wish those things to take place which be most agreeable to themselves'. In other words, she continued to see, or pretended to see, the issue as one between her private conscience and that of Warwick and his friends. This was the error which Scheyfve had warned her against in January – repudiating the authority of the minority government. Perhaps she had not had time to consult him on this occasion, or perhaps her 'old illness' of which she complained, had prevented her from doing so. Since he did not report her renewed troubles until the 25th, it appears that she had not followed her usual practice on this occasion. On the

23rd her servants reappeared before the council, and flatly refused to act as messengers a second time. They were then imprisoned for contempt, and the council's attempt to send Mary a replacement controller of their own choice met with a similar refusal. Short of summoning Mary to London, and risking another major conservative demonstration, there was only one thing to be done, and the chancellor, Lord Rich, Sir Anthony Wingfield and Sir William Petre were sent in commission to Copthall bearing fresh letters from the king.

There then followed a celebrated confrontation, recorded in detail in the council register of 29 August.[54] There was nothing new to be said on either side. The commissioners declared that the king's patience with his recalcitrant sister was exhausted, and that henceforth no service must be said in her house except that authorized by law. Mary, for all her professions of humble obedience to the king, treated his representatives with a mixture of petulance and contempt. She made it perfectly clear that she did not recognize them as bearing any valid authority for the task which they had undertaken, and reminded them scornfully that her father had 'made the more part of you almost from nothing'. Reverting to her earlier stance, she declared that, in matters of conscience, she would obey her brother when he came of age, but not before. Meanwhile, she relied upon the emperor's protection, and 'hys Ambassadour shall knowe how I am used at your handes.' Up to a point, her arguments were cogent enough. It had been a foolish move, she pointed out, to endeavour to control her through her servants, while she was at liberty to receive or dismiss such servants at her pleasure. Equally, it was unconvincing to represent the king as old enough to decide matters of faith when they would not have admitted his capacity to handle more mundane affairs. At the same time, much of her response was sheer histrionics. When the king's letters were presented, and again when she gave Rich a ring as a token for her brother, she knelt with every profession of humility. In the process of protesting against the arrest of her officers, she declared, 'I am sickly, and yet will not dye willingly . . . but if I chaunce to dye I will protest openly that you of the councell be the causes of my death. You gyve me fayre wordes,

[54] *APC*, III, 347; Foxe, *Acts and Monuments*, VI, 21–2; *APC*, III, 333, 336, 340; the commissioners' instructions are also printed by Foxe, VI, 22–3.

but your dedes be always ill towards me.' Finally, as they rode away, she leaned from her chamber window to protest that she was not used to keeping her own accounts, and ended with the parting shot: 'I pray God to send you to do well in your sowles and bodies to, for some of you have but weak bodies.' It was a performance of great spirit, but little dignity, which has sometimes been described as 'hysterical'. More likely it was a calculated and public gesture of defiance, and if so, it worked. The council did not retreat, but neither did it punish her contempt. Her officers remained in prison until the spring of the following year, and the ban on the mass was never lifted, but in practice the compromise of the summer was allowed to return, and Mary enjoyed the consolations of religion in the privacy of her own chamber.

Scheyfve, in what must by then have been a reflex gesture, appeared on 4 September to make his inevitable protest, but on this occasion he met with an unexpected response. Having heard him out, the earl of Warwick declared that on a matter of such consequence, the king himself must be consulted, and he would have to return for his answer later. When he came back, the earl declared that Edward had insisted that his laws must be obeyed, and that no one, least of all his sister, could be exempted.[55] Scheyfve clearly allowed his scepticism to show, because Warwick observed sharply that in his judgement the king had as much authority as if he were forty. Whereupon the ambassador sensibly declared that he had no commission to discuss the nature of the king's authority, and passed on to other matters. So, by the middle of September, the intent of the council was clear. They were going to insist upon the maxim which Stephen Gardiner had recognized from the beginning: 'A king's authority to govern his realm never wanteth, though he were in his cradle.'[56] It may still have been a fiction that Edward was making his own decisions, but it was a fiction with a specific

[55] Scheyfve to the emperor, 12 September 1551; *Cal.Span.*, x, 360; *Chronicle*, 80. Edward's personal involvement in these conflicts with his sister is very hard to assess. When she was not there, he seems to have been genuinely indignant about her mass, and her disobedience. When talking to her he usually took a much more conciliatory line, which has increased the impression that he had little hand in writing the severe letters which were sent under his name, but may mean no more than that he was abashed by her presence.

[56] Gardiner to Cranmer, 12 June 1547; Gardiner, *Letters*, 299.

purpose, and one which Mary consistently refused to perceive. The emperor's declining grasp, however, spelt danger to this new confidence, because the renewal of war with France in October, instead of diminishing the danger of Imperial intervention in England, actually increased it. In a most interesting and significant letter to the bishop of Arras on the 5th of that month, Mary of Hungary outlined a new strategy to take advantage of Mary's stubborn partisanship. The French, she pointed out, were counting on English friendship because of the manner in which the emperor had been obliged to aid the king's sister in defying his laws.

> We must therefore have a port in that country at our disposal, either by force or through friendship. Many people are of the opinion that the kingdom of England would not be impossible to conquer, especially now that it is a prey to discord and poverty. It seems there are three persons who might try their fortune, conquer the country and marry our cousin, if she is able to hold out with his Majesty's favour.[57]

This could be done 'under colour of taking the king out of the hands of his pernicious governors . . . If they had already got rid of the king, we could intervene with the pretext of avenging him, or some other excuse easily to be devised.' The three persons alluded to were the Archduke Ferdinand, Dom Luis of Portugal and the duke of Holstein. In the case of Ferdinand, the emperor would have to foot the bill, which would be a major disadvantage, while Dom Luis and the duke of Holstein might call upon their brothers, the kings of Portugal and Denmark respectively. Mary was the bait, and possibly also the means of entry. Once an invader had landed, the main Imperial fleet could be used to support him, and that would deprive the French of any advantage in the island. On the subject of Mary herself, the queen dowager was totally unsentimental: 'If the king or his ministers proceed to take the mass away from her, she will be obliged to put up with it. She has no means to resist, and would be a victim of force, so that she would be blameless in God's sight.' Looked at from this point of view, the princess's mass was not a matter of her own salvation, nor of the emperor's family honour, but of preserving a useful and potentially invaluable bridgehead in England in the interests of Habsburg strategy.

[57] *Cal. Span.*, x, 377.

It is not surprising that Mary of Hungary should have believed that an Anglo-French alliance was imminent. Simon Renard, the Imperial ambassador at the court of Henry II had reported in June that Henry's councillors were repeatedly reminding the English that the emperor had tried to get Mary out of England during the previous summer, in order to use her against them. This was not strictly true, but the princess's position as an Imperial pawn was generally appreciated, and Edward's councillors had not succeeded in neutralizing her as her father had done. On the other hand the English council knew perfectly well that the country was in no fit state to go to war, and the earl of Warwick's policy was one of disengagement. He had already retreated, from both Boulogne and Scotland, and had no intention of inviting the emperor to exploit his domestic difficulties.[58] Consequently, during the autumn of 1551 the rhetoric of conflict gradually petered out. At the end of October Mary was invited to attend the reception of the queen dowager of Scotland at court. She sent her excuses, on the grounds of her 'constant ill health, which at present is worse than usual', but admitted to Scheyfve that the real reason was fear of religious coercion. It appears that Charles was not particularly pleased to receive this news from his ambassador, because in early December he sent her word that it would be wiser to attend when given the opportunity. Mary responded that she would visit the king after Christmas, as she was wont to do, but would not submit to any 'outrageous rite which might cause her to offend'. Her priests were still being harassed, she complained, and she had lodged her habitual protest. In the middle of January, Scheyfve did the same, but it was almost a ritual game by this time, the council responding, as it was wont, that the king, like the emperor, insisted on having his laws obeyed. As Nicholas Wotton had told Charles months before, 'in England there is but one king, and the king hath but one law to rule all his subjects by. The Lady Mary being no king, must be content to be a subject.' There the matter was allowed to rest. Rochester, Englefield and Waldegrave were released from prison on 28 March 1552, and

[58] For a detailed examination of Warwick (Northumberland)'s foreign policy, see Jordan, *Edward VI: The Threshold of Power*, 116–81; also Beer, *Northumberland;* and D. E. Hoak, 'Rehabilitating the Duke of Northumberland', in *Tudor Rule and Revolution: Essays for G. R. Elton from his American Friends*, ed. J. W. McKenna and J. de Lloyd Guth.

returned to duty a fortnight later. In June, when Mary made another state visit to the court, escorted by a 'goodly company', she was well received and the subject of religion was apparently avoided. There was certainly no general relaxation in the drive for conformity, and the parliament of that year saw another Act of Uniformity which was even more distasteful to the conservatives than the last,[59] but Mary retained the very narrow ground of indulgence which was her last bastion of retreat. No more could be conceded and no more could be hoped for. Had Edward lived, conflict would no doubt have broken out again, but by the end of 1552 his deteriorating health had begun to create a general climate of uncertainty. The duke of Northumberland (as Warwick had become in October 1551) began to make conciliatory gestures to Mary. In December he authorized the payment of over £500 to help repair some of the dykes on the more exposed parts of her Essex lands; an investment, perhaps, in anticipation of the exchange of these lands with the Crown a few months later.[60] He also began to keep her informed of public affairs. In February 1553 she was received at court in a manner which suggested a new emphasis upon her position as heir apparent, being met an hour's ride out of London by the earl of Warwick, Lord William Howard, and a hundred horsemen. The king was too ill to see her for several days.

Below the surface, nothing had changed. At what point Northumberland began to face up to the possibility that Edward would not outlive his minority we do not know, but it was probably not until the late spring of 1553.[61] In March Mary was still asking the emperor to force the council to enlarge the scope of her religious freedom, and professing her total submission to his will. She had long since informed her brother's advisers that she would not marry without her cousin's consent, and there were, in consequence, no serious negotiations after Portuguese interest fizzled out in 1550. The ruling families of Ferrara,

[59] Statute 5 and 6 Edward VI cap.1; *Statutes of the Realm*, IV, 130–1. This replaced the conservative Prayer Book of 1549, which was virtually a translation of the Sarum Use, with a second book of a more markedly Zwinglian character. C. W. Dugmore, *The Mass and the English Reformers.*

[60] *APC*, IV, 188.

[61] Jordan, *Edward VI: The Threshold of Power*, 494–532, presents an interpretation largely exonerating Northumberland of any deep laid conspiracy. The older view is represented by A. F. Pollard, *The Political History of England, 1547–1603* (1913). See also C. S. L. Davies, *Peace, Print and Protestantism* (1976).

Brandenburg and even Poland, expressed interest at one time or another, and Ferrara was mentioned several times, but no powers were issued, and no details were ever discussed. While Elizabeth made herself thoroughly at home in the new regime, so that her favour and her frequent presence at court were often commented upon, Mary remained firmly alienated. Her public position was perfectly clear. She stood for the religious settlement that her father had bequeathed, and the traditional Burgundian alliance. No mention was ever made of the unity of Christendom, nor of the papal authority, nor of the dissolved religious houses. It is misleading to speak of Mary during these years as a catholic. There is no evidence at all that she communicated with the *Curia* either directly or indirectly, in marked contrast with the representations which were made on her behalf in 1536. There is no doubt that her religious stand was popular, but of the 'conservative front' which the council feared, between herself, provincial magnates such as Arundel, Derby and Shrewsbury, and the Henrician party among the gentry, there is no discernible trace. To a government set upon protestant reform, Mary was an obstacle and a threat, but she was a domestic threat – at least to all appearances. What made her an alien element was her attitude towards the emperor. The council knew perfectly well that she had sheltered behind him in every hostile political situation for nearly twenty years, but that was an understandable strategy in the circumstances. What was not appreciated was the extent of her emotional dependence, a dependence which became much more marked when her problematic relationship with her father came to an end. Despite her financial independence, her estates and clientage, Mary scarcely made a move of any significance between 1547 and 1553 without consulting the Imperial ambassador. It is not surprising that Mary of Hungary regarded her as an exploitable asset, or that the French described her as being 'altogether of the Emperor's allegiance'. She was also the heir to the throne by the unchallenged terms of Henry VIII's will, and as the summer of 1553 advanced the prospect of her succession began to cause acute alarm in some well-informed quarters.

5

Annus Mirabilis

(1553–1554)

The death of Edward VI on the evening of 6 July 1553 was expected, and a merciful release. The council had known for about two months that his days were numbered, and the event had been anticipated numerous times in popular rumour. Nevertheless, when the news was formally announced to the lord mayor and aldermen of London two days later, the country was plunged into a political crisis. Mary was the heir, by the terms of her father's will, which had also received statutory authorization, and her accession was generally expected. However, several weeks earlier, by means which are not entirely clear, Edward had become convinced that his half-sister must on no account succeed him. Scheyfve reported at the time that the duke of Northumberland was plotting to seize the Crown, and it has been generally believed since that his influence was responsible for the king's decision.[1] The evidence for this view is strong, but circumstantial. Edward had been very much dominated by the duke after the latter had seized power in the autumn of 1549, but it is not certain that his ascendancy was still complete in the spring of 1553, when the king was fifteen and beginning to find his feet in the political arena. Although Mary had never wanted to believe it, Edward's protestantism was a genuine commitment, embraced with the passionate intensity of adolescence, and he was also fully aware of his sister's obstinate conservatism. On the other hand, if the king was mainly responsible for the

[1] Scheyfve to the emperor, 11 June 1553; *Cal.Span.*, XI, 49. For a somewhat different view, see Jordan, *Edward VI: The Threshold of Power*, 513–27.

attempt to exclude Mary, it it hard to see why he should have passed over his protestant half-sister Elizabeth in favour of so obscure a claimant as Jane Grey. Jane's hereditary claim was inferior to that of her mother, Frances, who was the elder daughter of Henry VIII's sister Mary and Charles Brandon, duke of Suffolk. And both were inferior to Elizabeth, who was placed after Mary in their father's will. Jane Grey's only advantage, apart from the fact she had shared some of Edward's schooling as a child, was that she was already married. However, since her husband was Guildford Dudley, the duke of Northumberland's fifth son, the benefit of that would accrue mainly to the Dudleys. It is not hard to see why the document which the king presented to his law officers on 12 June, to form the basis of his will, should have been attributed to the duke's influence.[2] Nevertheless all the direct evidence suggests that it was the king himself who invoked the allegiance of the reluctant in order to get his 'Device' accepted by the privy council.

That 'Device' has been the subject of exhaustive scholarly analysis, and it is now accepted that a number of crucial amendments had been made as the king's demise became imminent.[3] Those amendments were not made in Edward's own hand, because he was by then too weak to write, but he clearly knew of them and approved them. Originally the succession had been settled upon any son who might be born to Frances and her husband Henry Grey, duke of Suffolk. That idea had been set down early in the year, before the king's health was known to be desperate, and indicates a settled intention to elevate the Suffolk line before any question of Jane's immediate claim arose. It may then have been discovered that Frances was no longer capable of bearing a son, because all reference to her and her heirs male was removed. At some time after Jane's marriage to Guildford Dudley on 21 May, the succession was directed to 'the heirs male of the Lady Jane', a format which still anticipated a time span of many months. But the document which was presented to the law officers about three weeks later had been altered to read 'the Lady Jane and her heirs male'. This provision had neither law nor logic to commend it, and looks like a scrambled improvis-

[2] Petyt MS xlvii, f.316; J. G. Nichols, *Literary Remains of King Edward VI*, II, 571–2; Jordan, *Edward VI: The Threshold of Power*, 1515–16.

[3] *Literary Remains of King Edward VI*, II, 571.

ation produced by a rapid deterioration in the king's condition. A sharp political struggled resulted. Not only did the judges demur – Montague and Gosnold in particular arguing that the king's mere will could not overturn an act of parliament – but several senior councillors were apparently in favour of allowing Mary to succeed on certain conditions.[4] The first of these positions was sounder than the second. Not only did a statute require parliamentary repeal, but Edward, as a minor, was not even capable of making a valid will. On the other hand it could be sensibly argued that, even if Mary agreed not to alter the religious establishment, there was no way in which she could be held to her promise once in possession of the Crown. Scheyfve, well informed about these developments, reported to the emperor on 19 June that the princess was much perplexed, and earnestly sought his advice as to what she should do. Ironically, Charles's advice, which never reached her, was to accept a conditional offer if one were made. Even with so high a stake as the English succession in play, he could not commit resources to Mary's support and relief, and relied as he had always done in the past on diplomatic pressure to promote her interests. On 23 June he anticipated Scheyfve's request by issuing instructions to three special envoys, de Courrières, de Thoulouse and Renard, who were ostensibly to commiserate with the king on his illness. In fact they were intended to rally support for Mary, and to offer her every assistance short of actual cash or troops.[5]

However, if Charles had intended to exploit the divisions and uncertainties among the English councillors, he was too late. His envoys did not arrive until the day of the king's death. The privy council, and a substantial body of peers, household officers and other dignitaries had sworn on 21 June to uphold the king's will, and they had the enthusiastic support of the French ambassador, Antoine de Noailles. Northumberland had taken Noailles into his confidence on 26 June, realizing that the emperor would do everything in his power to overturn the 'Device', and that only

[4] Historical Manuscripts Commission, MSS of Lord Montague of Beaulieu, 4; Jordan, *Edward VI: The Threshold of Power*, 516; Scheyfve to the emperor, 19 June 1553, *Cal. Span.*, XI, 57.

[5] The emperor's instructions to MM de Courrières, de Thoulouse, and Simon Renard; 23 June 1553; *Cal.Span.*, XI, 60–5. Scheyfve had requested such a mission in his letter of the 19th.

French pressure could keep him too busy to intervene.[6] Charles had anticipated this reaction, and his instructions to his envoys make it clear that their prime objective was to counter French influence: 'You will take such steps as you think necessary to defeat the machinations of the French, and to keep them out of England.' The succession of Mary was only the most obvious means to that end. If Northumberland and his party appeared to be strongly entrenched, then they were to reassure him about the emperor's intentions. A bargain, which would have accepted the princess's exclusion in return for a formal alliance and a guarantee of good treatment for her, was distinctly implied. Of course, it would be better if they could overcome English fears of a foreign king, and persuade them to set aside Edward's will. To this end, they were authorized to declare that Charles favoured an English marriage for his cousin, which ran contrary to everything he had previously said on the subject, and is another indication of the extent to which he regarded Mary as an exploitable asset. The special ambassadors' first report, written on the morning of 7 July, was full of sound information and erroneous judgements. They knew that Edward had died 'between eight and nine o'clock' the previous evening, and that Mary, warned of the imminence of his demise, had already departed from Hunsdon on a pretext of sickness among her servants, and was heading for Kenninghall.[7] They also knew the terms of Edward's will, the fact that Northumberland intended to arrest her if possible to forestall popular revolt, and that Mary intended to proclaim herself queen forthwith. Since they had had no chance to speak to Mary, she must have sent them word of her intentions as soon as they arrived.

In spite of Scheyfve's earlier claims, the princess had certainly not waited for Imperial advice on this occasion. Had she done so, the ambassadors would have urged caution. The king's death had not been publicly proclaimed, and if the news were false she

[6] Noailles to Henry II, 28 June 1553, Archives de Ministère des affaires étrangères, IX, f.34: E. H. Harbison, *Rival Ambassadors at the Court of Queen Mary*, 43.

[7] Ambassadors to the emperor, 7 July 1553; *Cal.Span.*, XI, 72–6. The source of this advance warning is unknown. The claim made in Sir Nicholas Throgmorton's autobiography relates to the news of the king's actual death a few days later, sent by 'her goldsmith'. *The Chronicle of Queen Jane and of the first two years of Queen Mary*, ed. J. G. Nichols, 1–2.

would be running headlong into a trap. Moreover, they could see no prospect of success for her bid: 'All the forces of the country are in the Duke's hands, and my Lady has no hope of raising enough men to face him . . . The hope that my Lady builds upon English support for her claim is vain, because of religion.' Although Scheyfve signed this dispatch, the other ambassadors outranked him, and it seems likely that these views represented their rapid appraisal of the situation, rather than his experience.[8] On the following day, when the news of Edward's demise was officially released, the council knew that Mary was heading for Kenninghall, and hopefully declared that she was 'in flight', intending to escape overseas – a plausible enough story in the light of recent events. By 10 July it was known in London that she had proclaimed herself queen. What had prompted Mary to this unprecedented speed and resolution of action? It is clear that she had no shortage of sympathizers at court, or within the council, at this time. Whatever doubts may have been aroused by her unmarried state, or by her religious stance, she was the heir by the law which most acknowledged. On the other hand, she had never acted upon English advice before, and made no secret of her distrust for all those who had been associated with her brother's government. It is possible that resolute counsel may have come from Mary of Hungary, who, as we have seen, was much more prone to take a bold line than Charles – but there is no evidence to substantiate such a view. It is also possible that she may have acted less out of ambition, or a sense of justice, than out of fear. *Aut Caesar, aut nihil*: unless she gambled on her claim and won, she faced certain imprisonment and almost certain death. Queen Jane, with her precarious claim based upon a small religious minority, and the military strength of the Dudleys, could hardly have allowed her to live in peaceful retirement. If some had expected the emperor to recognize her in 1547, how much stronger was that likelihood now! However, the likeliest motivation in this supreme crisis of her life came from her conscience; that dogged sense of duty which had so often before driven her into conflict with authority.

According to Robert Wingfield, who was directly involved in these dramatic events, and wrote his account some time in 1554,

[8] *Cal.Span.*, IX, 74. Scheyfve had earlier shown himself more optimistic about Mary's chances.

Mary was at Euston Hall, near Thetford, when she received the first news of Edward's death on 8 July.[9] The messenger is described as 'her goldsmith, a citizen of London', who has been identified as one Robert Raynes. The princess was cautious, and would not allow the news to be proclaimed. She may have distrusted the messenger, but common prudence would have required corroboration in a matter of such importance. On the 9th she rejoined her main household at Kenninghall, and the king's death was confirmed the same day. Mary immediately summoned her servants, and proclaimed herself queen 'by divine and human law', amid scenes of loyal enthusiasm. Although Wingfield says that she consulted her advisers, the only counsel to hand were her normal household officers, and she had clearly decided upon her course of action at least several days earlier. Writing to the council in London on the same date (9 July) she charged them upon their allegiance to 'cause our right and title to the crown and government of this realm to be proclaimed in our city of London, and other places as to your wisdom shall seem good.'[10] Predictably, her messenger, Thomas Hungate, was imprisoned, and her claim repudiated over the signatures of twenty-three councillors, including some, such as Winchester and Arundel, who were thought to be sympathetic to her cause. Mary and her supporters did not wait for this daunting news, but immediately sent out messengers 'to draw all the gentlemen of the surrounding countryside to do fealty to their sovereign'. In other words, she mobilized her affinity, and the initial response was so exceedingly swift that the men in question must have been ready and waiting for the word. Within two days she had been joined by Sir Henry Bedingfield, Sir John Shelton, John Huddlestone, Sir Richard Southwell, Sir John Mordaunt, Thomas Morgan, Sir William Drury and a number of other Norfolk and Suffolk gentlemen. They came with their followers, armed and provisioned. Some, like Southwell, arrived 'amply provided with money'. They were not magnates, but they immediately formed the nucleus of a well-disciplined military camp. To the thirty or so gentlemen of her household who were with her

[9] Robert Wingfield of Brantham, 'Vita Mariae Reginae' ed. D. MacCulloch, *Camden Miscellany*, XXVIII, 203/251 and n. She may have mistrusted the news, knowing it came from Throgmorton.

[10] Foxe, *Acts and Monuments* VI, 385.

on 9 July, at least another thirty, with their retinues, had been added by the 12th. On that day, deciding that Kenninghall was too small and too difficult to defend, Mary moved her headquarters to Framlingham castle in Suffolk.[11]

How all this was achieved can only be inferred, because it is nowhere fully described. Wingfield ascribed it to spontaneous love for Mary and the righteousness of her cause, but it takes very careful organization to create such effective spontaneity. Mary herself may have known very little about it. Administration was not her forte, as she had confessed to her brother's commissioners, and she did not really need to know. What she was required to do was to make her own decision to claim the Crown. The organization of the coup was best left to others. So who were those others? John Foxe hinted darkly that disaffected members of the London council were behind Mary's success, but the detailed timetable does not support such a view. The most likely candidates are the chief household officers, Rochester, Jerningham and Waldegrave.[12] They were conspicuously loyal to Mary, had every reason to hate Northumberland after their spell in the Tower, and had all the necessary connections in East Anglia. They were not men of great power, but they gambled on a swift response of moderate strength triggering off a much larger movement, and they won. What they did was exactly what was required in the confused and uncertain situation following Edward's death. There was widespread popular support for Mary, or at least dislike of the duke and his schemes, but it required tangible and traditional leadership to make it effective. Mary's proclamation alone would not have achieved that. In the absence of any suitably resolute and sympathetic noblemen, a group of well-organized gentlemen had to do instead. The critical days were 12–14 July, because if the momentum of the first three days could not be maintained, there would have been little more that the loyal East Anglian connection could have done, and Mary's rebellion would have been pinned down and defeated. However, the momentum was sustained, and even increased. Wingfield's narrative contains a number of stories of

[11] Wingfield 'Vita Mariae', 206/255.

[12] Sir Francis Englefield was not with Mary at Framlingham, and only joined her on 24 July at Ipswich. According to Wingfield this was because he had been imprisoned for espousing her cause, but no other details are given. Wingfield, 'Vita Mariae', 220/269.

how particular men of power were won over by the energy and commitment of Mary's servants – Sir Thomas Cornwallis, the earl of Sussex, and Lord Wentworth. Once it was known that two rival queens had been proclaimed there must have been many men of substance in great indecision. Most no doubt postponed commitment until it was clear who was going to win, but those who were caught in the open and forced to decide might be swayed by all sorts of immediate circumstances. On 15 July the indefatigable Henry Jerningham brought off the most successful stroke to date, when he persuaded the captains of five royal ships lying in the Orwell to declare for Mary.[13] By then the tide was running strongly, and Wingfield lost count of those who were daily joining the Framlingham camp. On the 16th a command structure was created for what was becoming a sizeable host. The earl of Sussex became commander, Lord Wentworth earl marshal, Bedingfield knight marshal and Sir Edmund Rous sub-marshal. Regular military exercises commenced, and a disciplined army began to form. Meanwhile, sharp local struggles were being waged for the allegiance of particular towns and villages. The records of Ipswich, Lowestoft and Great Yarmouth all bear witness to hasty changes as the fortunes of Mary's followers improved.[14] Her most determined and energetic opponent in the region was Lord Robert Dudley, Northumberland's fourth son, whose own base was in Norfolk. Lord Robert's affinity was not large, but at first his agents enjoyed considerable success, and it was not clear until about 16 July that his father's cause was rapidly becoming hopeless.

In London the foreign diplomats watched with incredulity, and the council which had appeared so solidly for Jane on 9 July, began to fall apart. On 12 July Lord Cobham and Sir John Mason visited the Imperial ambassadors, and informed them that as their commission had been to the deceased king, they had no further business to detain them in London. Renard, who was the diplomatic brains of the mission, realized that there was an element of bluster about this brusqueness. He already knew that

[13] Ibid., 210/258. Wingfield says five; four days later the Imperial ambassadors reported that seven ships had defected. *Cal.Span.*, XI, 95.

[14] R. Tittler, and S. L. Battley, 'The local community and the crown in 1553: the accession of Mary Tudor revisited', *Bulletin of the Institute of Historical Research*, LVII, 131–9. Tittler argues that there is clear evidence of anti-Marian enclaves in the fenlands until well into August.

Northumberland had decided to take up Noailles's offer of French assistance, and that Mary was assembling a substantial force. He did not yet believe that she could win without Imperial reinforcements, and suggested that Flemish warships should be sent to Harwich. He was still thinking in terms of evacuation, but was sufficiently aware of the changing situation to be determined that he and his colleagues should stay put. Although they had managed no direct communication with Mary, he rightly perceived that their continued presence was an encouragement to her supporters. If his own account is to be believed, he also succeeded in throwing Cobham and Mason off balance with a disarming response to their threats. The emperor, he declared, had no intention of interfering, but could not help finding their proceedings very strange. After all, Mary was the lawful heir, and he feared that they were the victims of a French conspiracy which was aimed to place Mary Stuart on the throne, using Jane simply as a temporary expedient.[15] Their fears that Mary would alter the laws and religion of the kingdom, and marry a foreigner, were misplaced, because the emperor would encourage her in none of those courses. Whether by good luck or shrewd judgement, his words made a considerable impression upon two men who were, in any case, inclined to be sympathetic to Mary. They withdrew their ultimatum, and invited the ambassadors to await the result of further deliberation in council. The following day they were summoned to meet what purported to be the whole council, but was in fact that part which was beginning to come round to Mary's side – the earls of Bedford, Arundel, Shrewsbury and Pembroke, and secretary Petre. Northumberland, Suffolk, Northampton, and the rest of the hard core of Jane's party, were never told about these consultations. Renard, who already knew that Henry Dudley was departing for France that same day as Northumberland's personal envoy, embroidered his story of conspiracy by inventing dispatches which he claimed had been intercepted disclosing the duke's secret commitment to Mary Stuart.[16]

Events were moving with confusing speed. By 12 July Northumberland knew that a military operation of some kind would be needed against the rising in East Anglia, but believed that it

[15] Ambassadors to the emperor, 12 July 1553; *Cal.Span.*, XI, 85.
[16] Harbison, *Rival Ambassadors*, 49–50.

would be small-scale. By the morning of the 14th, when he left London at the head of 600 men, he had reason to fear that his force, drawn mainly from his own and his friends' retainers, would not be sufficient, and endeavoured to arrange for reinforcements. The stronger the rumours of Mary's power became (and they had exaggerated her host to 30,000 by the 16th)[17] the more openly everyone, from the citizens of London to his former allies on the council, began to distance themselves from him and his protégée. As the duke moved north-east to Cambridge over the next two days, his position suddenly disintegrated. Although they feared his military reputation, instead of being intimidated into joining him, the local gentry, such as Sir William Waldegrave, Ambrose Jermyn and Edmund Wright, gathered their followers and rallied to Mary. No reinforcements came. By the 18th his own men were deserting, and on the 19th he learned that the council in London had proclaimed Mary behind his back. This dramatic change may have been partly occasioned by Renard's successful stratagem, but he probably overestimated both his own influence and the international preoccupation of the English. So nervous was the duke of Suffolk by the evening of the 16th that he had the gates of the Tower locked, and the marquis of Winchester brought in from his London lodging at midnight. However, his apprehensions had nothing to do with the emperor. News had arrived of the defection of the royal ships, of the fact that the earls of Sussex and Bath had joined the princess, and that she was being proclaimed as far apart as Gloucester, Oxford and Yorkshire.[18] The protestant front, upon which Northumberland had largely relied, and which the Imperialists had believed to be effective,

[17] John Stow, *Annales* (1592) (STC 23334), 611; Jordan, *Edward VI: The Threshold of Power*, 528.

[18] *The Chronicle of Queen Jane,* 9–10. It is difficult to be sure how far this widespread support for Mary was spontaneous, and how far it was triggered off by news of what was happening in East Anglia. Mary had certainly sent letters to urban and county officials all over England and Wales, and her messengers would no doubt have improved upon the size of her following. The sheer scale of that operation argues a lot of forethought. The physical process of writing so many letters would have taken several days. Robert Tittler has shown that there was widespread support for Mary, particularly in the Home Counties, within a few days of her self-proclamation, but not that this was independent of what was happening in East Anglia. Tittler, *Reign of Mary I*, 10.

had simply failed to appear. Nicholas Ridley had denounced both Mary and Elizabeth in a sermon on the 9th, but the radical John Hooper had declared for Mary, and Sir Peter Carew had taken the initiative in proclaiming her in Devon. At some point between 16 and 19 July the earls of Arundel and Pembroke were able to leave the Tower, and took themselves to Baynard's castle, Pembroke's London residence. There they were joined by most of the councillors remaining in London – Shrewsbury, Bedford, Paget, Cheyney, Mason and Petre. The lord mayor and aldermen were summoned, and the decision was taken to proclaim Mary queen.

The marquis of Northampton, the earls of Huntingdon and Warwick, Lords Grey and Clinton, Sir John Gate and a number of other gentlemen, were still with Northumberland at Cambridge, but their position was much weaker than such a roll-call might suggest. By the evening of 18 July Mary had more men, and probably more artillery and provisions at Framlingham, than Northumberland and Suffolk combined, but Sussex was her only major noble supporter and her only experienced military commander. Much therefore depended upon the attitude of the earl of Oxford, the most powerful man in Essex. His continued allegiance to Jane could have given Mary's force a difficult passage to London, especially if he had joined Northumberland at Cambridge. According to Robert Wingfield, he was forced into Mary's camp by his own servants, persuaded by one of her eloquent messengers.[19] There may well be an element of truth in the story, but it is also reminiscent of the stories told by men such as Sir Robert Constable to account for their involvement in the Pilgrimage of Grace. If Mary won, the circumstances of his joining her would not be held against him, if she lost, he had at least some kind of a defence to fall back on. As it turned out, Oxford's defection was decisive, and coincided with the defection of most of the London council. By the morning of 19 July the Imperial ambassadors had decided that there was probably going to be a civil war in England, and that if Mary could survive the first armed encounter, she might prevail because of her popular support. They commended her cause to the emperor, but were prepared to withdraw, as they felt that there was little that they could do to help her. Later the same day,

[19] Wingfield, 'Vita Mariae', 215/264.

Shrewsbury and Mason called on them and informed them of the proclamation of Mary in London. They were astonished, and suspected treachery: 'we thought we saw what they might be trying to do; namely to induce my Lady to lay down her arms, and then treacherously overcome her or encompass her death by means of a plot.'[20] It was to be several days before they finally concluded that God had used the fickleness of the English to work a notable miracle. The following morning the duke of Northumberland, who had abandoned his advance on Bury St Edmunds when he heard of Oxford's desertion, himself proclaimed Mary at Cambridge, and what could still have been a violent campaign, ended without a blow being struck.

Ironically, the great triumph of Mary's life, and one of the most notable events in the history of the Tudor monarchy, had come about without any practical help, and with very little moral support, from the person upon whom she had always been most heavily dependent. The French ambassador, as surprised as anyone by the suddenness of Northumberland's collapse, and now faced with the distasteful prospect of being reviled as his principal accomplice, assessed the new queen's likely stance. The emperor, he declared, had very little call upon her gratitude, because 'in all her own miseries, troubles and afflictions, as well as in those of the queen her mother, the emperor never came to their assistance, nor has he helped her now in her great need with a single man, ship or penny.'[21] This was not entirely fair, but Noailles was right in believing that Mary's sense of obligation would not be diminished by the circumstances of her elevation to the throne. The simple fact seems to have been that, during the actual succession crisis, the international complications cancelled each other out. If Northumberland had not appealed to the French, his position would probably have remained stronger. If Mary had been actively assisted by an Imperial invasion, her popularity would almost certainly have been much reduced. In the immediate situation, it was Mary who represented self-determination, not Jane. It was also Mary who represented law, and her father's will. Her success was the

[20] *Cal.Span.*, XI, 95.

[21] Noailles to Montmorency, 3 August 1553; Archives du ministère des affaires étrangères, Paris. *Correspondance Politique, Angleterre*, IX, f.53. Harbison, *Rival Ambassadors*, 54.

triumph of conservatism over innovation, and the remarkable thing about it was not its ease, but its difficulty. Given the revolutionary implications of the intrusion of Jane Grey onto the throne, the extent of her initial recognition was remarkable. Henry VIII had never done such violence to customary law. Had he been willing to do so, he could have saved himself a vast amount of trouble and expense. Not even the radical protestants were convinced that tests of godliness could be applied in such a manner, and Edward's 'Device for the succession' exalted the will of the king to an unprecedented level of authority. Yet it almost worked. Charles V would have accepted it, the great majority of the nobility would have accepted it, and there was far more popular acquiescence than traditional accounts have allowed. It failed, partly because Mary herself showed unexpected resolution, and a decisiveness which contrasts starkly with her behaviour during the abortive escape plot of 1551; and partly because her affinity was strong enough to throw down an initial challenge. The fact that armed men were rallying to her within hours of her arrival at Kenninghall was critical. As soon as it was clear that Mary was willing and able to make a fight of it, the position began to change. In spite of Robert Wingfield's stories about loyal servants and seamen forcing their masters into Mary's camp, his own narrative also makes it clear that what counted most was gentry initiative and strength. It was, as E. H. Harbison observed many years ago, the 'third estate' which rallied to the cause of legitimacy, and which so impressed Continental observers with the peculiarities of English politics.[22]

The rapidity of her success created its own problems for Mary. It was reasonable to suppose that those who had demonstrated their support for her cause before 19 July had also demonstrated a willingness to fight for her, and that the reality of their commitment was not in doubt. However, as soon as Northumberland had surrendered, there was no means of telling the belated loyalist from the nimble time-server, except possibly by the distance he had travelled. As Mary inspected her forces at Framlingham on 20 July, still unaware that they would serve

[22] They were accustomed both to noble factions and to peasant risings, but this was neither. The lead appeared to them to come from the gentry and the towns, and modern research has confirmed this. Harbison, *Rival Ambassadors*, 55.

only a ceremonial purpose, the first of these new adherents began to arrive. Lord Paget and the earl of Arundel brought the news from London, and were immediately received into favour. They represented an invaluable accession of political experience, and Arundel was dispatched the next day with the sensitive and responsible task of arresting the fallen Northumberland and those who were too closely associated with him to stand any chance of successful defection. On the same day arrived a number of others, of various provenance – the earl of Oxford and Lord Rich, with 'goodly companies'; Lord Clinton, Lord Grey of Wilton, Sir John Clere, James Croft, and others whom Wingfield specifically identified as 'fugitives from Northumberland's army'.[23] The reception of these men must have depended to a large extent on Mary's snap judgement, and the logic is not always apparent. Oxford, whose transfer of allegiance had been of considerable importance, never became a councillor, or received any other position of trust; whereas Lord Grey 'who was so repentent of his misdeed that he obtained a well-merited pardon from the gracious queen', was immediately dispatched to assist Arundel, and subsequently re-appointed to his charge as captain of Guisnes. By 24 July, when Mary disbanded the bulk of her army and began to move towards London, her first council, already numbering about twenty, had come into existence. Apart from Oxford, Grey and Clinton, it contained all the peers who had so far made their personal submissions, but the majority were members of her earlier household or affinity, and only Paget and Arundel had recent experience of high office.[24]

Over the next few days, as she moved first to Ipswich and then to her own former residence at Newhall, a steady procession of peers, councillors and other notables sought her out, and decisions had to be made about their reception. How this was done can only be conjectured. Perhaps Lord Paget had already insinuated himself into her confidence and become the new queen's chief adviser, pehaps she was still listening to her old

[23] Wingfield, 'Vita Mariae', 217/266.

[24] There are a number of detailed discussions of the formation of Mary's council. Loades, *The Reign of Mary Tudor,* 70–85; A. Weikel, 'The Marian Council revisited', in J. Loach and R. Tittler, *The Mid-Tudor Polity, 1540–1560,* 52–73; and D. E. Hoak, 'Two revolutions in Tudor government: the formation and organisation of Mary I's privy council' in *Revolution Reassessed*, ed. D. Starkey and C. Coleman, 87–116.

servants Rochester and Waldegrave. The aged Thomas Heneage was well received, although he was long past further service and died shortly after. Nicholas Bacon was pardoned, probably on the intercession of his wife,[25] and Henry Neville, Lord Abergavenny, was welcomed. But Sir William Cecil was committed to prison, and the earl of Rutland arrived as a prisoner before being sent to the Tower. With the benefit of hindsight, it looks as though Mary was following a generous and self-confident policy of conciliation, proceeding severely against only a handful of the most guilty conspirators, delivering salutory lessons to the less guilty, and receiving as many as possible with pardon or welcome. This may have been so, but would not explain why relatively insignificant men like Sir John Gates and Sir Thomas Palmer were pursued to the death, while the duke of Suffolk was pardoned almost immediately on the intercession of his wife. On 31 July the queen reached Ingatestone, the home of Sir William Petre, and spent the night there. After this, Wingfield's chronology becomes a little vague, but it was between then and her arrival in London on 3 August that Mary had to make most of her decisions about her brother's former councillors. The marquis of Winchester and the earls of Bedford, Shrewsbury and Pembroke all presented themselves during this period as (probably) did Sir Thomas Cheney and Sir John Mason. Not all were received with equal warmth, although all seem to have been equally involved in the counter-plot which had led to the London proclamation on 19 July. Bedford and Mason were admitted to favour at once, but Winchester, Shrewsbury and Pembroke were upbraided for their lack of zeal on the queen's behalf, and kept in uncertainty of their futures for several days. At the same time the earl of Huntingdon and Viscount Hereford were imprisoned, and Lord Darcy placed under house arrest.

The one influence which seems to have been in complete abeyance throughout this period was that of Charles V. Having received the news of Mary's proclamation in London, on the following day the ambassadors dispatched a secretary to Mary,

[25] Wingfield, 'Vita Mariae', 222/270. Wingfield describes Ann Bacon (who was also Cecil's sister-in-law, as 'once' having been 'a waiting woman of Queen Mary's', but she seems to have been very recently in Mary's service, and was a member of her privy chamber by the time of the coronation.

warning her not to disband her forces, and asking to be appointed a time and a place for audience.[26] She replied on about the 22nd, apparently assuring them that she would not reduce her army 'nor trust the people with whom [she] now had to do', and asking for their advice about her late brother's funeral. The ambassadors' priority was very clearly revealed in their written response on 24 July. After warning her at some length against celebrating a requiem mass for Edward, they went on:

> Your Majesty will know that his Imperial Majesty ordered us to endeavour to efface the Council's suspicions by assuring them, as assure them we did, that they were wholly mistaken in believing that his Majesty desired a foreign marriage for you, or to wish you to make any innovations . . . Now if your Majesty were to set about ordering religion by means of the late King's funeral, you would furnish the Council with an opportunity for saying that his Majesty's words had been disproved by events.[27]

What Mary thought of this oblique reference to her dependence upon Imperial support, we do not know, but she did not act upon the advice; nor indeed did she retain her army. When she met the ambassadors at Newhall on the 29th, the talk was mostly about Henry Dudley's arrest at Calais, on his way back from his mission to the French court, and about the immediate threat to Calais which seemed to be posed by the Constable's military preparations. However, later the same evening, at the queen's instigation, an interview took place which was to have a profound effect upon the course of her reign. She sent the ambassadors word that one of their number might go to her privately in her oratory 'entering by the back door to avoid suspicion'. His colleagues chose Simon Renard for this crucial assignment, and Renard's account of what transpired marks the beginning of Mary's last, and most important, relationship with an Imperial envoy.[28] Renard did his best to gloss over the fact that they had done virtually nothing until her success was assured, and then,

[26] Ambassadors in England to Prince Philip, 20 July 1553; *Cal.Span.*, XI, 105.

[27] *Cal.Span.*, XI, 117–19.

[28] Ibid., 129–35. Renard subsequently convinced himself that he had engineered Northumberland's fall, and had been responsible for restoring England to 'union, concord, and devotion to the emperor'. C. Weiss, *Papiers d'état du cardinal de Granvelle*, in *Collection des documents inédits sur l'histoire de France*, (Paris, 1844–52), V, 21. Harbison, *Rival Ambassadors*, 50 and n.

presuming upon her gratitude for over twenty years of moral support, proceeded to advise her upon the vital issues of religion, her marriage and foreign policy.

What he actually said appears to have been sensible and conventional. She should commence by consolidating her position, remembering how unstable her subjects had just shown themselves to be. She ought not to rush her religious policy, 'but rather to recommend herself by winning her subjects hearts, showing herself to be a good Englishwoman, wholly bent on the kingdom's welfare'. At the same time, because the greater part of government 'was not within a woman's province', and because she would need aid, comfort and protection, she should marry as soon as possible. The emperor would be happy to advise her, should she wish it. In response Mary was neither evasive nor ironic. She repeated the expressions of gratitude to Charles which she had uttered so frequently before in less momentous circumstances. As a private individual, she declared, she had no desire to marry, but she now recognized it as a public responsibility. After God, she desire to obey no one but the emperor, whom she had always looked upon as her father, and was 'determined to follow [his] advice, and choose whomsoever [he] might recommend'. As for religion, she could not accept the ambassadors' cautious advice. It was well known that she had rejected the recent innovations, and had continued to have her mass celebrated in private. Religion had been changed since her father's death, by the will of the late protector, and she had to declare herself a Christian. She was determined to have a mass celebrated for her brother, to discharge her own conscience 'and out of respect for the will of the late king Henry, her father'. She would force no one to go to mass, but meant to ensure that those who wished could do so. They then went on to discuss the threat to Calais, and the representations which were already being made on behalf of the fallen duke of Northumberland.

There were a number of remarkable features about this interview. The first was that it took place at all. It was not unknown for ambassadors to receive secret audiences, but to consult an ambassador as though he were a secret counsellor, upon the domestic affairs of the kingdom, was a most unusual step for a monarch to take. Presumably Mary felt herself bound by her given word not to marry without her cousin's consent, but was unwilling to reaffirm that commitment in front of her own council. If Renard is to be believed – and he had at this point no particular reason to falsify his testimony – Mary was far from satisfied with the integrity of her normal advisers. Referring to her intended religious policy, she declared that:

> she would use their dissimulation for a great end, and would make their consent prevent them from plotting against her . . . She could not help being amazed by the divisions in the council, whose members were accusing one another, trying to disculpate themselves, chopping and changing in such a manner that she was unable to get at the truth of what had happened.[29]

If this is really how the queen felt about her chosen councillors within a few days of having selected them, then her original expectations must have been unrealistically high. In the circumstances such bickerings were to be expected, and the fact that they were all genuinely loyal to their sovereign would not have made them of one mind, even over so straightforward a matter as the date of her entry to London. Renard was subsequently to justify his own position on the grounds that the English council was totally untrustworthy; but the foundation for that conviction, which emerged for the first time in this interview, appears to have been no more than Mary's inability to cope with a normal level of dispute and disagreement. Her religious stance, on the other hand, was a good deal more resolute than either Renard or the emperor could welcome. At the same time, it was based firmly upon her father's settlement. No reference was made by either party to the pope, the jurisdiction of the Church or religious foundations. The mass appears to have been the only issue, and this was consistent both with her later proclamation of 18 August, and also with the assurances which she was alleged to have given to the men of Suffolk who rallied to her during the critical early days of her bid.[30] It was also consistent with everything which she had said to Somerset and to her brother's commissioners during the troubled days of the previous reign.

On 3 August, the day after the emperor's ambassadors completed their account of their first personal encounter with the new queen, Mary entered London, and took possession of her kingdom. It was a day of unrestrained celebrations, and all observers commented upon the size and magnificence of her retinue:

[29] *Cal. Span.*, XI, 131–2.
[30] Foxe, *Acts and Monuments*, VI, 387.

> The nomber of velvet coats that did ride before hir, aswell strangeres as otheres, was 740; and the nomber of ladyes and gentlemen that folowede was 180. The earle of Arundell did ride next before hir, bearinge the sworde in his hand, and sir Anthony Browne did beare up hir trayne. The lady Elizabethe did follow hir nexte, and after hir the lord Marquess of Exeter's wyfe.[31]

According to one estimate, her total escort numbered about 10,000, in spite of the fact that she had dismissed most of her Norfolk and Suffolk following. There were a few sour touches. The French ambassador was conspicuous by his absence. Winchester, Shrewsbury and Pembroke, still unconfirmed in royal favour, hovered anxiously on the sidelines, and Mary seems to have lacked the theatrical instinct to make the most of the occasion. The Imperial ambassadors considered that 'her manner, her gestures, her countenance were such that in no event could they have been improved', but the Tower chronicler noted that although she listened to an oration on behalf of a hundred poor children, 'she sayd nothinge to them'. On arriving at the Tower she was greeted by three long term prisoners, the duke of Norfolk, the bishop of Winchester and Edward Courtenay (whose mother, Gertrude, was riding in the queen's company). She formally released them with suitably gracious words; but of instructive political pageantry, such as that which was to accompany Elizabeth's entry five years later, there was little or none. The time had probably been too short to make such preparations, and perhaps that was what the councillors had been arguing about a few days earlier. On 25 July the duke of Northumberland, his sons, and the marquis of Northampton had disappeared into the Tower, their ignominious entry requiring an escort to protect them from the fury of the mob. To those citizens who had witnessed both scenes the message would have been clear enough, and artificial drama superfluous.

Over the succeeding weeks, as Mary gathered up the threads of government, a number of priorities jostled in her mind. Appointments to her council, and to the major offices of state, were largely completed by the end of August. The council, as we have seen, had been assembled in a somewhat piecemeal fashion, as circumstances had required. This process continued after the

[31] *The Chronicle of Queen Jane*, 14. Henry Machyn's account is similar, but refers to 1000 velvet coats and 3000 horse. *Diary*, 38–9.

entry to London.[32] For high office, on the whole the queen chose men of experience, irrespective of their antecedents. Stephen Gardiner emerged from the Tower to become lord chancellor; the earl of Bedford continued as lord privy seal, and Sir William Petre as principal secretary. After about three weeks of anxious uncertainty, the marquis of Winchester was confirmed as lord treasurer. Such a strategy was probably inevitable, but it did not make for a harmonious team. Those who had been most forward in Mary's cause at first, and who had taken serious risks on her behalf, regarded their more experienced colleagues as crypto-traitors, and bitterly resented their advancement. Paget and Gardiner were old enemies, and the most solid of the conservative peers, such as Shrewsbury, Pembroke and Derby, continued to be unsure of their favour, even after admission to the council. Given her own lack of political experience, what Mary needed was an established regime in working order, such as her father had inherited. The circumstances of her accession made that impossible, and what she assembled was a difficult, nervous, cross-grained bunch of men, who needed a lot of driving and coaxing. Within her household, on the other hand, and particularly within the chamber, public considerations were less important, and she was better able to please herself. With the exception of Sir Thomas Cheyney, the treasurer, all the chief officers were replaced on the legitimate grounds that they had been close associates of the duke of Northumberland. The earl of Arundel became great master and lord steward, positions formerly held by Northumberland himself.[33] The earl of Oxford recovered his hereditary (and purely ornamental) office of lord great chamberlain from the marquis of Northampton. Sir John Gage became chamberlain in place of Lord Darcy, and Henry Jerningham took over the sensitive position of vice-chamberlain and captain of the guard from Sir John Gates.

It has recently been said that 'almost all' Mary's household officers 'like the ladies of her privy chamber, were taken from her

[32] Loades, *Reign of Mary Tudor*, appendix, records the dates of the council oaths.

[33] Soon after this, Mary abolished the office of lord great master, which had been a Cromwellian innovation of 1540, and Arundel continued as lord steward. Loades, *The Tudor Court*, 51.

old princely household'.[34] This represents a serious misunderstanding, because Mary had not had a household of princely dimensions since 1533, and the establishment which she had run since 1547 could not have filled more than a corner of the royal chamber. What is probably true is that she found places in her court for all those of her old servants who wanted them. Robert Rochester, the former controller of her personal household, replaced Sir Richard Cotton in the same post; and Edward Waldegrave became master of the great wardrobe. Other gentlemen similarly placed included Roger Lyngons, as a gentleman of the privy chamber, Thomas Hungate as an esquire of the body, and George Tyrell as a gentleman waiter.[35] There were almost certainly more, but no complete household list survives from the early part of the reign. However, only Jerningham, Rochester and Waldegrave were given household offices of any responsibility. Sir Edward Hastings, who received the important preferment of master of the horse, had never been a servant of Mary's although he had been a strong and early supporter. A number of former servants were also given positions outside the household; Sir Francis Englefield as master of the wards, William Cordell as solicitor general, Richard Wilbraham as bailiff of a royal manor and Robert Strelly as chamberlain of the Exchequer. Altogether, Mary brought thirty-three new servants onto the check roll of the domestic household, including five new departmental sergeants, which must have just about absorbed her entire Newhall establishment.[36] Such generosity, which is entirely in keeping with her long record of care for her menials, would have represented an increase of about 15 per cent to the wage bill. The proportion of the chamber and privy chamber servants after 1553 who had former connections with the queen may have been as high as 25 per cent, but was certainly no more, and that would include a significantly higher rate among the ladies and gentlewomen. Mary's accession inevitably transformed the privy chamber, turning it from a centre of political power and intrigue

[34] J. Murphy, 'The illusion of decline: the Privy Chamber, 1547–1558' in *The English Court*, ed. D. Starkey, 141.

[35] PRO LC2/4/2.

[36] R. C. Braddock, 'The Royal Household, 1540–1560' (Ph.D., Northwestern, 1971), 82–5. For the identified posts given to Mary's known pre-1553 servants – see appendix.

into a glorified boudoir. Seven ladies, thirteen gentlewomen and three chamberers took the place of the six lords, four principal gentlemen and eighteen gentlemen who had served Edward VI in his latter days.[37] The male establishment was reduced to five gentlemen and seven grooms, who were also reduced to the functions of messengers and door-keepers. Only two, John Norris, the chief usher, and George Brodyman, the keeper of the privy purse, were persons of any consequence. Three of the ladies and gentlewomen, Eleanor Kempe, Susan Clarencius and Frideswide Strelly, had certainly been in Mary's service in the immediate past, and two others, Ann Bacon and Jane Dormer, probably had. Lady Waldegrave and Lady Jerningham were the wives of servants, while Mary Finch and Barbara Hawke returned from pre-1547 days. Cecily Barnes, another old retainer, does not appear on the early lists, but had returned to Mary's service by 1557. Lady Catherine Brooke, the wife of Sir David Brooke, chief baron of the Exchequer, was another who returned after a long absence; in 1516 she had appeared as Catherine Pole, the young princess's nurse.[38] At the same time, a significant number have no traceable connections with the queen before 1553 – Lady Elizabeth Bridges, for example, Mabel Brown, Mary Clarke, Dorothy Broughton, Jane Russell and Elizabeth Gilbourne. Sybil Penne belongs in a special category, having been Edward VI's nurse, and presumably well known to Mary, although never in her service. Rather more than half of the original privy chamber had been close to Mary in one way or another in her earlier life, and seem to have been drawn about her like a comfortable cloak as she commenced the last and most demanding period of her life.

It is not known how quickly these initial appointments were made.[39] The entire chamber and household establishment was completed in time for the coronation entry on 29 September, and

[37] D. E. Hoak, 'The king's Privy Chamber, 1547–1553', in J. de Lloyd Guth and J. McKenna, *Tudor Rule and Revolution*, 87–108. PRO LC2/4/2.

[38] See above, p. 29. The long service record, however, must go to Beatrice ap Rice, 'the Quene's Laundress', PRO LC5/49 f.52.

[39] Henry Machyn, *Diary* (39), seems to say that Hastings, Jerningham and Rochester were all named to their posts on 5 August, but he also says that Winchester was named lord treasurer the same day, which is over a week before he took the council oath.

probably much sooner. There were very few displacements from the household, and the majority of the outer chamber staff also kept their places. A high level of continuity was normal, except in the sensitive privy chamber, so Mary would not have needed to spend much time or thought except on building up her intimate service from about half a dozen to some four times that number. As a priority the privy chamber would have been quickly replaced by the major public issues of religion and marriage. Both were extremely delicate and extremely urgent.

At first the queen's religious position seems to have been very simple. She wanted to restore the mass and the other elements of traditional liturgy. The mass was, and had been for many years, the centre of her personal spirituality. When Renard first met her in her oratory, he noticed that her eyes constantly strayed to the sacrament reserved upon the altar. She also believed, rightly, that the majority of her subjects felt as she did. At the same time, she was unable to understand that those who disagreed, or at least many of them, did so out of religious conviction which was at least as strong as her own. Like Stephen Gardiner, and possibly through his influence, she regarded 'the new religion' as a by-product of political conspiracy, a convenient ideological 'front' for those who had seen an opportunity to seize power during Edward's minority.[40] Consequently, she seems at first to have been inclined to ignore the protestants, believing that once they were deprived of the coercive power of the state, they would shrivel into insignificance. Neither the emperor nor his ambassadors shared this somewhat facile optimism. They had started by believing that the protestant convictions of the English were so strong and widespread that they would frustrate her bid for the Crown, and although that quickly proved to be erroneous, they continued to urge extreme caution, while professing the warmest admiration for her intentions. The initial bone of contention was Edward's funeral. For the peace of her own conscience, Mary declared her intention to have him buried with traditional rites. The ambassadors were horrified, pointing out that, as the late king had lived and died a professed heretic, such attentions would do him no good, and might 'cause her Majesty's subjects to waver in their loyal affection'.[41] In a secret memorandum of 2

[40] J. A. Muller, *Stephen Gardiner and the Tudor Reaction*; L. B. Smith, *Tudor Prelates and Politics*, 99; Loades, *The Oxford Martyrs*, 58–9.

[41] *Cal. Span.*, XI, 134.

August, they advised her to let him be buried in the reformed fashion, since custom would allow her to absent herself from such a contaminating ritual, after which she could hold whatever private service she felt best. In a report of 8 August, the day before the interment took place, they reported that the queen would act upon their advice 'with the consent of her whole council'. There had already been some protestant demonstrations in London, and angry murmurings among the yeomen of the guard, so they felt that their caution had been entirely justified. What is not at all clear is whether Mary had actually sought the advice of her own council before deciding upon this course of action. On 9 August Cranmer and John Scory of Chichester laid the king to rest 'with scant ceremony', and Gardiner celebrated a requiem mass in St Peter's chapel in the Tower. Thereafter mass was to be celebrated daily in the chapel royal, and the traditional rites were restored.[42]

Edward's funeral had not been a major issue, but it had exposed some significant features of the new reign. In the first place, there was lively protestant feeling, both within the city of London and also among the royal household. The same people who had rallied to Mary, and had turned out to cheer her only a week before, were by 10 August demonstrating against the mass, assaulting priests who insisted upon celebrating it, and even staging a major riot which threatened to bring the queen's wrath down upon the lord mayor.[43] At the same time the emperor's ambassadors were treating Mary as though they were her natural and proper advisers. When she acted as they wished, as on this occasion, they praised her wisdom and discretion, when she acted independently, they blamed the factiousness or inadequacy of her council. On 27 August they wrote, in an early example of what was to become a typical refrain, 'The said council does not

[42] *Cal. Span.*, XI, 156. A later report referred to 'six or seven masses a day' being celebrated in the chapel. On the general magnificence of later Marian services, see H. M. Hillerbrand, 'The early history of the Chapel Royal', *Modern Philology*, XVIII, 1920.

[43] There are a number of contemporary accounts of this riot, which was provoked by a sermon of Gilbert Bourne, condemning the imprisonment of Edmund Bonner, the bishop of London, by Edward VI's council. The fact that Bonner had been warmly welcomed on his release a few days earlier is illustrative of the divided opinion of the city. Wingfield, 'Vita Mariae', 225/272; Machyn, *Diary*, 41; Foxe, *Acts and Monuments*, 391–2.

seem to us, after mature consideration, to be composed of experienced men endowed with the necessary qualities to conduct the administration and goverment of the kingdom.' Within a few weeks of her accession these ambassadors, and particularly Simon Renard, were exploiting the emperor's special relationship with Mary to make themselves into a secret council, and to undermine the mutual confidence which she needed to establish with her own subjects. Renard must have been much easier to deal with than a quarrelsome privy council, and Mary lacked both the will and the experience to keep him at arm's length. At the same time the religious disturbances in London confirmed them in their pessimistic view of the English character, and encouraged them to urge the queen to trust good catholics – like themselves – in preference to the unstable English. Recent research has shown that London was deeply divided on religious issues at this time, and that outside London the queen's proceedings were generally welcomed,[44] but neither Mary nor those to whom she was most disposed to listen had any real understanding of the nature of the religious situation with which they were dealing.

Nevertheless, by the beginning of September, it was generally agreed that a good start had been made. The well-publicized apostasy of the duke of Northumberland, following his trial and conviction for high treason on 18 August, 'edified the people more than if all the catholics in the land had preached for ten years', and the arrest of a number of radical preachers in London 'very much quieted' the city. The altars had been set up again in St Paul's, and mass celebrated, an example followed in a number of other churches 'not by commandment but by devotion of the people'. The refugee protestant congregations had begun to withdraw, and Mary was under strong pressure to expel those that remained. On 18 August the queen had made her first official pronouncement on the subject of religion, inhibiting preaching, and condemning the use of 'new found' terms of abuse, such as 'papist' and 'heretic'.[45] A settlement of religion

[44] S. E. Brigden, 'The Reformation in London in the Reign of Henry VIII' (Ph.D., Cambridge 1979), is particularly good on the different traditions of the various parishes in London. Loades, *Reign of Mary Tudor*, 148–77.

[45] P. L. Hughes and J. F. Larkin, *Tudor Royal Proclamations*, (New Haven, 1964–9), II, 5. There are a number of other texts and accounts of this edict.

'by common consent' had been promised, and in the meantime, no coercion was to be applied. However, at some point during the first week of September, the queen dramatically altered this reasonably hopeful situation. She informed her cousin's ambassadors that she intended to restore the church in England and Ireland to the obedience of the apostolic see 'as they were before the changes we know of took place'.[46] For the last month she had been addressing secret representations to the pope, asking him to remit all ecclesiastical censures against the kingdom in order to facilitate this task. They were astonished, having told her from the first that 'we thought she should not go beyond the reinstitution of the mass, holy communion and matters relating thereto, reverting to the condition in which they were at the time of the late king Henry's death.' It seems that Mary had sent her initial request to Julius III in the same letter which had announced her accession, and since she had clearly not consulted the Imperial ambassadors before taking this step, it is an open question whether she had taken any advice at all. As her letter was known to Cardinal Pole, at Maguzzano by 7 August, it must have been sent well before her entry to London, and probably before the end of July. Consequently, if the matter had been discussed, it would have been with her 'Framlingham' council, that is mainly her old household officers. If so, they must have kept the secret from their colleagues, because if Lord Paget had found out about it, it would certainly have come to the ambassadors' ears.

Mary took this decision, as she seems to have taken her decision to claim the throne, out of a compelling sense of duty and in consultation with her God. At no time since her crisis of conscience in 1536 had she made any recorded allusion to the papacy or its authority, and it must have seemed that the pope's refusal on that occasion to give her any special absolution had caused her to despair of the apostolic see. Throughout her struggle with her brother's council she had stood by her father's settlement, and it was in the knowledge of that fact, at least as much as in their perception of English religion, that the ambassadors had given their advice. Mary's attitude also seems to have

[46] Ambassadors to the emperor, 9 September 1553, *Cal.Span.*, XI, 216. For Mary's secret negotiations with the pope, see Giacomo Soranzo to the Council of Ten, and Henry Penning's report; *Cal. Ven*, V, 790, 813.

taken Julius by surprise, because although he expressed the warmest satisfaction, his only immediate action was to authorize his legate in Germany, the cardinal of Imola, to send his secretary to England on a fact-finding mission.[47] The person who welcomed Mary's initiative with unrestrained enthusiasm was Reginald Pole. As soon as he heard the news, he wrote immediately to the pope soliciting a mission to England, partly on the grounds that he was Mary's cousin and understood his fellow countrymen, and partly that no time should be wasted, when souls were daily perishing outside the communion of the church. On 13 August he launched the first of a long series of exhortations to the queen, begging her to end the schism immediately, in the interests of her subjects' salvation and her own entitlement to the Crown.[48] Julius granted Pole the English mission, with the title of legate, but took no steps to implement it until he should be better informed. Meanwhile, Mary herself had begun to form some impression of the difficulty of what she had undertaken. In conversation with Imola's secretary, Gianfrancesco Commendone, about the middle of August, she repeated her request for a relaxation of sanctions, and admitted that the task was likely to prove more difficult that she had thought. There were bad laws to be repealed, and many practical factors to take into account. The pope had no more loyal daughter than herself, but she would have to choose a more mature time to declare the fact.[49] Commendone reported direct to Rome at the end of August and recommended caution.

By the time the matter was openly discussed between them, the queen and the ambassadors shared much common ground. They urged her not to let the legate come before parliament had been consulted: 'it will be difficult and indeed almost impossible to make those who are in possession of church property yield it up: there will be a general feeling of apprehension that the Orders are to be reinstated.' She must realize that the question of papal authority was odious, much more so than the mass.[50]

[47] Pole to the cardinal of Imola, 13 August 1553; *Cal. Ven.*, v, 768.

[48] Pole to Julius III, 7 August 1553, ibid., 764; Pole to Mary, 13 August, ibid., 766; Pole to Julius III, 13 August, ibid., 767.

[49] Pole to Girolamo Muzzarelli, 8 September 1553; *Cal.Ven.*, v, 785. Penning's report, ibid., 813.

[50] Ambassadors to the emperor, 9 September 1553; *Cal.Span.*, XI, 218.

The queen was reluctantly convinced. Whatever her private conscience might suggest, she could not even treat her brother's legislation (which she had already denounced as 'no true laws') as *ultra vires*, let alone her father's. On 11 September she wrote to the Venetian ambassador, who was acting as honest broker, to inform the cardinal of Imola that no legatine mission should be sent until the time was more propitious. By the middle of September the consistory in Rome had been informed that in England 'the schismatics are greater in number than the heretics, and all enemies of the church of Rome', an assessment which caused Julius to divert Pole's northern mission in the direction of a more immediate goal – Franco-Habsburg peace. How much the English council knew about these critical deliberations is not at all clear. Renard habitually dealt direct with the queen, unless the matter was formal or ceremonial, and Mary seems to have told her own councillors little or nothing of what transpired. There must have been rumour and speculation, because one of the reasons alleged by Jane's supporters for her exclusion had been that her allegiance to the 'old religion' might mean the return of popery.[51] More recently, Peter Vannes, the ambassador in Venice, had also picked up some report, and had written to the council warning them not to let the queen be 'too fervent a Papist'. As late as 9 September the Imperial ambassadors believed that she had not consulted her council, because they urged her to keep the whole matter secret from everyone except Gardiner, 'so that malicious people may not seize the occasion for worse plottings and machinations'. Mary had, of course, the perfect right to consult, or not to consult, whom she chose, but since her councillors had to execute her policies once they were decided upon, their views had considerable importance. This was to become increasingly apparent over the succeeding twelve months.

The emperor's cautious advice on the question of religion is normally seen as self-interested, because of his desire to avoid civil conflict in England while he strove to set up a suitable marriage alliance. In fact his attitude antedated any question of such a marriage, and was based rather upon an exaggerated fear of the strength of English protestantism. His main concern, and that of the bishop of Arras, who was largely responsible for his

[51] Ambassadors to the emperor, 10 July 1553; *Cal.Span.*, XI, 80.

policy during the prolonged bouts of illness and lethargy which afflicted him at this time, was to ensure the support of England against France.[52] If Mary were to stir up religious strife in England by hasty or ill-considered policies, she would greatly reduce her usefulness to him, marriage or no marriage; and if she were to be overthrown the new regime would inevitably look to France for support, as Northumberland had done. Had Mary done what Charles expected her to do, there would have been little risk, but as soon as he became aware of her true intentions he redoubled his efforts to cause delay, and began to press the marriage as a matter of great urgency. His advice to her to seek a match in England had never been entirely honest. It was what he had deemed necessary at the time to reassure potential enemies. While his ambassadors were still urging such a course in England, he was writing secretly to his son Philip in Spain, suggesting that he might disentangle himself from his Portuguese negotiations and try his luck in England instead: 'if they were to make a proposal to me we might delay it in such a way as to suggest to their minds the possibility of approaching you.'[53] Philip responded favourably. The prospect of becoming king of England was attractive to him, in spite of the dubious reputation of its inhabitants. As soon as Charles was aware that Mary had virtually remitted her choice of bridegroom to him, he instructed Renard to proceed delicately along the path which was already mapped out in his mind. When his brother Ferdinand raised the possibility of such a match for his own son, the emperor replied mendaciously that such a decision was a matter for the English council, who might well reject a foreign marriage. In fact, once again, the English council was not consulted, although Lord Paget fortuitously suggested Philip, apparently on his own initiative.

Arras seems to have expected Mary to pay more attention to English opinion than she actually did, and thus created a problem for the emperor which need not have existed. Obviously

[52] Loades, *Reign of Mary Tudor*, 109–22; Harbison, *Rival Ambassadors*, 44–56. The bishop of Arras was Antoine Perrenot de Granvelle, later Cardinal Granvelle. For his control over Imperial policy at this time, see M. J. Rodríguez Salgado, *The Changing Face of Empire*, 79–83.

[53] Emperor to Philip, 30 July 1553; *Cal.Span.*, XI, 126. He had opened this gambit by saying that he expected the English to remember the old betrothal to himself, but that he was not inclined to marry again.

the French would oppose any Habsburg marriage proposal as soon as they got wind of it, but Antoine de Noailles was forced to keep a low profile after his involvement with Northumberland, and only presented his new credentials on 6 August. It was to be another month before he first heard of any negotiation involving Philip. The rival whom the Imperial amabassadors feared was Edward Courtenay, the son of Mary's old supporter the marquis of Exeter, and created earl of Devon on 3 September. Courtenay was a personable and well- educated young man, a catholic, and of royal blood. His mother, Gertrude, the dowager marchioness, was also a close companion of the queen, and referred to as her 'bedfellow'. Courtenay was certainly favoured by Stephen Gardiner, the lord chancellor, with whom he had passed some part of his imprisonment in the Tower, and by a number of Mary's old servants. He was also thought to be favoured by the influential ladies of the privy chamber, notably Susan Clarencius. The earl of Pembroke was rumoured to have given presents to Courtenay and his mother to secure their intercession with the queen, and his own admission to the council. Renard distrusted the queen's ladies, claiming that they were 'able to get from her more than she ought to grant them',[54] and that they 'did nothing but chatter of marriage'. However, all these anxieties were unreal, fuelled only by Mary's bashful reluctance to commit herself, and her unwillingness to discuss the matter frankly with her advisers. In spite of all the speculation, as far as can be ascertained, she never had the slightest intention of considering Courtenay as a partner. At twenty-seven he was rather young, but what was more serious, he had spent over half his life in prison, and was simply intoxicated by unaccustomed freedom. He was quickly revealed as dissolute, reckless and unreliable. His peerage was a tribute to his father's memory, not his own worth, and the queen quickly came to regard him with contempt. Noailles wasted time and money entertaining him, and Gardiner did his best to conceal his faults, but as the only domestic candidate for the queen's hand, he was a broken reed. Cardinal

[54] *Cal.Span.*, XI, 189. He was particularly apprehensive of the influence of Susan Clarencius, who was, he claimed, a 'second mother' to Courtenay. Clarencius was, in spite of her low rank, 'Chief' gentlewoman of the privy chamber, as mistress of the robes. Renard later admitted that she had supported Philip 'to the uttermost'. Loades, *Tudor Court*, 56.

Pole, who was also mentioned, would have been more acceptable to Mary, but he was at the other end of Europe, and had no intention of abandoning the clerical life.[55]

By the beginning of September the real issue was not who Mary would marry, but whether she would marry Philip or not. In many ways her old suitor Dom Luis would have made a more suitable husband, but the emperor blocked his way, as he did that of the young Archduke Ferdinand. Mary had professed herself willing to marry on his advice, and he had nominated his son. As far as we know, the negotiation had not proceeded beyond hints and suggestions, when the ambassadors reported on 4 September that the council was doing its best to force the queen into the open by insisting that she held all audiences in public. On that day Mary refused to see Don Diego de Mendoza for fear of being drawn into a public discussion of the matter. 'This gave us clearly to understand', Renard wrote, 'that the council's suspicions all turn upon this point of the Queen's marriage.'[56] Rumours were flying in all directions, and the matter was openly discussed in every tavern. The ambassadors did not know what to do next. They had no explicit commission to negotiate a marriage, communication with the queen was difficult, and broad hints were being dropped by the council that it was time they went home. Gardiner was being particularly difficult. He knew that Mary would marry only on the emperor's advice, and he also knew that when the ambassadors had first arrived, they had declared it to be Charles's wish that she should marry an Englishman. Surely, therefore, the emperor would bless a union with Courtenay. So why did she not silence all the malicious tongues by saying so? The queen did not know how to respond. No formal proposal had been received from Philip, or on Philip's behalf, and neither modesty nor policy would permit her to make the first move, or the first mention of his name. She affected to believe that he was already contracted to the infanta of Portugal, and declared that she would not, in any case, marry a man she had never met. By 8 September, when Renard sent an informative report to the bishop of Arras, he had at least consolidated his confidential relationship with the queen. She had even gone so far as to suggest that he might visit her in

[55] Ambassadors to the emperor, 4 September 1553; *Cal.Span.*, XI, 198–207.
[56] Ibid., 201.

disguise, in order to conceal their interviews both from the council and from his own colleagues.[57]

Renard was forced to mark time. His instructions were to head off any other negotiation in order to leave the way clear for Philip, and to encourage the queen to think about him, but not to make a specific offer until it was finally certain that the Portuguese negotiation could be evaded. He was extremely successful. In the course of one discussion he succeeded in informing Mary that the prince was 'an old married man', with a son of six or seven; to which she replied 'that she had never felt that which was called love, not harboured thoughts of voluptuousness' – an apparently inconsequential remark, which told its own story. It was not until about 15 September that Renard finally received word from Arras that Philip was definitely available, and he could go ahead. At the same time, the emperor recalled de Courrières, de Thoulouse and Scheyfve, leaving Renard a clear field, and the full status of resident ambassador. Unfortunately for him, however, his negotiation was anticipated by some shrewd guesswork on the part of his opponents. On 7 September, Noailles had been secretly informed that a firm proposal had been made, whereby Philip would live in England, renouncing all other titles, and would bring the Low Countries to the English Crown as a dowry.[58] There was no truth in the report, but he believed it, having no reliable source of inside information. The next day he wrote in great agitation to Henry II, 'ce seroit pour vous et les vostres une perpetuelle guerre', and urged an ultimatum to the effect that Philip's landing in England would be deemed an act of war.[59] Henry was in no position to make such a threat, but he authorized Noailles to oppose such a marriage by all the means in his power. Since the French had no plausible alternative to offer, what this meant in practice was a sustained attempt to 'de-stabilize' England, by supporting agitators and malcontents of all kinds, by financing the publication of anti-Spanish propaganda, and by encouraging Courtenay to make as big a nuisance of himself as possible. As this

[57] Renard to the bishop of Arras, 7 August 1553. *Cal.Span.*, XI, 153.

[58] R. A. de Vertot, *Ambassades des Messieurs de Noailles*, II, 143–4. The news was apparently brought by a minor English courtier named Sir John Leigh. Harbison, *Rival Ambassadors*, 76–7 and n.

[59] Noailles to Henry, 7 September 1553; Vertot, *Ambassades*, II, 144–5.

campaign developed, Renard became increasingly neurotic, finding French agents and rebellious heretics at every turn:

> 'To tell you between ourselves what I think of her [Mary]', he wrote to Arras, 'I believe that if God does not preserve her she will be deceived and lost either by the machinations of the French, the conspiracies of the English, by poison or otherwise. The Lady Elizabeth is greatly to be feared ... I hear that she already has her eye on Courtenay as a possible husband ... This is very dangerous; and I foresee that Courtenay's friends, who include most of the nobility, are hatching some design which may later menace the queen.'[60]

There was a great deal more in the same vein. Once the proposal had actually been made, Mary required very little persuading to accept Philip, and coyly confessed that she was already 'half in love' with him after seeing his portrait. Renard was right in claiming that the real difficulty of his mission lay in persuading the English council and people to accept the match. However, he and Mary between them created most of that difficulty. They were the real conspirators; meeting secretly, passing tokens and feeding each other doubts and suspicions. Not that there was much point in such elaborate precautions. Noailles was sure he knew what was going on, even before he did, and most of the English council were merely offended by the obvious implication that the queen did not trust either their wisdom or their discretion in a matter of such importance.

The only Englishman who was in Renard's confidence was Lord Paget. He was known to be in favour of a Habsburg marriage, and had already suggested Philip. Moreover, Renard knew that he had an axe to grind, 'to make good the loss and damage he suffered at the hands of his enemies and those who wished him ill'. One of those enemies was the lord chancellor, the chief promoter of Courtenay's interest. Nevertheless, Paget's comments were shrewd and responsible, as befitted his ability and experience. He warned Renard of the disadvantages to England of a king who could not speak the language, and who would have other realms to care for. The English had no desire to become involved in war with France, and would restrict the powers of any foreign king within the realm.[61] He also advised

[60] Renard to the bishop of Arras, 9 September 1553; *Cal.Span.*, XI, 227.
[61] Renard to the emperor, 5 October 1553; *Cal.Span.*, XI, 265.

the ambassador to encourage his master to involve other members of the council in the negotiations, but this tactful prompting was ignored. Paget may well have been looking to advance his own interests, but there were real advantages in the Spanish marriage proposal. Philip was a man of considerable political experience, with the habit of command. He had ample resources of his own, could overawe the English factions, and would in due course control the commercially vital Low Countries. Paget must also have realized by the time he spoke to Renard that Philip's attractions for the queen, as Charles's son and as an unsullied catholic, would prove irresistible. Consequently, although the emperor initiated the negotiation as a means of exploiting Mary's dependence for his own purposes, the marriage could also be turned to England's gain, if the terms were right and the main hazards of foreign domination could be avoided. Renard formally proposed the match to the queen on 10 October. On 28 October, trusting that the emperor had acted out of loving care for herself and her realm, she accepted the proposal, bursting into tears as she did so. The following day, in the presence only of Renard and Susan Clarencius, she swore on the sacrament to marry the prince of Spain.[62] By that time all her councillors knew what was afoot, and several of them made individual attempts to dissuade her, but it was some time before they discovered that her decision had actually been made. Only on 16 November, when she rejected a petition from the House of Commons to marry within the realm, did it become public knowledge.

Mary's attitude to the vital question of her marriage contains some puzzling features. Although she was so deferential to the emperor's judgement, it was she rather than Charles or Renard who was reluctant to have the matter openly discussed in council. Even former intimates such as Englefield and Waldegrave were pleading Courtenay's cause to her as late as the end of October. In spite of Renard's earlier fears, her ladies, particularly Susan Clarencius and Frideswide Strelly, seem to have encouraged her in her inclination towards Philip. It may be that they realized, better than either Renard or her councillors, the emotional strain which the whole process caused her. She knew that she could be signing her own death warrant by embarking

[62] Ibid., 319, 327.

upon procreation at the age of thirty-seven and after a long history of gynaecological disorder. It is not surprising that she berated the Speaker and his delegation on 16 November, declaring that 'to force her to take a husband who would not be to her liking would be to cause her death, for if she were married against her will she would not live three months, and would have no children.'[63] Her speech was a mixture of imperious rage and sheer petulance, produced by the frustration of not being able to communicate the fact that this was a highly personal matter, as well as a decision of state. What she had needed was not advice but emotional support, and of the men with whom she had had to deal, only Renard had dimly perceived that fact. At the same time, having decided to marry, not only because of the succession but also in order to have her husband's support in the duties of government, she could still say that although 'she would wholly love and obey him to whom she had given herself, following the divine commandment, and would do nothing against his will; but if he wished to encroach in the government of the kingdom, she would be unable to permit it.'[64] She had wept through sleepless nights before 'the inspiration of God' had come to her, but she had not even started to resolve the problems which she would have to face as a result of her decision.

Meanwhile, Mary had set aside her problems in the gorgeous pageantry of coronation. On 27 September she had arrived by water at the Tower, accompanied by her sister Elizabeth, and on the 29th processed through the city of London to the old palace of Westminster. The citizens had spent the last two weeks trimming the conduits, hanging the streets and rehearsing their children in the various speeches and songs which were to grace the pageants of the day. One of these, at the conduit in Cornhill, featured 'iii children clothed in womens apparell', representing Grace, Virtue and Nature. Several of the pageants, as was customary, were provided by the foreign communities, the Genoese, the Hanse and the Florentines. The themes seem to have been strictly traditional and anodyne, and the splendour of the occasion consisted more in the magnificent clothing and accoutrements of the queen's chariots and horsemen than in any

[63] Ibid., 363–4; Vertot, *Ambassades*, II, 269–70; Harbison, *Rival Ambassadors*, 92–3; *TTC*, 14.

[64] Renard to the emperor, 12 October 1553; *Cal.Span.*, XI, 288.

particular subtlety of 'device'. A small fountain in Gracechurch Street ran with wine, and the queen was presented with £1000 in gold, but if she made any speech or other notable gesture, it was not recorded.[65] Her mere appearance was sufficient to gratify the crowds, 'in a gown of blew velvet, furred with powdered armyen, hangyng on her hed a call of clothe of tynsell besett with perle and ston . . . that the value therof was inestymable'. Dark fears for her safety, rumours of weapons being stockpiled, and of the likelihood of heretical demonstrations, were all blown away in the loyal enthusiasm of the day. On 1 October she was crowned by the bishop of Winchester, Cranmer, in the Tower, and Robert Holgate of York being equally *personae non gratae*. All those peers who were not sick or in prison took part, and the ceremonies lasted from ten in the morning until five in the afternoon. Only Gardiner and Mary knew that she had sent for a special chrism from Flanders, to avoid using oil that had been consecrated by schismatic hands. Twenty fresh knights of the Bath were created, starting with the earl of Devon, and ending with her old servants, Robert Rochester, Henry Jerningham and William Dormer.[66] At the enormous banquet which followed her coronation Mary was served with no less than 312 dishes. A total of 7112 dishes were offered to the whole company, of which 4900 were declared 'waste', and presumably distributed to the expectant citizens.[67]

Ironically, but inevitably, Mary was shadowed throughout these days of triumph by her closest blood relative, her half-sister Elizabeth. Younger, and much more beautiful than the queen, her appearance attracted many favourable comments. Renard regarded her as a menace, and believed her to be intriguing with the French, the heretics and every other disaffected group. There is, and probably was, no evidence to substantiate his suspicions, but she was certainly a reluctant attender at mass, and Mary neither trusted her nor liked her. A few weeks later, in a discussion with Renard over the succession, Mary made it clear

[65] *The Chronicle of Queen Jane*, 27–31; Machyn, *Diary*, 45–6; S. Anglo, *Spectacle, Pageantry and Early Tudor Policy*, 319–21.

[66] PRO SP11/1/16.

[67] BL Add.MS 34320 f.97; 'An ordinarie for the coronacion of the high and mighty princess Queen Mary the first'. This document also gives the list of the special servitors appointed for the banquet, none of whom seem to have had any prior connection with Mary.

that she did not want Elizabeth to follow her on the throne, in the event of her dying unwed or childless. Her religion was suspect, and she was too like her mother.[68] Neverthless, she was the heir by Henry's much vaunted will, and she had behaved with scrupulous correctness during the dangerous days of July, turning up with her retinue to greet Mary on the 25th – just before her absence would have been noteworthy or suspicious. For the time being she did not greatly matter; her relations with Courtenay were pure speculation, and the queen's marriage might well relegate her to the political fringes, but she already had a following, and the more controversial Mary's political and ecclesiastic programme became, the stronger that following appeared.

Parliament met on 5 October. There had been those within the queen's council who had wanted to summon it before the coronation, but such a course would have cast doubt upon the legitimacy of her title, and was rejected. By the middle of the month some of her aspirations and convictions were beginning to turn, first into debates, and then into statutes. A Treason Bill, with the queen's signature already on it, was handed down from the Lords to the Commons on 12 October. Its intention was to return treason to the basic definition of 1352, and it was not retrospective, but in spite of the queen's obvious support, it was controversial. The main reason, according to Mary herself, was the members' conviction that this was a prelude to the restoration of papal authority. They would not accept 'the abolishing ... of that law that gave the title of supremacy of the church in the realm to the Crown, suspecting that to be an introduction of the Pope's authority ... which they cannot gladly hear of'.[69] Their suspicions were well founded, and Gardiner had made no secret of the intention in his opening address, but the Bill did not immediately affect either property or jurisdiction, and it was eventually accepted on 19 October. For some curious reason, having accepted this Bill and two others restoring the Courtenay family, Mary then closed the first session on 21 October, thus losing several other measures which were under discussion. Dr Loach attributes this to sheer inexperience, but since the effect

[68] *Cal.Span.*, XI, 393. Mary's preferred choice at this stage was Margaret Douglas, countess of Lennox.

[69] Renard to the emperor, 15 October 1553; *Cal.Span.*, XI, 294.

was to give an appearance of great importance to the Courtenay restoration, the subtle Gardiner may well have been responsible.[70] The two principal measures of the second session, which began on 24 October were the Act declaring Henry VIII's marriage to Catherine to have been valid, and that repealing the bulk of Edward's religious legislation, including the Act of Uniformity, and that authorizing the marriage of priests. In the circumstances these could hardly be controversial, and seem to have been seen by some as reducing any possible claim that the queen's legitimacy depended upon the pope. The second was a different matter. Uncontroversial in the Lords, from which all the protestant bishops had been excluded, it was fiercely debated in the Commons, who spent eight hours on it on 8 November. Its opponents succeeded in forcing a divsion, but lost by 270 votes to 80. Renard chose to conclude that the protestants were weaker than he had feared, but the significant fact was less their numbers than their extraordinary determination in the face of the queen's clearly expressed intentions. Although Mary bungled her interview with the Commons delegation, because she lost her temper, by the time parliament was dissolved on 5 December, she had good reason to be satisfied with the progress of her policies. Protestant services would cease to be legal on 20 December, her council was reconciled to her choice of bridegroom, and her mother's good name had been publicly restored by the very institution which had humiliated her.

The price which she was paying for these successes was less evident, and is hard to assess, even now. On the day that parliament rose a dead dog was thrown into her presence chamber, tonsured like a priest, and similar minor acts of vandalism and contempt were reported in London and elsewhere. A petition was presented from Kent 'for the retaining of the present services', and seditious broadsheets circulated, calling upon 'Noblemen and gentlemen favouring the word of God' to reject the 'hardened and detestable papists [who] follow the opinions of the said queen'. On the other hand, popular ballads celebrated her virtue and piety, giving her the affectionate nickname of 'marigold'.[71] A general policy of clemency towards Northumber-

[70] J. Loach, *Parliament and the Crown in the Reign of Mary Tudor*, 77.

[71] William Forrest, *A newe ballade of the Marigolde* (1554) (STC 11186); *Cal.Span.*, XI, 173. For other examples of this conflict of views see Loades, *Reign of Mary Tudor*, 162–3.

land's followers, which resulted in only two executions apart from the duke himself, had been well received and was probably necessary. As Renard had somewhat sourly observed, if she had executed all those who had been guilty in some measure, she would have had few subjects left. Stormy relations with France were inevitable as one of the prices to be paid for the Spanish marriage, but the marked hostility of the English themselves to Spain must have come as something of a surprise. The Londoners, whose opinions were the most noticeable and forcefully expressed, had little direct contact with Iberia, and Catherine's Spanish servants never seem to have attracted the sightest hostility. Renard (who had no great love of Spaniards himself) blamed 'the manner in which your Majesty's own subjects [of the Low Countries] complained of their arrogance ... and the unfortunate stories told by several exiled and refugee Spaniards who live over here'.[72] The emperor had anticipated a general hostility to all foreigners, and Renard had been thoroughly briefed to expect that, but this specific hatred was unexpected. It probably arose from contemporary opinion in Germany and the Netherlands, and presented Noailles with an excellent basis upon which to build his propaganda campaign against the marriage. Although the riots which Renard feared did not materialize in response to the withdrawal of the Prayerbook services, by the end of 1553 the 'universal love' which Mary had reputedly enjoyed during her brother's reign was less in evidence. Power and responsibility were not compatible with unanimous popularity; nor had Mary taken any particular pains to create an image for herself with which her subjects would identify. In her own eyes she stood for 'normality' against 'innovation', and for 'truth' against 'error', but no concerted campaign of either visual or written propaganda had so far presented her in that light. Two splendid entries into London had been almost entirely wasted in that respect. Only the Florentines had compared the queen with Judith triumphing

[72] Renard to the emperor, 11 December 1553, *Cal.Span.*, XI, 425. Many of these exiles were probably fugitives from the Inquisition. The 'Reneger incident' of 1545 also seems to have left a bitter legacy on both sides, as the Inquisition moved against English merchants in Spain. G. Connell Smith, *The Forerunners of Drake*.

over Holofernes, and their erudite allegory passed almost unnoticed by English commentators.[73]

By the end of November Mary's decision to marry Philip had produced a number of tangible consequences. Throughout the month, Renard was engaged in detailed discussions with the English council, closely supervised by both the bishop of Arras and the council of state. Having achieved his main objective, and being realistically sceptical of Mary's ability to bear children, Charles was disposed to be generous with terms. The English (and this applied equally to Paget and Gardiner, despite their differences) were determined to drive a hard bargain, knowing that strong safeguards for English interests would be essential if the treaty was to be acceptable. By the end of the month a draft had been produced, providing for a future union of England and the Netherlands, should the marriage prove fruitful, and safeguarding the rights of Don Carlos, Philip's existing son, in Spain and the Indies. In the event of Mary's dying first without heirs, Philip would have no claim to England.[74] He was to observe all the laws and customs of the realm, not intrude his own servants into English offices, and not involve England in the perpetual Habsburg struggle with France. On 27 November the council of state in the Netherlands accepted this draft, and on 7 December the English council followed suit, well pleased with the efforts of their negotiators. Neither Mary nor Philip was directly involved in these discussions, but the queen certainly knew more about what was going on than the prince did. On 29 November he wrote briefly, expressing satisfaction with Mary's response, and offering to come as soon as she was ready. His letter crossed with one from his father, urging him to reach England by February, or March at the latest, bringing with him a carefully selected retinue who would know how to behave in a foreign land: 'it is impossible to exaggerate the importance, both

[73] Anglo, *Spectacle, Pageantry and Early Tudor Policy*, 319. The only person who does seem to have picked it up was Leonard Stopes, whose *Ave Maria in Commendation of oure most vertuous Queene* contained the lines

Our Iwell oure ioye, our Judith doutlesse
The great Holofernes of hell to withstand ...

[74] There are a number of texts of this treaty. That which was proclaimed on 14 January is Hughes and Larkin, *Tudor Royal Proclamations*, II, 21–6. Philip did have a remote hereditary claim in his own right, but that was not alluded to, except in propaganda.

for present and future purposes, of gaining popularity and goodwill.'[75] He seems to have known nothing of the detailed terms until a copy of the final treaty was sent to him in January.

Almost simultaneously, on 26 November, a meeting was held in London of some six or seven gentlemen, several of them members of the House of Commons, who decided that, since persuasion had failed, the marriage must be opposed by force. Over the following month the conspiracy cautiously spread, drawing in the duke of Suffolk (who seems to have learned nothing from his quite unmerited escape during the summer), his brothers Thomas and John Grey, and possibly the disgruntled earl of Devon. Noailles had been receiving indirect approaches from English malcontents since at least the middle of November, and was involved in the conspiracy from the first. He believed that he was dealing with a powerful resistance movement, which could sweep Mary from her throne, but Henry II was more sceptical, and was no more prepared than the emperor had been in the summer to commit precious military resources to a wild goose chase in England.[76] The conspirators, who seem to have been led by Sir James Crofts, were equally wary, remembering how little good the French had done Northumberland. The English, they warned each other, 'could as evil abide the Frenchmen after that sort as the Spaniards'. So, after rejecting an original proposal to assassinate the queen, they began to plan a fourfold rising. One element was to be led by Crofts in Herefordshire, a second by Sir Thomas Wyatt in Kent, a third by Sir Peter Carew and the earl of Devon in the South West, and the fourth by the duke of Suffolk in Leicestershire. The objective was never clearly formulated, but it does not seem to have been a demonstration aimed at forcing a change of policy, as the Pilgrimage of Grace had been. The council later claimed that it was a protestant plot aimed at reinstating Jane Grey, who was still in the Tower. However, the evidence does not support this. Jane Grey and her cause were thoroughly discredited, and although there was certainly protestant involvement, all the recognized leaders of the reformed community adhered to their

75 *Cal.Span.*, XI, 398, 403.

76 PRO KB27/1174 rex 5, KB8/29; *TTC*, 20–4. Harbison, *Rival Ambassadors*, 113–19.

declared principles of non-resistance, and rejected it.[77] The aim was almost certainly to depose Mary and replace her with Elizabeth, possibly married to Courtenay. The cause to which the conspirators appealed when forced into the open was the same as that to which they had appealed in their intrigues with Noailles – the exclusion of the Spaniards.

Renard got wind of the conspiracy before Christmas, and so did Paget. 'Before Easter', the former wrote, 'there shall be such a turmoil in England as never was seen.' However, they had little hard information, and Renard had cried wolf before, so nothing was said to the queen. On 27 December the emperor's commissioners arrived to complete the marriage treaty, and there were some hostile demonstrations 'so hatfull was the sight of ther coming in'. On 14 January Gardiner announced the signing of the treaty to the whole court in the presence chamber at Westminster, itemized its terms.

> 'Theis newes', wrote a contemporary chronicler, 'although before they were not unknown to many, and very moche mysliked, yit being nowe in this wise pronounced, was not onley credyted, but also hevely taken of sondery men, yea and therat allmost eche man was abashed, loking daylie for worse mattiers to growe.'[78]

Meanwhile, a series of leaks and disclosures caused both Gardiner and Renard to decide that some precautions would have to be taken, and forced the conspirators themselves into premature action. Renard alerted the queen on 18 January, and Courtenay confessed his role in the affair to Gardiner on the 21st. For the next two weeks confusion reigned. Wyatt was in Kent trying to raise his friends and neighbours by the 19th, and they issued a proclamation denouncing the marriage on the 25th. Suffolk rode down to Leicestershire for the same purpose, and Sir Peter Carew endeavoured to stimulate an anti-Spanish panic in Devon. Crofts never seems to have left London. Most of this activity

[77] 'The troubles of Thomas Mowntayne, rector of St. Michael Tower-hyll, in the reign of Queen Marye, written by himself'; *Narratives of the days of the Reformation*, ed. J.G. Nichols (Camden Society, LXXVII, 1859), 218–33. The involvement of protestants in Wyatt's rebellion has recently been urged afresh by M. R. Thorp, 'Religion and the Wyatt rebellion of 1554', *Church History*, XLVII, 363–80; and by W. B. Robison, 'The national and local significance of Wyatt's rebellion in Surrey', *Historical Journal*, XXX, 769–90.

[78] *The Chronicle of Queen Jane*, 35; *TTC*, 100.

quickly fizzled out, without any specific action by either the queen or the council. Devon did not respond to Carew's attempts, and he fled to France, while the earl of Huntingdon (not long pardoned for his involvement with Northumberland) took the opportunity to re-establish himself in grace by arresting Suffolk and sending him up to London.[79] However, by the 25th Wyatt was in arms with between two and three thousand followers. Attempts to raise a loyal force to oppose him in Kent had failed, and the queen had no immediately available army to interpose between the rebels and London. Renard was convinced that disaster was imminent, and denounced the English council in unmeasured terms for their divisions and incompetence: 'the councillors reproached one another... quarrelling, taking sides and blaming one another.' Some blamed Gardiner's zeal in pressing the religious reaction, others Paget and Arundel for having engineered the marriage. Renard suspected some of the council of secretly favouring Elizabeth and Courtenay, and believed with some justice that Gardiner was trying to protect the latter from the consequences of his own folly.[80] In fact these furious dispatches tell us more about Renard than they do about the council. He seems to have seen himself as a kind of St George, battling with the dragons of factiousness, heresy and French intrigue, to rescue his master's favourite cousin from her unsatisfactory subjects. On 31 January he reported that the queen had sent for him in great perplexity and grief, because she could not make her council provide her with a guard, and 'begged your majesty ... to remember her in her present need'. The council rejected his offer of Imperial troops, knowing perfectly well that they could not be sent in time to do any good, and that rumour of their coming would only make the situation worse.[81] They were in fact doing their best to raise troops, and his suspicion of disloyalty amongst them was totally unwarranted. There had been differences of opinion at first, and the desertion of the London trained bands on the 28th had been a major setback, but by the 31st the soldiers, led by Pembroke and Clinton, were confident of their ability to handle the situation, and were begging the queen to trust in them. On 1 February

[79] BL Egerton MS 2986 f.11; *TTC*, 100.
[80] Simon Renard to the emperor, 27 March 1554; *Cal.Span.*, XII, 174.
[81] *Cal.Span.*, XII, 65. *TTC*, 66–8.

'a-bowt iii of the cloke at after-non the Quen grace cam rydyng from Westmynster unto yeldhall with mony lordes, knyghtes and ladyes, and bysshoppes and haroldes of armes.'[82] There she made a resolute speech, declaring that her marriage was undertaken 'with consent and advisement of the whole council', and she would not allow it to take precedence over her marriage to the realm. Nor would she leave London 'although by her council she had been much moved to the contrary'. The citizens cheered her, and her resolution may, in fact, have prevented them from opening their gates to Wyatt a week later.

In such circumstances Mary, like her father, and her sister later, could rise to the occasion. Nevertheless, reading between the lines of Renard's neurotic and self-important letters, it can be seen that the real trouble in this crisis was not the council, but the queen herself. She not only insisted that Renard should be consulted and informed about every step taken, but made it clear that she had more confidence in him than in anyone else. When he complained that the council were not being entirely frank with him, she sent for Paget and upbraided him with failing to observe her wishes. Paget declined to explain, begging her to address her question to the whole council, but it seem clear that the council regarded the ambassador's presence as intrusive, and his closeness to the queen as a direct reflection upon themselves. Mary never seems to have understood this, and the situation remained unchanged when the crisis was over. On 3 February Wyatt arrived with his force in Southwark, but found London bridge held against him, and remained on the south bank for three days, while some of the protestants in his force sacked the bishop of Winchester's library. Late on the 6th, he suddenly moved upriver to Kingston, and crossing Kingston bridge, advanced on London in the small hours of the morning. According to Renard, there was panic at the court, and the council sent to the queen between two and three in the morning, advising her to escape by river. 'She', he continued, 'without losing her presence of mind for a moment, sent for me.'[83] Whether by his advice or not, she remained at Whitehall, and was present in her gallery to encourage her gentlemen pensioners to feats of daring when the

[82] Machyn, *Diary*, 53; there are several versions of the speech; Procter, *Wyates rebellion*, 77, Foxe, *Acts and Monuments*, VI, 414–5.
[83] *Cal.Span.*, XII, 86.

court briefly came under attack. It was a mere skirmish, over before it had begun, and within a few hours the rising had collapsed, but Mary's courage had made a good impression, even upon reluctant admirers such as Edward Underhill.[84]

Thus, by the 8th of February the queen was for a second time the victor over rebels. This time she was less clement, about one hundred of them being executed, including most of the ring-leaders who were caught. Suffolk and his daughter both died, as did Wyatt and Guildford Dudley. Elizabeth and Courtenay were arrested on suspicion of complicity, and lodged in the Tower. Some of the queen's more ardent supporters began to celebrate her victories in print, as John Procter in his *The Historie of Wyates rebellion*, and John Christopherson in *An exhortation to all menne to take hede and beware of rebellion*.[85] To them, this renewed evidence of divine favour marked her out as a chosen vehicle of God's grace, so that her marriage, no less than every other aspect of her policy, had to be seen as expressions of His will. Mary herself seems to have shared this view, and the sense of mission with which she had come to the throne was significantly strengthened. In practice, however, little had changed. The marriage remained very unpopular – so much so that Wyatt became something of a popular martyr – and Renard, Paget and Gardiner continued to give the queen conflicting advice. The ambassador wished to seize the opportunity to remove both Elizabeth and Courtenay by trial and execution, representing them as a threat to Philip's security. Gardiner endeavoured to protect Courtenay, as he had done all along, and Paget strove to protect Elizabeth. Renard's concern was genuine, and a legitimate part of his duties, but he again abused his position by endeavouring to force the queen's hand. He greatly exacerbated the ill-feeling between Gardiner and Paget by consistently denigrating the chancellor, not only in his dispatches to Charles and Arras, but also to Mary herself. He took it upon himself to lecture Gardiner over his dealings with the French, and tried to

[84] Edward Underhill, 'The narrative of Edward Underhill', in *Tudor Tracts*, ed. A.F. Pollard, 188–91.

[85] *Short Title Catalogue of books printed in England, Scotland and Ireland and of English books printed abroad, 1475–1640*, by A. W. Pollard and G. R. Redgrave; revised by W. A. Jackson, F. S. Ferguson and K. F. Pantzner (1976–86), 20407, 5207.

interfere with the programme for the second parliament of the reign, which met on 5 April. The only person who could have put a stop to this behaviour was the queen, but her confidence in Renard does not seem to have wavered, and she took his representations seriously. She remonstrated with her councillors, both individually and collectively, and eventually complained that she spent half her time shouting at them. The ambassador did not succeed in securing the execution of either Courtenay or Elizabeth,[86] but his influence remained very great, partly because of the power which he represented, his undoubted skill and persuasiveness, and partly because he appeared to control the timetable of the marriage.

In fact this was not the case. When Philip learned the terms of the marriage treaty, he was deeply annoyed. He considered them dishonourable, and contemplated abandoning the entire project. In the end the lure of a crown was too great, and he contented himself with making a formal but secret disclaimer, on 4 January, declaring that he did not consider himself to be bound by the terms of a treaty which had been negotiated without his knowledge: 'he intended to grant the said power [to ratify the treaty] and swear to observe the articles in order that his marriage with the said queen of England might take place, but by no means in order to bind himself or his heirs to observe the articles.'[87] For this reason, and partly because of genuine difficulties over money and ships, Philip abandoned his early intentions of coming swiftly with a small retinue. Mary then made it clear that she was not prepared to marry in Lent. The weeks passed, and there was no direct communication between the royal couple. Philip did send the formal powers for his betrothal to take place *per verba de praesenti* on 6 March, but it must have been a very disappointing occasion for Mary. Not only did her prospective husband not write, nor send any message, but he was represented at the ceremony by his father's councillor the count of Egmont, who had already headed the negotiating commission, and the magnificent ring with which she was presented came

[86] Loades, *Reign of Mary Tudor*, 129–30; the acquittal of Sir Nicholas Throgmorton on 17 April may have frustrated any chance of convicting suspected plotters who had not resorted to arms. Loach, *Parliament and Crown*, 92, 98.

[87] *Cal.Span.*, XII, 4–6.

from the emperor and not his son. Renard became agitated, and pointed out that the prince's silence was causing scandal and concern. As late as 16 February Philip had written to Renard as though he still intended to come soon, but on 27 March he told the emperor he would come with 3000 men and 1500 horses, an entourage which would take a long time to assemble and embark, as well as bringing 5000 or 6000 soldiers to reinforce the army in the Netherlands.[88] The ambassador had no control whatsoever over these developments. He had sent Philip a watered-down account of the Wyatt rebellion, representing it as a minor religious agitation. The prince probably knew better from other sources, but there is no suggestion that his delay was caused by fear over his reception. Having decided to come with a full household, and a large enough fleet to protect himself from interception by the French, he had no choice but to take his time, and simply did not bother to keep Renard informed.

The uncertain prospect of Philip's coming further aggravated the disagreements between the councillors themselves. It was generally and understandably believed that his arrival would make major changes in the distribution of power and confidence, so there was much jockeying for position. Both the imprisonment of Elizabeth and the failure to bring her to trial were consequences of these manœuvrings.[89] Gardiner wished to secure at least her disinheritance by statute, a proposal to which Paget and his allies were bitterly opposed. The queen herself, firmly convinced of the religious explanation for the Wyatt rising, was eager to free herself from the title of Supreme Head. She had not used the title in her official style since Christmas, and its subtantive powers were necessary for her programme of catholic reform, but she fully accepted Pole's contention that 'for a woman to call herself head of that multitude which constitutes the church, is forbidden both by divine as well as natural law.' Gardiner, still smarting from his setbacks over the marriage and the Wyatt rebellion, saw this as an excellent opportunity to recover Mary's confidence. He knew perfectly well that the main

[88] Ibid., 103–5; 176. This change of plan was largely prompted by Mary of Hungary's insistence that he must bring both money and reinforcements. Rodríguez Salgado, *The Changing Face of Empire*, 84.

[89] *Cal.Span.*, XII, 166–7; when Renard refers to 'the heretics' by this time, he tends to mean anyone who is opposing Gardiner – in this instance Paget, Arundel and Pembroke. *The Chronicle of Queen Jane*, 71.

stumbling block would be the secularized church lands, but believed that he could, by restoring the authority of the bishops, make some progress towards re-establishing the hierarchy. This, he seems to have believed, would have set up a satisfactory bargaining position to deal with the main issue. It might also have the great additional advantage of restoring traditional ecclesiastical jurisdiction before Philip's arrival, thus avoiding the problems which would result from bringing the pope back 'in the Prince of Spain's retinue'. This was something that both he and Pole were anxious to avoid, and Mary may also have appreciated their anxiety. Gardiner does not, however, seem to have been entirely frank with his council colleagues about his preparations for parliament, because of the double purpose of his proposals, and the result was a major disaster. The main object of the session was to ratify the marriage treaty, and that was done without difficulty. A related act was also passed, as we have seen, declaring the queen's title and authority to be the same as that of her male predecessors. This was a consequence of doubts which had been raised by some common lawyers over the nature of the queen's 'estate' in the realm, because if it had been the same as that of an heiress to a normal property, it would have been surrendered to her husband on marriage.[90] However, beyond that point harmony broke down. Gardiner's bills do not survive, but from contemporary comment it appears that their intention was to revive the laws against heresy; 'this Parliamente is lyke to be armed with penall lawes', as one member reported.[91] From the records it appears that there was a good deal of debate and redrafting, but on 26 April the main Bill to restore episcopal jurisdiction over heresy passed the Commons and went to the Lords.

Paget and his allies among the councillors were angry and alarmed. Angry because they felt they had been deceived by the chancellor over his intentions; and alarmed partly because they envisaged strong opposition to the implementation of such a measure, and partly because they saw themselves overtaken in the race for power. On 1 May, as a result of a campaign orchestrated by Paget, the Lords rejected the Bill on a division.

[90] D. M. Loades, 'Philip II and the government of England' in *Law and Government under the Tudors,* ed. C. Cross, D. M. Loades and J. J. Scarisbrick, 177–94. See above, p. 2.

[91] Longleat, Thynne MSS II, f.195; Loach, *Parliament and Crown*, 94.

The main motive for their action seems to have been the general fear that it represented a covert attack upon their rights in former Church property. Whether that fear was justified we do not know, in the absence of the Bill, and of any draft. It was almost unprecedented for a council quarrel to spill over into parliament in this way. The queen was furious and Renard was dumbfounded. The ambassador drew the inevitable, and quite unjustified, conclusion that his erstwhile ally had been suborned by the French; but the true explanation was that Mary simply did not know how to manage her council. There had been plenty of indications of that before, but this fiasco was conclusive proof, and what followed provided further confirmation. Until March, Renard had been consistently opposed to the chancellor, and friendly to Paget, but by the end of that month he had concluded that 'the confusion is such that no one knows who is good or bad . . . loyal or treacherous.'[92] By early May, and as a result of the parliamentary session, he had completely changed sides, and on 13 May he wrote a letter to the emperor which reveals that his neurotic fears had now transferred themselves to Paget and his friends.

> The queen is being urged to imprison Paget, and twelve men have undertaken to protect her if she will consent, and order Arundel and Pembroke to be arrested as well. The queen has taken council with the High Treasurer, the Chancellor and the Controller . . . the Earl of Sussex shall be sent to Sussex, the Earl of Huntingdon to his country, the Earl of Shrewbury to the North, and the Earl of Derby to his country.[93]

Paget was certainly in disgrace, and had been forced to withdraw to his estates, but the aspersions cast upon his loyalty were quite unfounded. Renard's willingness to believe (or possibly invent) stories about his intrigues with seditious heretics reflects no great credit upon the ambassador's judgement, or perceptiveness, when confronted with the baffling twists of English politics. Philip's dilatoriness, and a damaging quarrel with his own secretary, had perhaps worried him into over-reacting. No story was too fantastic to be believed: the dowager queen of Scotland was advancing upon the borders with a great army; Cardinal

[92] Renard to the emperor, 22 March 1553; *Cal.Span.*, XII, 164–70.
[93] Ibid., 250–4.

Pole was calling himself duke of York, and claiming the Crown; French agents were active among the English nobility. Noailles's correspondence confirms none of these fears, and he was certainly doing his best to upset the security of England.[94] Unfortunately, Renard's influence over the queen continued to be great, and in June he persuaded her to allow Imperial agents to open the correspondence of Sir John Mason, her ambassador in Brussels, on the grounds that he was intriguing with Paget. Since Paget was by this time back at the council board, although not in favour, his action was doubly improper.[95] Renard's commitment to his master's cause was total, but it was the queen's business to preserve her own freedom of action, and this incident seems to indicate that she was not aware of any such option.

Meanwhile, in spite of all doubts and uncertainties, and in spite of the bluster of the French ambassador, the preparations for Philip's coming went steadily ahead. In early April a joint commission was set up to adjudicate disputes involving Philip's servants, in the hope of stamping out possible trouble between the different nationalities before it got out of hand. By the end of May an English household, some 350 strong, had been named for the new king, headed by the earl of Arundel, who was to provide unity of control by being lord steward both for the king and the queen. Philip's English chamber was headed by Sir John Williams as chamberlain, and John Huddlestone as vice-chamberlain, who had both been among Mary's earliest and loyalest supporters, although certainly not the highest in rank. The sons of seven leading peers, were, however, appointed as gentlemen of the privy chamber, together with three 'aids', who were clearly interpreters.[96] No chapel or stable establishment was provided, it being understood that the prince would bring his own. Early in May, there still being no word from Valladolid, the fleet began patrolling the western approaches to provide a suitable escort and reception, and about the middle of June Philip's household was mobilized and sent to Southampton to await his coming. On 14 June Renard reported that the queen was having a Garter insignia 'worth 7 or 8000 crowns' prepared

[94] Jehan Dubois had accused Renard of accepting bribes from Englishmen to obtain favours from Mary. The bishop of Arras was investigating the charges during March and April. *Cal.Span.*, XII, 178–80. Loades, *Reign of Mary Tudor*, 136–7.

[95] *Cal.Span.*, XII, 289.

[96] Ibid., 297. The whole of Philip's household swore a special oath of loyalty to him. *Acts of the Privy Council*, V, 31. 2 June 1554.

for her husband, but that there were few other signs of welcome or anticipation. This may well have been less the result of indifference than of prudent economy, because although Philip's harbinger, the marquis de las Navas, reached Southampton on 11 June, there was still no sign of the prince himself. Las Navas did, however, bring with him a magnificent jewel – the first token which Philip had sent to Mary – and she welcomed him with emotional enthusiasm. The English nobility were courteous, and Renard's more nightmarish visions of a resisted landing and sea battles with the French, began to appear as insubstantial as in fact they were. On hearing of his arrival, Mary left London on 16 June, and met las Navas at Guildford the following day.[97] She then proceeded by way of Farnham to Bishop's Waltham, where she awaited Philip's arrival. However, the days turned into weeks, and he did not come. The purveyors of the royal household faced terrible problems, and Renard began a new vein of lamentation: 'The officers appointed for his highness' service have been living at Southampton at great expense for a long time', he wrote on 9 July, 'and are now beginning to leave that place, speaking strangely of his Highness.'[98] The fleet had run out of victuals, and everyone was running out of patience, when at long last, on 20 July, the Spanish fleet dropped anchor in Southampton water. Leaving his ship off Portsmouth, Philip proceeded by barge to Southampton itself, where he was greeted in pouring rain by the assembled English nobility.

It was twelve months, almost to the day, since Mary had been proclaimed in London, and in spite of all the problems and alarms, it had been a year of extraordinary success. She had secured, albeit in secret, the papal absolution which she had failed to obtain in 1536, and claimed to have craved ever since. She had restored most of the traditional ecclesiastical order, removed the protestant bishops and married clergy, and replaced them (for the most part) with good catholics.[99] And she had used

[97] *Cal.Span.*, XII, 283. Las Navas informed the queen that Philip was due in two weeks.

[98] Ibid., 309.

[99] Mary had considered replacing the protestant bishops in time for the first parliament in October 1553, but had not done so. A campaign of deprivations followed the passage of the first act of repeal, and a large number of bishops were replaced in time for the second parliament. Loades, *Oxford Martyrs*, 124–5; *Reign of Mary Tudor*, 176–7. For the role of Pole in these replacements, see *Cal.Ven.*, V, 453–4, 471–2.

the power of her office to push through, against a great deal of varied opposition, the marriage treaty which she wanted. She had survived a fairly serious rebellion, and outfaced French threats of war. Her health had stood the strain of hard work and responsibility remarkably well, and now she stood on the threshold of the marriage which had eluded her for over twenty years. In conversation with Pole's private envoy Henry Penning, some time in September 1553, she had 'said . . . fervently that did she not believe herself called by God to that dignity [the Crown], in order to be of some use to this poor country, she would rather elect to be her laundry maid's serving-wench'.[100] By the summer of 1554 she had done much to discharge that duty, and had been well served in the process by advisers whose loyalty and diligence was often greater than she gave them credit for. On the other hand, her general rapport with her subjects had declined rather than improved. The more they had seen of her, the less enthusiastic they had become. The Venetian, Soranzo, signing off his English embassy in August 1554, wrote, 'The queen, being born of a Spanish mother, was always inclined towards that nation, scorning to be English, and boasting of her descent from Spain'.[101] Considering the way in which she and her mother had been treated, perhaps that was only human, but it was a message which was beginning to be picked up in the alehouses and market-places, and not only in London. It remained to be seen whether that would matter in the long run. Wyatt's failure suggested that it might not; but the extent to which England had been ruled for twelve months by the Imperial ambassador in his master's interest was not an entirely hopeful sign.

[100] *Cal. Ven.*, v, 429.
[101] Ibid., 532.

6

Philip and Mary

(1554–1557)

Apart from the weather, Philip could hardly complain of his welcome to England. The earls of Arundel, Derby, Shrewsbury and Pembroke, together with other councillors, had gone out to meet him in 'a barge richly adorned and gilt', and Arundel had invested him with the Garter on board his own ship. No sooner had he landed than a messenger from his father delivered the emperor's surrender of the kingdom of Naples into his hands, 'whereat the English lords were greatly pleased'. It was a time for calculated graciousness, and Philip rose to the occasion with unaccustomed skill. The same evening he delivered a long discourse to the assembled English council, explaining that 'He had not left his own countries to augment his estate or the greatness of his power . . . for God . . . having summoned him to be the husband of the queen their mistress, he would not refuse His divine will, and for this purpose he had crossed the sea to live with the said lady and them.'[1] It is to be hoped that they understood him, because he was not fluent in any language but Spanish, and there is no mention of an interpreter, but his demeanour at least was friendly and reassuring, and his own servants felt that he had excelled himself as an emissary of goodwill.

Fortunately, there were a number of things which the English did not know as they responded to his charm and imposing appearance during these early days. They did not know that he had repudiated the limitations of the marriage treaty, or that the

[1] *Cal.Span.*, XII, 293.

emperor had written a few weeks earlier that God must have guided the project with His own hand, 'and I trust it will prove a factor of weight in our endeavours to serve Him and guard and increase our dominions.' Above all, not even the earl of Bedford, who had gone to Spain in embassy and returned with the prince, knew that he was actually under orders to spend no more than six or eight days in England before making his excuses and joining his father in the Low Countries. These instructions, sent on 29 June, had been the result of the unexpected fall of Marienbourg to the French, and confirm the nature of the emperor's priorities.[2] Even if Philip had wanted to obey his father's wishes, however, he would not have been able to do so, because the English had prepared a stately schedule which could not be hurried. He may well have received private word that his presence with the army was not really necessary, for he showed no sign of haste or impatience, although it was not until 2 August that Charles reconsidered the situation, and told him to stay where he was.

He spent three days at Southampton, recovering from the rigours of his journey, and becoming acquainted with at least some of his English household, before riding to Winchester with a magnificent escort, both English and Spanish, on the 23rd. There, at the bishop's palace, Mary, who had once declared that she would never marry a man she had not seen, waited to discover what God had bestowed upon her. In spite of getting soaked on the road, Philip proceeded straight to the cathedral, where he heard Gardiner sing the Te Deum, before seeking his quarters at the deanery. There he changed, and after supper, at about ten in the evening, was brought privately through the garden to the palace 'where her grace verye lovyngly, yea, and most joyfullye receyved him'. They chatted together for about half an hour under the hopeful scrutiny of no more than a dozen courtiers, before he departed, repeating his carefully learned valediction 'Good night, my lordes all'.[3] They are the only words of English he is ever known to have uttered. Nobody knows what

[2] Ibid. Philip must have known of the French retreat by 22 July, because he landed his horses in England, and sent on to the Netherlands only the 4000 infantry reinforcements which he had brought with him for that purpose. *Cal.Span.*, XIII, 8.

[3] *The copie of a letter sent into Scotlande* (by John Elder); *The Chronicle of Queen Jane*, Appendix X, 140. There are several other accounts of this meeting.

their private feelings may have been about this first encounter, but probably Mary was more impressed than he was. She certainly did not make a very dazzling impression upon the Spanish courtiers. 'She is rather older than we were led to believe,' one of them later commented, while another described her as 'a perfect saint, who dresses badly'. 'Rather handsome than otherwise' was the most flattering description, while Ruy Gomez, who was Philip's closest confidant, and the person most likely to know his mind, shortly after praised his master's tact and skill in dealing with a woman from whom no physical pleasure or satisfaction was to be expected.[4] If Mary was daunted by the prospect of her first sexual encounter, she was far too well trained to show it, and whatever she may have confided to the old friends in her privy chamber was never repeated or recorded. The following day, which was given over to the exchange of polite formalities, he visited her again, when they 'pleasantly talked and communed together'. The question of the language used in these encounters is an interesting one. They clearly did not use an interpreter, and the natural assumption is that they spoke Spanish. However, Mary can have had little occasion to use her mother's tongue since Catherine's death, and her fluency in speech may be doubted. The Venetian ambassador, Giovanni Michieli, later reported explicitly that she understood Spanish, but did not speak it. So it may well be that she used French, of which she had an excellent command, and which he was perfectly capable of understanding.[5] In the circumstances, such bilingualism would have been no bar to communication.

On Wednesday 25 July, which was St James's Day, their nuptials were celebrated in Winchester cathedral, with all the pomp of which the English church and state were capable, and with careful political showmanship. Before the ceremony began, Don Gomez Suarez de Figueroa, representing the emperor, publicly repeated his donation of the kingdom of Naples, and handed over the patent in a silver-gilt casket. The lord chancel-

[4] Ruy Gomez to Francisco de Eraso, 27 July 1554; *Cal.Span.*, XIII, 2. Physical descriptions of Mary by the Spaniards were uniformly unflattering; 'not at all beautiful', 'small, and rather flabby than fat' etc. The Spaniards found English women generally ugly, badly dressed, and bold in their demeanour.

[5] This assumption is strengthened by the fact that she used the marquis of las Navas as an interpreter when talking to the duchess of Alba, who may well not have been at home in French. *Cal.Span.*, XIII, 12.

lor then praised the emperor's generosity, and reminded his hearers that the terms of the treaty had been confirmed, both by parliament, and by Philip's ratification before the earl of Bedford in Spain. The bride was given away by the marquis of Winchester, and the earls of Arundel, Derby, Bedford and Pembroke, in the name of the whole realm; 'then all the people gave a great shout, praying God to send them joy.' As soon as they had 'closed hands', and were formally man and wife, 'immediately the sword was presented before the king, borne by the Earl of Pembroke', and Gardiner proceeded to the mass. At the end of the ceremony, and to the sound of trumpets, Garter king of arms proclaimed their styles in Latin, French and English (but not Spanish) 'King and Queen of England, France, Naples, Jerusalem and Ireland, Defenders of the Faith; Princes of Spain and Sicily; Archdukes of Austria; Dukes of Milan, Burgundy and Brabant; Counts of Habsburg, Flanders and Tyrol.' After the marriage feast, held in the bishop's palace, the royal couple danced in the German style. So far, it had been a very public celebration, but the climax was to be different. As one of Philip's gentlemen wrote soon after, 'the bishop of Winchester blessed the bed, and they remained alone. What happened that night only they know. If they give us a son, our joy will be complete.'[6] Dynastic politics had manœuvred Mary into the same position that her mother had occupied thirty-five years before, and the future of England again depended upon the outcome.

It was a time for triumph and rejoicing. Even the sceptical Edward Underhill managed to make off with an outsize venison pie from the banquet, and for several days the city of Winchester was given over to feasting and celebration upon an unprecedented scale. According to custom, Mary remained invisible, while Philip went sightseeing, and, more seriously, transacted other business with his Spanish councillors and advisers. Eventually, on 31 July, they set out on a leisurely progress towards London, spending two nights at Basing and one at Reading, before reaching Windsor on 3 August.[7] There Philip was duly

[6] *Cal.Span.*, XIII, 11. Even the published accounts of the wedding had a romantic touch. Mary's wedding ring was a plain hoop of gold 'because maydens were so maried in olde tymes'; John Elder's *Letter*, 141.

[7] Extract from a *Journal of the Travels of Philip II* by Jean de Vandenesse; *Cal.Span.*, XIII, appendix, 443.

installed as a knight of the Garter, and held a chapter of the order. On the 11th, they moved on to Richmond, and news arrived that the French had besieged Renty. This provoked a large-scale exodus of the king's Spanish and Italian followers, who were given leave to go and serve in the campaign, but they saw little action, because the siege was raised only a few days later. At Richmond the king and queen marked time, waiting for word from London that the preparations for their state entry were complete. On the 17th they moved to Suffolk Place in Southwark, and at two o'clock on the following afternoon crossed London bridge, and processed through the city to Whitehall. Work had been going on since the end of May upon the pageants and scenes which greeted them, and great care had been taken to ensure a suitable welcome for the king, since London had quite a lot to prove in that respect. The result was splendid, and must have been very expensive – particularly the giant figures of Corineus Brittanus and Gogmagog Albionus on London bridge – but not particular original or subtle. Philip was very much the centre of attention, and the verses which the giants displayed between them were typical of the theme which was to recur all along the way:

> O noble Prince, sole hope of Caesar's side,
> By God appointed all the world to guide,
> Most heartily welcom art thou to our land,
> . . . . . .
> But chiefly London doth her love vouchsafe,
> Rejoysing that her Philip is come safe.[8]

There were some six or seven of these set pieces, one of them showing the king's descent from John of Gaunt, and the others

[8] Unica Caesareae stirpis spes inclite princeps
Cui Deus imperium totius destinat orbis
Gratus et optatus nostras accedis ad oras
. . . . . .
Te tamen in primis urbs Londoniensis honorat,
Incolumenque suum gaudet venisse Philippum.

Elder, *Letter*, 146. For a full discussion of the pageants of this occasion, see Anglo, *Spectacle, Pageantry and Early Tudor Policy*, 327–38. Elder translated all the verses into English, but they appear to have been displayed in Latin only, a sufficient indication of their purpose.

somewhat conventional scenes of royal virtue and piety.[9] Philip was pleased, and wrote soon after that he had been received with universal signs of love and joy.

The reality was less comfortable. Even the flattering pageantry had not been without a touch of discord, as the observant Gardiner spotted the words 'verbum dei' on a book held by the painted figure of Henry VIII. Two of the devisers of this scene had been the late king's printer, Thomas Berthelet, and his successor, Richard Grafton, who had held a patent for many years to print English Bibles, and had lost his position for printing Jane's proclamation. That the aldermen of London had entrusted the city's welcome to two citizens of such antecedents was both ironic and significant. The pageants themselves had in some cases been erected upon sites recently vacated by the scaffolds bearing those Londoners whose opposition to the regime had been too openly expressed. On 20 August, two days after the entry, the city chamberlain was instructed to take them down, to avoid vandalism. Whatever Philip might pretend, or his publicists declare, his first month in England had been very far from a honeymoon, except in the most literal sense. The first and most immediate problem had been caused by the fact that he found himself with two households. Ruy Gomez, who was nothing if not prejudiced, blamed this fiasco on Renard and Arras. 'The ambassador', he wrote 'gets everything into a muddle. However, I do not blame him, but rather the person who sent a man of his small attainments to conduct so capital an affair as this match, instead of entrusting it to a Spaniard.'[10] This was hardly fair, but was clearly a defensive move, since the prime fault seems to have lain with Gomez himself, who had not troubled to inform Renard what retinue the prince would be bringing. The English servants had immediately taken up their duties, in accordance with instructions, and before he knew what was happening, Philip found his meals being served by strangers with whom he could not even converse. Spanish complaints were

[9] Including one of the 'foure most noble Philips' (Philip of Macedon, Philip 'the Arabian', alleged to have been the first Christian emperor, Philip the Good of Burgundy, and Philip the Bold). Anglo, *Spectacle, Pageantry and Early Tudor Policy*, 332–3.

[10] Ruy Gomez to Eraso, 23 August 1554; *Cal.Span.*, XIII, 35. This letter was written with one eye on the recipient, because Eraso disliked and distrusted Arras.

immediate and bitter. Even the duke of Alba was not able to discharge his duties as major-domo; 'todos andaramos bein vagamundos y sun hacer falta' – we are all hanging about here with nothing to do – as one gentlemen confided to a friend in Spain.[11] Before he reached London, Philip had solved the problem in the obvious way – by dividing his service between the two households – but the result was very expensive and satisfied nobody. From the complaints which continued to be made, it seems that he retained his Spanish gentlemen for personal attendance, and placed more formal service in the hands of the English. The Spaniards continued to feel themselves slighted and dishonoured in public, while Lord Fitzwalter, an English gentleman of the privy chamber who spoke Spanish, protested that he had so little access to the king that he was getting out of practice with the language!

Philip seems to have done his best (and much better than his father expected) to placate the English and to discipline his own followers, but the hostility between the two nations was mutual and implacable. Most of the Spanish courtiers had never wanted to come to England, and some had come at great personal cost. They came, partly out of loyalty to their prince, and partly because the marriage had been represented to them as a decisive blow against France. The excessive number of these nobles and gentlemen was quickly reduced by the repellent effects of the English weather and the attractions of campaigning in the Low Countries. Philip was wise enough not to detain them when they asked permission to go. By the time the court reached London, over eighty had departed, as had the Italians and Flemings. The main problem, however, was not with the courtiers themselves, but with their dependants and hangers-on. The 'artisan and vagabond Spaniards' who followed the court acted rather like the travelling 'fans' of a modern football team, attracting violence even when they were not responsible for inciting it. Charles had also warned his son not to allow his servants to bring their wives with them, because of the danger of friction with the influential ladies of the queen's privy chamber. Some came, nevertheless, but their experience seems to have confirmed the wisdom of the Emperor's advice: 'Dona Hieronima de Navarra

[11] *Tres Cartas de lo sucedido en el viaje de su Alteza a Inglaterra*, Primera Carta, 91.

and Dona Francisca de Cordova ... have not yet seen the Queen', ran one report of 17 August, 'and are not going to see her, for they have not joined the court because they would have no one to talk to, as the English ladies are of evil conversation.'[12] The duchess of Alba did see the queen, and indulged in a prolonged exchange of courtesies which left them both sitting on the floor.[13] Although the encounter seems to have been amiable enough, it was not repeated, and at least one Spanish observer believed that the duchess was deeply dissatisfied with her reception.

The main trouble arose, as might be expected, in London. The Spaniards had complained, almost from the moment of landing, of the number and audacity of English thieves. It was best to go abroad in company, and to go early to bed. Even the king's own belongings had been plundered, and the council did not seem to be able to do anything about it. As the court approached London the complaints grew louder, and there were some unpleasant incidents. Some innkeepers refused to accommodate Spaniards, and hurled insults at them. Others were content to overcharge for everything they provided. The friars were particularly subject to abuse:

> for the English are so bad, and fear God so little that they handle the friars shamefully, and the poor men do not dare to leave their quarters ... [the crowd] tried to tear their cloaks off the backs of Don Pedro de Cordova and Don Antonio his nephew, who are *comendadores*, asking what they meant by wearing crosses, and jeering at them.[14]

Given their total ignorance of the language, it is possible that some Spaniards over-reacted to what was primarily curiosity, but the hostility which they identified was certainly present. French-inspired propaganda had helped to create this situation, but there were a number of other ingredients. One was the rooted Spanish conviction that all Englishmen were 'como gente barbara e muy heretica', who executed monks and nuns for

[12] *Cal.Span.*, XIII, 33. Charles had originally warned that 'even soldiers' would get on better with the English than Spanish ladies.

[13] Ibid. The reason for this curious outcome was that neither would allow the other to take a lower seat. One of the duchess's complaints was that she was not lodged at court, but it is not at all clear that anyone in England knew she was coming.

[14] Ibid. *Comendadores* were members of the Spanish military orders.

amusement, and had no fear of God or his saints. This Black Legend went back to the sufferings of Catherine of Aragon, and the dissolution of the monasteries; and whereas it increased their admiration for Mary, it did nothing at all to assist her relations with her own subjects. Another problem was the entrepreneurial spirit which prompted a number of Spaniards to run the risk of opening booths and other temporary shops, in defiance of the privileges of the London merchants. That these shops were eventually closed by the council in October, rather than sacked by the mob indicates that the discipline of the capital may not have been as bad as it was represented.

By the time that the court moved to Whitehall for the winter, on 28 September, certain features of the new regime had begun to emerge. On 23 August the king had issued patents to twenty-one English pensioners, conferring annuities of between £75 and £500. The beneficiaries were all noblemen and councillors, and the only surprise was the complete omission of the lord chancellor. Paget, who had not recovered the queen's favour, was making his way back as the king's man, and received one of the highest annuities at £375.[15] Simon Renard, the *éminence grise* of the first year of the reign, found that his confidential relationship with the queen had come to an end. Disliked by Philip, and confined to his proper ambassadorial functions, he was soon complaining bitterly of his lot, and asking to be recalled. Charles took the view that his unrivalled knowledge of English affairs made him a valuable asset to the king, and kept him at his post, but although he bombarded Philip, Alba and Ruy Gomez with unsolicited advice, they do not seem to have paid any attention, and his reports of the situation became increasingly jaundiced and pessimistic. 'They' [the English], he wrote on 18 September, 'loudly proclaim that they are going to be enslaved, for the queen is a Spanish woman at heart and thinks nothing of Englishmen, but only of Spaniards and bishops.'[16] He continued to enlarge upon the divisions within the council, and its general failure to

[15] Archivo General de Simancas, CMC la E, Legajo 1184. Renard had already distributed some rewards in March, and drawn up a pension list for the king's guidance, which Philip followed closely, but not exactly. *Cal.Span.*, XII, 158; 315–16. For a fuller discussion of these pensions and their significance, see Loades, 'Philip II and the government of England', 177–194.

[16] *Cal.Span.*, XIII, 49.

impose any kind of discipline or respect. These reports need to be treated with even more caution than those of the previous year, when, for all his nervous distortions, he did at least know what was going on. Other observers who were closer to Philip, spoke of him 'settling' the affairs of the kingdom at this point, and claimed that the alarmist tales being circulated in Spain and the Netherlands were greatly exaggerated. The king and queen gave every public appearance of being well pleased with each other, and took part together in masques and entertainments of a kind which had not been seen since before the onset of Edward VI's last illness. Writing 'newes from the courte' to Sir William Cecil on 12 October, Francis Yaxley reported,

> The king and queenes maiesties be in helthe and meary ... they daunsed together on Sunday night at the courte. There was a brave maskery of clothe of gold and sylver wheryn the maskers weare dressed as marryners whereof the fyrst was I thynke my lorde admirall.'[17]

A 'cane-play' involving the king and some of the Spanish lords was planned for the following Thursday. All was quiet in the capital, apart from the usual crop of maliciously inspired rumours. Most important of all, the queen was convinced that she had conceived, a belief shared by her physicians. Stories to this effect were quickly and deliberately put about, to rally loyalty and affection, and to provide a distraction from tales of Spanish armies and popish clergy invading the realm.

> Nowe singe, nowe springe, oure care is exil'd
> Oure vertuous Queene is quickened with child

wrote one ballad-monger, who clearly expected to make a profit from this royal event. When Philip appeared at his wife's side for the opening of parliament of 12 November, he got the nearest thing to a warm greeting which he was ever to receive in England.

The queen's supposed pregnancy was in many ways the most important development to take place in the autumn of 1554, and it partly concealed the unsatisfactory nature of Philip's position in England. His own servants were quick to point out that he had no real authority, and urged him to withdraw until he could

[17] BL MS Lansdowne 3, f.92.

persuade or force the English to receive him in a manner befitting their notion of sovereignty. He had not been crowned, the terms of the marriage treaty prevented him from filling English offices with his own men, and all he was expected to do was to disgorge money, for which the English had an insatiable appetite.[18] There was a good deal of substance in these protests. Philip did not even receive the protection of the treason laws until January 1555, and it was consistently made clear to him in small ways that he was seen primarily as a consort. Most surprisingly, he was given no English patrimony, and consequently had neither revenue nor patronage of his own. Such an endowment was not precluded by the marriage treaty, and by analogy with a female consort, should have been the normal practice. Why Mary did not make this provision by exercising her prerogative is something of a mystery. She professed both warm affection and also dutiful obedience towards her husband. 'This marriage and alliance', she wrote to the Emperor, 'renders me happier than I can say, as I daily discover in the king my husband and your son, so many virtues and perfections that I constantly pray God to grant me grace to please him, and behave in all things as befits one who is so deeply embounden to him.'[19] But despite this, and despite her later claims that the kingdom needed his strong hand, she took no practical steps to grant him any effective authority. Perhaps she was deterred by the evidence of her subjects' hostility, which caused her great personal distress and anger, but as Paget later told the emperor, that hostility was much stronger among the people than among the nobility, and Mary was not in other ways influenced by evidence of popular opinion. Perhaps she did not perceive a need, realizing the extent of Philip's other resources. In the winter of 1554–5 there was every reason to adopt a waiting policy. Delicate and protracted negotiations were under way by September which were to lead to the restoration of papal authority in January. It was critically important not to upset aristocratic opinion over property issues while that settlement hung in the balance. Above all, there was the vital question of the unborn

[18] *Cal.Span.*, XIII, 31. Ruy Gomez believed that the council had divided into 'two new factions', one for the king and the other for the queen, a reflection, perhaps, of the fact that several were looking to Philip for patronage. Ibid., 35.

[19] *Cal.Span.*, XIII, 28.

child. The symptoms of her pregnancy developed with apparent normality, and on 23 November Renard added a postscript to one of his routine dispatches to say that 'she has felt the babe' – presumably what the English called 'quickening'.[20] Mary's age, and the hazards always attendant upon sixteenth-century childbirth, made it imperative that proper provision should be made for the custody and education of the heir in the event of the queen's death.

A Bill 'for the limitation of treasons', which probably dealt with this subject, was discussed on several occasions in the House of Commons during late November and early December, before being dropped as unsatisfactory. A new Bill for the same purpose then appeared on 20 December. This time the queen, and possibly also the king, had been consulted. Mary, reverting to her old habits, instructed Petre, Rochester and Englefield to consult Renard about the draft, which they duly did, although they refused to show it to him.[21] This placed the ambassador in difficulty, because the emperor, aware of complaints which had been made about his activities in March and April, had instructed him not become involved in parliament matters. He resolved this dilemma (after a fashion) by agreeing to discuss the measure as it impinged upon the marriage treaty, and then reporting the results of his discussions to Philip. His main concern was that the plan proposed was too restrictive upon the king, who should have, he believed, a legal right to act as guardian and regent, irrespective of legislation. This Bill was heavily amended in committee, and as it eventually emerged from the House of Lords on 16 January was very much simpler than the measure which had been discussed with Renard. It conferred the custody, not only of the heir but also of the realm, upon Philip; until the fifteenth birthday of a daughter, or the eighteenth of a son. It also extended to him the immediate protection of the treason laws.[22] Renard regarded this as a considerable success – and the result of his own advice – but Philip was not pleased. In the first place the Act insisted that the terms of the marriage treaty should remain in force during any

[20] Renard to the emperor, 23 November 1554; *Cal.Span.*, XIII, 102.
[21] Renard to Philip, December 1554; *Cal.Span.*, XIII, 128–31.
[22] Statutes 1 & 2 Philip and Mary, c.10; Loach, *Parliament and the Crown,* 117–19.

such regency; and secondly the treason laws were to protect him only for the duration of his marriage, leaving any regency situation to take care of itself. The whole passage of the Act had been controversial, particularly in the Commons. Several members had shown their distrust of Philip's good faith over the treaty – with every justification as we now know – and when someone had suggested that he should be given a full right of succession in the event of Mary's death, the proposal had been rejected out of hand.

By January the queen's health was giving cause for concern. On the 18th she excused a very brief and conventional note to the emperor on the grounds that her physical condition did not allow her to do more. Also, Philip was becoming restless. He had had at least one eye on the business of the Netherlands throughout the autumn, holding regular consultations with Alba, Figueroa and Eraso, the emperor's secretary. Ruy Gomez travelled regularly to and fro, bypassing Renard, much to the latter's chagrin, and Arras had to remind the king as delicately as possible that there was still much to do in England in the wake of so momentous a parliament.[23]

Philip seems to have felt, with some justification, that he had done his duty in England. Not only had he begotten a child upon the queen, but he had also successfully reconciled the most important schismatic state in Europe with the see of Rome, a task which many had declared to be impossible. By the summer of 1554, Julius III had recognized that some unpalatable concessions would have to be made if England were to be recovered. It had frequently been pointed out to him, and most recently by Commendone, that heresy was only a part of the problem, and that English hostility to the papacy was political rather than theological. He was also well aware that the emperor was stalling, not wishing to take any risks in a potentially volatile situation until his son was safely installed as king. Consequently the news that Philip was finally on his way to England, and the patent failure of Pole's alternative mission for Franco-Habsburg

[23] Quite apart from her supposed pregnancy, Mary's health continued to be fragile. In August 1554 the Venetian Soranzo had reported that her constitution was weak, and that she suffered from headaches and palpitations, so that she often took medicine and was let blood. *Cal.Ven.*, v, 532. *Cal.Span.*, XIII, 131.

peace, prompted him to take a fresh initiative. He augmented the cardinal's powers, to give him authority to negotiate on the question of church property, and instructed him to give English affairs priority.[24] Pole naturally assumed that the way was now clear for his return to his native land, and sent an envoy to the bishop of Arras to complete the formalities. Arras quickly divined that his powers only enabled him to negotiate each case of expropriated church property on its individual merits, thus excluding any possibility of a general settlement. This was useless, but neither Arras nor Charles said so explicity, for fear of sacrificing the advantage which had been gained. Instead they spoke in terms of the king's recent arrival, and his need to assess the situation and consult the English council. Pole, by this time at Dillinghem, near Brussels, came close to despair. He knew Mary's views, and had been secretly consulted by her on a number of issues over the previous six months; he had even confirmed her episcopal appointments, in violation of the strict law of *praemunire*.[25] But he also knew that he could not proceed to England without the support of both the emperor and the king, and that that support would not be obtained without what he considered to be a betrayal of the church – an undertaking to grant a general and unconditional absolution. On 24 September he directed an eloquent plea to Philip, full of scriptural allusions about Peter knocking at the door, and disingenuous amazement at the deafness of such pious princes.[26]

On 12 October the king responded, although not quite in the manner which Pole had envisaged. Realizing that only the pope could actually order Pole to give the necessary absolution, he sent instructions to his father's envoy in Rome, Don Manrique de Lara, to open direct negotiations with Julius. At the same time he sent Renard across to Brussels to persuade the cardinal into a more co-operative frame of mind. Both missions were successful, although the first turned out to be much the more straightforward. On 7 November Julius wrote, not to Philip but to the emperor because Charles had intercepted the dispatch, much to his son's annoyance:

[24] Loades, *Reign of Mary Tudor*, 176–7.

[25] *Cal.Span.*, XIII, 53; *Cal.Ven.*, V, 453–4, 471–2; Loades, *Reign of Mary Tudor*, 176.

[26] *Cal.Span.*, XIII, 53; Ibid., 63–4.

> We immediately called together those of the cardinals, whom on account of their learning, prudence and piety we considered best qualified to discuss this question, and when we had exposed your Majesty's wishes to them, they all agreed with us that it would be far better, for all reasons human and divine, to abandon all the church property, rather than risk the shipwreck of this undertaking.[27]

Instructions to this effect had been immediately dispatched to Pole. Before this news arrived, Pole had been persuaded to give just enough ground for Philip to risk admitting him to England during the parliament, which was about to meet on 12 November. The cardinal had not changed his views, but he had been willing to agree that his own powers were sufficient, without further reference to Rome, and that he would not exercise any jurisdiction without the king and queen's consent.[28] This latter point was crucial, since it guaranteed at least that he would not make a difficult situation worse. The English council, which seems to have worked closely with the king on this issue, agreed on 3 November to admit Pole to the country, although as a papal envoy in the first instance, and not as legate, and on the 5th Lord Paget and Sir Edward Hastings were sent to the Low Countries to escort him. At this point the cardinal was still an attainted traitor, and his legatine status unlawful, so it is somewhat surprising to find a proclamation dated 10 November instructing all the king and queen's subjects to submit to his authority 'in such cases of spiritual jurisdiction for the reformation of their souls as in the time of the said twentieth year of the reign of our said father King Henry VIII was, or with his consent might have been, used and expressed'. Furthermore, on the same day a licence was issued under the Great Seal for the exercise of the same jurisdiction.[29] Since not even Foxe protested at what appears to have been a gross constitutional impropriety, we should probably conclude that the proclamation was not issued upon its ostensible date. Patents under the Great or Privy Seal were frequently backdated, but proclamations not normally

[27] *Cal.Span.*, XIII, 79–80. For a detailed discussion of this curious twist to the negotiation, see Rodríguez Salgado, *The Changing Face of Empire*, 97.

[28] Pole's reports to Julius III; *Cal.Ven.*, V, 582–3, 584–6; Loades, *Reign of Mary Tudor*, 323.

[29] Hughes and Larkin, *Tudor Royal Proclamations*, II, 48–9; *Calendar of the Patent Rolls*, Philip and Mary, II, 311.

so, and the explanation may lie in another quirk of Mary's conscience. The queen had always believed, along with Pole, that the statutes passed against the catholic faith had been *ultra vires*. She had appeared to accept those of her father, but had made it clear within a month of her accession that her conscience did not really accept the path of parliamentary repeal to which political circumstances constrained her. The wording of this proclamation strongly suggests that it was issued on her initiative, rather than Philip's, and perhaps it was intended to make the same point that Henry VII had made when he dated his reign from the day before the battle of Bosworth.

The public action of reconciliation commenced on 17 November, with the introduction of a Bill to repeal Pole's attainder. The members knew perfectly well what was in the wind, because Philip's consultations with the council had not been secret, and Gardiner's opening address had referred explicitly to the confirmation of true religion. The Bill passed through both Houses in five days without controversy, and on the afternoon of 22 November the king and queen took the unusual step of going to the House of Lords in person, so that the Act could be perfected before Pole, who was already well on his way, actually arrived. The cardinal had landed at Dover, and as he rode across Kent his escort had been augmented by the earl of Shrewsbury, Lord Montague and Lord Cobham, for the purposes of both honour and security. Significiantly, he did not attempt to enter London in the conventional way, but arrived at Whitehall stairs by river from Gravesend. The king greeted him at the stairs, and led him ceremonially to the presence chamber, where Mary was so moved by his appearance that she declared the babe had leaped in her womb, as had the unborn John the Baptist at the greeting of Our Lady.[30] Pole had been in exile for twenty years, and his household was largely Italian, so he found it much easier to take the high moral ground than did those who had struggled through the difficult years, but his conviction that he understood the English and their problems was not well founded. He was lodged across the river at Lambeth, a deliberate gesture of intention as far as the queen was concerned, and within two or three days his new powers and instructions arrived

[30] Loach, *Parliament and the Crown*, 105–9. Elder, *Letter*, 153; Prescott, *Mary Tudor*, 287.

from Rome, to everyone's satisfaction. On 28 November he appeared before both Houses of Parliament at Westminster, and addressed them on the subject of his mission. The queen, he declared, was the symbol of the unquenchable faith of her people, preserved by God for this very hour,

> And see howe miraculously God of hys goodness preserved her hyghness contrarye to the expectacyon of manne. That when numbers conspyred agaynste her, and policies were devised to disherit her, and armed power prepared to destroye her, yet she being a virgin, helpless, naked and unarmed, prevailed and had the victorye over tyrauntes.[31]

The king also had come like another Solomon to build the temple which his father had willed but been unable to accomplish. The Holy See had always held the ancient church of the British in particular regard, and it was no part of his intention to impose conditions upon the return of the prodigal son:

> I cum to reconcyle, not to condemne. I cum not to compel but to call agayne. I am not cum to call anything in question already done, but my commission is of grace and clemency to such as will receive it . . .

As recorded by John Elder, and by Foxe, it was a noble and moving speech, and must have been particularly gratifying to Philip as it concentrated entirely upon the spritual and pastoral purposes of the reconciliation, and not at all upon the legal and technical processes. Nothing was said about the vexed question of papal suzerainty, nor about taxation, nor about the actual status of the secularized lands. The last hurdle seemed to have been cleared, and two days later the members of both Houses presented themselves at Whitehall, when Gardiner submitted on their behalf, a joint petition to the king and queen, 'as persons unsullied by heresy or schism' to intercede with the cardinal for his absolution:

> So as thys noble realme, wyth all the members thereof maye in unitie and perfecte obedience to the Sea Apostolike . . . serve God and your majesties to the furderance and advancemente of hys honoure and glorye.

[31] Elder, *Letter*, 157; Foxe, *Acts and Monuments*, VI, 570.

Pole then pronounced the solemn sentence amid scenes of high emotion, and the twenty-year schism was brought to an end.[32]

To Mary, this must have been the greatest moment of her life. After years of struggle, not to mention some very straight spiritual counsel from Pole, her conscience was now at peace. Her accession to the throne, and her marriage, had been but means to this end, and the conception of her child the means by which God intended to protect His work beyond her own lifetime. It is not surprising that she was described by one observer as being fatter, and having a better colour, than when she was married, a sign that she was as happy as she was reported to be.[33] But Philip had borne the brunt of the work, and when Mary wrote to the emperor on 7 December informing him of what had happened, she also declared truthfully that their success had been largely obtained by his wise guidance. Apart from his wife's gratitude, Philip's reward came mainly from outside England; in eulogistic writings like *Il felicissimo ritorno del regno d'Inghilterra alla cattolica unione;* and in a decisive (if temporary) increase in Habsburg prestige and influence at Rome. However, it soon transpired that absolution was far from the end of the schism, except in the most superficial sense. Now that the 'possessioners', as Pole significantly called them, had been absolved from ecclesistical penalties, what was their own spiritual status, and what was the status of their lands? Although the petition to the king and queen had been an unequivocal statement of intent, the Henrician statutes had not yet been repealed, and in the process of repeal those two questions would have to be addressed. Pole's position was quite clear: 'this dispensation was a mere permission *ob duritiam cordis illorum*',[34] and did not absolve from the guilt of the offence. In other words Christian consciences could only be discharged by returning what was, in effect, stolen property. Similarly, he did not accept that the original statues which had dissolved the monasteries had conferred any valid title upon the Crown. Consequently the Crown

[32] Elder, *Letter*, 163; Foxe, *Acts and Monuments*, VI, 572. Rullo to Seripando, 1 December 1554, Carlo de Frede, *La Restaurazione Cattolica in Inghilterra sotto Maria Tudor*, 57.

[33] *Cal.Span.*, XIII, 110. Ibid., 117.

[34] *Cal.Ven.*, VI, 10. BL Add. MS 41577, ff.161–6; J.H. Crehan, 'The return to obedience: new judgement on Cardinal Pole', *The Month* NS XIV, 221–9; Loach, *Parliament and the Crown*, 108–10; Loades, *Reign of Mary Tudor*, 325–8.

had held no valid title to transmit to the purchasers and grantees. This would have left the 'possessioners' titles entirely dependent upon the dispensation which had just been granted. Since no pope could bind his successors in a matter of this kind, that was hardly satisfactory; and indeed, later in 1555, Julius's successor, Paul IV, revoked all such dispensations; a measure from which England was specially exempted after a lot of effort.[35]

It is not surprising, therefore, that there was some very hard talking in council on 21 and 22 December, as the draft Bills to be placed before parliament after Christmas were discussed. Pole declared bluntly that no temporal power had any jurisdiction over ecclesiastical property, while the common lawyers argued that all property was subject only to the authority of the Crown in parliament.[36] From their point of view any statute not repealed was good and binding in law, and whereas the parliament had agreed to repeal all acts made 'against the See Apostolic of Rome', it had no intention of touching those which had dissolved the monasteries. Furthermore, Pole's dispensation would only be pleadable in a court of law if it were embodied in the Act of Settlement. Both sides quoted precedents, and called on the highest principles. On the whole, Pole did better on the principles, and the lawyers on the precedents. These exchanges were recorded by Ludovico Priuli, Pole's secretary, who must have been present, and could probably follow the lawyers' arguments much less clearly than he could his master's. Mary was present but not, apparently, Philip, who would have been unable to understand the discussion without an interpreter. On the first day the queen made two recorded interventions; first to tell the lawyers that if they intended to be guided by precedents from her father's or her brother's reign, she would abdicate; and second to announce in general terms that she supported the cardinal's position unreservedly. Her councillors, Priuli noted, were greatly dismayed.[37] On the second day, however, as the drafts were examined clause by clause, the tone was quite different, and in the end the lawyers won on most points of substance, particularly over the inclusion of the dispensation in the Act. Pole

[35] *Rescissio Alienationum*, *Cal.Ven.* VI, 189; see also R. H. Pogson, 'Cardinal Pole, Papal Legate to England in Mary Tudor's Reign' (Ph.D., Cambridge, 1972), 147–9.

[36] Loach, *Parliament and the Crown*, 109–10.

[37] BL Add. MS 41577, ff.161–6; Loach, *Parliament and the Crown*, 111.

argued strenuously that the authority of parliament was as nothing beside that of the Holy See, but the council did not agree with him. In the end he managed to avoid conceding the point of conscience, because the statute merely recorded that the two Houses had asked the property might be enjoyed 'without scruple of conscience', and not that such a request had been granted. On the other hand it was roundly declared that 'the title of all Landes Possessions and Hereditaments' could be pleaded only in the royal courts 'and none otherwise'.[38]

In giving her assent to such an Act, the queen surrendered the position which she had taken up on 21 December, in much the same way as she had given up her original intention to hold a public requiem for her brother. Perhaps in this case Philip persuaded her, as Renard had done earlier. His priorities certainly seem to have been different, pehaps because his own conscience was not touched by what had happened in England. He was prepared to make any concession to the property holders that was consistent with the restored jurisdiction of the church, and the eventual statute thus reflected his view more accurately than it did either Mary's or Pole's. By the time that parliament was dissolved on 16 January, the policies represented by Mary's marriage, and by her return to the catholic church had, by and large, been embodied in statute, and had thus received the consent of the realm in its highest and most tangible form. The medieval heresy laws had been restored, and the last 'religious' attainders repealed. In spite of the setbacks, and of the compromises which she had been constrained to make, this was the high-water mark of the queen's success. However, it was one thing to make good laws, and quite another to enforce them.

There is very little evidence of what Mary thought about the secular government of her kingdom. Its international aspects she seems to have left largely to Philip, gradually abandoning separate English diplomatic representation, except at Rome. When Stephen Gardiner died in November 1555, Philip wished to promote Lord Paget in his place, but the queen did not concur and the post went instead to the innocuous Archbishop Heath. Paget did, however, follow the earl of Bedford as lord privy seal, again on Philip's initiative. In distributing her patrongage, she was generous in small ways to her old and loyal servants, but the

[38] Statutes 1 & 2 Philip and Mary, c.8.

major grants were reserved for traditional magnate families which had fallen into disfavour under her father – the Howards, the Courtenays, and above all the Percys. The creation of Thomas Percy as earl of Northumberland in 1557 represented an extremely conservative, almost reactionary, policy towards the government of the north and the defence of the Scottish border,[39] but it would be hard to claim that it was typical of Mary's attitude towards regional administration in general. Most of the evidence relating to the queen's involvement in the implementation of policy is circumstantial, and her opinions have to be deduced.

By contrast, her views on ecclesiastical affairs are well known. She discussed them freely with Renard, Commendone and Penning, each of whom reported faithfully and at length. At some point during the third parliament she also drew up a memorandum on the subject for the benefit of her council. The reason for this unusual proceeding is not clear. Her intervention in the discussion of 21 December had been emotional and unhelpful, and she may have felt more in control of herself on paper. More likely she feared that her physical condition might preclude any more such sessions, and she wished her position to be clearly known:

> touching good preaching, I wish that may supply and overcome the evil preaching in time past. And also to make sure provision that none evil books shall either be printed bought or sold without just punishment therefore. I think it should be well done that the universities and churches of this realm should be visited ... Touching punishment of heretics, methinketh it ought to be done without rashness, not leaving in the meanwhile to do justice to such as by learning would seem to deceive the simple ... especially within London I would wish none to be burned without some of the council's presence, and both there and everywhere good sermons at the same. I verily believe that many benefices should not be in one man's hands.[40]

There was little in this programme from which Pole could have dissented, also it is very difficult to tell whether the queen or the cardinal was the main inspirer of the persecution which began in

[39] Loades, *Reign of Mary Tudor*, 97–8; *Cal.Pat.*, II, 495. The endowment was in excess of £3000 p.a., PRO SP12/1/64. On the policy involved see also P. Boscher, 'The Anglo-Scottish Border, 1550–1560' (Ph.D., Durham, 1985).

[40] BL Cotton MS Titus C VII, f.120.

earnest in February 1555. Nevertheless there were differences of emphasis between them. Mary, as this passage makes plain, believed in the power of good preaching, as well as in discipline, while Pole was unenthusiastic. In his view sermons, even good ones, only stirred up controversy. The business of good Christian laymen was to be obedient and to discharge their religious obligations, not to argue about theology, which was the business of the clergy. He was more concerned with how people behaved than with what they believed. When Pole convened his legatine synod in November 1555, preaching did not feature highly among its priorities, and the evidence suggests that in this respect the queen's wishes were not much observed.[41] Both were anxious to improve the educational standards of the clergy, but neither was responsive to the new theological ideas and spiritual techniques being developed in Europe by the Jesuits and the Dominicans. Pole had spent most of his life in the ferment of catholic reform, but was radically out of sympathy with the direction which it was taking.[42] Mary probably knew of it only by report, and took her opinion from Pole. Her taste in devotional literature certainly embraced some recent Continental writing, but did not run to controversial theology.

The religious policy to which Mary was so deeply committed, and which Pole was mainly responsible for implementing, was backward-looking rather than innovative, drawing its inspiration from the Christian humanism of John Colet and Thomas More. But although there was nostalgia for the supposedly palmy days before 1529, many aspects of traditional medieval piety did not reappear. The last edition of the *Legenda Aurea* had been published in 1527, and very few saints were celebrated in print, in spite of official promptings to revive their images and patronal festivals. The whole emphasis of English spirituality had become less ceremonial and more scriptural over the previous twenty years, and although Pole condemned this change, he did not withdraw the Great Bible, and the primers which had replaced the traditional books of hours continued to have the

[41] *Reformatio Angliae ex decretis Reginaldi Poli* (1565) (Bodley MS film 33); J. P. Marmion, 'The London Synod of Cardinal Pole' (MA, Keele, 1974); Loades, *Reign of Mary Tudor*, 346–8.

[42] Fenlon, *Heresy and Obedience in Tridentine Italy*, 116–74.

new scriptural emphasis.[43] The small pieties of obits and lights, the substance of much popular religion, returned with the mass, and a few chantries and colleges were re-established by pious benefactors. However, the Henrician changes had been widely and deeply accepted. Bonner's manual of catholic orthodoxy, *A profitable and necessarye doctryne*, was modelled on *A necessary doctrine and erudition* of 1543, and his homilies on those of Cranmer. The spirituality of 1555 was that of Richard Whitford rather than that of John Myrc – let alone Caesarius of Heisterbach.[44] Significantly, Mary made no attempt at all to revive the great pilgrimage shrines, which had flourished right up to the 1530s. Images of St Thomas of Canterbury reappeared, but the shrine remained desolate, as did Walsingham, Glastonbury and a host of lesser centres. Since the queen never went on pilgrimage herself, her subjects showed no inclination to revive the habit. When she wished to express her gratitude to God for her victories over Northumberland and Wyatt, she gave additional endowments to the universities of Oxford and Cambridge. Mary was not interested in any cult, old or new, except that of the blessed sacrament. Throughout her marriage service, as one observer noted, her eyes never left the host, and it was the strength of this devotion which was largely responsible for her reputation for sanctity, the 'miraculous Mary' of John Procter. It was neither financial constraints nor shortage of time which prevented the queen from re-establishing at least one of the shrines of Our Lady, but lack of inclination.

In other respects her generosity to the church was significant, but not overwhelming. During the discussion of the settlement, in December 1554, she had expressed her intention to discharge her conscience by restoring all ecclesiastical property in the

[43] D. M. Loades, 'The spirituality of the restored catholic church under Mary' (forthcoming). Mary's devotional reading, as revealed by her surviving books in the Royal Library, has been described as 'in the main stream of devout humanism', had also included presentation copies of some works by Philip's theologians Pedro de Soto and Alfonso de Castro. T. A. Birrell, *English Monarchs and their Books from Henry VII to Charles II*, Panizzi Lectures, 1986 (British Library, 1987), 21.

[44] Richard Whitford's *The Werke for Householders* (1535) was a manual of practical piety for the laity. John Myrc's *Libei Festivalis*, which went through a number of editions before 1520 was a liturgical guide for the clergy. Caesarius's *Dialogus Miraculorum* (thirteenth century, printed 1475) saw the direct hand of God in every event, however trivial.

hands of the Crown – and thus also setting an example to her tight-fisted subjects. However, it was not until her fourth parliament, in December 1555, that she managed to secure an Act for the restitution of first fruits and tenths, and she continued to sell former monastic property for her own purposes throughout her reign. Naturally her councillors, and her parliaments, argued strongly against any diminution of the royal revenue – with good reason – but it is hard to avoid the conclusion that Mary placed the re-endowment of the church fairly low in her order of priority.[45] When sixteen former Benedictine monks, under the leadership of John Feckenham, the dean of St Paul's, presented themselves at court in March 1555, and requested permission to return to the regular life, the queen was genuinely delighted, but it took eighteen months to gratify their ambition. There were a number of reasons for this. In the first place the canonical status of the men themselves had to be clarified, particularly after the Bull *Praeclara* finally extinguished the ancient houses in June 1555. More important, Mary wished to use this initiative as the basis for a wider policy of restoration, and set up a commission consisting of Gardiner, Winchester, Rochester and Petre to confer with Pole for that purpose.[46] The result was very disappointing. Between April 1555 and August 1557 six new houses were established, four for men and two for women. But the total number of religious was barely one hundred, and the whole endowment (which came entirely from the Crown) a little over £2000 a year, significantly less than the value of the estates granted to the re-established earldom of Northumberland.[47] The main reason for this seems to have been that the queen would not take any initiative herself, but rather waited for groups of religious to appear, as the Benedictines had, before deciding

[45] Michieli to the doge and senate, 27 October 1555; *Cal.Ven.*, VI, 229. In the short term most of the revenue returned in 1555 was absorbed by the obligation to pay monastic pensions, which was also returned. R. H. Pogson, 'Revival and reform in Mary Tudor's church: a question of money', *Journal of Ecclesiastical History*, XXV, 249–65; Loach, *Parliament and the Crown*, 137–8. The lands and revenues returned by Mary were listed shortly after her death, with a view to their recovery. SP12/1/64. The statement of intention attributed by Foxe to 28 March 1555 was never put into effect. Foxe, *Acts and Monuments*, VII, 34.

[46] Loades, *Reign of Mary Tudor*, 353.

[47] SP12/1/64. See above.

what support to give them. Such groups tended to be small, and ageing, many of them returning from exile abroad, but even so, £180 a year to the Bridgettines of Syon was hardly munificent, nor £133 6s. 8d. to the Franciscan Observants at Greenwich. Only the Benedictine house eventually established at Westminster in November 1556 was a major foundation, with a revenue of £1460.[48] It seems that Mary's enthusiasm for the religious life was distinctly limited, and neither Philip nor Pole did much to help. There was no attempt to introduce any of the new orders from the Continent, and Pole specifically rejected an offer from Ignatius Loyola. He did attempt to bring in two members of the reformed house at Monte Cassino to inject some rigour into Westminster, but they did not come, and there was little vitality in any of the restored communities. Feckenham's regime was sober and dignified, but more like a cathedral chapter than a monastery,[49] and the smaller houses, even the Carthusians, made very little impact. New vocations were few, and in the overall context of the revived catholic church, the regulars failed to make any significant contribution. Whether the queen could have altered that situation by giving a more positive lead must remain a subject for debate.

Mary was to make a number of other benefactions. She restored Manchester College, the hospital of the Savoy, and the guild of St Faiths in London, but it is difficult to discern any selective policy behind her gifts, apart from an enthusiasm for education. Pole was compelled, partly by the situation which he found, and partly by papal policy, to give a high priority to discipline and administration, and the queen seems to have been content to let his legatine mission run its course.[50] Having stated her views and priorities, she does not seem to have made any great effort to impose them. Like Pole, she was much concerned to improve the quality of parochial life, and the decision to build up the cathedrals as spiritual powerhouses, which can be discerned towards the end of the reign, may have been partly hers. Equally positive was the decision to return almost 500 advowsons to

[48] *Cal.Pat.*, III, 354.

[49] M. C. Knowles, *The Religious Orders of England*, III, 431–3; *Memorials of Father Augustine Baker*, ed. J. McCann and R. H. Connolly; Catholic Record Society, XXXIII, 95–6.

[50] Loades, *Reign of Mary Tudor*, 321–55.

episcopal control, which was realized in a number of grants during 1557 and 1558.[51] It is now generally recognized that the catholic restoration was, in some respects, very successful. The number of priestly vocations recovered dramatically, and there is plenty of evidence that former religious habits were re-establishing themselves by 1558. However, the queen's own role in this appears surprisingly passive, considering the strength of her convictions. When she had said in August 1553 that she did not want to constrain men's consciences, she was being a good deal less than honest, but it is probably true that she saw her role as an enabling one – creating the political circumstances in which the proper ecclesiastcal authorities could do the job which God had assigned them. She was more than willing to place the authority of her Crown at the service of the true church, but did not consider it to be any part of her function to interfere in policy decisions, once these had been returned to lawful hands.

During the early spring of 1555, Mary's health, and her approaching confinement, loomed increasingly large upon the political horizon. Early in January she was reported to be nervous and depressed by the possibility that Philip would depart for the Low Countries before their child was born, and Renard took it upon himself to write a solemn admonition to the king upon the subject. By 20 April she had withdrawn from public life and no one was allowed to enter the privy apartments except her women. At that point her delivery was expected by 9 May, and there was a lot of jostling for position as the council tried to neutralize the various threats as they perceived them. Renard believed that some firm pronouncement should be made about the succession, and although he did not like the prospect, advised that Elizabeth should be recognized, in order to minimize the danger of civil strife.[52] This was not done, but a further move by Gardiner to have her excluded was defeated. About the middle of April she was released from house arrest and brought to court – or more accurately, her house arrest was transferred from Woodstock to Hampton Court. Some, both among her enemies and her friends, thought that it would be better if she were out of the country, but a proposal to marry her to the duke of Savoy came to nothing, and she was kept under close surveil-

[51] *Cal.Pat.*, IV, 401, 420, 449, 399, 402, 437, 439, 450.
[52] *Cal.Span.*, XIII, 165–6.

lance instead. Courtenay, another potential troublemaker, was released during Holy Week on the understanding that he should immediately depart abroad, and he set off for the Imperial court at the beginning of May. On 30 April Henry Machyn expressed the nervous tension of the period when he wrote in his diary

> the last day of Aprell tydynges came to London that the Quen grace was delevered of a prynce, and so ther was grett ryngyng thrugh London, and dyvers places Te deum laudamus songe; and the morow after yt was tornyd odurways to the plesur of God. But yt shall be when it plesse God, for I trust God that he wyll remember ys tru servands that putt ther trust in hym.[53]

On 22 May Ruy Gomez confided to Eraso that he could see no signs of an imminent birth. The queen was wandering around the privy garden 'and she steps so well that it seems to me that there is no hope at all for this month.' Her physicians were saying that it could be any day, but Mary herself did not expect to give birth until early June. The tension was not confined to England. Thanks partly to Pole's continued efforts, and partly to Mary's diplomatic intervention at an earlier date, a Franco-Imperial peace conference with English mediation assembled at the village of La Marque between Calais and Gravelines on 23 May. The negotiations quickly got into difficulties, and one of the reasons was Mary's condition. The birth to her of a healthy son would have given the Imperialists an immense advantage; conversely, if mother and child both died, Philip would be left in 'mid-air', for Elizabeth was generally expected to favour France.

At the end of May a series of letter blanks was prepared, announcing the queen's safe delivery to all corners of Europe. On 1 June Mary was reported to be feeling some pain, but not enough to take to her bed, and the physicians were predicting a birth on 6 June. However, 6 June came and went, and the anxiety began to mount. In the queen's chamber a cradle stood ready 'very sumptuously and gorgeously trimmed', and Mary ceased to go out at all. Disconcerting rumours began to spread. The queen was not really pregnant at all, but seriously ill; some said she was already dead. Others believed, or purported to believe, that the whole thing was a fraud in the interest of Philip. Foxe reported that on 11 June a certain Isabel Malt, who had

[53] Machyn, *Diary*, 86. There were several other false alarms.

been safely delivered of a son, was approached by Lord North to part with him in secret.[54] A substitution plot had been spoken of in unsympathetic quarters since March, and Noailles had been told that Mary's condition was merely the result of a tumour. On 3 May, in response to another rumour of a successful delivery, one John Gillam of Hereford was reported to have said, 'Now that there is a prince born, his father will bring into this realm his own nation, and put out the English nation.' This view was shared by the Venetian Giovanni Michieli when he wrote that after the birth King Philip would no longer be an alien in the realm, and that a complete change in his political relationship with the queen and her council was to be looked for.[55] At the same time, a redeployment of Imperial troops in the Netherlands, which was probably occasioned by the forthcoming peace conference, was reported to be a precaution to enable Philip to secure himself and his interests in the event of the queen's death. By the end of May Noailles was again convinced that the pregnancy was false, and that her midwife, not daring to tell her the truth, was deceiving Mary with stories of mistaken calculations from day to day. She was alleged to be spending long hours sitting on the floor of her chamber, in such a position that she could not possibly be carrying a child.[56] Nevertheless Renard, in spite of his anxiety, continued to be resolutely optimistic. While admitting that everything depended on the queen's safe delivery, he believed the stories of inaccurate prognosis, and reported as late as 29 June that the queen was as well as she had ever been during his stay. She was undoubtedly with child. He was mistaken, and early in July, without any explicit statement, the trappings of confinement began to be removed. By 10 July she was again conducting business, and getting some much needed fresh air after spending over two months in the same stuffy and insanitary palace, while the weather got steadily warmer.

July 1555 must have been a strange and difficult month for those close to the queen. Whatever her attendants may have

[54] Foxe, *Acts and Monuments*, VII, 126; 'concerning the childbed of Queen Mary, as it was rumoured among the people', which also prints the texts of several prayers issued at this time for the queen's safe delivery.

[55] *Cal. Ven.*, VI, 107.

[56] Vertot, *Ambassades*, VI, 89; Noailles, Avis, 29 May 1555; Prescott, *Mary Tudor*, 308.

thought, and in spite of resuming many of her normal activities, Mary clung to her hope with an obstinacy that was as pathetic as it was unreasonable. In the middle of the month she wrote to Sir John Mason, her ambassador in Brussels, instructing him to deny reports that she was not with child, although some of her own councillors also wrote privately, dissociating themselves from her opinon.[57] Not only did she desperately want a child, for both personal and political reasons, but she was also well aware that Philip was waiting only for her condition to be resolved before departing to the Netherlands. As late as 25 July her physicians, and some of her women, were keeping up the pretence, although it was becoming an increasingly dangerous farce, and reflects no credit upon either their professional competence or their moral courage. At some point between then and 4 August the symptoms of pregnancy must have diminished to the point at which even Mary became convinced that she had been deceived. Nothing was said in public, and of her private anguish the merest glimpse has remained on record, as she confided to Frideswide Strelly her anger at the flattery and lies by which she had been surrounded.[58] Understandable as it was, such a comment was hardly fair, because her self-deception had been the most determined, and it had been virtually treasonable to share the doubts which were being openly expressed by heretical writers and French agents. There was still no official pronouncement, but on 4 August the court moved to Oatlands, a much smaller residence than Hampton Court, and the large retinue of rockers and other occasional nursery staff were dismissed. Whether Mary's own intense desires had created a phantom pregnancy, or whether it was a symptom of some major physical disorder, is not clear. There were rumours of her having been delivered of 'a shapeless mass of flesh', but these were probably put about by enemies who wished to demonstrate that she was under the curse of God for persecuting His saints. Given her medical history, a cyst or tumour, as suspected by Noailles, is a possible explanation, and might help to account for the further delusions which she was to suffer in the last year of her life.

[57] Badoer to the doge and senate, 21 July 1555; *Cal. Ven.*, VI, 138–9.
[58] BL Sloane MS 1583 f.15; J. M. Stone, *Mary I, Queen of England*, 351.

The realization of her failure was bitter, because although Mary herself still trusted in God to heed her prayers for a child, she knew perfectly well that neither her subjects, nor her friends, nor her husband expected those prayers to be answered. She was now thirty-nine, and in a state of physical and emotional collapse. The long-term credibility of what she had achieved since the summer of 1553 was in serious doubt. And in an age which saw the fortunes of childbirth, like the fortunes of war, as a barometer of divine approval, her standing with the Almighty had been called in question. Whether to hide his chagrin, or merely to escape from an atmosphere of hysterical despondency, on 8 August Philip went off to Windsor for a few days on his own, and on the 26th he departed for the Low Countries. Mary accompanied him as far as Greenwich, riding through London in a litter, to the delight and relief of the majority of the citizens who had feared that she was on her death-bed.[59] Philip had done reasonably well in England and it was not his fault that Mary had failed to give him another heir. He had made little impact on the internal affairs of the country, partly out of indifference and partly for lack of opportunity, but in the last days before his departure he had finally reorganized the council in an attempt to reduce its clumsiness and division.[60] He had pardoned and reconciled many former opponents of the regime, and he had paid his pensioners regularly and in full. There were members of the council who were principally his men, particularly Paget and Pembroke, and his presence, if not his active intervention, had done much to calm the feuds which had disturbed the first year of Mary's reign. Jousts and tournaments of a traditional kind had improved his relations with the English aristocracy at large, and he had enlivened the court with the masques and revels necessary to its prestige and appeal.[61] Above all, he had maintained a very convincing show of affection and support for the queen, which cannot have been easy, because, as one of her earlier biographers had observed, she was neither attractive nor

[59] *Cal. Ven.*, VI, 200, 204; Machyn, *Diary*, 93.

[60] Loades, 'Philip II and the government of England' in *Law and Government under the Tudors*, 190.

[61] Anglo, *Spectacle, Pageantry and Early Tudor Policy*, 339–43; R. C. McCoy, 'From the Tower to the tiltyard: Robert Dudley's return to glory', *Historical Journal*, XXVII, 425. See also below.

frigid.[62] They did not always agree on policy issues, but she deferred to his judgement more often than not, and the strength of her affection for him was the talk of every court in Europe. There is no doubt that by August 1555 he was extremely anxious to escape from the demands of a difficult and taxing situation in England for which the sacrifices suddenly seemed no longer worthwhile. Aware of Mary's fragile emotional state, he spoke soothingly of an absence of a few weeks, and left most of his household behind, but many suspected that his return would be long delayed – if it ever took place at all.

The failure of Mary's pregnancy had not been the only setback to Habsburg plans in the summer of 1555. Pope Julius III, whose relations with the emperor had been consistently good, had died in March, at a time when the French and Imperial factions in the *Curia* had been finely balanced. Pole, who like Del Monte, had been one of the three legates at the opening of the Council of Trent, was expected by many to succeed him. However, the cardinal of England was not really interested, and Charles was unenthusiastic after experiencing what he considered to be Pole's indiscreet zeal over the English mission. As a result Marcello Cervini was elected in April as Marcellus II. Cervni had been the third of the Tridentine legates, and like Pole and Del Monte, stood broadly in the humanist tradition of the *spirituali*. Both Pole and the emperor welcomed his election, and he immediately renewed the former's powers in England. However, he died after only three weeks in office, and in the unexpected conclave which followed Imperial policy collapsed in disarray. Philip had already made it very clear to Manrique de Lara that he considered 'the Theatine Cardinal' (Gian Pietro Carafa) to be totally unacceptable, but unfortunately he had not expressed positive support for any alternative.[63] Carafa was a Neapolitan, an extreme zealot who had re-established the Roman Inquisition at his own personal expense, and a fanatical hater of all things Spanish. De Lara was quite clear that the best way to keep Carafa out would be to support Pole, but neither Charles nor Philip was willing to do so, and he narrowly failed to obtain a majority on the first vote. His friend and fellow moderate Giovanni Morone similarly failed on

[62] Prescott, *Mary Tudor*, 312–13.
[63] *Cal.Span.*, XIII, 155; Loades, *Reign of Mary Tudor*, 231–2.

the second vote; at which point the Imperial party broke ranks, and Carafa was elected. This was bad enough in itself, but the new pope very rapidly discovered the nature of Philip's instructions, and all the diplomatic advantages which the king had gained from the reconciliation of England disappeared in a matter of hours. By the beginning of June the reports from both Rome and England were so encouraging to them that the French delegation was recalled from La Marque, and the negotiations collapsed. Charles was a sick and disappointed man, and the time had come to start laying down his responsibilities. Already his brother Ferdinand was conducting with the Lutheran princes those negotiations which he knew to be necessary, but which revolted his catholic conscience. On 25 September the signing of the religious peace at Augsburg was to mark the effective end of his thirty-six-year reign. When Philip arrived in Brussels on 8 September, the first task which confronted them both was the transfer of power in the Low Countries.

The king's departure from England was far less momentous for the realm than it was for the queen. Mary, who had by no means recovered from the trauma of the summer, was weak and depressed. She consoled herself by writing constant messages of affectionate enquiry and small news, while immersing herself in business to an extent which Pole considered to be yet more damaging to her health. Michieli's prediction that all business would cease with the king's departure was true only of those international affairs which had always been Philip's main preoccupation. Just after the middle of September Renard also departed, having originally been given leave to withdraw in March.[64] As the emperor was handing over his powers, and the king had his own means of keeping in touch with English affairs, there was no longer a role for him, and he was not replaced. Cardinal Pole was now Mary's comforter and closest confidant. For some time after the end of August he lived at court, but he was not a member of the council, and played no part in the regular processes of secular government. The so-called 'council of state' which Philip had set up in August, consisting of Gardiner, Thirlby, Paget, Arundel, Pembroke, Winchester,

[64] Pole to Philip, 5 October 1555; *Cal. Ven.*, VI, 205–6. Soranzo had observed in August 1554 that she rose at dawn, ate nothing until past noon, and transacted business until after midnight; *Cal. Ven.*, V, 532–3. *Cal. Span.*, XIII, 247.

Rochester and Petre, seems to have existed mainly for the king's benefit. It sent him regular memoranda in Latin about English affairs, and consulted him on a variety of issues, but left no mark upon the normal records of administration, which were entirely unaffected by the king's absence. Although Michieli reported great uncertainty about Philip's intentions, officially he was expected to return for the parliament which was due to meet on 21 October, and in the preparation for which he had shown unexpected interest. He did not come, because of the extraordinary complexities which accompanied his father's hand-over of power, but instead wrote an apologetic letter to the council, pleading pressure of other business, and urging them to their accustomed loyalty and diligence.[65] By the end of September the members of the king's English chamber, who had accompanied him to Brussels, were anxious to return home, having no function to perform. They had witnessed the solemn transfer of authority in the Netherlands from Charles to Philip on 25 September, which was probably the main reason for their presence, and were allowed to leave in ones and twos over the next month. At the same time, Philip's Spanish household also began to leave England. Those who remained moved from Hampton Court to Whitehall at the end of October, under the leadership of Don Diego de Acevedo, and awaited the king's orders. In early December they were instructed to join him in the Low Countries, and set off on the 20th. Philip's confessor, Alfonso de Castro, had preceded them, and a report written on 18 December by the Venetian ambassador in Brussels, Federico Badoer, reflects the conflicting emotions of the moment:

> The king's confessor . . . has repeated a variety of foul language uttered by the English, indicating their illwill towards his Majesty and the Spanish nation [and says] that on seeing him and the rest of the royal attendants depart, they made great rejoicing well-nigh universally; and he [also says] that the queen's wish again to see the king is very great, nay boundless.[66]

[65] PRO SP11/6/28. 15 October. There is some doubt about whether this letter was ever received, as it does not feature in the records of either House.

[66] *Cal. Ven.*, VI, 285. De Castro had earned himself a minor niche in English history by preaching in February 1555 against the burning of heretics, presumably on Philip's orders, since this does not correspond with what is known of his views. Foxe, *Acts and Monuments*, VI, 704.

De Castro himself had orders to proceed to Spain, and this had caused her additional anguish, as she understood it to indicate that the king would not return to England for a long time.

The withdrawal of virtually the entire Spanish presence between the end of August and Christmas relieved the English council of a major problem. Although tension between the nations had fluctuated from month to month, it had never been entirely absent. Within a month of the king's arrival there had been 'knife work in the court', as one Spaniard reported, and both sides were appealing to the lord steward and the *alcalde* – Philip's judicial officer. Thereafter there had been a steady stream of incidents. Machyn records a number of instances of Englishmen being hanged for robbing or murdering Spaniards, and some of Spaniards suffering the same fate for killing Englishmen.[67] There were also a number of pardons for similar offences. In September 1554 there had been a brawl near the court in which several lives were lost, and in October a rumour (probably spread by the French) that Philip intended to seize the Tower to London had caused panic in the city. At the end of May 1555 another major brawl took place, involving 'upwards of 500' men and five or six deaths, while on Corpus Christi (13 June) a mob had attacked the church in which a number of Spaniards were worshipping, and had only been placated with great difficulty.[68] According to Michieli the English were nearly always the aggressors, and nearly always got the worst of the exchange – an outcome which may have had something to do with the fact that the Spaniards understandably went about armed. Philip was angered, and Mary both angered and distressed by these incidents. The council seems to have done its best, but the co-operation of the mayor and aldermen of London was not quite wholehearted, and in the absence of a police force such expressions of popular feeling very easily got out of control. To that extent, Philip's departure was a disappointment to his enemies for, as one of them later confessed, it was much less easy to provoke a demonstration by crying 'no Spaniards' when they

[67] Machyn, *Diary*, 69, 72, 79 etc. Loades, *Reign of Mary Tudor*, 215–16.

[68] *Cal.Ven.*, VI, 85, 126; 27 May and 1 July 1555. 'It is a cause of great sorrow to the Queen if they maltreat a Spaniard, greater than if she herself had to suffer', wrote Juan de Barraona, one of Philip's gentlemen. C. V. Malfatti, ed., *Four Manuscripts of the Escorial*, 92–3.

were not around to assaulted.[69] Anti-Spanish invective in print was less affected by this absence, and a number of extremely virulent attacks maintained the momentum through 1555 and 1556, sustained principally by the fear that Philip had designs on the English succession in the event of Mary's death. Some of these were clearly protestant works, such as *A supplicacyon to the quenes maiestie* and *A shorte treatise of politike power*, which lamented the state of English religion under the heel of Antichrist. Others, however, scarcely mentioned religion, including those most abusive to Philip personally. *A warnyng for Englande* concentrated upon 'the plague that shall light upon the English nobility yf the Kyng of Spayn obtaine the dominion of Englande', while Bradford's *Copye of a letter* mocked the queen's physical unattractiveness by referring to Philip's exploits with 'bakers daughters and other poor whores' in Antwerp, and accused her of trying to tempt him back with political favours.[70]

The issue which particularly concerned these pamphleteers was the question of the king's coronation. The coronation of a consort was normally at the discretion of the sovereign, and was a question of favour and circumstance. Of Henry VIII's six queens, only the first two had been crowned. But a male consort was a different proposition. Philip held the crown matrimonial, the powers of which were defined by the marriage treaty. Coronation was not mentioned in the treaty, and nobody really knew whether it would make any difference or not. Renard wavered between believing that it was a mere matter of courtesy, and the conviction that it would make a substantial difference to Philip's authority. As long as there was a prospect of issue, and the king's regency rights were acknowledged, a coronation was a matter of secondary importance, but after the failure of Mary's 'pregnancy', it became the only possible route whereby Philip might stake his own claim to the kingdom. He had tentatively explored the situation during the third parliament, but found

[69] Loades, *Reign of Mary Tudor*, 238. During the last critical period of Mary's supposed confinement policing of a kind was provided by the retainers of those nobles who were thought to be particularly loyal. *Cal.Ven.*, VI, 57. These were probably the 'troops' also referred to as standing by in case of trouble.

[70] *STC* 3480. 'Will ye crowne the king to make him live chast with his wife contrary to his nature ...' There were about a dozen of these personal attacks. See S. R. Maitland, *Essays on the Reformation* (1898), chs 7, 8.

that his interest aroused immediate suspicion, and also fear that it was another device for dragging England into the Franco-Habsburg war. At that point the matter was not pressed, but after his return to the Low Countries, the king seems to have renewed his efforts in a more determined way. The evidence for this pressure comes mostly from the reports of Federico Badoer, and needs to be treated with a certain caution, but it it consistent both with Philip's known ambition, and also with the frequently expressed fears of the English. On 13 October Badoer wrote that the king of England had informed his wife that he was most anxious to gratify her wish for his return, but that he could not do so without being given an honourable share in the government of the realm.[71] On the 27th he reported Mary's response; that the parliament was full of violent opposition, and that she had hesitated to propose his coronation, preferring to effect it after the parliament, with the aid of a select group of peers and others. He had apparently replied by advising her not to take any risks. At the end of December no progress had been made on any front, and Mary had sent a special message 'apologising for her non-adoption of any of the resolutions desired by him in the matter of the coronation, or with regard to waging war on the Most Christian King [of France]'.[72] She was, she declared, surounded by enemies, and knew it would be impossible to resolve either of these important matters without greatly endangering her Crown. She begged him to return, and the emperor had seconded her plea, but Badoer had heard that he was not inclined to oblige, and was feeding her with empty hopes.

If Badoer was accurately informed, this was a curious exchange. Parliament had no right to be consulted over a coronation, and the Venetian's words may indicate no more than a general anxiety on Mary's part. At the same time, the hint of hysterical exaggeration has an authentic ring. Philip was using his emotional hold over the queen, and her desire for his return, in an endeavour to force her to abandon some, at least, of the restrictive clauses of the marriage treaty. She, on the other hand, could not afford to breach the treaty openly by giving him the kind of powers which he sought. A coronation, effected by her simple prerogative, might have seemed an obvious compromise;

[71] *Cal. Ven.*, VI, 212.
[72] Ibid., 227, 299–300.

but it did not happen, in spite of the fact that Philip kept up his pressure until April. The problem is rather like that of the non-existent patrimony: however unpopular it might have been, such a move would have been within the terms of the treaty by which the English parliament set such store. But that did not happen either; nor did Mary pay any attention to Philip's two nominations – Paget and Wotton – for the vacant chancellorship. It is hard to avoid the conclusion that, genuinely as the queen wanted her husband back, she wanted him on her own terms. He, having let his conditions be known, could not afford to return without loss of face, unless either the circumstances changed, or his need of her help became imperative. Popular opposition to Philip's coronation in England was certainly real, and was one of the main reasons behind the so-called 'Dudley conspiracy' which was to be unearthed in the spring of 1556, but it was no stronger than the original opposition to the marriage, which Mary had successfully defied. Perhaps, with her health and morale weakened by the events of the summer, Mary was no longer in control of herself or the political situation by the end of 1555. Or perhaps she was not really anxious to involve Philip in the government of England on equal terms, but was too emotionally dependent to be honest about it.

Pole seems to have done his best to protect the queen from additional stress during the latter part of the year, but it was no easy task. The parliament which met from October to December was a particularly difficult one. The commons argued fiercely about church revenues, about the subsidy (the first one to be asked for in the reign) and about religious exiles. In the end they did the council's bidding on each of these issues except the last, but succeeded in making a very disaffected impression upon outside observers, particularly the Italians and the Fench.[73] The main reason seems to have been not the uniquely unruly composition of the House, nor even the unusually controversial nature of the agenda, but the collapse of council management following the death of Gardiner in November. The chancellor had been an awkward and cantankerous servant (as Henry VIII had found him), but he had been loyal and extremely skilful, and he was not adequately replaced. For two months the Great Seal

[73] Loach, *Parliament and the Crown*, 128–58; *TTC*, 180–6; Harbison, *Rival Ambassadors*, 273–9.

was in commission, and on 1 January Nicholas Heath was appointed to the vacant post. If the death of Gardiner was a political loss, and noticed rather than felt, another and more personal loss for Mary was in prospect. By the time Charles V handed over the Netherlands to his son he was a very sick and tired man, and there was much talk of his imminent departure to retirement in Spain. In October a fleet of English ships was prepared to escort him down the Channel, and there was speculation about whether he would land briefly in England to bid his cousin farewell. In the event, his departure was delayed for almost a year, which may have been the lethargy of a sick man, or possibly his final unease about the arrangements which he was making. He had been expected to surrender Spain and Sicily to Philip, and the Empire to Ferdinand almost immediately. But a quarrel with his brother over the Imperial vicariate of Milan, which he was determined to bestow upon Philip, postponed that hand-over indefinitely. At the same time, as the transfer of Spain hung fire, there were rumours of similar disagreements with his son. These were, or were reported to be, personal rather than political. Philip was alleged to be out of favour, because he was altogether too fond of masquing and amusements.[74] The stories were circumstantial, but numerous. A certain Madame d'Aler was referred to, and on 18 December Badoer reported that the king had masked and gone 'to his usual revels'. His lifestyle was being carefully concealed from Mary, because she was nervous and easily distressed. In all probability Philip, who was only 28, considered himself to have had a very dull and frustrating time in England, and his relaxation was embroidered by malicious gossip. Whatever the English pamphleteers may have thought, he was never given to promiscuity, and there may well have been other reasons for Charles's hesitation. The transfer eventually took place in early January 1556, and Philip promptly began a dispute with the English council about the priority of his titles. The king now had not merely another realm to care for, but a vast empire as well, and the chances of his returning to England receded still further into the distance.

The harvest of 1554 had been poor, and that of 1555 worse, so that by the New Year there was dearth, and a risk of famine. When parliament closed on 9 December Sir Anthony Kingston,

[74] *Cal. Ven.*, VI, 271–2, 277–8.

who had been responsible for securing the defeat of the council's measure against religious exiles, was committed to the Tower for two weeks, and Noailles reported that Mary was visibly angry and frustrated.[75] It was widely believed that the queen had intended to use this session to make Philip's kingship a reality, and that she had been unable to do so. This was probably a misunderstanding, but it contributed to a growing impression outside England that Mary was not really in command of her realm. English prestige also suffered a substantial blow when the truce of Vaucelles between France and the Habsburgs was concluded on 6 February, without either the participation or knowledge of the English council. In view of the mediating role which Mary and Pole had attempted to undertake at La Marque, Charles had been in favour of involving them again, but neither Henry nor Philip agreed. The English were not belligerents, and therefore had no right to take part except as mediators – a role in which they had previously failed. It is not surprising that Henry was unwilling to accept Mary as impartial, and Philip was still annoyed by her failure to mobilize England in his support. So the queen's reputation was slighted. There was a bitter reaction at the English court, and even Mary was resentful.[76] Although it seems clear that it had been the French who had been mainly responsible for the form of the negotiations, the English, significantly, blamed Philip, and to a lesser extent Pole. At the end of January there were rumours that the king would return and that Spaniards were coming in again at every tide. Whoever these may have been, they were not Philip's harbingers, and he made no attempt to come and soothe his wife's ruffled dignity.

Mary's fortunes were very low in the early part of 1556. At the beginning of March a widely ramifying conspiracy was discovered, involving a plot to rob the Exchequer and to invade England with an army of mercenaries and exiles from France. The motivation was mainly hatred of the Spanish connection, and the object to depose May in favour of Elizabeth.[77] The

[75] *APC*, V, 202–3; Vertot, *Ambassades*, V, 205. *TTC*, 185–6.

[76] Loades, *Reign of Mary Tudor*, 235–6; part of the difficulty was caused by the fact that Charles had wanted the English to be involved, and his joint declaration with Philip on 27 December had called upon the queen and the legate to take the matter in hand. *Cal.Span.*, XIII, 255.

[77] *TTC*, 176–217.

substance of the plot was an intrigue conducted in France by Henry Dudley, the same man who had carried Northumberland's plea for assistance in July 1553. Before Christmas he had been warmly received at the French court, but after the truce of Vaucelles Henry became less enthusiastic about such adventures, and Dudley was dismissed with empty promises. It was this rebuff which forced the conspirators to fall back on their contingency plan to rob the Exchequer, which in turn led to their discovery. As the arrests and interrogations went on through March and April, the council became increasingly alarmed. Small fry like John Danyell and Thomas White led on to slightly larger fish, such as Richard Uvedale, the captain of the Isle of White, and John Throgmorton. A number of substantial gentry were arrested – Sir Nicholas Arnold, Sir Anthony Kingston, Sir William Courtenay and Sir John Pollard. There were rumours that some members of the council were implicated, and several of Elizabeth's servants were questioned. Eventually thirty-five men and one woman were indicted, and ten were executed.[78] That this somewhat shadowy conspiracy claimed far more victims than Northumberland's attempt to divert the succession is a measure of the extent to which 'mercifull Marye' – so praised throughout the first year of her reign – had become disillusioned with the practice of clemency. Antoine de Noailles was finally expelled as *persona non grata*, and according to one report was lucky not to find himself in the Tower.

How serious a threat the Dudley conspiracy presented is arguable. What is clear is that it gave the government an appearance of instability. Michieli was probably correct when he observed that, although there was much discontent, the people chiefly responsible were 'private gentlemen', the nobility and 'principal personages' being loyal.[79] However, this was not much comfort to those who remembered that the 'principal personages' had also appeared to be loyal to Queen Jane. It was for that reason that Continental observers tended to overemphasize the extent of the disaffection in England, and their opinions are disproportionately represented in the surviving evidence. There was probably little chance that Dudley's invasion, had it materialized, would have triggered a major

[78] Ibid., appendix IV.
[79] *Cal. Ven.*, VI, 283.

insurrection. When Thomas Stafford tried a similar attack just over a year later, he was defeated without difficultly by local forces. But the numerous alarms, of which this was the most serious, depressed the queen and sapped the morale of the regime. While Dudley's accomplices were falling over each other to confess, Mary made another attempt to persuade Philip to return. In the middle of March Sir John Mason, acting on the queen's instructions, asked whether she should maintain the fleet which was standing by to escort him, and added that she needed the comfort of his presence; nor should the king yet despair of having heirs.[80] Philip made further excuses, and bland professions of affection, but his Spanish courtiers were franker. They could see no reason why he should gratify a wife who had done nothing to gratify him, and expend money and effort for nothing. In early April she tried again, her envoy on this occasion being no less a person than Lord Paget. Paget's instructions were to represent the urgent needs of the kingdom. Badoer, who reported his mission, believed that he had been chosen because he was in favour with Philip, and did not need to mince his words. He also understood that Mary's patience had been wellnigh exhausted by the contemptuous treatment to which she had been subjected by her consort.[81] At least some of his entourage could see the point, and urged him not to turn her angry remonstrances into hatred. Either Philip had complete confidence in his power over Mary, or he was becoming indifferent to her and her kingdom, because he did not return, and his political credit among the English nobility began to ebb away.

As she had done so often in the past when her mind was troubled, Mary turned for the last time to the emperor. In April she wrote

> I thank you humbly for remembering me where the return of the king my husband is concerned, as I have seen not only from your letters, but also by the messages brought by Lord Fitzwalter . . . I implore your Majesty most humbly for the love of God, to do all that is possible to permit it. I see every day the end of one negotiation and the beginning of

[80] Ibid., 376. In this connection the queen's age was delicately adduced as another reason for haste.

[81] Ibid., 401–2. Mary was, he understood, 'beyond measure exasperated' by Philip's treatment.

> another. I beg your Majesty to forgive my boldness, and to remember the unspeakable sadness which I experience because of the absence of the king, which emboldens me thus to write to you, who have always shown me a more than paternal affection.[82]

The following month she wrote again, in a similar vein, following a visit to Brussels by Sire Henry Jerningham, and in July was driven to reproach: 'as your Majesty has been pleased to break your promise in this connection . . . I must perforce be satisfied, although to my unspeakable regret.' These are the letters of an emotionally dependent woman to a respected older relation, not those of one sovereign to another, and indicate something of the tension between the private and the political person which Mary was never able to resolve. It was not Charles's fault that the queen remained unsatisfied. By this time he had relinquished most of his responsibilities, and had neither the will nor the authority to order the actions of his son. How much persuasion he tried is not clear, but with the hand-over of power in the Netherlands safely accomplished, and the virtual certainty that Mary would bear no children, his efforts would have been more out of personal affection that political interest, and probably carried little weight. The French believed that Mary's distress would lead to a breakdown of relations between husband and wide, and retailed stories that she had gone around the privy apartments defacing portraits of Philip.[83] If the report of this very understandable reaction was authentic, the mood did not last, and on 10 September she wrote again, in a rather different vein professing that her main concern was not for her own personal satisfaction, but for the good of her kingdom. Unless Philip returned great danger would ensue for lack of his firm hand. This plea does not seem to have been prompted by any particular crisis in English affairs, and may have been no more than an attempt to shift the pressure point. If the king ever heard of it, it must have struck him as ironic that, having failed to provide him with an effective role when he was present, Mary was now claiming that his participation in government was essential for the security of the realm[84] It is unlikely that the

[82] *Cal.Span.*, XIII, 260; ibid., 271.

[83] Giacomo Soranzo, ambassador in France, to the doge and senate, 14 April 1556; *Cal.Ven.*, VI, 410.

[84] *Cal.Span.*, XIII, 276.

emperor ever received this letter, because he had sailed from Flushing for Spain on 17 September, and a relationship which the queen had enjoyed for as long as she could remember, effectively came to an end.

French and Italian reports from the summer of 1556 cast a very gloomy light on English affairs, and particularly upon Mary's state of mind. She was alleged to be living in fear of assassination, her palace filled with armed men, and only five women sufficiently trusted to 'keep the queen's chamber'.[85] Gilles de Noailles, who had replaced his expelled elder brother in the French embassy, declared that she was looking ten years older, and heard on good authority that she was sleeping very badly, spending her time in 'tears, regrets, and writing letters to bring back her husband'. The Dudley conspiracy seems particularly to have unnerved her. She 'rages against her subjects, for she is utterly confounded by the faithlessness of those whom she most trusted, seeing that the greater part of these miserable creatures [the conspirators] are kith and kin or favoured servants of the greatest men of the kingdom, even of Lords of the Council'.[86] In consequence, she was trusting nobody but Hastings and Montague, who were inadequate support in such a dangerous situation. Noailles was hearing what he wanted to hear, and his stories need not be taken at face value. Anti-Spanish and anti-catholic propaganda continued to appear in London, and no doubt Mary was much angered by John Bradford's shrewd and malicious gibes, if she ever read them. More substantial, and much more representative, was the same author's concern that Philip and Mary were planning to divert the succession from Elizabeth.[87] The queen must have been uneasily aware that her sister was enjoying the same kind of popular support that she herself had enjoyed when she had represented an 'opposition' policy during her brother's reign. There was a good deal of disaffection, and much of it focused on Elizabeth. After Dudley came the minor conspiracy of Cleobury,

[85] Vertot, *Ambassades*, v, 361–3.

[86] Ibid.; Prescott, *Mary Tudor*, 344.

[87] 'if ever the king should have a just title to the crown, and obteine it, he would knocke that most vertuous Ladi Elizabeth's Grace sure ... either banished the land or els put to deth miserably.' Like Northumberland, he claimed, Mary was trying to divert the succession from the rightful heir.

the Suffolk schoolmaster, demonstrations against the religious persecution, and a large number of individual cases of seditious words.[88] On the other hand, none of these incidents presented a serious threat, even to public order, let alone to the security of the Crown. Cleobury and his accomplices were apprehended by the local people 'wt oute any commandment', and the records of the English council and court give no hint that the situation was out of control in the way which the French seem to have hoped.

The truth appears to have been that during the summer, and particularly during July and August, Mary was in a condition bordering upon hysterical collapse, and greatly exaggerated the challenge which she was facing. The French, who were looking for any opportunity to prise apart the Anglo-Habsburg alliance, were doing their best to make her situation as difficult as possible, and added further exaggerations of their own. Noailles, for example, received and passed on rumours that Philip was negotiating with the pope to get his marriage dissolved.[89] There was no truth in such reports, but they were well calculated to disturb the queen's mental balance still further if they reached her. That there was a 'siege mentality' at court in this period is confirmed by a curious entry in the council register for 6 August:

> This daye my Lordes of the Counsaill, upon consideration of the state of thinges at this tyme, resoved for the preventing of all inconveniences that might happen, and savegarde of the king and queenes majesties' persones if nede shulde require, that Mr. Controller, in thabsence of the Lord Stewrde, and Mr. Treasourer and Mr. Vicechamberlain in thabsence of the Lorde Chamberlayne, shuld tomorrowe in the morning call bifore them thofficers of the Howsehold and the Yeomen of the Garde, and other their majesties ordinary servantes under their charges, and to enquire what armure and weapon eche of them hathe.[90]

The said servants were then to be instructed to prepare such armour and weapons, each in accordance with his degree, as should be prescribed for them by Michaelmas at the latest. Such a mobilization was not a routine muster, and would normally

[88] Cleobury issued a bogus proclamation at Yaxley in Suffolk, declaring that Mary was dead, and 'ye Ladye Elizabeth Queene'; *APC*, v, 316, 29 July 1556; Strype, *Ecclesiastical Memorials*, III, 336. Loades, *Reign of Mary Tudor*, 281–2.

[89] Vertot, *Ambassades*, v, 361–3; *Cal.Ven.*, VI, 410.

[90] *APC*, v, 320.

have occurred only when the monarch intended to go to war in person. So someone expected either an assassination attempt or serious disorders in the immediate vicinity of London. The harvest of 1556 was the third failure in a row – one of the worst sequences in the century – with resulting dearth and hardship, but even with such promising material to the hand of the agitator, there was no violence of any significance. The root of this panic, like the root of the French reports, probably lay more in the queen's state of mind than in any objective need for such precautions.

By October Mary had to some extent recovered. On the 19th Michieli reported her to be overjoyed because Philip had given orders to some of his household to proceed to England, and had renewed his long-standing promises. Unfortunately for her, the reasons behind this apparent change of heart had nothing to do with Mary. The king had spent quite a lot of time and energy during the summer defending the commercial interests of his Flemish subjects, his Portuguese friends, and even the Hanseatic league, against English encroachments. He had accused the Merchant Adventurers of being in league with heretical conspirators, and his relations, both with the English council and the city of London, were worse than at any time since the marriage.[91] On the other hand, his need of English support and assistance was becoming desperate, and some attempt to repair his neglected political position in the island had to be made. The main reason for this urgency went back to the disastrous papal conclave of May 1555. Contrary to what some had expected, Paul IV had at first behaved sensibly, even amiably, towards England. He had confirmed Pole's legateship, exempted the country from the rigorous terms of the Bull *Rescissio Alienationum*, and waived the customary annates for the confirmation of episcopal appointments;[92] all necessary measures of assistance for the newly re-established church. On the other hand, his political relations with Philip had followed the predictable course, through tension to hostility. By the autumn of 1555 Pole had already been worried that reports of ill will between the king and the pope were encouraging the English malcontents, and his

[91] *Cal. Ven.*, vi, 718; BL Lansdowne MS 170 f.129; Loades, *Reign of Mary Tudor*, 238–9.

[92] Loades, *Reign of Mary Tudor*, 349.

anxiety was increased when Paul warned him somewhat pointedly about getting involved in secular affairs. In early December the eventual papal sentence against Thomas Cranmer left the archepiscopal see of Canterbury vacant, and Pole was nominated by the pope himself, with many gracious words on his worthiness. However, about a week later Paul had entered into a secret treaty with the king of France, and there was talk of an attack upon the kingdom of Naples.[93]

Nothing so dramatic occurred, and indeed the truce of Vaucelles followed a few weeks later, but the underlying tension continued as Paul harried known Imperial supporters within the *Curia*, and promoted his objectionable nephew, Carlo Carafa. After Cranmer's execution on 21 March 1556, Pole was duly installed as archbishop, but as if to reinforce his point about secular and spiritual functions, on 10 April the pope named two new legates to negotiate a Franco-Habsburg peace, thus superseding Pole in one of his previous functions. As both the emissaries he appointed were known to be pro-French, the cause of peace was not served and Habsburg-Papal relations continued to deteriorate. By the end of July the situation had become so bad that Simon Renard (by this time ambassador in France) drew up a list of Imperial grievances, including the charge that the Vicar of Christ had mobilized 10,000 men, and was threatening to kill all the Spaniards he could catch.[94] Far from making peace, Paul was doing his best to disrupt the truce which already existed, and to provoke Philip into open war. At the end of June Pole, who could see himself becoming stranded between two hostile powers, begged the king, for the good of Christendom, to find some other manner of expressing his indignation. But by this time the pope's behaviour had become, from the Habsburg point of view, outrageous and unacceptable, and on 6 September the duke of Alba invaded the Papal States from Naples, on the king's orders. Neither Mary nor her kingdom were parties to this dispute, but its effects were quickly felt, not only in Philip's renewed interest, but also in a virtual breakdown of communi-

[93] Cardinal of Siguenza to the emperor, 23 December 1556; *Cal.Span.*, XIII, 253–4; Bernado Navagero to the doge and senate, 20 December 1556; *Cal.Ven.*, VI, 290–1. Loades, *Reign of Mary Tudor*, 349–50.

[94] *Cal.Span.*, XIII, 272–4. For a discussion of the situation in Italy, see Rodríguez Salgado, *The Changing Face of Empire*, 151–4.

cations with Rome. Pole sought in vain for guidance as to how he should conduct himself, and was eventually informed in December by his old friend Giovanni Morone, the vice-protector of England, that the pope was refusing to dispatch English business on the grounds that Mary was as much an offender as her husband, and both were worthy of ecclesiastical censures.[95] The queen seems to have taken this disaster much more philosophically than Pole, perhaps because it removed any inhibition which she might have felt about co-operating with Philip to the best of her ability. Everyone believed that it was only a matter of time before the French intervened on the papal side, and Anglo-French relations reached a new low point in November when Henry Dudley was again discovered to have been conspiring with French assistance. This time he was exploiting his contacts among the English garrisons of the Calais Pale, and with the sizeable protestant population of Calais itself, in an endeavour to negotiate the surrender of those fortresses to France.[96] At the beginning of December the earl of Pembroke was sent across with reinforcements 'to secure the Pale', a move which the French chose to regard as provocative. At the same time a boundary dispute over St Englevert, on the fringes of the Pale, further increased tension and Michieli wrote that, in the event of any French attack upon the Low Countries, the queen would honour her father's treaties with the emperor.[97] Although Philip had still not visited England by the end of the year, his absence was no longer a source of indignation. The secret couriers were passing between them almost daily, and a fair number of his Spanish servants had quietly returned. By Christmas his English household was on standby, and there was no longer any reasonable doubt that he would come in the near future. Consequently, when the court moved from St James to Greenwich on 22 December to keep the festival, it was with a better prospect of good cheer than had seemed possible three months before.

There is little in the Revels or the household accounts to suggest an unusually lavish celebration. Mary's court was normally a rather dull and sober place, except when the king's presence injected a little more activity, but on this occasion there

[95] *Cal. Ven.*, VI, 618; VI, 847, 880.
[96] *Calendar of State Papers, Foreign, 1553–8*, 267, 273, 275.
[97] *Cal. Ven.*, VI, 907.

were some unspecified masques and plays. One of the latter seems to have been a laborious comedy by William Baldwin entitled 'Love and Lyve', in which all the characters had names beginning with 'L' – 'Leonard Lustyguts, an Epicure', 'Layies Lechery, a sumptuous whore', and so on. It ran for three hours, involved a cast of over sixty, and was described by its author as 'chargeable because the matter is stately, comprehending a discourse of the hole world'. Baldwin was a favourite entertainer, and his employment on this occasion confirms that Mary's spirits had improved considerably since the summer.[98] The New Year gift list for 1557 is unusually comprehensive, and although it cannot be taken as an accurate representation of who was present, it does indicate who was sufficiently in favour to be admitted to the privilege of exchanging tokens with the monarch.[99] (Appendix 2.) The list is headed, as might be expected, by the queen's kindred – Reginald Pole, Elizabeth, Anne of Cleves and Lady Margaret Strange. Of the earls, marquises and dukes only three did not participate, Francis Russell, earl of Bedford (who was in Zurich), Henry Clifford, earl of Cumberland, and William Somerset, earl of Worcester. Altogether twenty-seven peers, eighteen bishops and fifty-five ladies of rank appear, along with 171 other assorted courtiers and royal servants of varying status. Interestingly, the countess of Bedford was admitted, despite the circumstances of her husband's absence, and the elderly marchioness of Exeter, whose son had died abroad in disgrace and in suspicious circumstances.[100] Lord John Grey and Lord Robert Dudley, former

[98] A. Feuillerat, *Documents relating to the office of the Revels*, 215–17. Anglo, *Spectacle, Pageantry and Early Tudor Policy*, 341. Anglo points out that there is no proof that this play was performed at Christmas 1556, but it does appear in an undated Christmas list, and Baldwin's letter to Sir Thomas Cawarden, the master of the revels, is dated 1556.

[99] BL MS RP 294.

[100] Gertrude had been excluded from the court after her son's involvement with Wyatt, and subsequent imprisonment. He had gone abroad, with licence, in May 1555, and on 6 August he had written to his mother to congratulate her on her recall to the privy chamber (SP11/6/2). He had subsequently been suspected of involvement with Dudley, and was again in disgrace when he died in Venice in September 1556. There were rumours that he had been assassinated by English government agents. K. R. Bartlett, 'The English exile community in Italy and the political opposition to Mary I', *Albion*, XIII, 3, 223–41; Bartlett, 'The misfortune that is wished for him', *Canadian Journal of History*, XVI, 1–28.

opponents of the regime, appear, but not the latter's brothers, Ambrose and Henry, nor William Parr, the quondam marquis of Northampton. At the end of the list are some thirty names of those who received, but did not give, starting with the queen's seven maids of honour, and including such faithful old servants as Beatrice ap Rice and Randall Dodd. As a nominal roll of the court and council, this document contains few surprises, but it is eloquent of the extent to which Mary had succeeded in preserving at least the appearance of conciliation and consensus. In a more general context it had some unusual features. The Irish peerage was totally unrepresented, which may be indicative of a lack of interest in the affairs of that kingdom, although Mary had resurrected the earldom of Kildare in 1554. More surprisingly, the only diplomatic representative was the secretary of the French ambassador. No emissary came from Philip, nor apparently were any of his Spanish servants present at Greenwich at this time. The queen's gifts always took the standard form of plate, specially commissioned from Robert Raynes for the occasion, and graded in size according to the status and function of the recipient. The gifts which Mary received in return were much more varied and interesting, not having yet achieved the standardization which can be seen by the end of the century. Cash gifts were already normal for the peers and bishops, but many of the ladies gave garments, handkerchiefs or gloves, and inferior servants objects or commodities related to their trades. For example John Cawoode, her printer, gave 'a book in laten entitled vita christi', and John Soda, the apothecary, 'marmalade and cordyall'. These homely gifts give a domestic air to the record of what was, primarily, a ceremonial display of loyalty and duty. After such an extremely taxing and distressing year, there must have been comfort and reassurance for Mary in this familiar ritual.

However, the new year was barely two weeks old when the anticipated crisis in relations with France occurred. On 16 November the duke of Guise had gone to Italy to provide support for the pope against Philip, and it was only a matter of time before the truce in the Netherlands also broke down. That break came on 11 January, with an attack on Douai, and although England was still not directly involved, it did have treaty obligations towards Philip in that region, if he chose to invoke them.[101] At some point during January, probably when

[101] Loades, *Reign of Mary Tudor*, 241.

she received the news of the French attack, Mary put the whole question of her relations with France before her council, and received in return a lengthy memorandum of advice. From her point of view, knowing that Philip was going to press her for a declaration of war, it must have been a most discouraging and unwelcome document.[102] In their opinion, her councillors wrote, England was not bound by the treaties of 1542 and 1546 to intervene, because the war was the same one which had been going on when the marriage agreement had been drawn up, broken only by a truce, and not by a treaty of peace. They did not confront the possible response that, in that case, the marriage treaty had violated existing obligations. Even if the old treaties had been valid in this context, the attack still required to be 'certified', and that the king had not yet done, fortunately 'considering that the Queen's Majesty is not hable to do that the treaty requireth'. A fresh offer to mediate would reflect adversely upon the queen's honour, since the truce had been negotiated without her participation, and would also 'touch his majesties honour', unless he requested it. Even the threat to intervene, as a deterrent, was not practical politics, because the country was in no state to wage war and an empty threat to do so would simply expose the queen to ridicule and danger. It is not clear who prepared this *consulta*, which exists only in draft form, but it probably represented the majority view, and corresponds roughly with the line which the council as a whole was to take in subsequent discussions with the queen. Two main objections to hostilities were advanced; firstly that the realm was impoverished, having neither money, supplies nor able men for such an undertaking; and secondly that England had no interest in the war, which was being waged exclusively in defence of Habsburg interests in Italy and the Low Countries.

After three successive harvest failures, and with widespread sickness encouraged by malnutrition, there was undoubtedly substance in the first point. Moreover, after four years of struggle, an improvement in the Crown's financial prospects was at last in sight, and war would at least postpone the much-needed recovery.[103] The second point was more a matter of opinion, but at the same time it went to the very heart of the political tensions

[102] BL Cotton MS Titus C VII ff.198 *et seq.*
[103] Loades, *Reign of Mary Tudor*, 241–4.

which had existed since the beginning of the reign. From Mary's point of view, and even more from Philip's, England was not entitled to determine its own priorities in such a fashion. War and peace were prerogative matters, for the monarch to decide, and although an island (or rather, a part of one) England did not exist in isolation from Europe. Its church was a part of the universal church, and its monarchy a part of the great Habsburg connection. Philip, as king, was perfectly entitled to draw upon the resources of his English subjects, as upon those of his other realms. His father had had the same problem in Spain in the 1520s, and had eventually overcome triumphantly, so that Castile became the backbone of Habsburg financial and military power. Even if the marriage treaty prevented him from mobilizing the realm directly, he could do so indirectly, through the queen. Philip was prepared for opposition, but he was not prepared to let it stand in his way. On 2 February, having worked out a timetable for his visit to England, he sent Ruy Gomez across to explain and justify his own position, and to explore the possibilities. He was not to discuss English participation with anyone except Paget. Neither the queen nor the council as a whole was to be consulted as yet, except about the possibility of purchasing supplies of grain.[104] The king probably knew, or could guess, what line the English council would take. He probably also knew that Cardinal Pole, to whom Mary listened on every matter, secular or ecclesiastical, was of the same opinion. He could not therefore be sure how the queen would respond, after such a long separation, and having done so little to gratify him in the past. It would have to be his task to persuade Mary into the war, provided he could re-establish the personal ascendancy which he had enjoyed over her while they were together, but which might well prove to have been eroded by time, absence and neglect. On 8 March he set out from Brussels, and ten days later, crossed from Calais to Dover. On the 19th he rode in post to join the queen at Greenwich, and found her in a ferment of eager anticipation. His first political task was accomplished almost before it was essayed.

[104] *Cal.Span.*, XIII, 286–7.

7

Mary and Elizabeth

(1557–1558)

As Philip landed at Greenwich, at 5 o'clock on the afternoon of 20 March, 'ther cam a shype up by the tyde' which greeted him with a thirty-two gun salute, and cries of 'God save the Kyng and Quen'.[1] Mary had been meticulous in her preparations. The gentlemen pensioners had been mustered, the king's household recalled to duty, and every mile of his passage from Calais smoothed and hastened by the queen's ships and servants. The following day all the bells of London rang out, and every church was commanded to sing the Te Deum, to the glory of God, and by order of the bishop. When Philip came, however, his Spanish entourage could not be far behind, and as Henry Machyn noted with a hint of alarm, three shiploads of them reached the capital before the sounds of rejoicing died away. In the event, he had not insisted upon any conditions relating to the government of England; nor was the matter on his mind. Having assumed responsibility for the troubled kingdoms of Spain, he was no longer eager to encumber himself with responsibilities which he might well be unable to discharge.[2] On 23 March the ceremonies of welcome concluded with a ride through London from Tower wharf to Whitehall, with all the livery companies in

[1] Machyn, *Diary*, 129.

[2] The situation in Spain had become increasingly difficult after Philip's departure in 1554, but until January 1556 the regent, Juana, had been responsible to the emperor and not the king. The two main problems were war taxation and the depredations of the Barbary corsairs. Eventually, in 1559, the Cortes of Castile were to send a virtual ultimatum to Philip, and he returned to take charge in person.

their finery lining the route, and the sceptre borne before them by the lord mayor. After that, it was down to business, and the business, of course, was war. Philip's position was desperate, because although his armies were enjoying success in Italy, he was effectively bankrupt. His revenues were committed three years in advance, and credit was costing him 54 per cent. Informal sounding of individual councillors provided little hope or encouragement. Lord Paget was the leader of the war party, and he had some support from the military nobility, particularly the earls of Pembroke and Shrewsbury, but they were a small minority of the council as a whole. Moreover, the men whom Mary was most disposed to trust, Pole, Rochester and Heath, were the chief opponents of involvement. On 1 April Mary summoned the select council, no doubt thinking that would be more evenly divided and easier to deal with, and in Philip's presence set out the arguments in favour of war. Two days later the council responded with another *consulta*, repeating the verdict of their earlier paper: England could not, and should not, become involved in hostilities.[3]

However, the council did not make decisions in such matters, and the process of consultation was more designed to mobilize support than to put a major policy issue to a vote. The count of Feria apparently informed the new Venetian ambassador, Michel Surian, that the king could do what he liked with the English nobility, because they were all totally venal and would do anything for cash. He then added that Philip would not require a declaration of war, but merely money and a fleet. Since this conversation was held after the rebuff of 3 April, it looks as though Feria was preparing to make the best of a compromise solution. On 12 April the king admitted to Arras that the going was tougher than he expected, but his minister pressed him hard to insist on a complete break. The French were continuing to use their ambassador and his servants to foment trouble in England, and only a severance of diplomatic relations would bring that threat to an end.[4] Ironically, one of Philip's most effective allies in his campaign was his enemy Paul IV. Because he was at war

[3] François de Noailles to Montmorency, 5 April 1557; Aff.Etr. XIII, ff.182–3; Harbison, *Rival Ambassadors*. A Latin version, prepared for Philip's benefit, survives as BL Sloane MS 1786.

[4] *Cal.Ven.*, VI, 1004. *Cal.Span.*, XIII, 288, 289.

with the pope, the conscientious Pole remained at Canterbury, refusing to come to court, to take part in meetings of the council, or to have any communication with the king. This deprived the 'peace party' of its most influential statesman at a critical phase. There were constant rumours from Rome that Paul was about to deprive Philip of all his realms and dominions, as a schismatic and rebel against the Holy Church. His own advisers eventually persuaded him to think better of such a drastic course, but on 10 April he did recall all his legates from the Habsburg lands, including Pole specifically by name. Consequently, English hostility to the papacy, which had tended to undermine the king's position during his earlier residence in England, now ceased to be a significant factor. In all probability Mary would have declared war on France eventually, no matter what her council had said. She summoned individual councillors, and under pressure they began to give ground. The council was not a cabinet, and had no collective responsibility. The councillor's oath bound him as an individual to give his sovereign loyal and disinterested advice to the best of his ability, but not to act as a member of a team. Immediate financial assistance was mentioned, and a small expeditionary force, with the possibility of a full declaration of war later, if a good harvest relieved the desperate problems of dearth and malnutrition. However, in the event the opposition was overcome, and a declaration precipitated, not by pressure from the queen but by the curious episode of Thomas Stafford's raid on Scarborough.

Stafford was the second son of Henry, Lord Stafford and Ursula, the sister of Cardinal Pole. He was thus a grandson both of the last duke of Buckingham (attainted in 1521) and Mary's old governess, Margaret, countess of Salisbury (attainted in 1539). He appears to have been a turbulent and irresponsible young man.[5] Because of his ancestry he entertained high hopes of being restored to title and favour on Mary's accession, and when this did not happen, became involved first with Wyatt and then with Dudley. By the summer of 1554 he had escaped to France, where he spent his time quarrelling with his fellow-exiles, and soliciting money and employment from the king. In January 1557 Nicholas

[5] C. H. Garrett, *The Marian Exiles*, 294–5; *TTC*, 172–3. Garrett suggests that Stafford returned to England for a time in 1555–6, but the evidence of identity is not conclusive.

Wotton, the diligent and observant English ambassador in France, had reported that Stafford had adopted the full arms of England, and apparently regarded himself as a claimant to the throne. King Henry toyed with the idea of using him in his perpetual campaign of covert harassment against Mary, but drew back. In the first place he did not wish to provoke a war with England, and at the same time Stafford could have been a very difficult agent. His own claim would find little support, and would cut right across the claim of Mary Stuart, which the French had consistently supported. Nevertheless, by the beginning of April he had plans to seize a castle on the English coast, which Wotton tentatively identified as Scarborough, and was reported to be raising men and money in Normandy. On 23 April he appeared off Scarborough with two French ships, and landed a small force of between thirty and a hundred men. The castle was semi-ruinous, and had a garrison of only about a dozen men, who were quickly overpowered. Stafford then issued a lengthy and elaborate proclamation, declaring that the principal strongholds of the country were about to 'be delivered to xii thousand Spanyards before the king's coronation'.[6] He also proclaimed himself duke of Buckingham and protector of the realm, its laws, liberties and customs. His timing was disastrous. The earl of Westmorland was only about fifty miles off with a recently levied force on its way to the Scottish border. Within twenty-four hours Westmorland knew of the invasion, within forty-eight hours the council in London knew, and by 28 April the castle had been retaken. Stafford and his band were prisoners, having attracted virtually no support in the three days of their occupation, and the French had apparently offered a gratuitous provocation which the English council could not ignore.

There are a number of suspicious features about this incident. The French king strenuously denied involvement, and given the inevitable consequences of such an adventure at such a moment, he may well have spoken the truth.[7] The council had apparently not responded to Wotton's warning about Scarborough, but the

[6] Strype, *Ecclesiastical Memorials*, III, 515. For a full discussion of this episode, see Loades, *Reign of Mary Tudor*, 365–8.

[7] Soranzo (in France) to the doge and senate, 21 May 1557; *Cal. Ven.*, VI, 1104–8.

proximity of Westmorland and his force would have been a very fortunate coincidence. Moreover, the speed and certainty with which information travelled was in striking contrast to the conflicting rumours and reports which normally preceded reliable news of any untoward incident. Surian wrote to the Council of Ten on 29 April, with what looks suspiciously like a premature report of the government's success, containing propaganda overtones which were not normally present in his dispatches. In addition, the French ships which had conveyed the invasion force were commanded by Jean Ribault, a notorious adventurer who had once been in the service of Lord Paget. The evidence is not conclusive, but given the high stakes played for, it looks very much as though Ribault was a double agent who lured the foolish and unfortunate Stafford to his doom at the instigation of Paget and his allies in the English council.[8] As soon as the news of the raid reached London, Philip knew that he had won, and Bernardino de Mendoza wrote to the duke of Savoy, 'The necessary steps have been taken to deal with this matter, and it will result in war being declared . . .' It was not until 7 June that the English herald, Norroy, visited Henry to announce hostilities, but the decision had been taken by 1 May, and by the middle of the month preparations were already well in hand. Norroy insisted, in accordance with his instructions, that Mary's action was an autonomous response to English grievances against France, going back to Noailles's support for Wyatt, but the king laughed and declared that Mary did not mind how much she upset her subjects in order to gratify her husband.[9]

Henry's gibe was not unreasonable, because opinion in England was generally hostile to the war. The merchant community was distressed, not only by the loss of trade with France, but also by the inevitable increase in the depredations of French pirates once they had been converted into privateers. The prospect of war subsidies was bound to be unpopular, and, as Surian observed, the prevailing opinion (at least in London) was that the only beneficiaries would be the king and his hated Spanish followers.

[8] On Ribault see *Correspondance Politique de Odet de Selve*, ed. G. Lefèvre-Pontalis, 218–23; Harbison, *Rival Ambassadors*, 283–5; and L. Woodbury, 'Jean Ribault and Queen Elizabeth', *American Historical Review*, IX, 456–9. He was eventually killed trying to establish a Huguenot colony in the New World.

[9] *Cal.Span.*, XIII, 294–6; *Cal.Ven.*, VI, 1152–4.

There was another side to the picture, however, and this last fear was not altogether justified. There were two groups of Englishmen who could expect to benefit, and many of them did so. The first consisted of the nobility with military aspirations, who took a traditional view of their role, and their allegiance to the Crown. They expected to serve their king in arms, because their honour required it, and for that purpose it was not really relevant that their king was a foreigner. The codes of chivalry belonged to an older world, and took no account of national consciousness. So Pembroke and Shrewsbury had supported Paget in council; Pembroke, Rutland and Montague were to hold important commands in France, Shrewsbury and Westmorland on the Scottish border. Such employment was both honourable and profitable, and it is not surprising that there was no shortage of volunteers. The other group consisted of former opponents of Mary's government, now seeking rehabilitation. It had been noticed in 1555, and was noticed again in 1557, how the king secured the pardon and release of political prisoners who were also 'serviceable' men of war. The names of those in this category who served Philip in the campaigns of 1557–8 were very numerous: Ambrose, Robert and Henry Dudley, Lord Braye, Sir Peter Carew, Sir James Crofts, William Winter, Peter Killigrew, and many more. Foreign war was (and still is) a well-known method of sublimating internal tensions, and it has been argued that this war was particularly effective in reuniting a ruling class which had been deeply divided by the conspiracies of Northumberland, Wyatt and Dudley.[10] Since the war was to run into the following reign, we have no means of knowing whether that unity would have survived the renewed strains of peace. Philip was willing to employ even known protestants like Peter Killigrew and the earl of Bedford to fight the French. How he, and more pertinently Mary, would have used them when hostilities were over must leave some room for doubt.

Nevertheless, during May 1557 the preparations for war went ahead with reasonable efficiency, and even some enthusiasm, at first under the pretext of honouring the 1546 treaty. Good early summer weather promised a bumper harvest, and faced with a

[10] C. S. L. Davies, 'England and the French War, 1557–9', in *The Mid-Tudor Polity, 1540–1560*, ed. J. Loach and R. Tittler, 162. BL Stowe MS 571, ff.77–132.

sudden drop in prices, long-hoarded grain was released onto the market. The fear of famine receded, and it was to be some months before the even grimmer spectre of a lethal influenza epidemic arose to take its place. Most important, the fleet was prepared for action. This had always been the English contribution from which Philip had expected the most, and although he had been extremely disappointed to discover the run-down condition of the navy in 1554, he had taken effective steps to remedy the situation. Re-building had begun in the autumn of 1555, and the two new ships laid down at that time, the *Philip and Mary* and the *Mary Rose*, were ready for service by the beginning of 1557.[11] In the spring of 1556 the lord admiral had been instructed to hold musters of seamen, and a commission had been set up to make further recommendations. These were implemented in January 1557, when an ordinary peacetime budget of £14,000 was allocated to the treasurer of the navy, and overall control of administration was taken out of the hands of the lord admiral and given to the lord treasurer.[12] By June 1557 twenty royal ships were available, and Lord Admiral William Howard was able to lead his fleet in a combined operation with the Flemish fleet against Cherbourg. The second activity in which Philip was interested was the preparation of a small expeditionary force to serve with the main Imperial army in Flanders. In theory, this force was supposed to number 10,000 (by comparison with the 60,000–80,000 men under the command of the duke of Savoy). In fact its muster roll never seems to have risen above 7,500, but it was a well-equipped and well-organized expedition. Commanded by the earl of Pembroke, it was probably raised in the quasi-feudal manner normal for Tudor armies serving abroad, the nobles and gentlemen raising their own companies from among their servants and tenants. A remarkable proportion of the aristocratic colonels and captains were redeeming past misdemeanours, the highest ranking being Lord Robert Dudley, who commanded the artillery train. None of the queen's earliest and loyalest supporters took part, and Surian may well have been correct when he suggested that they were

[11] BL Cotton MS Otho E 321–42 ix, f.88. T. Glasgow, jun., 'The Navy in Philip and Mary's war, 1557–8', *Mariner's Mirror*, LIII, and 'The maturing of naval administration, 1556–64', *Mariner's Mirror*, LVI, 3–27.

[12] Davies, 'England and the French war', 164.

being deliberately kept at home, while potential troublemakers were dispatched to Flanders.[13] Apart from £5600 allocated from the Exchequer to supply this army at Calais, the whole cost of the expedition, amounting to about £48,000, was met from the king's war chest.[14] Given that the English were neither particularly experienced soldiers, nor skilled in the most recent tactics, it may well be that the real reason for this expensive gesture was political rather than military. Pembroke's force was more valuable to Philip as a symbol of his authority in England, and as a means of rallying aristocratic support to himself, than as a contribution to his physical power. Musters were also held, but in these the king had little interest. They were purely for home defence, and their armament was primitive. The most important consequence of what these assemblies revealed was the decision to legislate an improvement in the standard of provision, which was to be implemented in the parliament of 1558.

The prospect of war with France had its normal effect upon Anglo-Scottish relations, which was why the earl of Westmorland was on his way to the border at the end of April. Mary of Guise, who had been regent since 1554, was fully committed to the 'auld alliance', but her rule was becoming increasingly unpopular with the Scottish aristocracy. By the summer of 1557 many of them were viewing a resumption of hostilities against England with considerable distaste, feeling, as the earl of Cassilis put it during a border truce negotiation, no more French than the English were Spaniards.[15] Consequently on 18 July, over a month after the outbreak of war between England and France, a continuation of the peace between England and Scotland was solemnly proclaimed at Carlisle and Dumfries. However, the Scottish commissioners had acted without the approval of the regent, and within a fortnight the peace was broken by Scottish and French raiding parties attacking the east March. At the beginning of August the English council declared a state of *de*

[13] *Cal. Ven.*, VI, 1147. One or two courtiers, such as Lord Montague and Sir Thomas Cheney, appear in the coat and conduct lists, but not in the musters, so it is not clear whether they served or not. BL Stowe MSS 571, ff.77–132.

[14] PRO E404/109 MS 11, 12; BL Stowe MS 571, f.78. Loades, *Reign of Mary Tudor*, 373.

[15] *Calendar of State Papers relating to Scotland*, ed. J. Bain et al., I, 416. The agreements, proclamations and letters of the English commissioners are contained in BL Harley MS 289, ff.43–58.

facto war, and moved a part of its fleet to the North Sea. The regent ordered a general mobilization, and Mary appealed to Philip for the assistance of his own fleet. In the event, large-scale hostilities were averted, because both camps were divided. The Scottish host duly assembled, but after a few skirmishes the Scots lords refused to undertake either a large-scale invasion or a siege of Berwick, and the small French contingent was left isolated. On the English side, Philip, whose mind was wholly concentrated upon the campaign in Picardy, declined to send any assistance, and refused to make any declaration against the Scots. The earls of Shrewsbury and Westmorland kept the English borders in a state of alert readiness, but Henry was unable to send reinforcements from France, and the main consequence of this aborted campaign was that the recently established rapport between Philip and the English council was undermined by prolonged recriminations.

By the time this happened, the king had long since returned to the Low Countries. The main object of his visit had been accomplished by the declaration of war, and the partial mobilization which had accompanied it. There was no further talk of his coronation, and he was unwilling to be distracted from the main business of building up his army. On 23 April he attended a chapter of the Order of the Garter, held at Whitehall, and assisted at the election of three new knights, Lord Fitzwalter (who was something of a favourite with him), Lord Grey, and the queen's faithful retainer, Sir Robert Rochester.[16] He put in several days of hunting at Hampton Court, and took part in an unnamed court masque. He also witnessed a most unfortunate accident, when Sir Jacques Granado, showing off the paces of a horse in the privy garden, was thrown against a wall and killed.[17] Mary rejoiced in his presence, but too much had happened during the previous three years for her to be under any illusions. This time there were no emotional fireworks, and no public displays of affection. The royal couple went about their public life together for nearly four months, and there were few signs of the anti-Spanish demonstrations which had dogged Philip's steps two years before. His entourage was probably smaller and better disciplined, but he may also have succeeded

[16] Machyn, *Diary*, 132–3.
[17] Ibid., 135.

in conveying discreetly to the English council that he was no longer interested in increasing his role in the government of the realm. Popular rumours that he would use the war for that purpose seem to have died away once war was actually declared, and no one, except Mary herself, believed any longer that there would be a child of the marriage.

Another indication that the king was reconciled to a purely formal status in England for the duration of Mary's life can probably be seen in his changing attitude towards Elizabeth. In his valedictory 'narration', written in May 1557, Michieli declared that she had ingratiated herself with Philip during her enforced residence at court in April and May 1555.[18] He hinted discreetly at an amorous attraction, but the true explanation was probably political, and dated from the summer or autumn of 1556. Like Mary, Elizabeth had become an independent party in the first year of her brother's reign when, in accordance with the terms of her father's will, she had been put in possession of an estate worth over £3000 per annum, and had made Hatfield and Ashridge her principal residences.[19] She had appeared to be high in favour with Edward, and was generally thought to be of the reformed faith, so her exclusion from the succession, along with Mary, in the summer of 1553 must have come as something of a shock. Bitterly though the new queen may have regretted it, by restoring the order decreed in Henry VIII's will, she had also restored Elizabeth to the position of heir apparent, and those same sentiments of legitimacy which had helped to defeat the duke of Northumberland frustrated her every effort to change that situation. In November 1554, as we have seen, Mary had confided to Renard that she wished to exclude her sister from the succession, because of her personal distaste for Anne Boleyn's daughter, her conviction that the girl was a bastard, and partly because she regarded her as a secret heretic. The queen's suspicion and hostility was brought sharply into focus by the Wyatt rebellion. On the scaffold, Wyatt himself denied all reports that he had incriminated her, and no conclusive proof of her involvement was ever produced. However, the object of the conspiracy had certainly been to set her upon the throne in Mary's place, and for a time she was in very serious danger. Her most

[18] *Cal. Ven.*, VI, 1059.

[19] *Cal.Pat.*, Edward VI, III, 238; dated 17 March 1550, but with issues from Michaelmas 1547.

implacable enemy had been the influential Renard, who regarded her as a major threat to Philip's future security, and endeavoured to insist upon her trial and execution as a precondition of his coming to England. At the end of January she had been courteously but firmly interned at court, and towards the end of March dispatched to the Tower.[20]

Many years later, when she was resisting parliamentary pressure to name her successor, Elizabeth remembered this dangerous time:

> I am sure ther was none of them [the members] that was ever a second person as I have been, and have tasted of the practizes against my sister . . . Ther were occasions in me that tyme I stood in danger of my lyfe my sister was insensed against me that I did difer from her in religion, and I was sought for divers ways, so shall never my successor be.[21]

In fact Mary's personal anger had soon been appeased. The unfortunate and irrelevant Jane Grey had gone to the block, but no judicial action was taken against Elizabeth, and the queen, as so often happened, was bombarded with conflicting advice. On this issue the councillors had divided much as they had over Mary's marriage, but Renard found himself with different allies. The lord chancellor and the 'household' councillors – Rochester, Waldegrave and Englefield – who had originally opposed the marriage, now urged strong action against the princess, while Paget, Arundel, Pembroke, Shrewsbury and Sussex endeavoured to protect her. This was the beginning of Renard's rift with Paget, which was to be completed later by Paget's action in parliament. It was rumoured during April 1554 that Gardiner intended to introduce a Bill to disinherit her, but either the rumour was false or he was dissuaded, for no such measure was discussed. Although the end of parliament had left many of her friends under a cloud for a different reason, it brought about an easing of Elizabeth's situation. On 4 May she was placed in the custody of Sir Henry Bedingfield, and removed under his supervision to Woodstock between the 21st and 23rd. At first the council tried to insist that the princess should not be allowed to converse with any suspect person, nor to send or receive any message, but Bedingfield very reasonably pointed out that such

[20] Prescott, *Mary Tudor*, 255–6; Machyn, *Diary*, 57–8.
[21] BL Stowe MS 354, f.18.

a constraint was impossible to enforce with so many servants about, and her journey via Windsor and West Wickham turned into something like a triumphal progress.[22] Many of the local people along the way, whom Bedingfield described as 'very protestants', turned out to greet her, bringing so many presents of food and other small items that her servants became over-burdened. A few also had the temerity to ring the church bells 'for which they were commanded to prison'. If Mary was ever told of these events, they must have reminded her forcefully of some of her own experiences during the darkest days of her disfavour. Did they signify anything more than sympathy with a royal lady in distress?

Elizabeth spent the next eleven months at Woodstock, in honourable but frustrating confinement. She continued to draw the revenues of her estates, and was attended by her own officers and servants. Her cofferer, Thomas Parry, was forced to pay the expenses of Sir Henry Bedingfield and his sixteen servants, but the hundred soldiers who guarded her were paid from the Exchequer.[23] Sir Henry kept a diary of his dealings with his difficult charge, and seems to have performed his duties with an admirable blend of conscientiousness, patience and tact. However, the heir to the throne could not be kept under house arrest indefinitely, and the problem of what to do about Elizabeth nagged on through the summer and autumn of 1554. In November, while he was in Brussels, Paget claimed that she was no longer important, because of the queen's pregnancy, and should be married off to some minor German prince.[24] Whether this represented his real view may be doubted, but the claims of the marquis of Baden were canvassed, and also the possibility of a Spanish marriage—although the latter was rejected on the grounds that she might fall foul of the Inquisition and cause a scandal. The emperor was anxious to see her disposed of in such a fashion, but as Renard pointed out in November, it would be very difficult to persuade her to marry a foreigner. Unlike Mary, who had frequently expressed a desire to escape from England when the going got rough, Elizabeth knew that she could expect no welcome or support except from her own people. Consequently some of her friends in the council were willing to propose a

22 BL Cotton MS Titus C VII, ff.6–65.
23 Ibid.
24 *Cal.Span.*, XIII, 90.

match with Courtenay. This could have been politically dangerous, and Renard opposed it fiercely, as a device of the French and the heretics; but it could also have had the merit of stabilizing the succession by producing the male heir which the queen had not so far achieved. It would at least have made Courtenay less of a political maverick. However, since neither the queen nor Elizabeth herself was willing to countenance such a marriage, the suggestion remained in the conspiratorial undergrowth.

The problem had been no nearer to a solution when the dangers attendant upon Mary's putative confinement necessitated further action. At the beginning of March 1555 it had been proposed to release both Elizabeth and Courtenay, who was being held in similar confinement at Fotheringay, and to send them abroad to separate destinations – the earl of Devon to Rome and the princess to Brussels. Courtenay was indeed dispatched to Italy via Brussels at the beginning of May, but Elizabeth stayed in England. If Mary were to die in childbed, the only person who would benefit from the absence of the lawful heir would be Philip. The English council probably dissuaded the queen from such a course on the grounds that the consequence would be civil strife. On 29 April Michieli reported that Elizabeth was expected at Hampton Court the following day, because her presence was deemed to be the best guarantee of Philip's personal safety.[25] She arrived, under conditions of some secrecy which were presumably designed to prevent demonstrations, accompanied by only a handful of servants. Although reported a month later to be 'at full liberty', she remained with the court until it moved to Oatlands on 4 August, and was then given leave to withdraw to Ashridge. In one sense the failure of Mary's pregnancy had strengthened her position, but it also made her a more obvious target for those who wished to preserve the Imperial ascendancy. Philip may already have been contemplating a political understanding, which would help to account for the rumours of his attachment to her, but his father favoured a more binding arrangement. By the time that the king arrived in the Netherlands in September 1555 Charles was already contemplating a marriage between Elizabeth and his nephew Ferdinand 'so that he may succeed to that crown, as his

[25] *Cal. Ven.*, VI, 57.

Imperial Majesty's son has no hope of an heir by his consort'.[26] Philip may have been unsympathetic to such a scheme, for no serious negotiation resulted, although as late as July 1556 the French were still threatening counter-measures if the Habsburgs attempted to extend their tenure of authority in England by such means.

Rumours of marriage, enforced expatriation, and possible exclusion by statute continued to be associated with Elizabeth's name in diplomatic correspondence, but the next thunderbolt to strike the ground near her was the Dudley conspiracy. This did not present the same kind of danger as the Wyatt rebellion, because there was no suggestion of her personal involvement, but several of her servants were arrested and interrogated, including her 'Governess' Katherine Ashley, who was discovered to be in possession of protestant and anti-Spanish literature.[27] At the beginning of June 1556 the queen sent Hastings and Englefield to visit her sister, with a gift and smooth professions of concern at the disruption to her household. To minimize the inconvenience, Mary appointed a new governess, and placed the whole Hatfield establishment under the control of Sir Thomas Pope, who was considered to be a reliable catholic and devoted to the queen. In the same spirit, Elizabeth responded with professions of gratitude for such sisterly concern. Pope seems to have been less reliable than had been expected, or perhaps he succumbed to the princess's celebrated charm, because within a few weeks he was reported to be providing generous masques and entertainments for her amusement, and was relieved of his responsibilities in the middle of October. From 28 November to 3 December Elizabeth visited the court, basing herself at her own residence of Somerset Place. In a manner strikingly reminiscent of Mary's appearances at St John's, Clerkenwell, 'came rydyng thrugh Smythfeld and Old Balee, and thrugh Fletsrett unto Somerset place, my good lade Elisabeth's grace the queen's sister with a grett compene of velvett cottes and cheynes, her graces gentyll-

[26] Licentiate Games (Ferdinand's ambassador in Brussels) to the King of the Romans, 29 September 1555; *Cal.Span.*, XIII, 251–2.

[27] *Cal.Ven.*, VI, 475; PRO SP11/8/54; later in the summer, after Cleobury's attempt, the council wrote to Sir Thomas Pope to acquaint the Lady Elizabeth with the misuse of her name – but that was a less serious conspiracy. BL Cotton MS Titus B II, f.139.

men, and after a grett compene of her men all in red cottes.'[28] Michieli estimated her retinue at 200 horsemen, and commented on both the 'infinite pleasure of this entire population', and the fact that no one came from the court to greet her officially, although many did so privately.

By the time that Philip returned to England, therefore, there was an uneasy truce between the two sisters, and no decisive poliical advantage had been secured by either. There was now little chance that Philip would choose to impose himself upon England in the event of Mary's death, and less still that there would be any heir of her body. On the other hand, there was no reason to suppose that the queen's death was imminent, or that Elizabeth should succeed in the near future. Pressure upon the princess to marry was again becoming intense, and it was suggested that her right to succeed should be confirmed in return for her agreement to wed Emmanuel Philibert, duke of Savoy.[29] Savoy had been dispossessed of his duchy by the French, and was consequently a loyal Imperialist, without the distraction of other responsibilities. There would have been some advantages to both sides in this arrangement. Elizabeth would not have been required to live abroad, and an Italian would probably have been a good deal more acceptable in England than either a Frenchman or a Spaniard. The unpredictable risks of an unmarried queen would also have been avoided, the Imperial connection maintained, and the future of the catholic restoration assured. On the other hand, Elizabeth did not need to have her claim confirmed, because it was generally accepted, and it is unlikely that she would have wished to commence her reign (whenever that occurred) committed in advance to the catholic church and the Habsburg alliance. So she insisted upon her general unwillingness to marry, and resisted every pressure. Consequently Philip had two battles on his hands in the spring of 1557; one being to bring England into the war, and the other to get Elizabeth

[28] Machyn, *Diary*, 120.

[29] *Cal.Span.*, XIII, 293. French objections to this proposal had been made clear as early as January. Ibid., 285. Philip's decision to abandon the English succession was signalled in a will, drafted in 1557, which ignored the marriage treaty, and left the Low Countries to Don Carlos. Rodríguez Salgado, *The Changing Face of Empire*, 83.

safely married. This second campaign reached an unprecedented climax at the end of March, when Christina of Denmark, the widowed duchess of Lorraine, and his own half-sister, Margaret, duchess of Parma, both visited the English court. For nearly a month these two extremely formidable ladies applied their powers of persuasion to the 23-year-old princess, but entirely without success.[30] Philip could have simply ordered her to accompany him on his return to the Netherlands in July, and he was widely reported to have that intention. On the other hand, the English council made it clear that they would oppose such a move, and in the circumstances the king did not wish to upset his somewhat reluctant allies. Nor did he particularly want to upset his queen, and Mary's hatred of her sister was by this time verging on paranoia.

Mary, Michieli reported, was driven by two emotions, love and hate. Her love for her husband was extreme, and 'separation, which to any person who loves another heartily, would be irksome and grievous, is assuredly so to a woman naturally tender.' Never a day passed in which this violent love did not generate both fear and anxiety, and the fear which afflicted her most was the dread of his renewed absence. At the same time her hatred for Elizabeth was such that 'although it is dissembled, it cannot be denied that she displays in many ways the scorn and ill-will she bears her.' The queen could never see her sister without reliving the insults and ignominy to which she had been subjected on account of Anne Boleyn.[31] She refused to believe that Elizabeth's professions of catholicism were genuine, and hated her doubly, both as a dissembler and a heretic. Worse was the willingness of so many of her subjects to dismiss the prospect of any other heir, and to accept this 'illegitimate child of a criminal' as their next queen; and worst of all was her husband's apparent willingness to do the same. Philip wished to marry Elizabeth to the duke of Savoy as the acknowledged heir, and that Mary was totally unwilling to accept. According

[30] *Cal. Ven.*, VI, 1024. The duchess of Parma was accompanied for a part of this visit by her son, Alessandro Farnese, later Philip's governor in the Netherlands. *Cal.Span.*, XIII, 448. The duchess also had other business to dispatch with the king, apart from Elizabeth's marriage, and departed highly dissatisfied.

[31] *Cal. Ven.*, VI, 1058.

to another Venetian report, written in the following year, the king's confessor, Fresnada, persuaded her to consent at some point during this visit, but within two days she had changed her mind, and thereafter remained implacable.[32] Elizabeth, she insisted, was not her father's daughter, and had no right either to the throne or to an honourable marriage. For the time being, Philip accepted defeat, but reports that the French were trying to persuade the pope to declare Elizabeth a bastard, and thus open the way to Mary Stuart, increased his determination. Other marriage projects were discussed, but the king was to revert to the Savoy match again in 1558, resuming the hopeless task of trying to persuade two women to accept a course which was equally distasteful to both of them for different reasons.

By the end of June, Mary's briefly renewed happiness was coming to an end. Not only was Philip on the point of departure, but his war with the pope was increasingly intruding upon the affairs of the English church. At first it had seemed that Pole's recall, like *Rescissio aliationum*, would be revoked in the face of persistent representations. On 21 May Mary wrote in her own name, and in that of Philip as king of England, pointing out how much damage would be done by the withdrawal of their legate at such a critical stage in the process of restoration. A few days later the council wrote to the same effect, and on 25 May, Pole himself wrote too.[33] However, the situation went from bad to worse. On 31 May Pole's friend Cardinal Morone was arrested on a charge of heresy, and by the middle of June the Roman Inquisition was proceeding against Pole on the same grounds. The cardinal was stunned by this display of malice from the authority in which he had always placed his principal trust, and the queen was equally appalled when Paul blandly informed her a few days later that he recognized the special needs of England, and had named a suitable legate in Pole's place. His nominee was William Peto, a senile Franciscan friar, who had once been a confessor to Catherine of Aragon, and had been exiled from England for her sake. By 1557 he was living in retirement at the revived Franciscan house at Greenwich, and was fit neither in mind nor

[32] Michel Surian to the doge and senate, 29 October 1558; *Cal.Ven.*, VI, 1537. Mary is alleged to have declared that Elizabeth resembled Mark Smeaton; Clifford, *Life of Jane Dormer*, 79–80.

[33] Strype, *Ecclesiastical Memorials*, III, 474–6, 476–80; *Cal.Ven.*, VI, 1111.

body for such a responsible task.[34] Mary was insulted, and when the papal nuncio bearing the official briefs reached Calais early in July, he was refused admission to the realm. Knowing the situation, Pole wished to obey the summons, intending to clear his name. However, Sir Edward Carne, Mary's ambassador in Rome, warned him that if he came he would disappear into the prisons of the Inquisition, and in Philip's absence his first duty was to Mary. The queen had no intention of allowing him to go, and on 26 July penned a strongly worded protest to the pope, expressing her amazement that a man who had performed such distinguished services for the church, and whose presence was so essential for the task in hand, should be withdrawn in the manner proposed.[35] At the same time Peto declined his intended preferment, on the legitimate grounds of age and incapacity. By the middle of August deadlock had been reached. English business could not be discharged in Rome, and papal directives could not be received in England. Mary instructed Carne that, if charges of heresy should be proffered against Pole, he was to insist that those charges must be investigated in England, as had been done in the case of the last archbishop of Canterbury, Cranmer. Should the pope reject such a demand, he was to leave Rome, declaring publicly that although England wished to remain loyal to the Holy See, it was impossible for the queen to obey the commands of the present pope.[36] In the event the charges were not made, and diplomatic relations were not broken off, but it is not surprising that rumours ran round the *Curia* to the effect that the English schism was about to be renewed.

Philip set off from London for the last time on 3 July. On this occasion Mary, whose health was less fragile than it had been two years earlier, rode with him on the way. They stayed one night at Sittingbourne and another at Canterbury, reaching Dover on the 5th. At three o'clock on the morning of the 6th they parted on the quayside. The king made a quick passage to Calais, arriving in the middle of the same day, and reached

[34] *Cal. Ven.*, VI, 1166; Loades, *Reign of Mary Tudor*, 430–1. *Dictionary of National Biography*.

[35] *Cal. Ven.*, VI, 1161, 1166, 1240; PRO SP69/11/655.

[36] Navagero (Venetian ambassador in Rome) to the doge and senate, 14 August 1557; *Cal. Ven.*, VI, 1248.

Brussels on the 9th. This time there seems to have been no pretence about an early return, although neither of them could have known that they would not meet again. Both accepted that Philip's widespread commitments would give him little time for English affairs, although the war would give them a common purpose and a working relationship. The king's Spanish household joined him in Brussels on 11 July, and his English household was again suspended, apart from his chamberlain, Lord Williams, and a small number of his gentlemen, who retained a token presence at the court. From Mary's point of view the blow of separation was probably softened by her awareness of the amount which she could contribute to the common cause. The fleet had already been in action; Pembroke's army followed the king across the Channel within a matter of days; even sharing the disfavour of the pope had its compensations – it was a sacrifice which might earn gratitude. In spite of Pole and his difficulties, the autumn of 1557 was not a period of despondency. On 10 August a French army advancing to raise the siege of Saint-Quentin was routed with heavy casualties – the most decisive victory to have been achieved by either side for several years.[37] Ironically Philip, who very much wanted battle honours and had never seen active service, missed the battle because he was waiting to lead the reinforcements which were being assembled. These reinforcements included the English, who were having problems with their wagon transport, and who consequently also missed the battle. However, neither the king nor the English missed the action altogether, because the town of Saint-Quentin held out until 27 August, when it was taken by storm. Although Pembroke's men were inexperienced, and not sufficiently disciplined for a long campaign, they fought well on this occasion, and their valour was generously praised until it became politically expedient to forget it.[38] On 12 September the pope finally accepted that the French were not going to be able to rescue him from the duke of Alba, and made peace, while in early October the long-threatened Scottish campaign against the north of England fizzled out in recriminations, as we have seen.

[37] Davies, 'England and the French war', 165–6. There are numerous descriptions of this battle.

[38] Juan de Pinedo to Francisco de Vargas, 27 August 1557; *Cal.Span.*, XIII, 317.

In the churches of London the Te Deums followed one another in rapid succession. No army stood between Philip and Paris, and in his retirement at Saint-Yuste the Emperor Charles V was anticipating a greater triumph than he had ever succeeded in achieving. In this general mood of euphoria it looked as though Paget's strategy of using a foreign war to mobilize aristocratic support for the king, and consequently to stabilize the government of England, was going to succeed. The summer musters, although they had revealed many deficiencies, had also involved noblemen and gentlemen actively in a function which identified them with the queen's policies, and put their loyalty on display. 'God prospereth the king's majesty in all his proceedings', declared the earl of Bedford, a man who would not hitherto have suspected the Almighty of such misplaced patronage.[39] However, it soon transpired that the successes of these months were ephemeral, and that the underlying problems had not gone away. Pembroke's force had been oversubscribed at one point, but there were rumblings of discontent in the fleet. At the beginning of August there was a mutiny of unknown dimensions, and the local authorities in the South West had to be ordered to assist with the impressment of seamen. Early in September a number of mariners and shipmasters were imprisoned on suspicion of betraying their vessels to the French, and later in the same month a brawl took place between English and Spanish seamen at Dartmouth.[40] Paul IV's withdrawal from the war made no significant difference to Anglo-Papal relations, which continued to be bad, and both Philip and Mary suffered from mounting financial difficulties. The king had defaulted on his obligations in June, with both Spain and the Netherlands protesting at overtaxation. The queen, whose financial policy had shown encouraging signs of success over the previous two years, was compelled to resort to a forced loan in September, and during October and November scores of men were referred to the council by the loan commissioners in the shires for their unwillingness or inability to pay.[41] At the same time, Philip's military advantage was short-lived. For about a month after the fall of Saint-Quentin the French would have been in no position to

[39] Davies, 'England and the French War', 166.
[40] *APC*, VI, 141–2, 171; Loades, *Reign of Mary Tudor*, 374.
[41] Loades, *The Reign of Mary Tudor*, 406.

resist a determined advance, but he had neither the nerve nor the resources to exploit the situation. During September he consolidated his position, capturing neighbouring fortresses such as Han and Catalet, and at the beginning of October began to move his regular forces into winter garrisons. By that time most of the English had already gone home. Mustered on 15 September, they numbered just over 6000 fit men, including the nobles and officers, having suffered nearly 1500 casualties by battle or sickness. By 10 October only 500 were left, and these were expected to depart in the near future.[42] Although it had done better than the sceptical Spaniards had expected, the value of the English expeditionary force had been more political than military, as this rapid process of disbandment makes clear. Moreover, by the end of October the ending of the war in Italy had brought the duke of Guise and his veteran troops back to the northern front; and Henry was determined to redeem the humiliation of Saint-Quentin with the minimum of delay.

In one sense Calais was an obvious target for such an enterprise. Half a dozen schemes had been prepared against the town during the previous four years, and its substantial protestant population was thought to have made it ripe for subversion. On the other hand, the fortifications were believed to be exceptionally strong, and the English set great store by retaining this last fragment of their once extensive French lands. Guise had at first been sceptical, but reconnaissance by the Italian mercenary Piero Strozzi some time in November apparently convinced him. The walls had been substantially rebuilt prior to Henry VIII's last French war, in 1539–42, but had not subsequently been repaired or maintained, and the castle was in ruins. Even more important, the garrisons were well below fighting strength – about 600 men in Calais itself, 800 at Guisnes, and mere handfuls at Hammes and Rysbanck, the critical fortress which guarded the entrance to the harbour.[43] These garrisons had been reinforced when there had been an alarm in December 1556, and again after the outbreak of war, in July 1557. But when it was thought that the campaigning season was over, the numbers had been heavily reduced as an economy measure. No one was expecting a serious attack in the middle of the winter, and the

[42] BL Stowe MS 571 ff.87–93.

[43] Davies, 'England and the French war', 170 and n.20.

opportunity was therefore too good to be missed. Surprise was the crucial factor, because, with the exception of the castle, the fortifications were not seriously decayed, and the place was well stocked with both arms and provisions. Although Guise kept his army divided until the last moment, the presence of 27,000 men on a war footing in Picardy could not be concealed, and there was a good deal of speculation during December as to the objective of the coming attack. Calais was mentioned speculatively, but the prevailing opinion among the Imperial commanders was that the duke would move against Luxembourg as soon as the weather permitted. However, on 18 December a reliable Imperial spy discovered the truth, and his information was promptly passed on to the duke of Savoy, commanding Philip's army, and to Lord Wentworth, the governor of Calais. Neither reacted with sufficient urgency; Savoy does not seem to have reacted at all. The English council was alerted on 24 December, and Wentworth finally sent an urgent appeal for reinforcements on the 26th. Had that appeal been promptly answered, with whatever forces were immediately available, disaster could have been averted, but instead the next few days saw bewildering changes of mind, both by Wentworth and the council. On the 29th he wrote again to declare a false alarm – Hesdin was the real objective. On the same day the council sent orders to the Channel fleet to proceed to Calais, and to the earl of Rutland to cross at once with a small number of men. On the 31st these orders were rescinded, and the same day Wentworth reiterated his appeal for urgent assistance. The next day, before either Philip or the council could respond, the whole French army swept into the Pale.[44]

Guise's tactics were as effective as his strategy. With the marshes frozen he was able to strike direct at Rysbanck which, almost unmanned, surrendered immediately on 2 January. The following day, when Rutland tried to enter the harbour, his ships were turned back by gunfire from the fort. That was the critical moment: enough English ships and soldiers were available to

[44] Lord Grey to the queen, 22 December 1557; queen to Lord Wentworth, 24 December; memorandum of intelligences, 26 December; council in Calais to the queen, 27 December, and enclosed reports; Lord Grey to the queen, 31 December; PRO SP69/11/695, 696 (i, ii), 698 (i-iv), 702. See also D. L. Potter, 'The Duc de Guise and the fall of Calais', *English Historical Review*, XCVIII, 481–512.

have frustrated the French attack, but the ships were not strong enough, or numerous enough, to force their way into the harbour under the Rysbanck batteries. Newnham bridge, on the fringe of the Pale, surrendered on 4 January, and Calais castle was taken by assault on the 7th. Lord Wentworth's will to resist was subsequently questioned, but he did make two determined and bloody attempts to regain the castle before deciding that his position had become untenable. Probably the failure of a force of musketeers from Gravelines to fight their way through to the town on the 6th had as much to do with his decision as the loss of the castle. As soon as Calais had fallen, energetic attempts were made to redeem the situation. Philip managed to get a small relieving force into Guisnes, but he could not instantly conjure a field army out of a collection of winter garrisons. Fresh musters were ordered in England on 5 January, when 500 Kentishmen were already on standby at Dover, and ships were impressed. However, a severe storm on the night of 9–10 January scattered and damaged the ships which had already arrived, and made an immediate counterstroke impossible. Time was now clearly on the side of the French, who held the initiative in every quarter. On the 16th the duke of Savoy announced that he was proceeding to the relief of Guisnes, but he never got there. On the 21st Guisnes surrendered after a brief but costly siege, and Hammes was abandoned, in both cases after mutinies in the garrisons had undermined the authority of the commanders.[45] The English plan had been to send 5000 men under the earl of Rutland to Dunkirk, and on 19 January Valentine Browne had been instructed to draw £10,000 from the mint, and proceed to the venue. However, by the 25th only 1200 men had assembled, and the fall of the last fortresses in the Pale deprived the expedition of its purpose. Ruy Gomez reported to Philip that the English troops were so few and of such poor quality as to be useless, and the king countermanded their orders.[46]

The whole story of the loss of Calais is, on the English side, a sorry recital of misfortune and incompetence. The government

[45] Earl of Rutland to the queen, 3 January 1558; Rutland, Tresham and Jerningham to the queen, 6 January 1558; duke of Savoy to Philip, 22 January 1558; PRO SP69/12/712, 715; *Cal.Span.*, XIII, 343; Davies, 'England and the French war', 173–4; Loades, *Reign of Mary Tudor*, 376–7.

[46] PRO E351/22; Philip to the privy council, 31 January 1558; *Cal.Span.*, XIII, 348.

subsequently salved its injured pride by indicting Wentworth and four of his officers for high treason in surrendering their trusts by prior arrangement with the enemy, but no conclusive evidence was ever produced. Strategically and financially, the Pale was no loss, as subsequent events were to demonstrate, but in 1558 and for at least a decade thereafter, English honour and self-esteem were deeply wounded. The mood of self-satisfaction, which had existed in both London and Brussels during the autumn of 1557, was rudely blown away by the events of January, and replaced by renewed suspicion and mutual recrimination. English complaints that Philip had failed to come to their assistance when he could have done so were almost certainly unjustified. However, other grievances were more substantial. No sooner had the French established themselves in Calais – and while the king was still urging the English council to make every effort to recover the place – than Flemish merchants were supplying and provisioning the garrison under licence from Philip himself. Feria, representing Philip in England during February and March, was acutely embarrassed, and urged the king to withdraw his safe-conducts.[47] The English were understandably angry, and reproached him constantly, but the Flemings had paid the king much-needed money for their privilege, and nothing was done. On 4 February Philip added insult to injury by instructing Feria to stop a proposed English voyage to the Portuguese Indies, 'as considerable prejudice might be done to the king of Portugal's interests, which narrowly concern me'. At the same time, while the English council was expressing alarm about the possibility of a sea-war with the Hanseatic League, the king was still backing the Hanse against the English merchants, and fobbing off the latter's complaints with bland professions of goodwill.[48] Nor would he make any declaration against Scotland, although repeatedly asked to do so, for fear of upsetting the Flemish merchants. It is not surprising that Feria admitted on 5 February that the English were not being treated with justice, and that there was substance in their complaints.

[47] Duke of Savoy to Philip, 9 January 1558; Feria to Philip, 22 February 1558; *Cal.Span.*, XIII, 323, 361–2.

[48] Philip to Feria, 4 February 1558; Philip to the privy council, 31 January 1558; *Cal.Span.*, XIII, 351, 348. For a further discussion of the quarrel with the Hanse, see Loades, *Reign of Mary Tudor*, 238–9.

On the other hand, he was most vociferous to complain about the English themselves, and his dispatches are full of representations about confusion, mismanagement and ill will. His first task, on 27 January, had been to discuss with the English council a proposal from Philip for a combined operation to recover Calais. The council expressed its appreciation to the king for the effort which he was willing to make, but declared that the task was beyond their resources. An army of 20,000 men would be required, which would take time to assemble. By the time it could be done, the French would have been able to make the town wellnigh impregnable, so that a campaign of at least five months would be needed, costing a minimum of £170,000. Existing garrison commitments amounted to £150,000 in a year, and another £200,000 would be needed for the fleet and coastal defence works. The country simply could not sustain such expenditure. Not only that, but there was a chronic shortage of suitably trained manpower, so that German mercenaries would be needed, even to defend the Scottish borders.[49] Feria was unimpressed, believing that the English were sulking and dragging their feet. The parliament which assembled on 20 January was generally anti-French in sentiment, and voted a subsidy with relatively little fuss. But it would only authorize the collection of the first half of the subsidy in 1558, and refused to place a total embargo on French trade. In many ways it was the most satisfactory of Mary's parliaments, and she prorogued it on 7 March for that reason, but it had not shown much enthusiasm for the war, and Feria regarded the subsidy as derisory.[50] The council, he complained, echoing Renard's words of four years earlier, was perpetually divided, and the councillors seemed to change their opinions and decisions with bewildering speed. One day Paget was saying that the country could easily produce 800,000 crowns (£200,000), the next he was full of doubts. Neither he nor any of Philip's other pensioners who had previously been willing to serve him was now prepared to lift a finger.

Feria's scornful jeremiad needs to be treated with the usual caution. His main grievance was that the English were not

[49] BL Cotton MS Titus B II, f.59; G. Burnet, *The History of the Reformation in England*, II, 324–5.

[50] Feria to Philip, 12 February 1558; *Cal.Span.*, XIII, 355–6; Loach, *Parliament and the Crown* 159–69; Loades, *Reign of Mary Tudor*, 386–7.

willing to accept priorities of policy laid down in Brussels. He also had no understanding of the true state of Mary's revenues. Nor were the manpower difficulties simply the result of low morale. Attempts to raise forces for the war were unsatisfactory after the summer of 1557, both in quality and quantity, but that was rather on account of the devastating influenza epidemic than of large-scale non-cooperation. Between the autumn of 1557 and the autumn of 1558 the mortality rate in some regions was three or four times the normal average, and the period has been described as the most serious demographic crisis of the century.[51] Equally important, the nature of the disease left a large number of the survivors debilitated, unfit both for normal work and for military service for many weeks after the crisis of the sickness was past. So it is not surprising that the musters held in the summer of 1558 could not raise the predetermined numbers of armed men. At the same time the English war effort was not as inadequate as Feria believed. The English fleet played an important part in Egmont's victory at Gravelines, raided the western islands of Scotland, and devastated the coast of Brittany.[52] When Philip was informed on 2 February that the council was so downcast and craven that the country could be taken by a hundred Frenchmen, he was being treated to rhetorical exaggeration of ridiculous proportions. What is reflected in these dispatches, and in other evidence of the period, is a further decline in the authority and prestige of the king. Damaged and undermined by neglect during the eighteen months from August 1555 to March 1557, that authority had been revived by Philip's presence. The advent of war had brought nobles and gentlemen to seek service and profit in his armies, and re-established the power of his supporters in the privy council. By February 1558

[51] A. G. R. Smith, *The Emergence of a Nation State, 1529–1660*, 55; F. J. Fisher, 'Influenza and inflation in Tudor England', *Economic History Review*, 2nd series XVIII, 120–30. 'What diseases and sicknesses everywhere prevailed! The like wherof had never been known before [which] ... began in the great dearth of 1556, and increased more and more the two following years. In the summer of 1557 they raged horribly throughout the realm and killed an exceeding great number of all sort of men ... In 1558, in the summer, about August, the same fevers raged again.' Strype, *Ecclesiastical Memorials*, III, 156.

[52] The Brittany expedition was not a success, but involved a substantial effort. There were also some 9000 troops kept on the Scottish border, and 1000 sappers were raised for Philip. Davies, 'England and the French war', 179.

disillusionment had again set in. The victorious campaign had been brief, and no Englishman had found a place in Philip's permanent military or civilian service on the Continent. His English pensions were falling into arrears, and Feria was bombarded with complaints 'as though I had been the treasurer'.[53] After the Calais fiasco Philip had insisted upon sacking the admiral, Lord William Howard, a move which caused a good deal of resentment, and had studiously ignored English interests and susceptibilities in other areas. When it came to defending themselves, the English were reasonably efficient. Two important statutes were passed by the 1558 parliament to improve the system of musters, in March a comprehensive system of lieutenancies covered all the English and Welsh counties for the first time, and by the summer modern and expensive fortifications had been undertaken at Berwick.[54] But when it came to prosecuting an active Continental war of the kind which both Philip and Feria wanted, neither the will nor the resources could be found.

Mary's personal reaction to this deteriorating situation can be only partly reconstructed. According to Pole, she received the news of the fall of Calais itself with stoical fortitude. On the other hand the popular tale, retailed by Foxe, that she declared Calais to be written on her heart, has an authentic sound to it. Although it was the duty of a Christian prince to accept such reverses as the inscrutable will of God, they could hardly be regarded as marks of divine favour. Her failure to bear a child, disastrous harvest and epidemics, and now military catastrophe, presented a real problem to a person of Mary's conscientious piety. Where had she gone wrong? One section of her subjects, of course, had no difficulty in pointing to the answer. To the protestants she was another Jezebel, a patron and promoter of idolatry, and a persecutor of the saints. In April 1557 Robert Pownall had published *An Admonition to the towne of Callays* in which he had declared:

> thy mother the staffe of thy defence is now so debilitated and weakened as well in worthy capitaines and valiante soldiers as in money, munitions

[53] *Cal.Span.*, XIII, 356. In March the sum owing was calculated at £2812 10s.; *Cal.Span.*, XIII, 373.

[54] Statutes 4 & 5 Philip and Mary, cs.2 and 3; *Cal.Span.*, XIII, 369; PRO E101/483/16; H. M. Colvin, *History of the King's Works* (1982), IV, 2, 613–64.

> and victuail, that she is scant able to defende & releve hir selfe muche lesse then to sueccour the in thy necessitie.[55]

These words must have seemed prophetic ten months later, and Pownall had ascribed the cause to the queen herself, 'another Athalia, that is an utter distroier ... of her owne subjects, a lover of strangers & an unnatural stepdame both to the and to thy mother England'. Pownall's argument, linking idolatry with foreign influence, was echoed by other protestant writers, most particularly Bartholomew Traheron and Christopher Goodman.[56] Traheron denounced Mary vehemently as a traitor to God and her country, and Goodman informed the English aristocracy that it was their failure to rebel effectively against such an evil ruler which had provoked the wrath of God. Mary and Pole were both aware of this propaganda, and their reaction was anger rather than distress. To them, it was rather their failure to exterminate such vipers which was being punished, and the loyal publicist Miles Huggarde reflected this view when he wrote:

> special causes there be whiche provocketh Goddes vengeance to light upon us, as chiefly infidelitie wherby God is most hainously dishonored, for the which we are most iustly punished; and also our rebellious murmuring against our regale rulers appointed of God to raigne over us.[57]

Both Mary and Philip blamed the heretics explicitly for the fall of Calais. In reporting its loss to the princess of Portugal, Cardinal Siguenza declared that Lord Wentworth and all those with him were known protestants, and another writer reckoned that there had not been ten good catholics in the whole town. But this conviction was never put into print to counteract the broadsides of hostile propaganda. By 1558 even Huggarde seems to have given up, but there is no sign that Mary ever doubted the correctness of the course which she was following.

Calais was a blow which could be turned, a temporary set-back, but childlessness was a fatal weakness in the queen's position. By Christmas 1557 she had again convinced herself

[55] *STC* 19078.

[56] Traheron, *A warning to England ... by the terrible example of Calece STC* 24174; Goodman, *How Superior Powers oght to be obeyd STC* 12020.

[57] *The Displaying of the Protestauntes STC* 13557 Sig.3v.

that she was pregnant, and in sending this happy news to Philip, declared that she had delayed her announcement this time in order to be absolutely sure.[58] The king naturally expressed the warmest satisfaction, but private reactions everywhere were of undisguised scepticism. On hearing the news in February the cardinal of Lorraine observed unkindly (and not quite accurately) that at least they would not have so long to wait this time, since it was eight months since Philip had left England. It is hard to know whether even Mary's own courtiers took her conviction seriously, because there was no repetition of the elaborate preparations for a lying-in, which had taken place in 1555. When a rumour reached the constable of France at the end of March that she had been delivered of a son, he had great difficulty in keeping a straight face. Nevertheless, on 30 March the queen made her will, 'foreseeing the great danger which by Godd's ordynance remaine to all whomen in ther travel of children'. This lengthy document (see appendix 3) with its numerous and generous bequests to all the religious houses in the realm, other charitable and pious foundations, and her loyal servants and familiars, is a fair reflection both of her character and her religious enthusiasm. The succession to the crown, she declared, 'shall wholly and entirely descend remayne & be unto the heyres, issewe and frewte of my bodye, accordyng to the laws of this Realme', with the guardianship and regency to Philip, who was also to be the chief executor of the will itself. By the end of April she knew that her hopes had again been disappointed, but despite the fact that she was now forty-two, and there was no prospect of an early visit from her husband, she refused to concede defeat by altering these arrangements.

To Philip this lack of political realism was extremely annoying. As Renard had pointed out to him in a memorandum of uncertain date, undesirable as Elizabeth was, alternative prospective heirs were worse, and the question of her marriage became more urgent with every month that passed.[59] If left to her own devices

[58] Surian to the doge and senate, 15 January 1558; *Cal. Ven.*, VI, 1427. Philip to Pole, 21 January 1558; *Cal.Span.*, XIII, 340.

[59] Notes in Renard's hand; *Cal.Span.*, XIII, 372–3. This document is dated by the editor March? 1558; but reference to 'a further examination of Stafford' means that it must have been written before the author heard of Stafford's execution, which had taken place on 28 May 1557.

she might marry an Englishman, restore the heretical church, and realign English foreign policy with France. Philip already believed that Mary's refusal to contemplate Elizabeth as her successor increased this danger by blocking the path to a suitable marriage. The king was as persistent as his wife was obstinate, and at some point during the spring of 1558 the question of the Savoy match was revived. By 1 May Mary already knew what was intended, and became extremely agitated when an embassy arrived from Gustavus Vasa of Sweden, soliciting the princess's hand for his son Eric, the duke of Finland. The Swedish ambassador behaved improperly by going to see Elizabeth without the queen's permission, and there was no chance of such a union with a quasi-Lutheran being acceptable to Philip, but the incident served to put the princess's status and future firmly back on the agenda.[60] An exchange of correspondence took place, of which only one letter survives, but that gives sufficient indication of Mary's distressed state of mind. Perhaps to put off a decision, or perhaps in an attempt to shift the responsibility, she offered to put the matter before parliament; to which the king replied that if parliament rejected it, he would hold her to blame.

> 'I beseech you in all humility', she wrote, 'to put off the business until your return ... For otherwise your Highness will be angry against me, and that will be worse than death for me, for I have already begun to taste your anger all too often, to my great sorrow.'[61]

Philip also urged her to re-examine the conscientious scruples which supported her objections, to which she responded that she had long before discussed the matter with Alphonsus (de Castro, one of the king's confessors), who had left her more confused than satisfied. What her conscience held, it had held for twenty-four years – that is, since Elizabeth's birth.[62] Only if Philip and the duke of Savoy both came to England could the matter possibly be resolved. Since the king had already tried direct persuasion without success, he did not rise to this bait, but the numerous visits which Feria paid to Elizabeth during his stay in

[60] Feria to Philip, 1 May 1558; *Cal.Span.*, XIII, 378–80.

[61] BL MS Cotton Titus B II, f.109; Strype, *Ecclesiastical Memorials*, III, ii, 418; Prescott, *Mary Tudor*, 377–8.

[62] Prescott, *Mary Tudor*, 377–8.

England – until the end of July – may have been partly in this connection. He never reported the content of these discussions, but usually expressed his satisfaction with them, so perhaps the princess was also taking refuge behind her sister's conscience, hinting at a willingness to comply, if only the queen could be persuaded. In public she continued to profess an unwillingness to marry, but Mary did not trust her on that issue any more than on any other.

The war spluttered on through the summer of 1558, without decisive advantage. Imperial victory at Gravelines was counterbalanced by French victory at Thionville. A joint English and Flemish naval expedition endeavoured to capture Brest, but was repulsed. In England the sickness continued, with high mortality, and no one came to London if they could avoid it. Peace negotiations had begun in May, but made no more progress than the war itself. William Peto was dead, and the pope made no effort to replace him, but Anglo-Papal relations continued to be difficult. Routine business languished, episcopal appointments were unconfirmed, and Paul's distrust of Pole was undiminished.[63] In these discouraging circumstances the cardinal and his bishops stuck manfully to their task, although in Feria's eyes they shared the same lack of animation that afflicted everything English. 'The Cardinal is a dead man', he wrote on 10 March, 'a good man, but very lukewarm', especially in the service of the king. Feria was an enthusiastic patron of the Jesuits, and believed that Philip should have taken the initiative in introducing the order to England. Perhaps the king did not share his enthusiasm, or perhaps he was unwilling to intrude upon Mary's jurisdiction. Nothing was done, and the persecution in England continued to be mainly a judicial and punitive process. It could hardly be described as a policy, because both Mary and Pole believed that it was their duty as Christian magistrates to punish heretics, and to eradicate them as a poison in the commonwealth.[64] They do not seem to have enjoyed much success. As one of his commissioners wrote to Bishop Bonner of London in April 1558, 'we

[63] Loades, *Reign of Mary Tudor*, 434 and nn.

[64] Stephen Gardiner, for whom the persecution had been a calculated policy of intimidation, had wished to abandon it for other methods in the summer of 1555; Foxe, *Acts and Monuments*, VI, 704. Loades, *Reign of Mary Tudor*, 332–4.

have such obstinat heretikes, anabaptists, and other unruly persons here [Colchester] as never was harde of.'[65] The burnings had never been popular, and occasional hostile demonstrations had occurred at such events since John Rogers had become the 'protomartyr' in February 1555. But the longer they went on, the more serious the problem became. In the summer of 1557 the sheriffs of Kent, Essex, Suffolk and Staffordshire, and the officers of Rochester and Colchester had all been in trouble with the council for failing to carry out the sentences of the ecclesiastical courts with sufficient expedition – a task which they clearly found distasteful. In August 1558 Sir Richard Pexsall, the sheriff of Hampshire, was bound in the large recognizance of £500 to answer for a similar offence, a penalty which must have been intended as an exemplary warning, since it appears to have resulted from a mere misunderstanding.[66] At the same time, Bonner was so nervous of 'tumults' that he was suggesting clandestine burnings, in the early hours of the morning, without the sheriff's presence. This was a far cry from the high-profile executions of the earlier days, which had been intended to intimidate the like-minded into submission.

In other ways the restored catholic church was doing quite well. Fabric was being repaired, altars and images reappeared, and above all ordinations had soared. But financial retrenchment was seriously affected by the war, as increased clerical taxation removed most of what had been gained by recovery and redistribution, and discipline continued to take precedence over evangelism. In time such a policy might have worked, but by the summer of 1558 time was running out for both Mary and Pole, and the queen had not taken the vital step which could have protected her achievement beyond her own lifetime. Warning signs of the queen's deteriorating health began to appear in May, but at first they had seemed no more serious than many earlier attacks. At the beginning of the month Feria had reported that she was weak and melancholy, and was sleeping badly, but attributed this to depression over the loss of her supposed pregnancy. On the 18th he referred casually to her 'usual ailments'. In early June she was 'worse than usual', but ap-

[65] BL Harlian MS 416, f.77.

[66] *APC*, VI, 135, 361, 371; Sir John Butler was fined for a similar offence on 7 August 1557; ibid., 144.

parently improved by the end of the month, when Philip specifically enquired because she had not written for several days, which was evidently unusual.[67] About the middle of August she developed a fever, which was also unusual for her. According to a report from Pole to Philip she took very good care of herself, and the symptoms had disappeared by early September. However, he was optimistic too soon. By the end of September she was ill again, and her condition began to give cause for alarm. A visit from the king, it was said, would be the most sovereign remedy, but for a great many reasons Philip could not come.

One of these reasons was that his father, the Emperor Charles V, had died at Saint-Yuste on 21 September. He had never abdicated his Imperial dignity, and so although the planned transition to his brother Ferdinand took place as a matter of course, there were some formalities to be attended to. More important, there was court mourning, and the proper celebration of his obsequies, which did not eventually take place until the later part of November. Mary probably never learned of the death of her long time protector and patron, because Philip himself did not receive final confirmation until 1 November, and by that time the queen's own condition was so serious that such bad news could well have had fatal consequences.[68] The other matter occupying the king's attention was the commencement on 8 October of a fresh round of negotiations with the French at Cercamp, during which Philip's relations with the English commissioners were distinctly delicate. One of the main sticking points was the return of Calais. The English felt that the king owed it to them not to make peace without Calais, and Philip was inclined to agree. On the other hand he desperately needed peace, and the French made it perfectly clear that they had no intention of surrendering their prestigious gain. Consequently, by the end of October there was a situation of crisis, caused both by the queen's health and by the deadlock over Calais.

[67] *Cal.Span.*, XIII, 398.

[68] Extract from *A Journal of the Travels of Philip II* by Jean Vandenesse, printed as an appendix to *Cal.Span.*, XIII; 'Tuesday (1 November), his Majesty being at Arras, had certain news, via France, of the death of his father.' The news had reached Paris 'by a Portuguese courier' on 18 October; *Cal.Ven.*, VI, 1534. Why such important information took so long, and came so circuitously, is not clear. Martin de Gaztelu had written direct from Saint-Yuste on 21 September, but presumably the message never arrived. *Cal.Span.*, XIII, 409.

17 New Hall, also known as Beaulieu, Mary's principal residence in the years before her accession.

18 Framlingham Castle, in Suffolk, where Mary rallied her forces in July set up her first council.

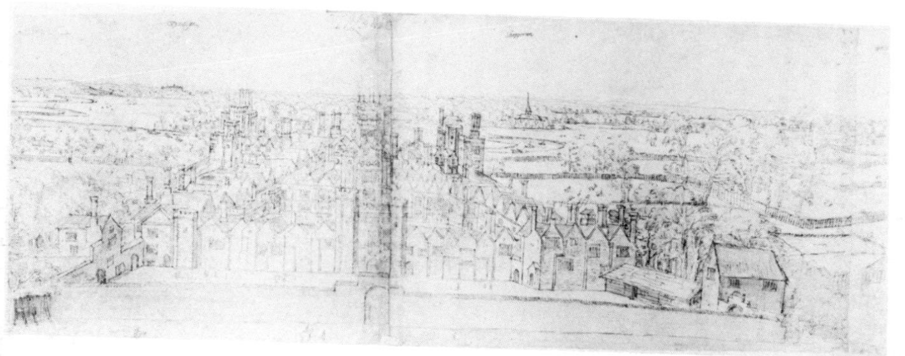

19 Oatlands, a small royal residence in Surrey, much favoured by Henry VIII. From a drawing by Wyngaerde.

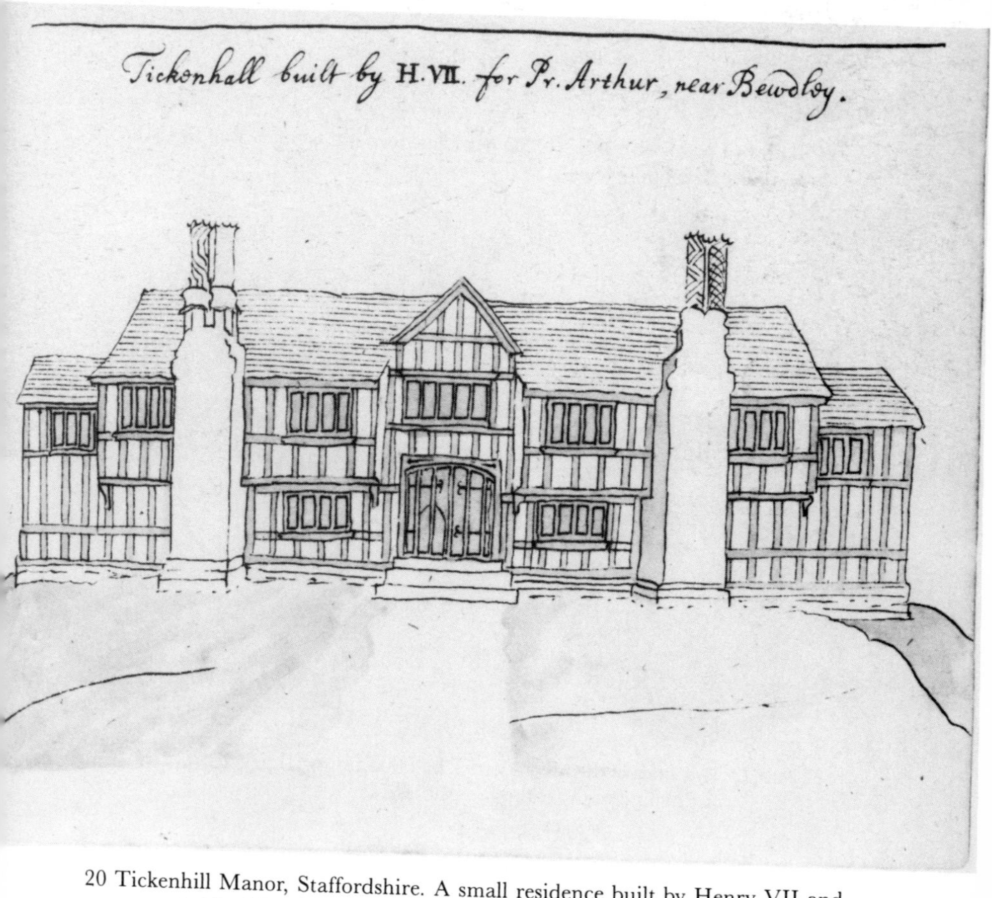

Tickenhall built by H.VII. for Pr. Arthur, near Bewdley.

20 Tickenhill Manor, Staffordshire. A small residence built by Henry VII and renovated for Mary's use during her time in the marches of Wales.

21 Ludlow Castle, Shropshire. The headquarters of the Council of the Marches, and Mary's main residence in the borders.

22 and 23 Two sides of the medal struck by Pope Julius III to celebrate the return of England to the catholic church in 1555.

24 and 25 Two woodcuts depicting Elizabeth's imprisonment after the Wyatt rebellion in 1554. The head emerging through the arras may be intended to represent Stephen Gardiner.

26 An allegory of the succession of Henry VIII, by Lucas de Heere. A piece of Elizabethan propaganda, representing Philip and Mary as the harbingers of war.

27 Thomas Cranmer, renouncing his recantation. From a woodcut in the 1631 edition of John Foxe's *Acts and Monuments.*

28 An Italian spinet c.1537. One of several instruments which Mary played with considerable skill.

29 Elizabethan jousting. The queen watching a tournament in the great tiltyard at Whitehall.

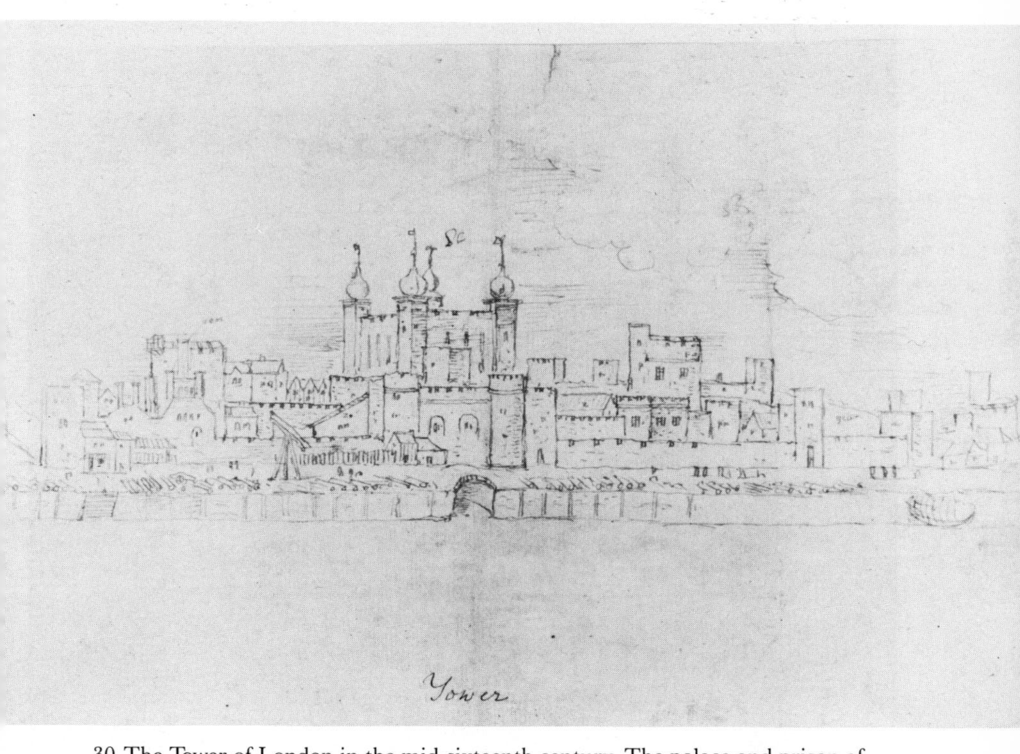

30 The Tower of London in the mid-sixteenth century. The palace and prison of monarchs. From a drawing by Wyngaerde.

31 Cardinal Reginald Pole, by an unknown artist. The son of Margaret, and Mary's cousin, he was a major influence on the queen in the last three years of her life.

32 The Emperor Charles V, by Titian. Although she only met him briefly in her childhood, he remained her chief protector and inspiration until his abdication in 1556.

33 and 34 The palace of Greenwich, by Wyngaerde. One of the most important and heavily used royal residences throughout the sixteenth century.

35 Portrait of an unknown man, thought to be Sir Henry Bedingfield, Mary's Vicechamberlain and Elizabeth's gaoler.

36 Obverse of a gold rial of Henry VIII.

37 Reverse of a gold rial of Mary.

38 The arms of Philip and Mary, from an eighteenth-century painting in Trinity College, Oxford.

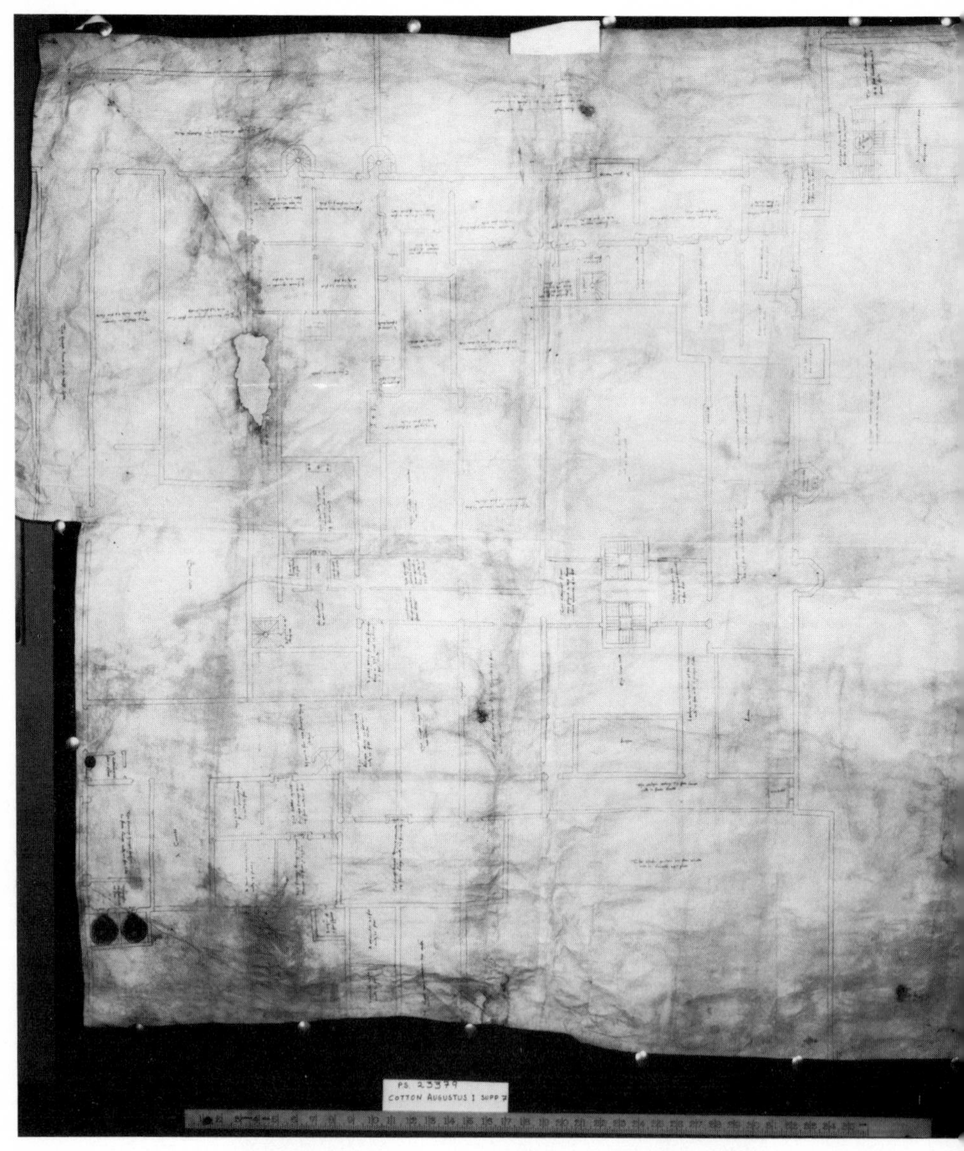

39 The Calais Exchequer, used as a residence by Henry VIII in 1520 and 1532.

Philip's agents in England, Alonso de Cordoba and Christophe d'Assonville, were not senior enough to cope, and it was decided to send Feria back, as a high-ranking councillor whom both Philip and Mary trusted. Feria arrived in London on 9 November, and immediately concluded that the queen's life was measured in days. As a result, the political situation was alarming. Feria had long believed that the king had wasted his assets in England by taking insufficient interest in the country, and by failing to build up an effective party in the council. His worst fears were confirmed by what he found on his return: 'they received me', he wrote, 'as they would a man who came with bulls from a dead Pope.'[69] Philip's pensioners had not been paid for over a year, with one or two favoured exceptions, and his English household had not been paid for two years, except for the archers of his guard, who also served the queen and were paid through her privy chamber.[70] Even Paget refused to see him privately.

All eyes were on Elizabeth, and when Feria reported on 14 November, most of his dispatch was devoted to her, her statements, her supporters and her likely policies. When he had seen her last, back in June, she had seemed grateful for the king's favour, and willing to be accommodating. Now, on the eve of her accession, her attitude was very different. She trusted entirely to the people, he declared, and rejected all suggestions that Philip's willingness to recognize her claim had strengthened her position. She amused herself at Feria's expense by reminding him how hard his master had tried to marry her to the duke of Savoy, 'and smiled at the thought of it'. The queen had lost the affection of her people, she continued, on the same train of thought, because she had married a foreigner. She was quite convinced that the Crown was hers, no matter what Philip or Mary might say, and acted accordingly. When he told her that the English commissioners at Cercamp were holding out for Calais, she replied that that was just as well, as she would have them beheaded if they made peace without restoration. Feria was clearly impressed, rather against his will as he was convinced she was a heretic. 'She is a very vain and clever woman', he concluded, '[who] must have been thoroughly schooled in the

[69] 'The Count of Feria's despatch to Philip II of 14 November 1558', ed. M. J. Rodríguez Salgado and S. Adams, *Camden Miscellany*, XXVIII, 320/329.

[70] By the end of 1558 £11,365 was owed. Archivo General de Simancas, Secretaria de Estado, legajo 811, f.124. PRO E101/428/9.

manner in which her father conducted his affairs . . .' He was also somewhat taken aback by her attitude over Philip's pensioners. She demanded a list of their names, and expressed grave reservations over the propriety of their continuing to receive money from one who would soon be a foreign ruler. Many of the council, he reported, were fearful, and convinced that they were about to lose their places, which made them hesitant and confused in the conduct of affairs. Cecil and Lord Robert Dudley were among those who would shortly take over their responsibilities.

By the time that Feria saw her, the last conflict of Mary's life was over. As late as 28 October she had made a codicil to her will, acknowledging her sickness, and the uncertainty of issue, but making no specific provision for the succession.[71] However, when the parliament reassembled on 5 November, anxious members of the Commons, knowing of her condition, took the initiative. Exactly how or when this was done is not clear. Feria believed that the Commons had sought a conference with the Lords, and that as a result a joint request had gone to the council to persuade the queen to 'accept Madam Elizabeth as her sister and heiress, and to inform her of this in loving terms'. The Journals record only that the Speaker William Cordell (who was a member of the council) was summoned to the queen on 7 November.[72] According to Feria, Cordell and Cornwallis had then been sent to Hatfield, where Elizabeth had received them graciously, and where her 'shadow government' was already assembling. The queen had made only two requests of her successor – that her debts be paid and religion preserved. It was a meaningless gesture, because everyone knew that Elizabeth would please herself. Difficult as her situation might be in some ways, and numerous as were the expectations focusing upon her, she was completely free from any obligation which could be enforced. Mary had failed to exclude her, in a campaign which had begun in a somewhat desultory fashion in the autumn of 1554, but had become increasingly determined and emotional as the reign progressed, and particularly from the start of 1557. The main result was a legacy of bitterness. 'She is highly indignant about what has been done to her during the queen's lifetime', reported Feria. Since she was usually very good at concealing

[71] BL Harley MS 6949 f.29; Stone, *Mary I*, appendix, 518–21.
[72] *Commons Journal*, 7 November; Loach, 170.

her emotions, particularly from those she suspected, this statement is testament to the strength of her feelings. All that Mary had succeeded in doing was to give her successor a powerful incentive to denigrate her reputation and undo her policies. It is not surprising that many of the council were apprehensive in the early days of November.

Mary was sufficiently conscious to recognize Feria when he arrived, and to understand his message, but not to read the letters which he brought with him. She was now mainly in the care of her women, being past the help of physicians, and she was fortunate in their loyal affection, which in some cases extended back over a quarter of a century. Eleanor Kempe, Susan Clarencius, Frideswide Strelly, Barbara Hawke and Jane Dormer had all served her before her accession, and are known to have had close personal ties. One of Mary's last recorded thoughts was for Jane Dormer, her young favourite and the only lady of the court apart from herself to find a Spanish husband. Jane was betrothed to no less a person than Feria himself, and Mary had deliberately delayed their nuptials in the hope of being able to attend. However, by the time that Feria arrived it was too late for that to happen, and the dying queen apologized for having stood in their way.[73] They were eventually married in December, after Mary's funeral, and Feria remained in England until April 1559 clearing up the residue of the king's business. Indeed the household which surrounded Mary on her deathbed was not very different from that which she had created in August 1553. Her elderly lord chamberlain, Sir John Gage, had died in the summer of 1556, and had been replaced by Sir Edward Hastings. Hastings' post as master of the horse was then filled by Sir Henry Jerningham, Sir Henry Bedingfield becoming vice-chamberlain. A more serious personal loss had been the death in November 1557 of Sir Robert Rochester, who had borne so much of the fury of Edward's council on his mistress's behalf. Rochester was probably not as close to the queen in the last two years of his life as he had once been, because of his reservations about her marriage, but he still received numerous marks of favour, including the Garter about six months before he died. He was replaced as controller by Sir Thomas Cornwallis. It was a very personal team. They had all risen to office and fortune through

[73] Clifford, *Life of Jane Dormer*, 69–70.

Mary's favour, and they all retired into private life or went abroad after her death. Whatever happened when Elizabeth came to the throne, there was little chance that any of Mary's friends and favourites would be left in the court, and they knew this perfectly well. Paget and Boxall, the secretary, were on reasonable terms with Elizabeth, but they were both conferring with Cecil during the last days of Mary's life, with a view to arranging a smooth hand-over of responsibility.[74]

The end finally came in the early morning of 17 November. Surrendering to the inevitable over the succession had brought Mary a kind of peace, and although those around her later reproached Philip for having hastened her death by his neglect, she does not seem to have been greatly troubled by his absence at the end. Perhaps she was too used to it. According to the testimony of Jane Dormer, written down long afterwards, 'She comforted those of them that grieved about her; she told them what good dreams she had, seeing little children like angels play before her, singing pleasing notes, giving her more than earthly comfort.'[75] During these last few days, the celebration of the mass was the centre of her conscious existence, as it had been the centre of her spiritual life for many years. So it must have seemed appropriate that she should die, having made the responses, at the elevation of the host, during that last celebration at six o'clock in the morning. Whether or not the story is true hardly matters. She died with the full consolations of the religion which had always meant so much to her, and in the presence of many of those who had loved her as a human and fallible woman. The illness which finally carried her off cannot be identified with certainty. She was not old, even by the standards of the sixteenth century, being three months short of her forty-third birthday. Her health had never been robust since adolescence, and it is natural to suspect that the same disorder which had disrupted her menstruation as a young woman, and given her two phantom pregnancies, finally killed her. Such a diagnosis would be consistent with Foxe's story of 'dropsy', and might indicate either a cancerous tumour or an ovarian cyst. On the other hand there is no suggestion that she suffered great pain during her last illness,

[74] 'The Count of Feria's despatch', 332. BL Cotton MS Vespasian F. xiii f.287 (conference between Heath and Cecil).

[75] Clifford, *Life of Jane Dormer*, 70.

and that same influenza which was laying low her subjects and keeping members of parliament at home on their sickbeds could easily have invaded the palace of St James.[76]

Whether Mary either wrote or sent any message of farewell to Philip is not known. Their relationship had become uneasy since the last clash over Elizabeth's marriage, and it may be significant that the affectionate bequest which she wrote into her will with her own hand in March, was not added to or mentioned in the codicil of October:

> I do humbly beseeche my saide most dearest lorde and husbande to accepte of my bequeste and to kepe for a memory of me one jewell, being a table diamond which themperours Majesty, his and my most honourable Father, sent unto me by the Count degmont.

Some other jewels of similar sentimental importance were also listed, but at that point Philip was also named as chief executor, and it was suggested that the jewels bequeathed should eventually pass 'to the Issue betwene us' which she was then expecting. By the time that the codicil was written, it had become clear that Philip would have no role in England after Mary's death, and could not therefore act as executor, so that role was given to Cardinal Pole, but no alteration was made to the terms of the bequest itself. Philip's own reaction to the news was so restrained as to appear callous: 'the queen my wife is dead. May God have received her in this glory! I felt a reasonable regret for her death.'[77] Hardly the language of emotional devastation. However, the king had recently lost both his father and his aunt, Mary of Hungary, whom he had known far longer, and with whom he had had much more in common. Also, the words quoted are from a hastily compiled letter, full of the preoccupations of state affairs. Philip had never felt the same attachment to Mary that she had felt to him; the whole arrangement had been primarily political from the start. Moreover, although Mary had expressed the greatest devotion, both to him and to his interests, she had not been particularly compliant when it came to obeying his wishes. At the same time, he was a relatively young man with only one son, and it was obvious that she would

[76] Loach, *Parliament and the Crown*, 169–70.

[77] Philip to the princess dowager of Portugal, 4 December 1558; *Cal.Span.*, XIII, 440.

have no children. Philip was too much of a Christian, and perhaps too much of a gentleman, to express it openly, but his principal reaction was probably one of relief. And that relief would have been greatly increased a few weeks later, when he learned that Elizabeth was safely installed, and expressing herself in terms of sisterly affection. On 27 December, after reading letters from the new queen, and receiving her envoy, Lord Cobham, he was able to write in warmer terms than he ever had to Mary, offering his friendly services, and declaring that her affairs would be to him as his own.[78]

Mary's body lay at St James's for almost a month after her death, while Elizabeth's officers took over the reins of power. Feria was distressed by the tone of the comments which were soon being made about her conduct of affairs. As early as 21 November he reported that the late queen was being blamed for having sent vast sums of money out of the realm to support the king's wars, and it seems likely from some of the memoranda which Cecil was preparing for the guidance of the new privy council that these rumours originated at the highest level.[79] There was, indeed, a certain amount of careless muddle in the hand-over. Mary's chamber had been full of state papers (which she had been too ill to attend to) at the time of her death, and some of Thomas Gresham's accounts were actually used for 'cering the corse', but the suspicion that Feria himself had spirited away 200,000 ducats (about £70,000) during that period was quite unfounded. Mourning a deceased monarch was always a somewhat sensitive issue, lest the new incumbent should take offence, and published panegyrics on Mary were far outnumbered by hopeful greetings to Elizabeth. But her passing did not go unlamented by the popular press, and *The epitaphe upon the death of quene Marie*[80] was a much more competent and moving piece than many such occasional offerings, conveying a genuine sense of loss and grief.

[78] Hatfield MSS, calendared in *Historical Manuscript Commission Reports*, IX, 13.

[79] A lengthy memorandum listed all the property which Mary had restored, and suggested the setting up of an enquiry under Lord Rich. At the same time a specific commission was established 'To consider in what points the realm hath sustained great loss during the late Queenes reign'; PRO SP12/1/57, 64.

[80] *STC* 17559; Society of Antiquaries Broadsheet 46, printed by Richard Lant.

She never closed her eare to heare
The righteous man distrest
Nor never sparde her hand to helpe
Wher wrong or power opprest.

The unknown author was not mourning a great ruler, nor even a lost opportunity, like those who had lamented the Godly Imp, Edward VI. He was remembering a woman whose virtues were on a very human scale, and for whom the images of power were less appropriate than the images of patience and suffering.

Her perfecte lyfe in all extremes
Her pacient harte did show
For in this world she never founde
But dolfull dayes and woe.

She was finally buried on 14 December in King Henry VII's chapel at Westminster Abbey, attended to the grave as she would have wished by Abbot Feckenham and his monks. The chief mourner was Margaret, countess of Lennox, her nearest surviving (and acceptable) relation, and the funeral sermon was preached by Bishop John White of Winchester.

He chose as his text the provocative sounding words of Solomon 'Laudavi mortuos magis quam viventes', but he was in fact not much concerned with the living, and his sermon was a panegyric in the traditional style:

> She was a king's daughter, she was a king's sister, she was a king's wife; she was a queen, and by the same title a king also . . . What she suffered in each of these degrees before and since she came to the crown, I will not Chronicle; only this I say, howsoever it pleased God to will her patience to be exercised in the world, she had in all estates the fear of God in her heart.[81]

The ceremonies were lavish and prolonged, extending over two days and costing the Exchequer £7763.[82] At the end, as was customary, her officers broke their wands of office and cast them into the grave. For most of them it was the actual, as well as the symbolic, end to their careers. Her cousin Reginald Pole, the prop of her later years, had followed Mary to the grave within a

[81] Strype, *Ecclesiastical Memorials*, III, 536–50.
[82] PRO SP12/1/32–3.

matter of hours, and Elizabeth, although she was for the time being scrupulously careful to maintain the status quo, had stopped the persecution on the day of her accession, and was already permitting protestant sermons to be preached from Paul's Cross. Ironically the only person in catholic Europe to be pleased by the turn of events in England was Pope Paul IV, for God had removed at a stroke both the semi-heretical cardinal and his pupil, and severed the links between England and Spain. It was to be some months before he discovered the truth, and his wrath was then blunted by the only ruler who could hope to exercise any influence over the new queen – Philip II.

8

The Historical Mary

Everyone who commented upon Mary's conduct of public affairs remarked upon her diligence and her piety. She rose before dawn, heard mass every day, ate frugally and transacted business incessantly, often until after midnight. As queen, she seems to have lost her youthful taste for hunting, and the entertainments of her court were sparse and unremarkable. The effectiveness of so much effort, on the other hand, is hard to assess. She was generous to petitioners, and had the reputation for never turning away anyone with a story of grievance or oppression. After the Wyatt rebellion she was besieged by the wives of the prisoners, and any pardons can be attributed to the effect of their intercessions. Even Jane Wyatt, whose cause was the most hopeless of all, found her sympathetic and easily moved.[1] Unlike Henry VIII, who disliked paperwork and wrote with extreme reluctance, Mary wrote, or at least drafted, many letters in her own hand, particularly to ambassadors. In consequence she was minutely well informed upon a whole range of business, from economies in the household to the conduct of a campaign in Italy. At the same time, both the Venetians and the Spaniards agreed that she enjoyed little real authority, and that all matters of importance were decided by the council, 'who are the lords of the kingdom'. This was partly what they expected to see because as Michieli observed after two and half years experience of the English court, 'Respecting the government and

[1] *The Papers of George Wyatt*, ed. D. M. Loades, (Camden Society, 4th Series), v 194. Jane's half-sister, Mary Finch, was a long-standing servant of Mary's.

public business she is compelled (being of a sex which cannot becomingly take more than a moderate part in them), according to the custom of other sovereigns, to refer many matters to her councillors and ministers.'[2] Unfortunately, as Michieli also noted – and both Renard and Feria concurred – she did not trust the majority of them. This was largely the result of her almost total exclusion from affairs of state throughout her adult life. Although she must have known many of her father's councillors well, those who had been her particular friends had usually fallen out of favour for that reason, and some, notably the marquis of Exeter and countess of Salisbury, had gone to the block. Although her relations with Protector Somerset had been good, she had skirmished incessantly with her brother's councillors, and regarded many of them as heretics and traitors. So she had come to the throne without any confidants at the highest political level. The nucleus of her original council, and the men to whom she was closest, were her household officers, Rochester, Waldegrave, Englefield and Jerningham. These men were good catholics, and good servants, but like their mistress they lacked experience of high office, and although she favoured them all with positions of profit and responsibility, she did not trust them with the guidance of the state – and rightly so.

Those who did have the relevant experience were a mixed group. Some, like Winchester and Bedford, were allowed to retain high offices because they succeeded in convincing her of the genuineness of their conversion; others, like Arundel and Paget, had not been closely associated with Northumberland, and had been the first of the existing council to make their submission. The duke of Norfolk, an almost accidental survivor of Henry VIII's last purge, had never been close to Mary, and was too old for a responsible position, as his failure against Wyatt made clear.[3] Stephen Gardiner, on the other hand, emerged from the prison to which he had been consigned by Somerset, with his faculties, and his appetite for office, unimpaired. Of all these men, he was the one whose position on the important issue of religion was closest to the queen's. But he was, or appeared to be, a recent convert to that point of view, and like all the others, his previous services to the Crown

[2] *Cal. Ven.*, VI, 1054.
[3] Loades, *Two Tudor Conspiracies*, 60–3.

debarred him from the full confidence of a monarch who was unable to forget the harrowing experiences of her own past. And these were only the acceptable ones. Many others had been too close to Northumberland, or too obviously protestant, for their services to be acceptable at all – the marquis of Northampton, Sir William Cecil, and Sir John Cheke. So although Gardiner and Paget, Winchester and Bedford, were all to be good servants and councillors to Mary in their different ways, there was not one with whom she felt personally at ease. She rewarded them with high office because she recognized their skills, and the offices had to be filled, but she was unable to put aside the past and accept the present at face value. In the first place it was seldom clear where the queen's confidence lay when her councillors disagreed, as they were bound to do. There were times when particular leading officers were clearly out of favour – as when Mary berated Gardiner for encouraging the Commons petition of November 1553, or Paget was rusticated for his behaviour in parliament in April 1554 – but usually the situation was much less clear. Mary tended to become confused or angry when there were disputes in council, or when the majority gave her unpalatable advice, as over the war in January 1557. There is no reason to suppose that Mary's council was any more factious or divided than most Tudor councils, because the large numbers which could have contributed to such an outcome were more apparent than real,[4] but the queen's attitude made the problem both more serious and more noticeable. The eruption of the quarrel between Paget and Gardiner onto the floor of the House of Lords in the second parliament was one of the most serious lapses of royal control to occur in the whole century. The other major consequence of the queen's distrust was her tendency to resort to personal favourites outside the council. The first and most obvious of these was Simon Renard. For all practical purposes Renard was Mary's chief adviser from August 1553

[4] As had been the case with the old royal council, before the changes of the 1530s, many of Mary's councillors seldom attended meetings, and some never. The average attendance between June 1554 and June 1557 was 10. Most of the councillors who were marginal for the purpose of meetings were active on commissions, or in local office. Loades, *Reign of Mary Tudor*, 257–8; some functions, particularly in relation to Philip, were also carried out by the smaller 'council of state' of six or seven members, and it was this body which began to use its own seal in May 1555. *APC*, v, 130.

until the arrival of Philip in July 1554. He was reasonably discreet, and there were many aspects of domestic policy into which he did not intrude, but his efforts to determine the fate of suspects after the Wyatt rising, and to manipulate the legislative programme of the second parliament, went far beyond the proper scope of his duties, and should not have been tolerated, let alone encouraged. The second favourite, and one of a completely different kind, was King Philip. By contrast with Renard, he had every right to be consulted, but exactly how much right (or capacity) he had to intervene in English affairs was unclear. By the terms of the marriage treaty, Philip had no independent jurisdiction in England, and could only do what Mary asked or allowed him to do. This was why both Spanish and Italian observers described his position as dishonourable, and why there was such a marked contrast between his role in the negotiations over church lands and his lack of involvement in other affairs. It was a situation which he found almost intolerable, but one which Mary either could not or would not remedy. Her attitude to her husband presents a number of problems. Ostensibly she was devoted to his interests, and anxious to defer as much as possible to his strength and wisdom. In reality, however, she did not carry out his wishes unless they corresponded with her own; so she supported him fully over the French war, but would not give him a coronation, or allow him to force Elizabeth into the Savoy marriage. On a number of issues she seems to have submitted more readily to the guidance of Renard than to that of Philip, but whereas Philip was his own man, Renard represented Charles V, and the emperor was a father-figure whose authority and benevolence Mary never questioned. The third favourite, and a marked contrast to the other two, was Cardinal Reginald Pole. Pole not only enjoyed the privilege of a kinsman, he also represented the pope, to whom Mary professed to be a loving and obedient daughter.[5] He had been out of England long enough to escape the contamination which affected all her regular English councillors, and in circumstances which inspired the highest confidence in his integrity. Moreover, he had a particular talent

[5] *Cal. Ven.*, v, 429. Pole's kinship with the queen also gave him a remote claim to the throne, and according to Strype there would have been a movement among the more determined catholics to advance him in Elizabeth's place if he had not also died. Strype, *Ecclesiastical Memorials*, iii, ii, 138. I have found no contemporary evidence for this.

for counselling the great, especially women, as he had demonstrated in the case of Vittoria Colonna. His name had been connected with that of the queen on a number of occasions in the past, and it had been said at one time that he was the only Englishman she would consider marrying. In 1554, in spite of his eminence in the church, he was still in deacon's orders, and was not ordained priest until the eve of his consecration to Canterbury in 1556. As long as Philip remained in England, Pole confined himself mainly to his ecclesiastical and diplomatic duties, but after the king's departure in August 1555, his role quickly and dramatically increased. He was given discretionary membership of the 'Select Council', which was to keep Philip in touch with English affairs, and was regularly accommodated at court in order to console Mary with his presence and advice. He was never sworn as a privy councillor, but was regularly consulted about a wide range of business. Michieli believed that he had been specifically briefed by the king to protect Mary from the quarrels and deviousness of her normal council:

> The truth is that, knowing the divisions which exist amongst them, her Majesty, in order not to be deceived and for the prevention of scandal, willed (with the king's consent) that Cardinal Pole should hear and have everything referred to him, it being evident that, whilst showing the utmost confidence in him, she distrusts almost all the others.[6]

Pole withdrew from this role temporarily while Philip was in England during 1557, and by the time he returned to duty his position had changed. The withdrawal of his legateship, and particularly the circumstances in which it happened, caused him great mental anguish, and left him dependent upon the queen in a sense which he had never been before. Moreover, much of the public business of the last year of the reign was concerned with the prosecution of a war of which he thoroughly disapproved. Consequently, although he continued to provide personal and emotional support for Mary in the crises of 1558, and to guide ecclesiastical policy, he seems to have become much less active in other affairs of state, and by August of that year his own health was declining into the illness which carried him off.[7]

[6] *Cal. Ven.*, VI, 1056. In October 1555 he was reported to be 'never out' of the queen's apartments at St James's; ibid., 217.

[7] On 6 September he wrote that he had been ill 'for some days' of a double quartan ague. *Cal. Ven.*, VI, 1529.

Because Mary had insufficient experience of managing her own affairs, and was psychologically dependent, her relations with her ministers and councillors were hesitant and inconsistent. This was largely a matter of self-confidence, and her effectiveness varied considerably, both with her mood and also with the state of her health. She was much prone to fits of what her contemporaries described as 'melancholy', which may have been a menopausal disorder, or a type of clinical depression. At these times her normal energy and application disappeared, and she would sink into lethargy. For some time after the failure of her pregnancy in July 1555, and again during the summer of 1556, she seems to have suffered from a hysterical condition, bordering upon collapse.[8] Nevertheless public business continued to be transacted; and since neither Renard, Philip, nor Pole was an executive chief minister in the sense of Wolsey or Cromwell, it must be concluded that this continuity was provided by the regular officers of state. Lord Treasurer Winchester, in particular, ran his department with only occasional reference to the queen. There was considerable continuity in financial policy from the latter part of Edward VI's reign, and the type of commission which had then been established to investigate methods of retrenchment reappeared again almost immediately after Mary's accession. Mary is known to have intervened directly in only two financial transactions. One was the decision to return spiritual revenues to the church in 1555, which was against the advice of her lay councillors and had a stormy passage through parliament. The other was the remission of the outstanding balance of the last Edwardian subsidy. This cost the Exchequer about £50,000 which it could not afford, and was the result of a moral and political decision on the queen's part. She was convinced that Northumberland had governed oppressively and unjustly, and that the subsidy had been mainly intended to provide inducements to his allies and rewards to himself and his friends.[9] Unlike Elizabeth, Mary was not much interested in financial

[8] See above, pp. 252, 266–7. Professor Tittler has ascribed these attacks to a 'probable hormonal imbalance'; *Reign of Mary I*, 80. Whatever the diagnosis, the condition was not treatable by contemporary medicine. At one point her doctors resorted to the bizarre (and surely desperate) expedient of bleeding her from the feet.

[9] P. L. Hughes and J. F. Larkin, *Tudor Royal Proclamations* (New Haven, 1964–9), II, 10; Loades, *Reign of Mary Tudor*, 186.

management on a day-to-day basis, and was content to leave such matters to her council. When she did intervene, her decisions were not based on financial considerations, and the consequences were always detrimental to the state of her revenues. Sometimes her known views could be evaded or ignored. In the spring of 1555 she was determined to return all church property in the hands of the Crown, and so informed her council; but this was not done, and former ecclesiastical lands continued to be sold, as they had been during the previous two reigns. Similarly in June 1556 she issued personal instructions 'that her pleasure was the lorde Treasourer the lord Privy Seal the Bysshop of Ely, Mr Englefield and Sir Edmund Peckham sulde take upon them the charge of the Mynt matters, and consider whiche waies maye best be devised for the reformacion of the coynes'.[10] A memorandum was drawn up for this purpose, but nothing was done because it was judged impracticable at that point to 'cry down' the existing coinage.

In other aspects of government the queen's direct involvement can be similarly traced, and the results are sometimes surprising. Having conducted a highly personal negotiation, of which her council was imperfectly and belatedly informed, which led to her marriage, she then played very little part in working out the terms of the treaty. Similarly, another matter very close to her heart, the reconciliation with Rome, began with a personal initiative. Thereafter, having accepted the emperor's arguments for caution and delay, she played no further part until the disagreements in council at Christmas 1555. The whole matter was handled by Philip in consultation with the council. She was sufficiently interested in parliamentary business to instruct her council to prepare carefully for each session, and to encourage more than normal care over the return of members, but seems to have played no part in the drafting of legislation, and not always to have known what her ministers intended.[11] On the other hand, she was frequently angry and distressed when things went wrong. The *venire facias* which was issued against 106 members of the Commons for absenting themselves without leave in January 1555 seems to have been the result of her own insistence, and the fact that it was not followed up may reflect the indifference (or

[10] *APC*, v, 284.
[11] Loach, *Parliament and the Crown*, *passim*; on the *venire facias*, 54–6.

realism) of her law officers. Both the second parliament in April 1554 and the fourth in December 1555 ended acrimoniously, with dissidents in disgrace or in the Tower. During the Wyatt rebellion, when her security was under direct threat, she behaved with exemplary courage, but does not seem to have had any clear views upon the strategy or tactics to be adopted. When the revolt was over, her main role was to mitigate the severity of the law against selected offenders, but when Sir Nicholas Throgmorton was acquitted by a London jury in April 1554 she was so upset that she took to her bed for three days out of chagrin. That experience may have hardened her, because when the Dudley conspirators were under investigation in May 1556, she was declared to be disillusioned with the results of clemency, and the proportion of offenders executed was certainly higher than in 1554. Several of the more positive and constructive aspects of the reign owed little more than acquiescence to the queen. It was a period of commercial initiative, following on from the steps taken under Edward VI, but whereas Northumberland had steered the council into very positive support for the Merchant Adventurers, Mary's attitude was much more ambiguous. Early in her reign, much to their annoyance, she restored the privileges of the Hanse, which Edward had abrogated. This may have been done out of deference to the wishes of the emperor, whose subjects many of the Hanseatic merchants were, or out of a general conviction that everything which Edward's council had done was wrong.[12] The somewhat ominous comment in London in November 1553 was that she 'intended to enrich foreigners by opening the gates of the country to them, and impoverish its unfortunate inhabitants'. The Merchant Adventurers did not give up, and their financial importance to the crown at length compelled Mary to take a more sympathetic attitude. Early in 1558 the Hanseatic privileges were again withdrawn, with the queen's consent, a move which landed the English council in a head-on confrontation with Philip, and cannot have improved relations between the royal pair. Several members of the council were among the founder members of the Muscovy company in 1555, but Mary herself had little interest in such matters, and gave her merchants no support when Philip rejected their appeals to take part in the Spanish Atlantic trade.

The aspect of policy in which the queen was most consistently

[12] *Cal.Span.*, XI, 315; Loades, *Reign of Mary Tudor*, 195–6.

and actively involved was naturally the settlement of religion. Renard noted within a few weeks of her accession that her first thought was to restore the church, 'to right matters at a stroke', a policy which he was convinced would lead to conflict, and even rebellion.[13] Using the emperor's authority, he persuaded her into a step-by-step policy, using a process of parliamentary repeal. This compromise approach worked reasonably well, but Mary chafed at the delay, and encouraged Gardiner in his various schemes to push the reaction along faster. The chancellor was anxious to negotiate, if possible, a reconciliation with Rome before Philip arrived, in order to avoid giving the catholic church a Spanish face. In this he was supported, from a distance, by Pole, and opposed by Paget and Renard. Mary sympathized strongly with Gardiner's urgency, but not with the reason for it, and in the event gave him no effective support. She stopped using the title Supreme Head at Christmas 1553, but used the power of the office with some zeal in the spring of 1554 to restore traditional practices and deprive married clergy, using the Henrician and Edwardian device of royal injunctions.[14] Once the papal jurisdiction was restored, and due process of law was again available, the queen set down in writing her priorities for the church in her realm. The punishment of heretics was to her a moral, not a political issue. These were evil men 'such as by learning would seem to deceive the simple' to their perdition. So although the authority used was Pole's, and the initial driving force came from Gardiner, it was the queen who decided that heretics should be burned, and lent the full weight of her royal authority to the process, which may explain why some were burned who had never been catholics, and were not technically liable to the penalty. Renard was highly alarmed, but his influence was in eclipse by the time the executions began, and his somewhat overemphatic warnings went unheeded. Philip took refuge behind his lack of constitutional authority, and it is very difficult to discover what he thought. There is no doubt that he approved of the burning of heretics in principle, but there are some signs that he thought this particular persecution unwise, and was scrupulously careful not to get involved. He knew perfectly well that the English did not, on the whole, regard

[13] *Cal.Span.*, XI, 216.

[14] W. H. Frere and W. M. Kennedy, *Visitation Articles and Injunctions* (Alcuin Club, 1910), II, 322–59.

heresy as a serious crime, and had no desire to give them any excuse to attribute this onslaught to his presence or influence.

Mary, on the other hand, was not pursuing a policy but fulfilling a duty. She was also, although she would probably not have admitted it, exacting a personal revenge; and the same was true of Pole. Not only had heretics and schismatics destroyed the peaceful and pious old England which they both imagined that they remembered; they had also destroyed Mary's personal happiness, and slaughtered the cardinal's family. To Gardiner, the actual burnings were evidence of failure. His intention had been to frighten leading protestants into submission, and thereby to discredit them and what they stood for. By the summer of 1555 this was clearly not working. The majority of victims were men and women of the artisan class, and their courage and integrity had actually improved the image of their cause. Gardiner then gave up his leading role, advocating civil disabilities, and other alternative penalties of the kind which were later to be used against catholic recusants. In November 1555 he died, but the momentum of persecution did not slacken. It was maintained primarily by the privy council, who harried the front line bishops, particularly Bonner of London, and constantly admonished justices of the peace to do their duty in support of the church.[15] This insistence reflected the personal wishes of the queen. Few individual councillors were zealous persecutors in any of their other capacities, as local magnates or justices. Nor were most of the bishops, who took endless pains to argue with and cajole their victims before resorting to the extreme penalty. Their own visitation articles, the records of visitations where these survive, and Bonner's *Interrogatories*[16] for churchwardens all tell the same story. There was much more concern at local level over discipline and church fabric than there was over heresy. Pole was occasionally willing to reprieve the condemned if they recanted at the last moment; but the queen, who was so willing to listen to pleas on behalf of those condemned for secular crimes, is not known to have countermanded the execution of anyone who had been 'relaxed' to her jurisdiction by the ecclesiastical courts.

[15] G. Alexander, 'Bonner and the Marian persecution', *History*, LX, 374–92. BL Cotton MS Titus B II, 51.

[16] *STC* 10117.

The most conspicuous example of the spirit in which both Mary and Pole proceeded was the case of Archbishop Thomas Cranmer. Cranmer had been deeply, although he claimed reluctantly, involved in the conspiracy of the duke of Northumberland, and had been duly condemned for high treason, along with Jane Grey, Guildford Dudley, and several other defendants, on 13 November 1553.[17] He was not executed, however, but remained in prison, still theoretically archbishop of Canterbury because his appointment had been confirmed by the pope. In April 1554 he was compelled to take part, along with Nicholas Ridley and Hugh Latimer, in a form of disputation in Oxford, which was designed to secure the condemnation of his theological views by academic authority. That having happened, he remained in prison in Oxford until September 1555, when at long last a Papal commissioner, in the person of Bishop James Brooks of Gloucester, arrived to conduct his examination. Being *legatus natus* by virtue of his office, he was technically of equal status with Pole, and could not therefore be condemned by his jurisdiction. That would not have impeded his execution for treason, but the queen had decided that such a course would be inappropriate for one who was guilty of so many crimes. Cranmer's effective trial took place in the Divinity School at Oxford on 30 September and 1 October 1555, and the results were transmitted to Rome for a final decision. On 16 October Ridley and Latimer were burned in Oxford, and Cranmer was compelled to witness their sufferings. A few days later he was reported to be showing signs of weakening, and Pole wrote, 'If he can be brought to repent, the church will derive no little profit from the salvation of a single soul.'[18] Pedro de Soto and a number of other zealous confessors in Oxford, thinking to perform a major service to the faith, worked on him through the winter. On 16 December he was finally and formally condemned in Rome, and sentence issued for his degradation and relaxation to the secular arm. When this news reached him in Oxford, he broke down, and between early January and 18 March signed a series of confessions and recantations, each more abject and explicit than the last. This news must have been communicated to Mary and

[17] *Fourth Report of the Deputy Keeper of the Public Records*, App. ii, 237–8; PRO KB8/23 Baga de Secretis.

[18] *Cal. Ven.*, VI, 256. A full account of Cranmer's trial and execution is given in Loades, *The Oxford Martyrs*, 221–31.

Pole, but they chose to ignore it. The ceremony of degradation took place on 14 February, and the writ *de heretico comburendo* was issued on the 24th. His Oxford confessors had naturally assured Cranmer that his life would be spared in return for these recantations, as that would have been the normal practice. However, as the days went by, and there was no sign of a halt to the proceedings, they began to doubt. At the beginning of March the former archbishop's first five confessions, witnessed by Henry Sidall of Christ Church and Juan de Villagarcia, were published in London – and promptly suppressed by the council.[19] This disclosure had placed the queen and the cardinal in an embarrassing position, because Mary had no intention of allowing the man whom she held to be primarily responsible for her mother's rejection, her own humiliation and the perdition of hundreds of thousands of English souls, to escape with his life. The preparations for his execution continued. At this point, according to Noailles, Mary and Pole were hoping both to exploit the recantations and to execute the penitent, and Foxe later took the same view: 'The Queen, having now gotten a time to revenge her old grief, received this recantation very gladly; but of her purpose to put him to death she would nothing relent.'[20] By 21 March, the date fixed for his burning, it had become clear to Cranmer that he had mortified his conscience for nothing. Right up to the last moment he was undecided as to what to do, and prepared an orthodox declaration to deliver at the stake. But when it came to the point he repudiated all his confessions, reaffirmed his protestant convictions, and died as another, and very conspicuous, martyr to his cause.

According to Michieli, reporting the event a few days later, Mary had never believed in the sincerity of Cranmer's recantations, and therefore considered him to be unworthy of pardon, a view which the ambassador considered to have been fully justified.[21] However, there is no doubt that the queen's reaction, whatever the thinking behind it, not only resulted in the punishment of one of her oldest and most detested enemies, it also deprived the church for which she cared so much, of a major

[19] *APC*, v, 247–9.
[20] Foxe, *Acts and Monuments*, VIII, 83; Vertot, *Ambassades*, v, 319.
[21] *Cal. Ven.*, VI, 434.

propaganda coup. Probably both Mary and Pole considered justice to have been done, and Gardiner was no longer around to draw attention to the political price.

This dramatic episode serves to illustrate an essential characteristic of the queen's attitude to government. Whatever the issue, her response was shaped and motivated by the dictates of her conscience. Because of the wrong he had done in the past, Cranmer was not a man of integrity; therefore he was not worthy of a pardon. Gardiner and Paget had both served her father after the break with Rome; therefore they were not worthy of her full confidence. She had betrayed her conscience in accepting her father's ecclesiastical supremacy; therefore it was essential to restore the papacy to its full honour and authority, although the methods and the timetable might be negotiable. She had committed herself to the care of the emperor as an alternative father, and in consequence was in honour and conscience bound to marry the man whom he selected for her. Her sense of duty was another expression of the same thing. As a woman, it was her duty to surrender the practical conduct of affairs into the hands of men, for whom God had intended them. As a wife it was her duty to be loving and obedient to her husband, to bear him children, and to help and support him to the best of her capacity. As a queen, it was her duty to see justice done, to listen to the complaints of the oppressed, and to ensure that good laws were made. She was incapable of political manipulation, and of self-interest in the normal sense. Hysterically indecisive when her conscience was not engaged, she could be both obstinate and ruthless when she saw a clear path of duty before her. Her personal relationships, and her management of policy rested upon the same foundation. Good people made good decisions. Conflicts of priority always induced great stress in her. In the early months of her reign her duty to restore the church was clearly at variance with her duty to respect the emperor's wishes, and she chose the latter course unhappily, knowing that it was not really satisfactory. Later on, her duty to Philip required her to recognize Elizabeth's right to succeed, and to provide her with a suitable marriage; but her conscience refused to permit her to acknowledge Elizabeth as her sister. Occasionally conscience or duty dictated courses which were frustrated by opposition or neglect. That may have happened over Philip's coronation; it certainly happened over the return of church goods, and eventually over the succession. On the broadest scale what was good for Mary's conscience was good for England, and it would not have occurred to her to apply any other standard. Having been brought up in a narrow world of much pain and unhappiness, obsessively concerned with her royal status and the consolations of her faith, it is not surprising that she failed to acquire an objective political vision.

For a similar reason her patronage was seldom dispensed in accordance with her own future interests. Over £12,000 per annum in lands went to families and individuals who had been broken by her father or her brother, and a further £800 in restoration to victims of her own attainders.[22] The names read like a roll-call of the mighty fallen: Howard, Percy, Courtenay, Pole, Seymour, Constable and Heron. She may have hoped for good service from the earls of Surrey, Devon and Northumberland, but only in the last case was a strategic consideration – the defence of the north – an important factor. Mary created new barons, such as Lord Williams of Thame, Lord Chandos, and Lord Hastings of Loughborough, and one new viscount, Montague, but no higher peerages apart from the restorations. In rewarding services to herself, Mary was generous in breadth rather than in depth. Her loyal servants, Rochester, Englefield, Waldegrave, Jerningham, Susan Clarencius and Frideswide Strelly, did very well in annuities, licences and preferential purchases, and the men received a wide variety of minor but lucrative offices in addition to their main ones. Sir Robert Rochester was a rich man, and a knight of the Garter when he died, but such a favourite might reasonably have hoped for a peerage. No fewer than twelve boroughs were chartered in 1554, most of them ostensibly for loyal service during the crisis of 1553,[23] and many small annuities were granted to obscure individuals for having appeared at Framlingham during those tense July days. By contrast, her most important peers and officers of state received little. Gardiner never got the cardinal's hat which he coveted; Paget received very little apart from his office. Arundel, Shrewsbury, Derby and Pembroke were rewarded mostly with the forgiveness of debts, or the payment of sums

[22] PRO SP12/1/64.

[23] R. Tittler, 'The incorporation of boroughs, 1540–1558', *History*, LXII, 24–42.

due.[24] Only the marquis of Winchester, with £400 a year in land, did particularly well at that level. Given that she was also increasing her income from the lands of attainted families such as Dudley, Grey and Parr, Mary was reasonably, but not conspicuously, generous. The distinctive feature of her patronage was not its scale but its distribution. Reginald Pole, who was amply provided for by other means, was given a personal estate of £1252 per annum in lands when his attainder was reversed. As with the Howards, the Courtenays and the Percys, this gesture surely indicates not only a desire to restore an old order swept away by the political storms of the previous twenty years, but also a conscientious attempt to remedy some of the innumerable wrongs which the queen believed her father to have perpetrated. Mary was doing what she believed to be right, rather that using her patronage as an instrument of policy.

Her religious foundations were also the fruits of conscience, but in a rather different sense. Any grand design which she and Pole may have harboured for the wholesale restoration of the monasteries dissolved between 1536 and 1540 foundered on the rocks of political opposition. When John Feckenham and his supporters petitioned to return to the cloister, the queen was genuinely delighted, and seems to have hoped for a much larger movement than actually took place, but her patronage was hesitant, and relatively small-scale. Even including two very late grants to the knights of St John of Jerusalem in England and Ireland, which amounted to £1863 per annum, the total annual revenue conferred upon religious houses was only £3982.[25] Even Westminster received less than half the endowment of the restored earldom of Northumberland, and Cardinal Pole's personal estate was greater than that of the other five houses put together. More would probably have come in due course, and the unfulfilled terms of Mary's will indicate as much, making small increases to the endowments of Syon and Sheen, and substantial cash bequests to all houses. Nevertheless, Mary did not pursue the restoration of the regular religious life with the energy which might have been expected, and the reason for this seems to have lain within her own spiritual experience. Unlike Pole, or Thomas More, she had not been influenced by the

[24] *Cal.Pat*, I, 184; Loades, *Reign of Mary Tudor*, 99.
[25] PRO SP12/1/64.

Carthusians, and her personal experience of the regulars was largely confined to friars. If she knew anything at all about the powerful new orders developing in Europe, such as the Theatines and the Society of Jesus, it was distantly and at second hand. The essence of Mary's faith lay in the sacraments, and particularly in the mass, rather than in the disciplined prayer and intercession which it was the purpose of monasteries to provide. Education had coloured her piety with contemporary humanism, and her priorities were those of the generation of Erasmus. Consequently monasteries and friars to her were a part of the proper furniture and equipment of a catholic church, rather than an essential aid to spiritual regeneration.

Pole did not dissent from this view, in spite of his youthful experience, and made no serious attempt to inject a greater sense of urgency into the queen's proceedings in this direction. The cardinal's own priority, after discipline, was clerical education. As chancellor of both Oxford and Cambridge, he visited them rigorously, and was instrumental in sowing the seeds of a new catholic intellectualism which was only to flower in the chilly climate of Elizabethan recusancy. His abortive legatine synod in 1555/6 drafted an extremely influential decree for the establishment of diocesan seminaries, which, again, was not implemented in his lifetime, but which provides a good indication of his thinking.[26] Even before Pole's arrival, the queen had begun to direct her own patronage in the same direction, with modest grants to the university of Oxford and Trinity College, Cambridge. The seed which Mary sowed on this ground turned out to be rather more fruitful than that bestowed upon the regular houses. Two Oxford colleges, Trinity and St John's, were founded by private initiative during her reign, and numerous schools, some by the queen herself and others by charitably minded subjects. The total bestowed by the Crown for educational purposes at this time is impossible to calculate, because of the many different, and often disguised, forms which it took, but the bequest of £1000 to the poor scholars of Oxford and Cambridge in the queen's will is indicative of the importance which she attached to such objectives. Again, there was nothing distinctive in this; Mary was following a fashion in charitable giving which

[26] *Reformatio Angliae ex decretis Reginaldi Poli* (Vat.Lat. 5968); Bodleian Ms film 33. P. Hughes, *The Reformation in England*, II, 235.

had been well established before she was born. The same was also true of parochial and other specialist foundations, such as Manchester College, and the Hospital of the Savoy. The regeneration of parish life was close to her heart, and again Pole was in complete agreement. So Mary set an example in restoring advowsons to the church, and relieving the financial pressure upon her bishops, both directions in which well-disposed gentlemen showed an inclination to follow. Consequently, although the abbey of Westminster represented the queen's largest single investment in the process of catholic restoration, it by no means expressed her real religious priority, which lay in the parishes, schools and universities. To a large extent this, too, has to be seen in terms of putting right things which had gone wrong, and repairing the 'face' of a catholic church, but ironically this was an investment which was to prove equally useful to her protestant successors, while the abbey of Westminster, the houses of Sheen and Syon, and the other regular foundations were again absorbed by the Exchequer.

When Michieli referred to the queen as 'apunto come una monaca et una religiosa'[27] he was describing the assiduity of her personal piety rather than her enthusiasm for the life of the cloister. Had she really wished to be a nun, her withdrawal from the world could have been hastened and facilitated at a number of times during her life. She knew this perfectly well, and had no intention of gratifying her enemies by pursuing such a course. Instead, it was her duty to become queen and to right some of the wrongs of a wicked generation. Nevertheless, piety was the most conspicuous feature of the image which she presented to the world. Piety, and courage, since not even her fiercest opponents denied that Mary could display the stoical determination of truly royal lineage. To Michieli she was also notable for her skill in languages, particularly Latin, and her music, and her 'wonderful grandeur and dignity'. He further credited her with a piercing and intimidating eye, and a powerful voice. As we have seen, other observers were less flattering, drawing attention to her plainness of face, lack of dress sense, and tendency to throw undignified tantrums when thwarted or distressed. She loved jewellery and rich fabrics, spending lavishly on both, but her lack of stature, and total absence of theatricality detracted from

[27] *Cal.Ven.*, VI, 1055.

the effect. In keeping with her general approach to life, Mary's presentation of herself was honest and unselfconscious. Unlike her father and sister, she seems to have made no attempt to project an image for the benefit of her subjects. Even her piety lacked the strenuous austerity of her grandmother Isabella, who was known as the 'crowned nun'. The contrast with Elizabeth is striking and informative. When the latter entered London for her coronation in January 1559, she took part in a public performance, in which she interacted with the presenters of the pageants, and indulged in a series of calculated gestures intended to gratify and impress. Moreover, within a few days the whole sequence of events was described in print for the benefit of those who had not been present, and embellished with the queen's speeches and other utterances, which even those present might have been unable to hear.[28] Mary's coronation entry is sparsely chronicled, and only parts of it can be reconstructed – mostly those parts which were provided by the assiduous Italian and German communities. If the queen indulged in any exchanges, either with the actors or with the crowd, they have gone unrecorded. She was, however, able to make a second attempt, along with Philip, after their marriage, in August 1554. As we have seen, this was much better recorded, and several descriptions survive, including one which was deliberately published. At the same time, the pageantry concentrated almost entirely upon the king, and again Mary seems to have been simply a mobile spectator.

It was hardly her fault that she did not indulge in grand progresses. Her reign embraced only five summers, of which one was taken up with her false pregnancy (1555) and another with a raging epidemic (1558). However, she did travel; to Winchester for her marriage in July 1554, and to Dover to say goodbye to Philip in July 1557. On neither of these occasions was much use made of the journey for public relations purposes. The wedding at Winchester and the banquet which followed were very lavish celebrations, but the pageantry did not match that of Charles V's visit in 1522, or the wedding of Arthur and Catherine in 1501. Philip was probably more aware than Mary of the importance of putting on a good show, and was not at all reluctant to appear in public, even in the uncongenial atmosphere of

[28] *The passage of our most dread Sovereign Lady, Queen Elizabeth* ... (*STC* 7589.5); A. F. Pollard, *Tudor Tracts*, 367–95.

England – something which he had learned since his first appearance in the Netherlands in 1549. The king was small of stature and, like Charles I later, preferred to appear mounted. Soon after his arrival in England, Figueroa reported that he had made a gallant figure on horseback, 'and the English were greatly pleased with his appearance, for a very different portrayal of him had been supplied by the French.'[29] Philip also appreciated, as Mary did not, the importance of military displays and sports. The queen's coronation was the only such event of the Tudor period not to be marked by a joust or tournament. Even the masquing which had been planned was put off until the Christmas following, for some unknown reason, and no jousts were held during the first year of Mary's reign. If she considered such spectacles to be unsuitable amusements for a woman, Elizabeth did not make the same mistake. Jousts became frequent again from 1559 onwards, and the Accession Day tilts of the later years of the century contributed substantially to the reputation and honour of Gloriana. The king's first attempt at such a show misfired rather badly. The *juego de canas* was a purely Spanish entertainment, and despite the magnificent costumes and mounts of the participants, the belligerent English found it poor sport; 'herlyng of rods on at anodur' as Henry Machyn commented disparagingly.[30] That was on 25 November 1554. By 18 December Philip had revised his strategy, and provided an orthodox foot tournament: 'a greet Tryhumph ... by the king and dyvers lordes both English-men and Spaneards in goodly harnes', reported the same observer. Over the next four months such events became numerous. Full-scale jousts were held on 23 January, at which the Anglo-Spanish team of defenders was led by the Dudley brothers, released from the Tower only the day before; and on 25 March the great tilt yard at Westminster witnessed the most lavish event to have been held there since the high days of Henry VIII:

> there was as gret justes as youe have seen ... the chalyngers was a Spaneard and ser George Howard; and all ther men and ther horsses trymmed in whyt, and then cam the kyng and a grete mene all in bluw ... and ther was broken ii hondred stayffes and a-boyff.[31]

[29] *Cal.Span.* XII, 319.
[30] Machyn, *Diary*, 76; McCoy, 'From the Tower to the tiltyard', 426.
[31] Machyn, *Diary*, 84; Alan Young, *Tudor and Jacobean Tournaments*, 31–2.

Despite his small size, the king took part in these exercises with considerable credit, being particularly skilled with his sword, but the queen did not appear. By 25 March she may well have felt that her physical condition precluded such excitement, but that can hardly have been the reason in January, let alone before Christmas. Mary, apparently, had no desire to witness the martial exploits of her knights, or to encourage them to break a spear in her honour. Going in solemn procession to hear mass at Westminster abbey or St Paul's was more in accordance with her notions of a suitable public appearance.

As in so many other respects, Philip's attitude towards martial display seems to have changed between his departure from England in August 1555 and his reappearance in March 1557. No tournaments or jousts are known to have taken place during his second visit, possibly because of his preoccupation with the business of real warfare, or possibly because he was no longer interested in attempting to improve his relations with the English aristocracy.[32] Had he wished, Philip could have found a number of ways in which to project an image for himself as king of England. He had genuine, although distant, English royal ancestry; he could have paid public homage to respected (and uncontroversial) English saints, like Edward the Confessor; and he could have learned at least a modicum of English. However, he did not pick up the broad hints which were dropped at his entry to London. He may have been more concerned not to offend his Spanish courtiers than he was to please the English, or he may simply not have perceived the need. Certainly he would not have learned any worthwhile lessons from Mary, who, although she enjoyed ceremony and splendour, seems to have had no notion of how to put it to constructive political use. She spoke, as Elizabeth did, of being wedded to her realm, but found no effective imagery to back up her words, and no one took her professions of Englishness very seriously. It has been frequently noticed that Mary's printed propaganda was feeble and hap-

[32] Young, *Tudor and Jacobean Tournaments*, 32, 115, quoting John Nichols, *Elizabeth*, I, 18–19, describes a tournament as taking place on 29 December 1557 before the king and queen, at which Elizabeth was present. Philip was not in England at that time, and there seems to be no other reference to a tournament on that date. The only 29 December that Philip was in England was in 1554, when there may well have been such an event – but Elizabeth was then under house arrest at Woodstock.

hazard by comparison with the sustained onslaught which she suffered from the protestants, and that she was more inclined to rely upon censorship and punishment than upon counter-attack.[33] She had no positive and effective riposte to the crude woodcuts of *Maria Ruyna Anglia* which portrayed a many-breasted queen suckling bishops, priests and Spaniards. It may well have been that political image making was not a matter of conscience. To punish those who insulted her and challenged her power was a matter of duty; to compel their respect and admiration by the positive virtues of her own performance was not. Indeed, it could have been represented as hubris by arrogating to the monarch a credit which should have been given to God. Mary's style, in this as in so many other matters, was a complete contrast to her sister's. Where Mary was a saint, and something of a martyr, Elizabeth was Belphoebe, Asterea or Gloriana. Where Mary was Griselde, Elizabeth was Deborah, or Diana. The contrast is equally well presented in the surviving portraits of the two women. The beautiful likenesses of Mary by Hans Eworth and Antonio Moro are honest representations, innocent alike of flattery and political purpose; while the Warwick and Ditchley portraits of Elizabeth are icons, artificial and unnatural, but pregnant with symbolism which all educated contemporaries would have understood, and most would have applauded.

It has often been said that, far from being 'bloody', Mary was the mildest and most merciful of the Tudors. Contemporaries as opposed in their sympathies as John Procter and Sir Nicholas Throgmorton praised her clemency,[34] and her willingness to restore forfeited goods and lands. One Italian observer declared that, if matters had been left in her hands, hardly any of the conspirators against her would have suffered the extreme penalty. The records, however, do not entirely support this testimony. Certainly many were pardoned who could hardly have expected clemency; William Parr, marquis of Northampton, Henry Grey, duke of Suffolk, and the three Dudley brothers

[33] Tittler, *Reign of Mary I*, 40–9; J. Loach, 'Pamphlets and Politics, 1553–1558', *Bulletin of the Institute of Historical Research*, XLVIII, 31–45; P. Took, 'Government and the Printing Trade, 1540–1560' (Ph.D., London, 1978). J. Loach, 'The Marian establishment and the printing press', *English Historical Review*, CI, 135–48.

[34] Nicholas Throgmorton, 'The legende of Sir Nicholas Throgmorton', BL Add. MS 5841, f.272; published in 1874 in an edition by J. G. Nichols. J. Procter, *The waie home to Christ*, *STC* 2455.

being some of the most conspicuous examples. On the other hand, about ninety died for their part in the Wyatt rebellion, as against 132 for the Pilgrimage of Grace, a movement almost ten times as large.[35] Twenty-seven were executed for Stafford's raid on Scarborough – about 10 per cent of those involved – and ten for the Dudley conspiracy, which did not result in any overt act of treason. It may be that Mary was personally reluctant to order executions, and her action at Easter 1554 when she issued a number of pardons against the advice of her council, on the pretext of a holy custom, suggests that such may have been the case. If so, her attitude was changing by the spring of 1556 when, according to Michieli, she explicitly ordered that Henry Peckham and John Danyell were to suffer 'by reason of the small fruit derived from her past indulgence'.[36] Her government certainly got harsher as time went by. Most of her conspicuous gestures of clemency came at the beginning, reflecting the need for reconciliation after a deeply divisive period, while Stafford's followers were treated with considerable severity. Moreover, the queen's direct responsibility for the burning of heretics is clear, and in some cases applied with a zeal which smacks of vindictiveness. Her own statement that they should be punished 'without rashness' reflected her complete conviction of the justice of such executions, rather than any tenderness towards the offenders. Mary regarded heresy as the most abhorrent of all crimes, because it corrupted the spiritual and moral values of the community, and because it invited the wrath of God for *lèse-majesté*. Her duty to protect her subjects, and to defend the church, required severity. And if she was ever inclined to weaken in that resolve, her own sufferings, and those of her mother, her lady governess and many of her friends, could be called upon to reinforce her convictions.

In many respects Mary was an amiable soul, and those who knew her well were devoted to her service. Beatrice ap Rice, Randall Dodd and Richard Wilbraham must have spent the best part of their lives in her household, while Susan Clarencius, Frideswide Strelly, Jane Dormer, Eleanor Kempe and many others served with equal devotion for shorter periods. She was constantly in demand as a godmother, and unfailingly punctilious in discharging her duties as such. After her accession she con-

[35] Elton, *Policy and Police*, 387; Loades, *Reign of Mary Tudor*, 282–3.
[36] *Cal. Ven.*, VI, 447.

tinued to lead an exemplary private life, and her court was probably freer from scandal than that of any other monarch in Europe. It was also one of the dullest. In spite of the excellent education which she had received, and the intellectual qualities which she still seems to have possessed, there was no great resort of scholars or artists to her service. Moro and Van den Wyngaerde, two of the more interesting talents of the period worked in England, and the latter left many fascinating drawings of London and of the royal palaces, but both were in Philip's service, not the queen's. Mary restored the full glory of the chapel royal, and maintained her father's and brother's musical establishment, but of the songs and poetry of courtly love which were to grace the court of Elizabeth, there was no hint. Plays were performed, and masks and dances took place, mostly during Philip's periods of residence. The plays tended to be rather heavy moralizings, like Udall's *Respublica*, more edifying to the spirit than lightening to the heart, or occasionally comedies.[37] The old customs of festivity were honoured. A Lord of Misrule duly appeared each Christmas, and Valentines paid their forfeits on 14 February. It was a very decorous and traditional establishment, overcrowded and expensive, but somewhat less mobile than was usual. A restless traveller in her younger days, as queen, Mary seems to have been more inclined to stay in one place than was normal. During the whole period from 28 September 1554 to 4 August 1555 the king and queen were at Whitehall or Hampton Court, and when Philip returned in 1557 his entire stay of three and a half months was spent at Whitehall, apart from a week at Greenwich over Easter.[38] Surprisingly, considering the strength of her convictions, and the care with which she vetted her privy chamber, a number of Mary's less intimate servants were protestants. Edward Underhill, a notorious evangelical, retained his place as a member of the band of gentlemen at arms, with the connivance of his comrades, in spite of several attempts to deprive him, and his own withdrawal to the north in 1555.[39] According to Underhill

[37] A. W. Reed, *Early Tudor Drama* (1926), 65–6. Anglo, *Spectacle, Pageantry, and Early Tudor Policy*, 340–2.

[38] *Cal.Span.*, XIII, 342–54.

[39] 'The narrative of Edward Underhill'; BL Harleian MS 425; A. F. Pollard, *Tudor Tracts*, 170–98. His place was given to Philip Brown in October 1553, but Brown never succeeded in making good his claim. *Cal.Pat*, I, 198–9.

there was no better place to 'shift the Easter time' (that is, to avoid receiving communion) than in the court. The reason for this was the underlying stability of the chamber and household, except at the highest level. The majority of Mary's ordinary servants had also served Henry VIII and Edward VI, and although most simply conformed to the wishes of the monarch for the time being, there were a number who dissembled, just as the catholics had done under Edward. Had the queen ever allowed a religious visitation of her household, she would have learned some unpalatable things about many of those who guarded her, served her food and cleaned her apartments. If heretics had been as subversive as she and her council professed to believe, Mary would have been constantly at risk, not least from those who were armed to defend her. Edward Lewkenor, one of her groom porters, died in prison for his involvement with Dudley; but if any plot was laid against the queen within her court, it has left not the slightest trace. Even those who most deplored the policies which Mary strove to implement, respected her personal integrity, and most of them accepted the lawfulness of her authority.

However, as soon as she was dead, such constraints disappeared. It was extremely tempting to represent her relatively early death as yet another judgement of God. Elizabeth had no more affection for Mary than the latter had shown to her, and within a few months a 'black legend' of corruption, mismanagement and national betrayal was being actively promoted. By a selective presentation of the evidence it could be plausibly claimed in 1559 that the late queen had given away £50,000 per annum in revenue within the space of three and a half years.[40] 'I never saw England . . . weaker in strength, men, money and riches,' wrote Sir Thomas Smith in 1560, skilfully and somewhat unscrupulously conflating the effects of war, dearth and disease. At the same time it was claimed that Mary had made sweeping changes to the commissions of the peace, in order to give her popish creatures an unwarranted ascendancy in the counties, and had sent large sums of money out of the country to finance her husband's wars. The last charge was totally unfounded, and the Spaniards were nearer the truth when they claimed that

[40] PRO SP12/1/64. This included £25,000 in spiritual revenue, which largely went to the discharge of monastic pensions, hitherto paid out of the Augmentations.

Philip had poured money into England for very little return. Manipulation of the commissions was a charge with greater substance, but the legitimate powers of the prerogative were never transgressed, and the development was much less sweeping than was claimed. Several other things which Mary had done left her posthumously vulnerable. Her love for Philip, veneration of Charles V and suspicious attitude to her own nobles and council were real enough, although in other circumstances they could easily have been forgotten. However, she had also lost Calais and burned nearly 300 protestants. With the friends, relations and disciples of these men and women increasingly secure in the possession of power after 1559, Mary could expect no mercy. Within days of her death her will was a dead letter. None of her main bequests was honoured. Philip does not even seem to have received the jewels which she left him, and no dole was given at her funeral, 'for that there should be no resorte of pore people for the annoyance of the Estates'.[41] Instead, money was sent by Elizabeth's almoner to every parish in London, where it could be conveniently filtered through the parochial funds, and detached from the late queen's memory.

A few years later, in 1563, John Foxe published what was to remain for centuries the most influential indictment of Mary and her policies:

> we shall never find any reign of any Prince in this land or any other, which did ever show in it (for the proportion of time) so many great arguments of God's wrath and displeasure, as were to be seen in the reign of this queen Mary; whether we behold the shortness of her time, or the unfortunate event of all her purposes.[42]

To the modern historian, these purposes were more frustrated by Elizabeth and by John Foxe and his friends than they were by the providence of God. Had Mary been succeeded by a like-minded person, even her childlessness need not have been a disaster, except in a purely personal sense. However, it is also true that Elizabeth was a pragmatist to her fingertips, and had she been convinced that Mary was fully supported by the political nation of England, her course would probably have

[41] PRO SP12/1/32. Philip gave instructions that all his wife's jewels were to go to her successor.

[42] Foxe, *Acts and Monuments*, VIII, 625.

been very different.[43] Circumstances gave the new queen the opportunity to take her revenge, and those circumstances included the genuine unpopularity of Mary's papalism and Spanish associations. Michieli's account of Mary in 1557 had been flattering rather than otherwise, but he concluded that the country was full of discontent, and that, much to her distress, 'the queen witnesses the daily decline of the affection evinced towards her universally at the commencement of her reign.'[44] As we have seen, Mary had not really applied political judgement to the situation which she had found in the summer of 1553, but had proceeded by a series of moral reflexes. Up to a point her instincts had been sound. Northumberland was unpopular, and so was the Swiss-tinted protestant establishment. What people had wanted was a legitimate Tudor and a return to the traditional forms of religion. But they did not want the pope, and they did not want a foreign king, although the majority had been willing to accept both when they represented the unequivocal will of their lawful sovereign.

John Strype in the seventeenth century, James Froude in the nineteenth, and to a lesser extent A. F. Pollard in the twentieth, all echoed Foxe's judgement,[45] and concluded that Mary had failed because she had sought to drive her people in a direction contrary to that which destiny had mapped out for them. Such determinism does not appeal today, and the emphasis of recent scholarship has been rather on the achievements of the reign – the sound administration, sensible financial policies and practical approach to ecclesiastical reconstruction. By a curious circular process, however, this brings the assessment back to one

[43] Although a protestant by conviction, Elizabeth was conservative by instinct. The main factors which seem to have prompted her to work for a fully protestant settlement, with all that that implied, were the evident unpopularity of the Spanish connection, her personal dislike of Mary, and the lack of any convincing display of catholic solidarity from the Lords and Commons. The Lords did not like the Bill of Uniformity, but no one, apart from Mary's bishops, objected to the Bill of Supremacy. N. L. Jones, 'Elizabeth's first year' in *The Reign of Elizabeth I*, ed. C. Haigh, 27–53.

[44] *Cal. Ven.*, VI, 1057.

[45] Strype, *Ecclesiastical Memorials*, III, 2; Froude, *The Reign of Mary Tudor;* A. F. Pollard, *Political History of England, 1547–1603* (1913). Catholic historians, such as Lingard and Philip Hughes, naturally dissented from this judgement, and ascribed Mary's failure largely to the shortness of her reign, a view echoed by several recent scholars. Tittler, *The Reign of Mary I*, 80–3.

of Foxe's fundamental propositions. Mary failed not because her policies were wrong but because by sheer misfortune she ran into the worst harvests and epidemics in the century, and died herself before her work had any chance to take root. To Foxe, however, it was precisely those misfortunes which proved how wrong she had been, and laid the foundation for the 'black legend'. Today the main question which is asked about Mary and her reign is whether they would have succeeded, given more time. In other words, whether Mary really misjudged her subjects in any fundamental way, or whether she fell foul of a temporary mood which would have vanished with the end of the epidemic and the peace of Cateau Cambresis. Professor Tittler in particular has argued that conservative supremacy was being gradually re-asserted in the counties and that, given the similar conservatism of the majority of the peerage, political opposition to a catholic government would have been overcome within a few years.[46] Other scholars have similarly argued that the traditional church regained much of the ground which it had lost, even within five years, and that, had Mary's reign continued, the English reformation would have been aborted from the top, as it had been initiated from the top.[47] Dr Loach has found little trace of organized opposition in Mary's parliaments, and much evidence of a sensible and constructive legislative programme. The troubles which undoubtedly afflicted the second and fourth parliaments were more the result of temporary breakdowns in council management than of any campaign of obstruction. Most of these arguments are sound, up to a point, and should certainly deter anyone from thinking of the reign either as 'sterile' or an 'inevitable' failure. However, what such arguments demonstrate primarily is that the Tudor machinery of government was in good working order, and given a few sensible appointments in key offices, could be relied upon to maintain discipline, deal with routine problems, and prevent opposition from getting out of hand. At the same time, it needs to be remembered that Mary

[46] Ibid., 72–9.

[47] R. H. Pogson, 'Reginald Pole and the priorities of government in Mary Tudor's church', *Historical Journal*, XVIII, 3–21. C. Haigh, 'From monopoly to minority; catholicism in early modern England', *Transactions of the Royal Historical Society*, 5th series, XXXI, 129–47. Loach, *Parliament and the Crown, passim.*

faced a number of problems, and that her success in dealing with them was uneven. There is no sign at all that the English were any more reconciled to the Spanish connection in 1558 than they had been in 1554. If anything, Philip was less popular after the fall of Calais than he had been at the time of his wedding, and his opportunity to build up a party among the English nobility had been wasted. Even a war against the generally unpopular French had not brought about any significant improvement in Anglo-Spanish relations, and had Mary continued to subordinate English political and commercial interests to those of Spain, she would certainly have faced increasing difficulties. The most likely solution to that problem would have come not from Mary but from Philip. Disillusionment with the relationship was not one-sided. By 1558 the king had concluded that England was an expensive nuisance. He also knew that Mary would never bear a child, and as a comparatively young man with vast territories and only one son, he could not afford to continue such an unproductive union. Although the French believed differently, there is no evidence that Philip had taken any actual steps to terminate his marriage by November 1558, but once his father's wishes no longer had to be respected, it would have been a reasonable course to follow. Whether Mary, whose emotional and hormonal balance had given such frequent grounds for anxiety, would have survived such a débâcle is another unanswerable question.

The succession was a further issue not capable of easy resolution. All the possible heirs were women, and each was fundamentally flawed from Mary's point of view. Only Mary Stuart and the countess of Lennox were reliable catholics; neither had any following in England, and neither featured in Henry VIII's Succession Act. Mary Stuart was also unacceptable to Philip. Catherine Grey, Jane's younger sister, was included in the Henrician Act, but had nothing else in her favour. Unless Elizabeth had actually died before Mary, her claim could not have been avoided, and the effects could only have been mitigated by the kind of marriage which Mary refused to contemplate. Given more time, she might have changed her mind, but there is no convincing reason to believe that the postponement of Elizabeth's accession by a few years would have made any fundamental difference.

Finally, there was the question of heresy. Persecution neither stamped out nor silenced the protestants during the three and a half years in which it was applied. The political tone of the protestant leadership changed significantly as the older generation of leaders went to the flames. The non-resistance principles of Cranmer and Latimer were, by 1556, being replaced by the revolutionary theories of Knox, Goodman and Ponet.[48] The development of a martyrology, and the appearance of a new generation of radical leaders, many of them without commitment to the royal supremacy, increased the danger of protestant insurrection. A situation similar to that in France or the Netherlands could easily have emerged in the 1560s. We simply do not know what would have happened if Mary had lived longer, but it should not be assumed that the government of Philip and Mary would have continued to function with increasing stability and success. The most important evidence lies not in the transitory circumstances of 1558, but in the character of the queen herself, which it has been the main purpose of this study to examine. Since the emotional crisis generated by her parents' divorce, and particularly by the events of 1532–3, Mary had guided herself by simple principles of right and wrong. The effect of her words and actions upon others, and their repercussions upon herself, constantly surprised and distressed her. As she grew older she learned to be less surprised, but her distress continued, and became shadowed by a steadily mounting suspicion of those with whom she had to deal. The men of the mid-sixteenth century were no more unprincipled that those of any other generation, but it was virtually impossible for anyone in office to act in accordance with Mary's simple rules of integrity. Charles V had the immense advantage of being a long way off, and of working through intermediaries. Mary knew very little of the moral compromises which his complex affairs demanded, and kept his image unsullied. This was psychologically satisfying to her, but it also meant that no one with whom she normally had to deal could live up to the standard of integrity which he represented in her imagination. This was even true of Philip,

[48] Goodman and Knox both claimed that a test of 'Godliness' should be applied in order to determine the legitimacy of authority. This was simply a mirror image of the catholic view that no heretic could wield lawful authority, but it was more radical than either Luther or Calvin would have advocated, and was aimed directly at Mary. W. S. Hudson, *John Ponet: Advocate of Limited Monarchy*; J. E. A. Dawson, 'The early career of Christopher Goodman, and his place in the development of English protestant thought' (Ph.D., Durham, 1978).

especially after 1555. In 1536, under extreme pressure, Mary had betrayed her principles. That surrender probably saved her life, but it was extremely damaging. Her sense of unworthiness, bred originally out of an admiration for her mother, increased her dependence upon the emperor, and made it virtually impossible for her to defy or ignore his wishes. At the same time, it made her more determined than ever to redeem herself when the opportunity arose.

Consequently, when the climax of her struggle came in July 1553, Mary knew what she had to do. Those who had attempted to deprive her of her heritage, and those who opposed her on issues to which her conscience was committed, were wicked men and traitors to God. *Vox populi, vox dei* said one of the emblems displayed at her coronation entry.[49] Ordinary people, with whom she had always enjoyed a rapport which was devoid of responsibility on either side, were the voice of God who spoke for her in that crisis, or so she believed. What then happened baffled her, because it did not conform to the simplified models of black and white with which she had consoled and sustained herself. Good men disagreed with things which she wished to do, and less good men supported her. The emperor manipulated her for his own purposes, as he had done for years, and convinced her that her own subjects, who had elevated her to the throne, were unreliable because they did not welcome his attentions. The husband whom she loved neglected her, and sometimes seemed curiously blind to the moral rectitude of her actions. In spite of years of loyal service and passionate devotion, God did not give her the child for which she longed, and sent plagues of all kinds to afflict her and her realm. Normal people live in a world of compromise. It is not that they lack a sense of right and wrong, but their actions are normally determined by their judgement of what is feasible. Mary was innocent of that kind of reaction. Her best intentions could be frustrated by circumstances, and occasionally her moral sense disorientated, but she was incapable of assessing the needs of her subjects except in terms of the imperatives which governed her own life. Had she restored religion as her father had left it, and married some lesser prince – Dom Luis or Ferdinand of Austria – both her life and her achieve-

[49] *The Accession, coronation and marriage of Mary Tudor* in C. V. Malfatti, ed. *Four Manuscripts of the Escorial*, 20.

ment might have lasted longer. Above all, if she had honoured Elizabeth and cajoled her into a suitable match, her work might not have been destroyed overnight by a vengeful successor with a grievance to indulge. However, the whole story of her life had made such options impossible, and left England with a piece of history which has the ingredients of pure tragedy. The nearest parallel is probably with Charles I, but Mary, who had lived much of her life as a martyr, was denied the consolation of dying as one.

Appendix 1

The Development of Mary's Household
(1516–1558)

A. Before 1525

Office	*Holder*		*Comments*
	1516	*1519*	
Lady mistress or governess	1 Elizabeth Denton 2 Margaret Bryan	Margaret, countess of Salisbury	Replaced by Jane Calthorpe in 1522
(Chamberlain)			Sir Philip Calthorpe? 1522
Treasurer	Richard Sydnor	Richard Sydnor	
Chaplain	1 Henry Rowle 2 William Atkinson	Henry Rowle	William Atkinson? 1522
Nurse	Catherine Pole	Catherine Pole?	
Gentlewomen	Alice Baker	Alice Baker Margery Parker Eleanor Hutton Margaret Cousen	
'Rockers'	Margery Parker Anne Bright Ellen Hutton Margaret Cousen		
Gentlemen		John Morgan Anthony Cotton Henry Dylock William Harryet Hugh Pennington Thomas Morgan	

A. Before 1525 *Con't*

Office	*Holder*		*Comments*
	1516	*1519*	
Valets		Roger Lee	
		John Kene	
		Richard Baker	
		Thomas Danstall	
		William Blakeney	
		John Spokysman	
		John Buttes	
		John Parker	
		John Rakes	
Grooms of the chamber		Richard Wood	
		John Bell	
		David ap Rice	
		Thomas Bedale	
Laundress	Avis Wood	Beatrice ap Rice	
Yeoman of the chamber		William Lambert	
Grooms of the household		William Wakerell	
		John Parre	
		Martin Aldewyn	
		Oliver Hunt	
		Thomas Inglyshe	
		Robert Harrington	
		William Sponar	
		John Warde	
		William Spore	
		Richard Maston	
		Michael Wales	
		Richard Younge	
			15 pages added in 1522

Note: Brackets indicate tenure uncertain.
Sources: 1515 *L&P*, II, 3802
1519 *L&P*, III, 970
1522 *L&P*, III, 1673

B(i) 1525–1533

Office	*Holder*		*Comments*
	1525 (unless stated)	*1533 (1 October)*	
Lady governess	*Margaret, countess of Salisbury	*Margaret, countess of Salisbury	10 personal servants
Ladies and gentlewomen	Lady Catherine *Catherine Pole Elizabeth Pole *Alice Baker Anne Knivett Frances Elmer Cecily Dabridgecourt Anne Reed —— de Bruxia Mary Fernando Anne Darnell Mary Dannet Mary Victoria (1526) Mary Fitzherbert (1526)	Lady Margaret Douglas Lady Maltravers Mrs Rider Mrs Frances Elmer Mrs Buttes Mrs Peter de Bruxia Mrs Giles Duwes Mrs Mary Browne	2 servants each
Chambereres	Alice Parker Helen Gwyn —— Baptist	Mrs Parker Mrs Knight	
Laundress	*Beatrice ap Rice	*Beatrice ap Rice	
[Master	The Marquis of Dorset]		*ref.: L&P* Addendum 458
Chamberlain	Lord Dudley *Sir Philip Calthorpe (1527) Lord Hussey (1530)	Lord Hussey	8 servants
Vice-chamberlain	Sir William Morgan *Sir Philip Calthorpe (1526)		4 servants
Treasurer of the chamber, receiver general and surveyor	*Richard Sydnor		4 servants (prior of Christchurch by 1532)

B(i) 1525–1533 *Con't*

Office	*Holder* 1525 (unless stated)	*Holder* 1533 (1 October)	*Comments*
Dean of the chapel and physician	Dr Wootton		3 servants
Almoner	Dr Burnell		3 servants
Schoolmaster	John (?Richard) Fetherstone Dr Wollman (1532)	Richard Fetherstone	3 servants
Chaplains	*William Atkinson John Parker	*William Atkinson John Parker	2 servants
Gentlemen ushers	*William Harriott *Roger Leigh John Corbet Richard Comme (1528)	Robert Christopher *Richard Baker	2 servants each
Cupbearer	George Dudley	Gawain Carew	2 servants
Carver	*John ap Morgan	Henry Jerningham	2 servants
Sewers	*Anthony Cotton	*Anthony Cotton Thomas Greville	2 servants
Sewers of the chamber	Thomas Marten *Richard Baker	Thomas Marten	2 servants
Gentlemen waiters	Peter de Briscia *Hugh Pennnington Thomas Preston Giles Suter Arthur Blunt Douvreux (Duwes?) *Thomas ap Morgan Richard Egerton Simon Buxton (1531)	Peter de Bruxia Giles Duwes *Hugh Pennington Thomas Preston Henry Rider Simon Buxton	2 servants each
Apothecary	Thomas Pereston		
Clerk of the closet	Richard Baldwin	Richard Baldwin	2 servants
Clerk of the jewelhouse	Henry Collyer	Henry Collyer	
Clerk of the revestry	Richard Higgins	Henry Collyer	officers combined

B(i) 1525–1533 *Con't*

Office	*Holder*		*Comments*
	1525 (unless stated)	*1533 (1 October)*	
Yeomen ushers of the chamber	Robert Chichester Richard Acton	Nicholas Palfrey	
Wardrobe of the robes	Jenkin Kent Thomas Palmer	John Kene Thomas Palmer	? same person
Wardrobe of the beds	George Bradley *John Bell Oliver Smith Thomas Masie	*John Bell Nicholas Newes	
Yeomen of the chamber	*William Blakney *David ap Rice Maurice Glyn Nicholas Purfrey David Lloyd Randall Write John Crack Thomas Griffiths Thomas Bulkeley John Raydon Meyrick Lewis Hugh Jones Giles Santon Ralph Diton	Christopher Wright *William Blakeney *David ap Rice Giles Santon Ralph Netton John Williams	
Grooms of the chamber	*Thomas Bedall Walter Bridges Charles Morley John Barnwell Robert Diton	Walter Bridges Robert Egerton Henry Woodward Randall Dodd	Porter
Minstrels	—— Aslandon	Gwilliam Browntance Thomas Pike David Lloyd	
Messengers	William Jordon William Beamon		
Steward	Lord Ferrers Henry Jernegan (1528)		6 servants
Treasurer	Ralph Egerton		6 servants
Controller	1 Sir Giles Greville 2 Sir Thomas Denys		4 servants *ref.: L&P,* Addendum 458
Cofferer	William Mackelow	William Cholmely	3 servants

B(i) 1525–1533 *Con't*

Office	*Holder*		*Comments*
	1525 (unless stated)	*1533 (1 October)*	
Clerk of the greencloth	Thomas Vaux		2 servants
Clerk Controller	Richard Tournegour	Richard Wilbraham	2 servants
Totals:			
persons†	304	162	
wages††	£741 13s. 4d.		
(In the original document household departments are listed in full)			

* Signifies a person in Mary's service before 1525 (see appendix 1A)
† Includes the council; see appendix B (ii)
†† Wages bill relates only to 1525; no bill is available for 1533

Note: Brackets indicate tenure uncertain
Sources: 1525 BL Harleian MS 6807 f.3
1533 BL Harleian MS 6805 f.7

B(ii) The council in the Marches (1525 unless stated)

Office	*Holder*	*Comments*
Lord president	John Voysey, bishop of Exeter	8 servants
Chancellor	Dr Deynton	5 servants
Learned counsel	John Port	Judge; 4 servants
	John Salter	3 servants
	George Bromley	"
	Sir Edward Crofts	"
	—— Audley	"
	Richard Halsall	Solicitor; 2 servants
Secretary	John Russell	2 servants
	John Uvedale (1533)	
Herald	Chester	2 servants
Pursuivant	Wallingford	2 servants
Sergeants at arms	William Lambert	2 servants
	Thomas Amyas	"
Armourer	William Armourer	
Gunners	–	–

Source: BL Cotton MS Vitellius C i f.23

C 1536–1547

Office	*Holder*	*Comments*
Gentlewomen of the chamber	Susan Clarencius (1536)	
	*Frances Elmer (1536)	
	Mary Baynton (1536)	
	Frances Baynham (1536)	
	Anne Morgan	
	Mary Fynche	
	Frances Jerningham	
	Elizabeth Sidney	
	Lady Eleanor Kempe	
	Barbara Hawke	
Chamberers	*Frideswide Knight (1536)	
	Cecily Barnes (1536)	
	Jane	the Fool
	Lucretia	the Tumbler
Gentlemen of the chamber	*Anthony Cotton (1536)	
	William Chichester (1536)	
	*Richard Wilbraham (1536)	
	*Randall Dodd (1536)	
	*Simon Buxton (1536)	
	Robert Chichester (? Rochester)	
Physician	Miguel de la Soa (1536)	Formerly in Catherine's service
Chaplain	*Richard Baldwin (1536)	
Apothecary	Juan de Soda	Formerly in Catherine's service
Yeomen of the chamber	George Young (1536)	
	*David ap Rice (1536)	
	*Christopher Wright (1536)	
	Thomas Grey (1536)	
	George Mountjoy	
Grooms of the chamber	Thomas Brow (1536)	
	*Walter Bridges (1536)	
	*Thomas Palmer (1536)	
	*Nicholas Newes (1536)	
Footmen	*Charles Morley (1536)	
	Robert ——	
Laundress	*Beatrice ap Rice (1536)	
Yeoman of the stables	Thomas Gent (1536)	

C 1536–1547 *Con't*

Office	*Holder*	*Comments*
Grooms of the stables	Thomas Bell (1536)	
	John Smythe (1536)	
	John Hythe (1536)	
	Nicholas Twydall	
	Thomas Crabtree	
Woodbearers	John Layton	
	William —— (1536)	
	Robert ——	
Keeper of the greyhounds	Christopher Bradley	
Porter	Thomas Deacon	
Others	*William Baldwin	'of the cellar'
	—— Spencer	'yeoman cook'
	Thomas Norton	'servant'

* Signifies a person in Mary's service before 1533
Source: BL Cotton Vespasian C xiv f.246

D 1549–1553

Name	*Status*	*1549*	*1550*	*1552*	*1553*
*Lady Eleanor Kempe	widow	+	+	+	
*Susan Clarencius	widow	+	+	+	
Margaret Cooke	widow	+	+		
*Robert Rochester	esquire	+	+		+
Francis Englefield	knight	+	+		
Edward Waldegrave	esquire	+	+		+
Griffith Richards	esquire	+			
*Richard Wilbraham	esquire	+	+	+	
*Henry Jerningham	esquire	+			+
Robert Strelly	gent	+			+
Thomas Matthew	gent	+	+	+	
Dr Howes		+			
William Cordell	gent	+	+	+	
John Alen	gent	+			
John Paschall	gent	+	+	+	+
Andrew Wadham	gent	+			
Roger Lyngons	gent	+	+	+	+
Richard Townshend	gent	+	+		
Thomas Hungate	gent	+	+	+	+

D 1549–1553 *Con't*

Name	*Status*	*1549*	*1550*	*1552*	*1553*
Thomas Poley	gent	+	+	+	+
Edmund Hennesley	gent	+	+	+	+
*Randolph Dodd	gent	+			+
John Goodaye	gent	+	+		
Thomas Horage	gent	+			
John Herle	gent	+	+	+	+
Gregory Lewker	gent	+	+	+	+
*Thomas Gent	yeoman	+	+	+	
*John Soda, apothecary	yeoman	+			
Cuthbert Miller	yeoman	+			
*Henry Collier	yeoman	+	+	+	+
*John Reynolds	yeoman	+	+		
Lionel Abygens	yeoman	+			
William Avery		+	+		
*Nicholas Twedall		+			
George Mungey		+			
George Tyrell	gent		+		+
John Bodye	gent		+	+	
William Hunt	gent		+		
Robert Eton	yeoman		+	+	
Peter Johnson	alien		+		
Gilbert Johnson	alien		+		
Thomas Borage	gent			+	
Thomas Wharton	esquire				+
Richard Freston	gent				+
Ralph Chamberlain	gent				+
Robert Peckham	esquire				+
John Bourne	gent				+
John Sulyard	gent				+
George Jerningham	gent				+
Edward Neville	esquire				+
Rice Mansfield (Manxell)	knight				+
William Grene	gent				+
George Brown	gent				+
—— Libb					+
—— Poley					+
—— Smith					+
—— White					+

* Signifies a person in Mary's service before 1547

Sources: PRO E179 69/65 (1549), 66 (1550), 67 (1552); R. Wingfield, 'Vita Mariae Reginae' f. 14r, ed. D. MacCulloch, *Camden Miscellany*, xxviii, 1984, 252–3 (1553)

E The women of the Queen's privy chamber

29 Sept. 1553	*15 Dec. 1553*	*26 Aug. 1557*	*17 Nov. 1558*
Ladies			
Lady Fortescue	Lady Bridges	*Lady Kempe	Lady Ann Wharton
Lady Peter	Lady Maunxell	Lady Peter	Lady Peter
*Lady Kempe	*Lady Kempe	Lady Strelly	Lady Jerningham
Lady Bridges	Lady Peter		*Lady Kempe
Lady Maunxell	Lady Brooke		Lady Cornwallis
	Lady Jerningham		Lady Waldegrave
	Lady Waldegrave		Lady Strelly
Gentlewomen			
Mrs Waldegrave	*Susan Clarencius	*Susan Clarencius	*Mrs Clarencius
Mrs Jerningham	*Mary Finch	*Mary Finch	Mrs Russell
*Mrs Clarencius	*Frideswide Strelly	Mary Thomas	*Mrs Dormer
*Mrs Finch	Mabel Browne	*Frideswide Strelly	*Mrs Bacon
*Mrs Stirley (Strelly)	*Ann Bacon	*Jane Dormer	Mrs Thomas
Mrs Barkley	Mary Clarke	Dorothy Broughton	Mrs Barbara Hawke
Mrs Browne	Sybil Penne	*Barbara Hawke	Mrs Rice
Mrs Bassett	Dorothy Broughton	Mary Bassett	*Mrs Strelly
*Mrs Bacon	*Barbara Hawke	Jane Russell	Mrs Babbington
Mrs Clarke			Mrs Penne
*Mrs Clarke			Mrs Southwell
*Mrs Boniham (Baynam)			*Mrs Cecily Barnes
*Mrs Dormer			Mrs Bassett
Mrs Pointz (mother of the maids)			
Chamberers:	Jane Russell	Elizabeth Babbington	Mrs Sturlocke
	Barbara Rice	Barbara Rice	Mrs Brodyman
	Elizabeth Golbourne	Elizabeth Sturlocke	Mrs Mackwilliams
	Elizabeth Skirlocke	Elizabeth Brodyman	

* Signifies that the person was in Mary's service before her accession

Sources: 29 September 1553, PRO SP11/1/26
15 December 1553, PRO LC5/49 f.23
26 August 1557, PRO LC5/49 f.103
17 November 1558, PRO LC2/4/2

F Former servants placed by Mary as queen

Name	*Position*	*Date of first service*	*References*
Eleanor Kempe	Privy chamber	before 1547	SP11/1/15
Susan Clarencius	Mistress of the robes	1536	numerous
Frideswide Strelly	Privy chamber	1533	SP5/49/23
Mary Finch	Privy chamber	before 1547	SP11/1/26
Ann Bacon	Privy chamber	before 1552	SP11/1/26
Frances Baynham	Privy chamber	1536	SP11/1/26
Jane Dormer	Privy chamber	before 1552	SP11/1/26
Barbara Hawke	Privy chamber	before 1547	LC5/49/23
Cecily Barnes	Privy chamber	1536	LC2/4/2
Beatrice ap Rice	Laundress	1519	*Cal.Pat*, I, 320
Robert Rochester	Controller of the household	1547(?)	numerous
Francis Englefield	Master of the wards	before 1549	*Cal.Pat.*, I, 249
Edward Waldegrave	Master of the great wardrobe	before 1549	
Thomas Wharton	Master of the henchmen	before 1553	*Cal.Pat*, I, 277
Richard Freston	Cofferer of the household	1553	*Cal.Pat.*, III, 195
Ralph Chamberlain	Esquire of the body	1553	*Cal.Pat.*, II, 161
Henry Jerningham	Vice-chamberlain	1533?	numerous
John Bourne	Principal secretary	1553	*Cal.Pat.*, I, 70
Richard Wilbraham	Bailiff of Farren Walsall	1533	*Cal.Pat.*, I, 83
Robert Strelly	Chamberlain of the Exchequer	before 1552	*Cal.Pat.*, I, 193
George Jerningham	Sewer of the chamber	1553	*Cal.Pat.*, II, 30
Thomas Matthew	Auditor of augmentations	before 1549	*Cal. Pat.*, I, 199
William Cordell	Solicitor general	before 1552	numerous
Thomas Poley	Esquire of the stable	before 1549	*Cal.Pat.*, I, 325
Rice Maunxell	Chamberlain and chancellor of South Wales	1553	*Cal.Pat.*, I, 270
Roger Lyngons	Gentleman usher daily waiter	before 1549	*Cal.Pat.*, I, 324
Thomas Hungate	Esquire of the body	before 1549	LC2/4/2
Randolph Dodd	Sergeant of the cellar	1533	*Cal.Pat.*, I, 299

F Former servants placed by Mary as queen *Con't*

Name	*Position*	*Date of first service*	*References*
John Herle	Esquire of the stable	before 1549	*Cal.Pat.*, I, 327
Thomas Gent	Yeoman of the stable	1536	*Cal.Pat.*, I, 56
John Soda	Queen's apothecary	before 1547	*Cal.Pat.*, I, 317
John Reynolds	Marshall of the hall	before 1549	*Cal.Pat.*, I, 383
Nicholas Twydall	Yeoman of the buttery	before 1547	*Cal.Pat.*, I, 325
George Tyrell	Gentleman usher daily waiter	1550	*Cal.Pat.*, I, 394
Robert Eton	Sergeant of the pantry	1550	*Cal.Pat.*, I, 281
William Grene	Yeoman of the chamber	1553	*Cal.Pat.*, III, 293
Thomas Borage	Queen's cook	before 1552	*Cal.Pat.*, I, 209
Thomas Palmer	Groom porter	1525	*Cal.Pat.*, I, 320

Note: Of those known to have been in Mary's service between 1547 and 1553, thirty-six are known to have been placed, and twenty-seven are not known. This latter group includes Henry Collier, whose earliest service went back to 1525. Several of those not placed were given annuities or other grants in reward for their services.

Appendix 2

The New Year Gift List of 1557

Name	*Gave*	*Received*
Cardinal Pole	A silver gilt salt (48 oz)	2 pieces of plate ($143\frac{3}{4}$ oz)
Lady Elizabeth	The fore part of a kirtell and a pair of sleeves of cloth of silver richly embroidered	3 gilt bowls, two cups and jug ($132\frac{1}{4}$ oz)
Lady Anne (of Cleves)	£20 cash	3 pieces of plate ($64\frac{1}{4}$ oz)
Lady Margaret Strange	£6 13s. 4d. cash	A gilt jug (18 oz)
Duke of Norfolk	A cup of crystal, garnished with silver and gilt ($35\frac{1}{2}$ oz)	A gilt cup ($26\frac{1}{4}$ oz)
Marquis of Winchester	£20 cash	A gilt bowl and cover (38 oz)
Earl of Arundel (lord steward)	£30 cash	A gilt cup ($61\frac{3}{4}$ oz)
Earl of Shrewsbury	£20 cash	A gilt bowl (30 oz)
Earl of Derby	£20 cash	A gilt bowl ($31\frac{1}{4}$ oz)
Earl of Huntingdon	£20 cash	A gilt cup ($22\frac{3}{4}$ oz)
Earl of Westmoreland	£20 cash	A gilt cruse ($17\frac{1}{4}$ oz)
Earl of Oxford (lord great chamberlain)	£10 cash	A gilt cup ($18\frac{1}{2}$ oz)
Earl of Rutland	£8 cash	A gilt cup ($16\frac{1}{4}$ oz)
Earl of Pembroke	£30 cash in a purse of gold	A gilt cup ($47\frac{1}{4}$ oz)
Earl of Bath	£10 cash in a purse of silver	A gilt cup ($21\frac{1}{4}$ oz)

Name	*Gave*	*Received*
Earl of Sussex	A gilt cup with a cover (23 oz) (given to the Bp of Bath the same day)	A gilt cup ($22\frac{3}{4}$ oz)
Viscount Montague	£13 6s. 8d. cash	A gilt cup ($19\frac{1}{4}$ oz)
Archbishop of York (lord chancellor)	£40 cash	2 gilt cups ($44\frac{1}{2}$ oz)
Bishop of Ely	£40 cash	A gilt cup and jug ($36\frac{1}{2}$ oz)
Bishop of Durham	£50 in velvet purse	A gilt bowl ($36\frac{1}{4}$ oz)
Bishop of Winchester	£50 cash	A gilt cup, bowl and salt (36 oz)
Bishop of Salisbury	£13 10s. cash	A jug and cruse (31 oz)
Bishop of Exeter	£10 cash	A gilt jug (15 oz)
Bishop of Chichester elect (Christopherson)	A book covered with red velvet	A gilt cruse (14 oz)
Bishop of London	£20 cash	A gilt bowl ($27\frac{3}{4}$ oz)
Bishop of Lichfield and Coventry	£13 6s. cash	A gilt jug ($16\frac{1}{4}$ oz)
Bishop of Norwich	£20 cash	A gilt cup ($25\frac{1}{4}$ oz)
Bishop of Oxford	£10 cash	A gilt jug (18 oz)
Bishop of Worcester	£20 6s. 4d. cash	A gilt cup ($24\frac{1}{4}$ oz)
Bishop of Bath	£20 cash	A gilt cup (24 oz) (*sic*) (given by the Earl of Sussex)
Bishop of St Davids	£13 6s. 8d. in a purse	A gilt jug (17 oz)
Bishop of Rochester	£10 cash	A gilt jug (15 oz)
Bishop of Bristol	£10 cash	A gilt jug ($15\frac{1}{4}$ oz)
Bishop of Gloucester	£10 cash	A gilt jug ($15\frac{3}{4}$ oz)
Bishop of Chester	£10 cash	A gilt bowl and spoon ($19\frac{1}{4}$ oz)
Dowager duchess of Norfolk	A cushion cloth fringed and tasselled with gold	A gilt cup (18 oz)
Duchess of Norfolk	A salt of silver gilt ($15\frac{1}{4}$ oz) (given to Viscountess Montague the same day)	A gilt jug ($17\frac{3}{4}$ oz)
Duchess of Somerset	A smock wrought all over	A gilt salt and gilt jug ($22\frac{1}{4}$ oz)
Marchioness of Exter	£10 cash in a purse	A gilt jug and salt ($29\frac{1}{4}$ oz)
Marchioness of Winchester	£10 cash	A gilt bowl ($24\frac{1}{4}$ oz)

Name	*Gave*	*Received*
Countess of Surrey	£5 cash	A gilt jug ($14\frac{1}{4}$ oz)
Countess of Arundel	£15 cash	A gilt cup ($26\frac{1}{4}$ oz)
Countess of Pembroke	£15 in a purse	A gilt cup ($25\frac{1}{2}$ oz)
Dowager countess of Bedford	£20 cash	A gilt cup and jug ($31\frac{3}{4}$ oz)
Countess of Bedford	£10 cash	A gilt cup ($22\frac{1}{4}$ oz)
Dowager countess of Oxford	Gilt salt and pepper (15 oz)	A gilt cruet ($9\frac{3}{4}$ oz)
Countess of Oxford	£5 cash	A gilt cruse (13 oz)
Countess of Huntingdon	£10 cash in a purse	A gilt cup ($18\frac{1}{4}$ oz)
Dowager countess of Shrewsbury	£10 cash in a purse	A gilt cup ($21\frac{3}{4}$ oz)
Countess of Shrewsbury	£10 cash	A gilt cup (21 oz)
Countess of Derby	£10 cash	A gilt cup ($21\frac{3}{4}$ oz)
Countess of Rutland	£6 cash	A gilt jug ($15\frac{1}{4}$ oz)
Countess of Bath	£10 cash in a purse	A gilt jug ($18\frac{1}{4}$ oz)
Countess of Hertford	6 handkerchieves worked with gold and silver	A gilt cruse ($9\frac{3}{4}$ oz)
Viscountess Montague	£6 13s. 4d. cash	A gilt salt ($15\frac{1}{4}$ oz) (given by the Duchess of Norfolk)
Lord Paget (lord privy seal)	£20 cash in a purse	A gilt cup ($33\frac{1}{4}$ oz)
Lord William Howard (lord admiral)	£10 cash	A gilt cup ($21\frac{3}{4}$ oz)
Lord Williams (lord chamberlain to the king)	£13 7s. 2d. cash	A gilt bowl and cruse ($38\frac{1}{4}$ oz)
Lord Clinton	£10 cash	A gilt cup ($21\frac{1}{4}$ oz)
Lord Cobham	£10 cash in a purse	A gilt cup ($21\frac{1}{2}$ oz)
Lord Rich	£10 cash	A gilt cup ($18\frac{1}{4}$ oz)
Lord Darcy	£20 in a purse	A gilt cup (27 oz)
Lord Stafford	£5 cash	A gilt cruse ($12\frac{3}{4}$ oz)
Lord Burgavenny	£5 cash	A gilt cruse (13 oz)
Lord Windsor	2 cruets of crystal garnished with silver (15 oz)	A gilt cruse ($12\frac{3}{4}$ oz)
Lord John Grey	5 handkerchieves wrought with gold and silver	A gilt cruse ($12\frac{3}{4}$ oz)
Lord Sandys	£10 cash	A gilt jug ($18\frac{1}{4}$ oz)
Lord North	£20 cash in a purse	A gilt bowl (28 oz)
Lord Robert Dudley	£10 cash in a purse	A gilt cup (20 oz)
Lady Paget	£10 cash in a purse	A gilt bowl ($21\frac{1}{4}$ oz)
Lady Burgavenny	£5 cash in a purse	A gilt cruse (12 oz)
Lady Clinton	A fair smock wrought with gold	A gilt cup ($13\frac{1}{4}$ oz)

Name	*Gave*	*Received*
Lady Howard	£5 cash	A gilt cup (14 oz)
Lady Braye the elder	2 smocks wrought with silk	A gilt cruse ($10\frac{1}{2}$ oz)
Lady John Grey	2 pairs of kid gloves	A gilt cruse ($8\frac{3}{4}$ oz)
Lady Anne Grey	45s. in a purse	A gilt cruse ($13\frac{1}{4}$ oz)
Lady Audeley	£4 cash in a purse	A gilt cruse ($10\frac{1}{2}$ oz)
Lady Sandys	£5 cash	A gilt jug ($13\frac{1}{4}$ oz)
Lady Butler	2 fair smocks wrought with silver and gold	A bowl and 'casting' bottle (21 oz)
Lady Manxell	£5 cash in a purse	A gilt cup (18 oz)
Lady Petre	£6 cash	A gilt jug ($17\frac{3}{4}$ oz)
Lady Jernegan (Jerningham)	£5 cash	A gilt jug (18 oz)
Lady Wharton	£10 cash in a purse	A gilt jug and 3 gilt spoons (24 oz) (the latter given by Cecily Barnes)
Lady Walgrave	£5 cash	9 gilt spoons ($18\frac{1}{4}$ oz)
Lady Hubblethorne (Huddlestone?)	5 handkerchieves of white work	A gilt cruse ($10\frac{1}{4}$ oz)
Lady Shelton	A cushion cloth edged with silver	A gilt cruse ($10\frac{1}{4}$ oz)
Lady Kempe	£10 cash in a purse	A gilt bowl and casting bottle ($23\frac{3}{4}$ oz)
Lady Freestone	£5 cash	A gilt cruse ($12\frac{1}{4}$ oz)
Lady Joslyn	2 smocks and 4 handkerchieves	A gilt cruse ($11\frac{1}{4}$ oz)
Lady Ratclyff	A comb case and a crystal glass	A gilt jug ($13\frac{3}{4}$ oz)
Lady Brown (justice Brown's wife)	49s. 6d. cash in a purse	A gilt cruse ($11\frac{3}{4}$ oz)
Lady Capell	A purse of gold and red silk	A gilt cruse ($8\frac{3}{4}$ oz)
Lady Mason	Ruffs wrought with silver	A gilt cup (15 oz)
Lady Grey of the Moat	A sacrament cloth	A gilt cup ($10\frac{1}{4}$ oz)
Lady York	Divers fruits, as six sugar loaves, orange water etc.	A gilt cruse (9 oz)
Lady Umpton (Unton) (Anne Dudley, widow of John, earl of Warwick, married to Edward Unton)	A 'wastercote' of white satin	A gilt jug ($13\frac{3}{4}$ oz)
Lady Gyfford	A cushion of needlework	A cup with a gilt cover (17 oz)
Lady Jane Seymour	A fair Flemish smock	(see under 'Free gifts')
Lady Mordaunt	£5 cash	A gilt cruse (11 oz)

Name	*Gave*	*Received*
Lady Stukely	£4 cash in a purse	A gilt jug (16 oz)
Lady Tyrell	A looking glass of crystal	A gilt casting bottle ($7\frac{1}{4}$ oz)
Lady Butler	£5 cash	A gilt jug (11 oz)
Lady Dyer	A corporas case of crimson satin	A gilt salt ($11\frac{1}{2}$ oz)
Lady Catesby	A combcase furnished with combs	A gilt salt (7 oz)
Sir Thomas Cheyney (treasurer)	£20 cash	A gilt cup ($33\frac{3}{4}$ oz)
Sir Robert Rochester (controller)	£66 15s. cash	A gilt pot and cup (78 oz)
Sir Henry Jernegan (Jerningham) (vice-chamberlain)	£10 cash	A gilt cup (24 oz)
Sir Edward Hastings (master of the horse)	£13 6s. 8d. cash	A gilt bowl (26 oz)
Sir William Petre (secretary)	£10 cash	A gilt cup ($23\frac{1}{4}$ oz)
Sir John Bourne (secretary)	£10 cash	A gilt cup ($21\frac{3}{4}$ oz)
Sir Francis Englefield (master of the wards)	A spice box of silver gilt ($21\frac{1}{2}$ oz)	A gilt cup (28 oz)
Sir Edward Waldegrave (master of the great wardrobe)	£10 cash	A gilt cup (26 oz)
Sir Edmund Peckham (treasurer of the mint)	£12 cash	A gilt bowl ($27\frac{1}{4}$ oz)
Sir Richard Southwell (master of the ordnance)	£10 cash	A gilt bowl ($23\frac{1}{4}$ oz)
Sir John Baker	£10 cash	A gilt cup and salt ($24\frac{1}{2}$ oz)
Sir John Hurlestone (Huddlestone)	£6 cash	A gilt cup ($15\frac{1}{4}$ oz)
Sir David Browke	£10 cash	A gilt bowl ($20\frac{3}{4}$ oz)
Sir Richard Sackvylle	£13 cash	A gilt cup ($24\frac{3}{4}$ oz)
Sir John Yorke	£8 cash	A gilt cup ($15\frac{1}{4}$ oz)
Sir Walter Mildmay	£5 cash	A gilt cup ($14\frac{3}{4}$ oz)
Sir William Raynesford	12 handkerchieves edged with gold	A gilt cruse (11 oz)
Sir Thomas Joslyn	£8 cash	A gilt jug ($16\frac{1}{4}$ oz)
Sir William Drury	£10 cash in a purse	A gilt cup (22 oz)
Sir Leonard Chamberlain	4 'wasticotes', 4 pairs of sleeves, 4 pairs of 'hosen of Guernsey make'	A gilt cruse (13 oz)
Sir Philip Parrys	£5 cash	A gilt cruse ($12\frac{3}{4}$ oz)

Name	*Gave*	*Received*
Sir John Mordaunt	£5 cash in a purse	A gilt cruse (11 oz)
Sir Henry Neville	A lute in a black velvet case with two tables painted, one of Charles V and Philip, the other of Ferdinand and his queen	A gilt jug ($14\frac{1}{4}$ oz)
Sir John Mason	A map of England stained upon cloth of silver in a wooden frame drawn with the Kings' and Queens' arms and a Spanish book covered with black velvet	A gilt cup ($22\frac{1}{2}$ oz)
Sir Richard Freestone (cofferer)	£5 cash	A gilt cruse ($13\frac{1}{4}$ oz)
Sir Anthony St Leger	£10 in cash	A gilt cup ($17\frac{1}{4}$ oz)
Sir John Alee	A primer covered with purple velvet	A gilt jug (15 oz)
Chaplains		
Dr Weston (dean of Windsor)	£10 cash	A gilt cup and cover (19 oz)
Peter Vannes	£12 6s. 8d. cash	A gilt bowl (17 oz)
Richards (clerk of the closet)	A superaltar of stone and silver	A gilt salt (11 oz)
Person Lewyn	A table of the passion	A gilt cruse (9 oz)
Knight	A book of prayers	A gilt cruse ($7\frac{1}{4}$ oz)
Dr Mallet (almoner)	A fair psalter and £5 cash	A gilt bowl ($20\frac{1}{4}$ oz)
Baker (confessor)	4 pairs of gloves	A gilt salt (3 oz)
Mrs Clarencius	£6 13s. in a purse	A gilt cup (22 oz)
Mrs Finch	£6 cash in a purse	A gilt bowl and spoon ($20\frac{1}{4}$ oz)
Mrs Russell	£4 cash in a purse	A gilt cup and spoon ($20\frac{1}{4}$ oz)
Mrs Sturley	£6 13s. 4d. in a purse	A gilt bowl ($18\frac{3}{4}$ oz)
Mrs Ryce	A partlett and ruffs of black silk	A gilt cup ($14\frac{3}{4}$ oz)
Mrs Barbara Hawke	6 'frowes kerchevers' plain	A gilt jug ($14\frac{1}{4}$ oz)
Mrs Babbington the elder	A smock fair wrought with black and gold	A gilt jug ($10\frac{3}{4}$ oz)
Mrs Babbington the younger (chamberer)	£4 cash in a purse	A gilt jug ($16\frac{1}{4}$ oz)

Name	*Gave*	*Received*
Mrs Bassett	66s. 8d. in a purse	A gilt jug and salt (16¾ oz)
Mrs Scurlock (chamberer)	A partlett, lining and ruffs	A gilt jug (14¾ oz)
Mrs Bacon	£4 cash	A gilt jug (15¾ oz)
Mrs Mary Tomew	£5 cash in a purse	A gilt jug (16 oz)
Mrs Frankwell	'Two greate bagges'	2 gilt cruses (15¼ oz)
Mrs Penne of Codyton	6 handkerchieves in a wooden box	A gilt jug (14 oz)
Mrs Penne that was King Edward's nurse	6 handkerchieves	A gilt cruse (13 oz)
Mrs Hemmyngs	6 handkerchieves and two sweet bags	A gilt cruse (7 oz)
Mrs Lewys Terlyng	A small picture of the Trinity	A gilt salt (6¼ oz)
Mrs Bell (silkwoman)	12 handkerchieves edged with gold	A gilt salt (5¾ oz)
Mrs Vincent	A stool of walnut set with 'bonework'	A gilt jug (18 oz)
Mrs Wilkenson (silkwoman)	A fair purse	A gilt cruse (10 oz)
Mrs Cecily Barnes (one of the privy chamber)	3 gilt spoons (4 oz)	A gilt cruse and spoon (12½ oz)
Mrs Anne Shelton	6 handkerchieves in a box	A gilt cruse (9 oz)
Mrs Stanton	8 'turquay' hens (delivered to the kitchen)	A gilt salt (10¼ oz)
Mrs Pawne	6 handkerchieves	A gilt salt (7¼ oz)
Mrs Caveley	A partlett and a pair of ruffs in black silk	A gilt salt (13¾ oz)
Mrs Danyell the elder	A combcase with combs and a chain	A gilt cruse (9¼ oz)
Mrs Brydeman (Brodyman) (chamberer)	A holywater sprinkler of silver and gilt	A gilt salt (14 oz)
Mrs Welsh	6 handkerchieves	A gilt salt (3¾ oz)
Mrs Mary Mytchell	74s. in cash	A gilt jug (13¾ oz)
Mrs Clyston	A smock wrought with black work	A casting bottle (7 oz)
Mrs Sturley of London	A partlett and a pair of ruffs	A gilt cruse (7¼ oz)
Mrs Preston	A fat goose and a capon (to the kitchen)	A parcel gilt spoon (1 oz)
Mrs Reymonde	2 swans and capons (to the kitchen)	A gilt salt (6¼ oz)
Mrs Zyzans	A pair of gloves wrought with silk	(joint gift with husband)

Name	*Gave*	*Received*
Mrs Henry Mynk	Pomegranates, oranges, lemons, and a portrait of the king	A gilt salt (6 oz)
Gent	2 'gynny cockes' scalded (to the kitchen)	A gilt cruse (7 oz)
Avis Byllyard	Small marchpanes, oranges and a basket of French pippins	A gilt salt ($4\frac{3}{4}$ oz)
Mrs Dormer	A smock wrought with black silk	A gilt cup ($16\frac{1}{4}$ oz)
Mrs Marchenes	2 night smocks wrought with black silk	A gilt jug ($10\frac{3}{4}$ oz)
Mrs Weddell	12 handkerchieves	A gilt jug ($13\frac{3}{4}$ oz)
Mrs Holland	2 handkerchieves	?
Mrs White	2 handkerchieves	A gilt salt (20 oz)
Mr Cordell (solicitor)	£7 cash	A gilt cup and cover ($23\frac{1}{4}$ oz)
Dr Owen	2 pots of conserve	A gilt jug (14 oz)
Dr Wendy	2 pots of conserve	A gilt jug ($14\frac{3}{4}$ oz)
Dr Hughes	2 pots of conserve	A gilt jug (14 oz)
Mr Rowland Scurlock	A pair of knives of damask work	A gilt cruse (12 oz)
Mr Michell Wentworth (master of the household)	2 fat oxen	A gilt jug (18 oz)
Mr Thomas Mildmay	£6 cash	A cup with cover (16 oz)
Bartholomew Compayne	£6 8s. 4d. cash	A gilt jug (15 oz)
Mr Thomas Stanley	£6 cash	A gilt salt ($13\frac{1}{2}$ oz)
White (sewer)	A standing cup or mazer with a cover and 14 pieces of strange coin	A gilt cruse (9 oz)
Sheffield (keeper of Greenwich House)	6 pomegranates	?
Nicholas Luzer	A table painted with the maundy	A gilt cruse (12 oz)
Keyme (locksmith)	An iron to hang the sacrament over the altar	A gilt cup ($11\frac{1}{4}$ oz)
Cawoode (printer)	A book in 'laten entitled vita christi and a little boke of exhortation to young men'	A gilt cruse (11 oz)

Name	*Gave*	*Received*
Smallwood (grocer)	nutmeg, ginger and cinnamon	A gilt cruse ($9\frac{3}{4}$ oz)
Nicholas Ursini	A fair clock in a case	A gilt salt ($12\frac{3}{4}$ oz)
John Overt (Greene)	A 'coser' covered with crimson velvet	A gilt salt ($13\frac{3}{4}$ oz)
Reyne Woolfe	A book called Georgius Agricola de re intellectua	A gilt cruse (13 oz)
Chappell (bedmaker)	A cushion of purple velvet	A gilt cruse ($11\frac{1}{4}$ oz)
Thomas Kent	6 handkerchieves	2 gilt salts (13 oz)
Knevet (sergeant porter)	A purse wrought with gold	A gilt cruse ($10\frac{1}{4}$ oz)
William St Barbe	A fair crossbow	A gilt jug ($18\frac{3}{4}$ oz)
Allen Bandeson	Another crossbow	A gilt salt (14 oz)
Henry Mylles (grocer)	A bottle of rose water, a sugar loaf, ginger and nutmegs	A gilt salt ($9\frac{3}{4}$ oz)
Nicholas, Andrew, Anthony, Mary, Edward, Dewice and John Peacock (the sagbuttes)	7 fans to keep off the heat of the fire	1 gilt cruse (11 oz)
Mr Babington	A book in French on how a king should choose his council	A gilt cruse ($10\frac{3}{4}$ oz)
Mr Norrys	12 handkerchieves	A gilt jug (19 oz)
Mr Thominoe	£5 cash in a purse	A gilt cruse ($12\frac{1}{4}$ oz)
Mr Frankwell	A pair of perfumed gloves	A gilt cruse (12 oz)
Mr Walter Earle	A book in English on war commentary	A gilt cruse ($9\frac{1}{4}$ oz)
John Soda	6 boxes of marmalade and cordyall	A gilt salt ($9\frac{1}{4}$ oz)
Kelly (plasterer)	A cake of spicebread	?
Body (clerk of the Greencloth)	A pot of green ginger and cinnamon	?
Lovell (gardener of Richmond)	A dish of 'loches' and a basket of apples	?
Pascall	A pair of gloves	A gilt salt ($9\frac{1}{4}$ oz)
Thomas Gresham	A bolt of fine holland in a case of black leather	A gilt jug (16 oz)
Thomas North	10 live partridges	?
Burrage (master cook)	A marchpane and 2 jellies	(see under Free Gifts)
Bettes (sergeant of the pastry)	A quince pie	(see under Free Gifts)

Name	*Gave*	*Received*
Harrys (fruiterer)	A basket of pomegranates, cherries, apples, oranges and lemons	A gilt cruse (17 oz)
Brown (hosier)	Three pairs of hose	A gilt salt ($6\frac{1}{4}$ oz)
Foster (fishmonger)	A casting bottle of silver gilt ($11\frac{1}{2}$ oz)	A gilt salt ($12\frac{1}{4}$ oz)
Myles Huggarde	A book written	A gilt salt (5 oz)
Philip Mainwaring	2 pairs of gloves	A gilt salt ($12\frac{1}{4}$ oz)
Francis Everard	2 pairs of gloves	2 gilt salts (12 oz)
Hymyng	A desk covered with crimson velvet	A gilt cruse (11 oz)
John De Molyn	A clock, copper and gilt	A gilt cruse ($13\frac{1}{4}$ oz)
John Basson and his brethren	A fair cittern	A gilt cruse ($11\frac{1}{4}$ oz)
Mark Bernard	A round(?) of damascene work with a box of perfumes in it	A gilt jug ($15\frac{1}{4}$ oz)
Armigall Wade	A glass of aqua composata	A gilt salt ($13\frac{1}{4}$ oz)
Holford (sewer)	A purse of green silk	?
The henchmen	A pair of gloves	?
Anthony Anthony	A pair of gloves in a box	A gilt cruse (13 oz)
Anthony Lambertyne	A pair of gloves	?
Giles Beraldus	A book of the passion written	?
Harry Ball	A pair of perfumed gloves	A gilt salt (4 oz)
William Smith	A fire shovel and fork	A gilt salt ($5\frac{3}{4}$ oz)
Alexander Zynzan	A box with the picture of Christ	A gilt cruse ($9\frac{3}{4}$ oz) (and for his family)
Zynzans two sons	2 pairs of gloves	
Richard Baker	A table painted of the woman of Samaria	?
Lawrence Bradshawe (surveyor of the works)	2 bolts of cambric	A gilt jug (13 oz)
The secretary to the French ambassador	4 French books bound in parchment	?
Haynes	A table with a picture of Christ and his mother	?
Childe	A little looking glass	?
Spylman Crosser	A castle of sugar	?
Robert Reynes	A cup of crystal garnished with silver	A gilt cup (13 oz)
William Treasurer	A pair of virginals	A gilt salt ($13\frac{3}{4}$ oz)

Name	*Gave*	*Received*
Curteys (alderman of London)	A table of needlework of the Maundy	A gilt jug ($18\frac{1}{4}$ oz)
Edward Neville	2 perfumers of silver with perfumes in them and two purses of green velvet	A gilt salt (10 oz)
Swete (painter)	A table painted of the Queen's marriage	?
Jacob Raynson (an Italian)	A chair of ebony, a turkey carpet, a silver basket and 10 medals in cases	A cup of crystal garnished with silver (given by the Duke of Norfolk ($35\frac{1}{2}$ oz)
Sebastian (schoolmaster of Pauls)	A book of ditties written	A gilt cruse (9 oz)
William (bitmaker)	2 bits	A gilt salt (8 oz)
Mr Sturton	A writing desk with silver ink and sand boxes. A chessboard and pieces	A gilt cruse (11 oz)
Shepherd (of the chapel)	3 rolls of songs	?
Richard Edwards (of the chapel)	certain verses	?
Lionel (porter of the Tower)	A handkerchief	?
Damacy (merchant)	A piece of fine Holland	A gilt cruse ($16\frac{1}{4}$ oz)
Burstead and his fellows (bowyers)	50 bows	?
George Starkey and his fellows (stringers)	2 gross and 4 dozen strings	?
John Smith and his fellows (fletchers)	5 dozen crossbow arrows	?
John Crote	1 dozen shafts	?
Thomas Lye and others	3 dozen arrows	?
Browne (instrument maker)	A fair lute	?
Edith Brydeman (Brodyman) (chamberer)	?	A gilt salt (14 oz)
Free gifts	–	
Lady Anne Somerset (one of the maids)		A gilt cruse ($9\frac{3}{4}$ oz)
Lady Jane Seymour (another of the maids)	–	A gilt cruse (9 oz)
Mary Howard (another of the maids)	–	A gilt cruse ($9\frac{1}{4}$ oz)
Mary Manxwell (another of the maids)	–	A gilt cruse (9 oz)
Cecily Arundell (another of the maids)	–	A gilt cruse (9 oz)

Name	*Gave*	*Received*
Margaret Cooke (another of the maids)	–	A gilt cruse (9 oz)
Dorothy Broughton (another of the maids)	–	A gilt cruse ($11\frac{3}{4}$ oz)
Beatrice ap Rice (laundress)	–	A gilt salt ($10\frac{1}{4}$ oz)
Mr William (Wilbraham) (master of the jewel house)	–	A gilt cup ($18\frac{3}{4}$ oz)
Mr Ryce	–	A gilt cup (18 oz)
Mr Bassett	–	A gilt salt ($14\frac{1}{4}$ oz)
Mr Kempe	–	A gilt salt ($10\frac{3}{4}$ oz) and parcel gilt spoons (4 oz)
Mr Ligons	–	A gilt jug (13 oz)
Mr Tyrell	–	A gilt cruse (11 oz)
Mr Damacy	–	A gilt cruse ($11\frac{3}{4}$ oz)
Mr Grene	–	A gilt cruse ($11\frac{1}{4}$ oz)
Mr Smith	–	A gilt cruse (11 oz)
Burrage (master cook)	–	A gilt salt (9 oz)
Mr Bristowe (clerk of the jewel house)	–	A gilt cruse ($15\frac{3}{4}$ oz)
Mr Halile (yeoman of the said jewel house)	–	A gilt cruse ($10\frac{3}{4}$ oz)
Mr Kyrkley (also yeoman of the said office)	–	A gilt cruse ($10\frac{3}{4}$ oz)
Edmund Peigeon (groom of the same office)	–	A gilt cruse (10 oz)
Dodd (sergeant of the cellar)	–	A gilt cruse ($7\frac{3}{4}$ oz)
Bettes (sergeant of the pastry)	–	A gilt cruse ($6\frac{1}{4}$ oz)
Christopher Moorehouse (groom of the privy chamber)	–	A gilt cruse (5 oz)
George Brydeman (Brodyman) (another groom)	–	A gilt salt (5 oz)
Stephen Hadnall	–	A casting bottle ($5\frac{1}{4}$ oz)
Thomas Longe	–	A gilt salt (5 oz)
Thomas Hobbes	–	A gilt salt ($11\frac{3}{4}$ oz)

There then follows an account of bullion delivered to Raynes, the queen's goldsmith, to be made into cramp rings (distributed on Good Friday 'as is accustomed'). Also various christening presents; and a gift to a woman of Bury for 'healing of Jane the fool her eye' and to Mrs Ayre 'for keeping of the said Jane during the time of her healing'. Also a gift of 97 oz of plate to Cardinal Pole at the time of his consecration to Canterbury.
Source: MS BL RP 294

Appendix 3

Mary's Will

MARY THE QUENE.

In the name of God, Amen. I Marye by the Grace of God Quene of Englond, Spayne, France, both Sicelles, Jerusalem and Ireland, Defender of the Faythe, Archduchesse of Austriche, Duchesse of Burgundy, Millayne and Brabant, Countesse of Hapsburg, Flanders and Tyroll, and lawful wife to the most noble and virtuous Prince Philippe, by the same Grace of God Kynge of the said Realms and Domynions of Engand, &c. Thinking myself to be with child in lawful marriage between my said dearly beloved husband and Lord, altho' I be at this present (thankes be unto Almighty God) otherwise in good helthe, yet foreseeing the great danger which by Godd's ordynance remaine to all whomen in ther travel of children, have thought good, both for discharge of my conscience and continewance of good order within my Realmes and domynions to declare my last will and testament; and by these presents revoking all other testaments and last Wills by me at onny time heretofore made or devised by wryting or otherwise, doe with the full consent, agreement and good contentment of my sayd most Dere L^d^ and Husband, ordeyn and make my sayd last will and testament in manner and forme following.

Fyrste I do commend my Soulle to the mercye of Almighty God the maker and Redeemer thereof, and to the good prayers and helpe of the most puer and blessed Virgin our Lady St. Mary, and of all the Holy Companye of Heven. My body I will to be buried at the discression of my executors: the interment of my sayd body to be made in such order and with such godly prayers, Suffrages and Ceremonies as with consideracyon of my estate and the laudable usage of Christ's Church shall seme to my executors most decent and convenient. Also my mynde and will ys, that during the tyme of my interrment, and within oon moneth after my decesse owte of this transitory lyfe, ther be distributed in almes, the summe of oon thousand pownds, the same to be given to the relefe of pore prysoners, and other pore men and whomen by the discression of my executors. And further I will that the body of the vertuous Lady and my most dere and well-beloved mother of happy memory, Quene Kateryn, whych lyeth now buried at Peterborowh, shall within as short tyme as conveniently yt may after my burial, be removed, brought and layde nye the place of my sepulture, In wch place I will my Executors to cawse to be made honorable tombs or monuments for a decent memory of us. And whereas the Howses of Shene and Sion, the which were erected by my most noble Progenitor K. Henry the Fyfte for places of Religion and prayer, the oon of Monks of th' order of Carthusians and th' other of Nunns Ordines S^{tae} Brigittae wer in the tyme of the late Scisme within this Realme clerly dissolv'd and defac'd, which sayde howses are lately by my said dere Lord and husband and by me reviv'd and newly erected accordynge to the severall ancyent foundacyons, order and Statutes, and we have restor'd and endow'd them severally with diverse Mannors, londs, tenements and hereditaments, sometyme parcell of ther severall possessions. For a further increase of their lyvyng, and to thentent the said Religious persons may be the more hable to reedifye some part of ther necessary howses that were so subverted and defac'd, and furnish themselves with ornaments and other thyngs mete for Godd's servyce, I will and give unto ether of the said Religious howses of Shene and Sion, the summe of fyve hundred pownds of lawfull money of Englond, and I further will and give unto the Pryor and Covent of the said house of Shene, and to ther Successours, Mannours, londs, tenements, sometyme parcell of the possessions belongyng to the same howse before the dissolucyon thereof and remayning in our possession, to the clere yerly valewe of one hundred pownds. And lykewyse I will and give unto the Abbesse and Covent of the said house of Sion, and to ther Successors, Mannours, lands, tenements and hereditaments sometyme parcell of the possessions of the said house of Sion, and remayning in our hands at the tyme of our decesse or of some other late Spirituall possessions to the clere yerly valewe of one hundred pownds, the which summe of 100^{li} to ether of the said houses and the said Mannours, londs, tenements and hereditaments to the said yerly valewe of C^{li} to ether of the said houses I will shall be pay'd, convey'd and assur'd to ether of the said houses within oon yere next after my decesse; requyring and chargyng the Religious persons, the which shall from tyme to tyme remayne and be in the said severall houses, to praye for my Soulle and the Soulle of my said most Dere and well-beloved husband the King's Maj^{ty} when God shall call hym to hys mercye owt of this transitory lyfe, and for the Soulle of the said good and vertuous Quene my Mother, and for the Soulles of all other our Progenitours, and namely the said Kynge Henry 5 as they were bounden by the ancyente Statuts and ordyenances of ther Severall foundacyons. Item, I will and geve to the Warden and Convent of the Observante Fryers of Greenwiche the summe of five hundred pownds. Item, I will and geve to the Pryor and Convent of the black fryers at St. Bartholomews within the suburbs of London, the sum of 400 Marks. And likewise unto the Fryers of the said Observante order beyng at Southampton, the summe of 200 pownds. Item, I will and geve unto the pore Nunns of Langley the Summe of 200^{li} pounds. All which said severall legacies unto the said Fryers and Nunns, I will that my Executors shall cawse to be payd to ther severall uses within oon yere next after my decesse, as well for the relefe and comfort, as towards the reparacyons and amendments of ther necessary howses, and to provyde them some more ornaments for their Churches, for the better service of Almighty God. Also I will and geve unto the Abbot and Cōvent of the said Monastery of Westminster the summe of 200^{li} pownds or else as many ornaments for ther Church ther, as shall amounte unto the Saide Summe of CC^{li} to be pay'd and deliver'd unto them within oon yere next after my decesse by my said Executors. And I will, charge and requyre the said Abbot and Cōvent, and all others the Fryers and Nunns and ther Cōvents above remembred, to pray for my Soulle, and for the Soulle of my said most Dere and well beloved Lord and husband, the King's Highnesse, by whose specyall goodnesse they have been the rather erected, and for the Soulle of my said most dere beloved mother the Quene, and for the Soulles of all our Progenitos with dayly Masses, Suffrages and prayers. Also I will and geve for and to the relefe of the pore Scolers in ether of the Universities of Oxinford and Cambridge the Summe of 500^{li} pownds, that ys to say, to ether of the said Universities the Summe of 500^{li} the which summe I will that my Executors shall delyver within oon yere next after my decesse unto the Chancellors and others of the most grave & wisest men of the same Universities, to be distributed and geven amongst the said pore Scolers, from tyme to tyme as they shall thynke expedient for ther relefe and comfort, and specyally to such as intend by Godds grace to be Religious persons and Priests. And whereas I have by my warrant under my Signe Manuell assigned and appoynted londs, tenements, and hereditaments of the yerly valewe of 200^{li} and somewhat more to be assur'd unto the Master and Brotherne of the Hospitall of Savoy, fyrste erected and founded by my Grandfather of most worthy memory Kynge Henry 7, my mynde will and intent ys, and I charge my Executors that yf the said londs be not assur's unto the said howse of Savoy in my lyfetime, that yt be done as shortly as maye be after my decesse, or else some other londs, tenements & hereditaments, sometyme parcell of the possessions of the said howse, to the said yerely valewe of 200^{li} and as muche other londs, tenements and hereditaments, late parcell of the possessions of the said howse, or of some other the late spirituall londs, as shall make up together with the londs I have before this tyme assur'd unto the said howse, and the which the said Master and his Brotherne doth by vertue of our former grant enjoye, the summe of 500^{li} of clere yerely valewe, which is agreeable with thendowment my said Grandfather indow'd the same howse with, at the first erection thereof. Willynge and chargynge the said M^{r} and his Brotherne and ther successors, not only to keep and observe the anciente rewles and statuts of the said howse accordynge to the foundacyon of the said Kynge my Grandfather, but also to praye for the Soulles of me, and of my said most dere Lord and Husband, when God shall call hym out of this transitory lyfe, and of the said Quene my Mother, and of all others our Progenitors Soulles. And forasmuch as presently there ys no howse or hospitall specyally ordeyn'd and provyded for the relefe and helpe of pore and old Soldiers, and namely of such as have been or shall be hurt or maymed in the warres and servys of this Realme, the which we thynke both honour, conscyence and charyte willeth should be provided for. And therefore my mynde and wyll ys, that my Executors shall, as shortly as they may after my decesse, provide some convenient howse within or nye the Suburbs of the Cite of London, the which howse I would have founded and erected of oon Master and two Brotherne, and these three to be Priests.

And I will that the said howse or Hospitall shall be indow'd with Mannours, londs tenements and hereditaments some tyme parcell of the Spirituall londs and possessions, to the clere yerly valewe of 400 Markes whereof I will, that the said M^{r} shall have 30 pownds by the yere, and ether of the said two brotherne 20^{li} by the yere, and the rest of the revenewe of the said londs, I will that my Executors shall limyt and appoynt by good ordynances and statuts, to be made and stablyshed upon the erection of the said Hospitall, how the same shall be us'd and imployed, wherein specyally I would have them respect the relefe succour and helpe of pore, impotent and aged Souldiers, and chefely those that be fallen into exstreme poverte, havyng no pencyon or other pretence of lyvyng, or are become hurt or maym'd in the warres of this Realme, or in onny servyce for the defence and suerte of ther Prince and of ther Countrey, or of the Domynions thereunto belongyng. Also I will and specyally charge the executors of this my present testament and last Will, that yf I have injuried or done wrong to onny person (as to my remembrance willingly I have not) yet yf onnly such may be proved, and lykewyse all such detts as I owe to onny person sens they tyme I have been Quene of this Realme, and specyally the lone money (the which diverse of my lovyng subjects have lately advanced and lent unto me) that the same injuries (yf onny be) and the said detts and lone money above all thyngs, as shortly as may be after my decesse be recompenced, restor'd and pay'd, and that doon, my mynde and will ys, that all such detts as were owing by my later Father, King Henry 8th or by my later Brother K. Edward the 6th, shall likewyse, as they conveniently may, be satisfyed and payd. And for as much as yt hath pleased Almighty God of hys infenyte marcye & goodnesse, to reduce this Realme unto the unyte of Christ's Church, from the which yt declyned, and during the tyme thereof diverse londes and other hereditaments, goods and possessions geven and dispos'd, as well by sondry of my Progenitors as by other good and vertuous people to sondrye places and Monasteries of Religion, and to other Ecclesiastical howses and persons, for the mayntenance of Godds servyce, and for continuall prayer to be made for the relefe both of the lyvyng and of the dedde, were taken away and committeed to other uses; I have before this tyme thought yt good, for some part of satisfaction thereof, and to be a piece of the dewtie I owe unto God, that some porcyon of the londs and hereditaments that were sometyme the goods of the said Church shold be restor'd ageyne unto good and Godly uses, and for the accomplyshing thereof I have, with the consent of my said most Dere Lord and Husband the Kyng's Majesty, and by theauthority of Parliament, and with the advyce and counsell of the Most Rev. Father in God and my right intierly beloved Cousyne Cardynall Poole, Archbp. of Cant. and Primate of Englond, who hath specyally travelled as a good Mynister and Legate sent from the Apostolique See to reduce this Realme unto the Unyte of the said See, Renounc'd and geven over as well diverse parsonages Impropriate, tythes and other Spirituall hereditaments, as also divers other profits and hereditaments some tyme belongyng to the said Ecclesiasticall and Spirituall persons and howses of Religion, to be ordered, used and imploy'd by the said most Reverend Father in God, in such manner and forme as ys prescribed and lymitted by the said Statute, and as to hys godly wysdome shall be thowght mete and convenyent. My mynde, will and pleasure ys, that such ordynances and devyses as the said most Revd Father in God hath made and devised, or shall hereafter make and devise, for and concerning the said parsonages, tithes and other Spirituall hereditaments (the which I have committed to his order and disposition) shall be inviolably observ'd. Requyryng my said Cousyne and most Revd Father in God, as he hath begun a good work in this Realme, soe he will (cheifly for God's sake and glory, and for the good will he beareth unto me, and to this my Realme, beynge his native Countrey) doe, as much as he maye, by Godd's grace, to fynishe the same. And Specyally to dispose and order the said Parsonages, tithes, and other Spirituall possessions and hereditaments commytted to his order, with as much speed as he convenyently may, accordynge to the trust and confidence that my most Dere Lord and Husband and I, and the whole Realme have repos'd in hym, and yn hys virtue and wysdome, for the which God shall rewarde hym, and this hys Countrey honour and love hym. And for hys better assistance in theexecution thereof, I will, charge and requyre my Executors, and all others of my Counsell, and the rest of my good and faythfull Subjects, that they to the uttermost of ther power be aydynge and assistynge unto my said Cousyne, as they tender the benefit of ther Countrey and ther own Commodyte. Furthermore I will and charge my said Executors, that yf onny person or persons have pay'd unto my use onny Summe of money for the purchase of onny londs, tenements and hereditaments the assurances whereof to them in my lyfe tyme ys not perfitted, that the said Person or Persons be, within such short tyme after my decesse as may be, either repay'd ther mony, or else have good assurances of the said londs, or of others of the like valewe, made unto them accordynge to the laws of this Realme. Also I will that my Executors shall within oon quarter of a year next after my decesse, destribute amongst my pore Servants that be ordinary, and have most nede, the Summe of 2000^{li}. willyng them in the destribution thereof to have a specyall regarde unto such as have serv'd me longest and have no certainty of lyvyng of my gifte to lyve by after my decesse. And as towchyng the dispocyon of this my Imperiall Crowne of England, and the Crowne of Ireland, with my title to France, and all the dependances, of the same, whereof by the mere provydence of Almighty God I am the lawful Inheritor and Quene: my will, mynde, and entent ys, that the s^{d} Imperiall Crowne of Englond and Ireland, and my Title to France, and all the dependances, and all other my Honours, Castells, fortresses, mannours, londs, tenements, prerogatyves and hereditaments whatsoever, shall wholly and entirely descend remayne & be unto the heyres, issewe and frewte of my bodye, accordyng to the laws of this Realme. Neverthelesse the order, Government and Rewle of my said issewe, and of my said Imperiall Crowne, and the dependances thereof, during the Minoryte of my said heyre and Issewe, I specyally recommend unto my said most Dere and well beloved Husband, accordynge to the laws of this my said Realme for the same provided. Willing, charging, and most hertily requyryng all and singular my lovyng, obedient and naturall subjects, by that profession and dewtye of allegiance that by God's commandment they owe unto me, beyng ther naturall Sovereigne Lady & Quene; And also desyryng them (per viscera Misericordiae Dei) that sens yt hath pleased hys devyne Majesty, far above my merits to shew me so great favour in this world, as to appoynte me so noble, vertuous, and worthy a Prince to be my husband, as my said most Dere and intirely beloved Husband the King's Majesty ys, whose endeavour, care and stodie hath ben, and chefely ys, to reduce this Realme unto the Unyte of Christ's Church and trewe Religion, and to the anncyente and honourable fame and honor that yt hath ben of, and to conserve the same therein; And not dowting but accordyng to the trust that ys repos'd in hys Maj^{ty}, by the laws of this Realme, made concernyng the Government of my Issewe, that hys Highnesse will discharge the same to the glory of God, to hys own honour, to the suerty of my said Issewe, and to the profit of all my Subjects; that they therefore will use themselves in such humble and obedient sort and order, that hys Majesty may be the rather incoraged and provoked to continewe hys good and gracious disposition towards them and this Realme. And for as much as I have no Legacy or jewell that I covet more to leve unto hys Majesty to reqyte the nobility of hys harte towards me and this Realme, nor he more desirous to have, than the love of my Subjects, I doe therefore once agayne reqyre them to bere and owe unto his Highnesse the same dewtie and love that they naturally doe and should owe unto me, and in hope they will not forget the same, I do specyally recommend the same dewtye and love unto hys Highnesse, as a legacye, the which I trust he shall enjoye. Also I will and geve unto my said issewe all my jewells, ships, municyons of warre, and artillery, and after my detts (and the detts of my said later Father and brother, King Henry 8, and King Edward 6.) satisfied and pay'd, and this my present testament and last will perform'd, I geve and bequethe unto my said issewe all the rest of my treasure, plate, goods and Chattells whatsoever they be. And callynge to my Remembrance the good and dewtyfull service to me doon by diverse of my lovyng Servants and faythfull Subjects, to whom, as yet, I have not given onny condigne recompence for the same, therefore I am fully resolv'd and determyn'd to geve to every of them whose names are hereafter mention'd such legacies and gifts as particularly ensueth.

[Then follow in the Will several particular Legacies to her women and other Servants about her, which in all amount to 3400^{li} among which she gives Dr. Malet her Almoner and Confessor, to praye for her the summe of 200^{li} and to the poor fryers of the Order of St. Dominick, erected and placed within the University of Oxford, to pray for her soul, her Husband's, Mother's, and all other her progenitours the summe of 200^{li}; besides all this she gives 20^{li} a year apiece to Father Westweek and Father Mecalfe and then it follows in her Will.]

And to thentente this my last will and testament may be the more inviolably observ'd, fulfil'd and executed, I will the Issewe of my bodye that shall succede me in the' Imperiall Crowne of this Realme upon my blessing, that he or she be no Impedyment thereof, but that to the uttermost of his or her power, they do permytt and suffer my said Executors to performe the same, and to ayd them in theexecution thereof. And yf ther shall be any imperfection in the assurances of the londes that I have devis'd and appoynted to the howses of Religion or to Savoye, or to the hospitall I mynde to have erected for the pore and maymed Souldiers, or onny negligence be in my Executors in the performance and execucyon of this my testament and last will, that then I will and charge my said Issewe on my blessing, to supply and accomplyshe all such defects and imperfections. And I charge my said Executors, as they will answer before God at the dredfull day of Judgement, and as they will avoyde such commynacyons, threatnyngs, and the severe justice of God pronounc'd and executed against such as are brekers and violaters of wills and testaments, that they to the uttermost of ther powers and wyttes, shall see this my present Testament & last will perform'd and executed, for the which I trust, God shall reward them, and the world commend them. And as yt hath stood with the good contentment and pleasure of my said most dere beloved Lord and husband the King's Majesty, that I should thus devise my Testament and last will, so I dowte not, but that his most noble harte desyreth and wysheth that the same should accordyngly take effect after yt shall please God to call me out of this transytory lyfe to his marcye. And havyng such exsperience of his gracyus faveure, zeale and love towards me as I have, I am fully perswaded that no person either can or will more honorably and ernestly travell in thexecution of this my Testam[t] and last will, then his Majesty will doo. Therefore I most humbly beseech his Highnesse that he will vouchsafe and be pleas'd to take upon hym the pryncipall and the chefest care of thexecutyon of this my present Testament and last will, and to be a patron to the rest of my Executors of the same in thexecutyon thereof.

And I do humbly beseeche my saide most dearest lorde and husbande to accepte of my bequeste, and to kepe for a memory of me one jewell, being a table dyamond which themperours Majesty, his and my most honourable Father, sent unto me by the Cont degment, at the insurance of my sayde lorde and husbande, and also one other table dyamonde whiche his Majesty sent unto me by the marques de les Nanes, and the Coler of golde set with nyne dyamonds, the whiche his Majestye gave me the Epiphanie after our Maryage, also the rubie now sett in a Golde ryng which his Highnesse sent me by the Cont of Feria, all which things I require his Majestye to dispose at his pleasure, and if his Highness thynck mete, to the Issue betwene us.

Also I reqyre the said most Reverend Father in God and my said most dere beloved Cosyn the Lord Cardynall Poole, to be oon of my Executors, to whom I geve for the paynes he shall take aboute thexecucyon of this my present Testament the summe of one thousande powndes. And for the specyall truste and good service that I have alweyes had and founde in the most Rev[d] Father in God, and my right trustye and right well beloved Councellour Nicholas Abp of Yorke, my Chancellor of Englonde, and in my right trusty and right wel beloved Cosyns William, Marques of Wynchester, L[d] Treasorer of Englonde, Henry Erle of Arundel, Henry Erle of Westmorland, Francis Erle of Shrewsbury, Edward Erle of Derbye, Thomas Erle of Sussex, W[m] Erle of Pembroke, and in my right trusty and well beloved Councellors Visc, Mountague, Edward Lord Clynton, highe Admyrall of Englonde, and in the Rev[d] Father in God and my right trusty and well beloved Councellors Thomas Bishop of Elye, Edward Lord Hastings of Lowtheborowghe, Lorde Chamberlayne of my Howsehold, S[r] W[m] Cordell K[t] M[r] of the Rowlles of my Court of Chancerye. I ordeyne and constitute them also Executors of this my present Testament and last Will, and I geve unto every of the said L[d] Chancellor, Lord Tresorer, etc., for their paynes and travell therein to be taken, the Summe of fyve hundred powndes. And unto every of the said Visc Montague, Lord Admyrall, etc., for their paynes likewise to be taken fyve hundred marckes.

And for the greate experyence I have had of the trothe fidelite and good servyce of my trustye and righte well beloved Servants and Councellors, S[r] Tho. Cornwallis K[t] Comptroller of my howsehold, S. Henry Jernegan K[t] Master of my horses, M[r] Boxall, my Chefe Secretary, S[r] Edward Waldegrave K[t] Chancellor of my Duchy of Lancaster, S[r] Francis Englefield K[t] Master of my Court of Wards and lyveries, and S[r] John Baker K[t] Chancellor of my Exchequer I geve unto every of them for ther paynes and good servyce to be taken, as assistants to this my said testament, and to be of Council with my said Issewe, the Summe of two hundred powndes. I do appoynte, name and ordeyne them to be Assistants unto my said Executors in thexecucyon of this my said Testament, and to be with them of the Council to my said issewe. And I geve unto every of my said

Servants and Councellors last before remembered whom I have appoynted to be assistants to my said Executors, as ys aforesaid, for ther good servyce and paynes to be taken and doon with my said Executors for thexecucyon of this my present Testament and last Will, the Summe of two hundred powndes, before geven unto ether of them.

Nevertheless my playne Will, mynde and entent ys, that yf onny of my said Councillors whom I have appoynted before by this my Testament to be my Executors of the same, shall at the tyme of my decesse be indetted unto me in onny Summes of money, or ought to be and stond charged unto me or to my heirs or Successors for onny Acc^ts^ or summes of money by hym or them receyved, whereof at the tyme of my decesse he ys not lawfully discharged. That the said Executor or Executors, who shall be so indetted or ought to be charg'd with onny such Acc^ts^ shall not, for that he or they be named & appoynted onny of my Executars, be exonerate and discharged of the said detts or acc^ts^, but thereof shall remayne charged, as tho' he or they had not been named of my said Executors, and in that respect only shall be excepted to all intents as none of my said Executors, to take any benefit or discharge of the said dette or acc^ts^.

And in wytnesse that this ys my present Testament and last Will, I have sign'd diverse parts of the same with my Signe Manuell, and thereunto also have cawsed my prevye Signett to be put, the Thirtieth day of Marche, in the yere of our Lorde God a Thousande fyve hundred fyfty and eight, and in the fourth yere of the Reigne of my said most dere lorde and husband, and in the fyfte yere of the Reigne of me the said Quene. These beynge called to be wytnesses, whose names hereafter followythe

HENRY BEDINGFELD JOHN THROKMORTON
THOMAS WHARTON R. WILBRAHM

MARYE THE QUENE

[Codicil]

MARYE THE QUENE.

This Codicell made by me Marye by the Grace of God Quene of Engl^d^ &c., & lawful wyfe to the most noble and vertuous Prynce Philippe, by the same grace of God, Kynge of the said Realmes and Domynions of Englond, &c., the twenty-eighth day of October, in the yere of our Lord God 1558, and in the 5th yere of the reign of my said most dere Lord and husbande, and in the Sixth yere of the reigne of me the said Quene. The which Codicell I will and ordeyne shall be added and annexed unto my last Will and Testament heretofore by me made and declared. And my mynd and will ys, that the said Codicell shall be accepted, taken and receyved as a part and parcell of my said last will and testament, and as tho' it were incorporate with the same to all entents and purposes, in manner and forme followynge.

Fyrste, whereas I the said Quene have with the good contentment and pleasure of my said most dere belov'd Lorde and husbande the Kyng's Majesty devis'd & made my said last will and testament, beryng date the 30th day of Marche last past, and by the same, for that as I then thowght myself to be with childe did devise and dispose the Imperiall Crowne of this Realme of Englond and the Crowne of Ireland, with my title to France and all the dependances thereof, and all other honours, Castells, Fortresses, Prerogatives and hereditaments, of what nature, kynde or qualitie soever they be, belongyng to this crowne, unto the heires, Issewe and frewte of my body begotten, & the government, order, and rewle of the said heire and Issewe I recommended unto my said most dere Lord and husband duryng the mynoryte of the said heire, accordynge to the lawes of this Realme in that case provided.

Forasmuch as God hath hitherto sent me no frewte nor heire of my bodie, yt ys onlye in his most devyne providence whether I shall have onny or noo, Therefore both for the discharge of my conscyence and dewtie towards God and this Realme, and for the better satisfaction of all good people, and to thentent my said last will and Testament (the which I trust, is agreeable to God's law and to the laws of this Realme) may be dewly performed, and my dettes (pryncipally those I owe to many of my good subjects, and the which they most lovyngly lent unto me) trewly and justly answered payed, I have thought it good, fealynge myself presently sicke and week in bodye (and yet of hole and perfytt remembrance, our Lord be thanked) to adde this unto my said testament and last will, viz. Yf yt shall please Almighty God to call me to his mercye owte of this transytory lyfe without issewe and heire of my bodye lawfully begotten, Then I most instantly desire et per viscera misericordiae Dei, requyre my next heire & Successour, by the Laws and Statutes of this Realme, not only to permytt and suffer theexecutors of my said Testament and last will and the Survivours of them to performe the same, and to appoynte unto them such porcyon of treasure & other thynges as shall be suffycient for the execution of my said testament and last will, and to ayd them in the performance of the same, but also yf such assurance and conveyance as the Law requyreth for the State of the londs which I have devysed and appoynted to the howses of Religion, and to the Savoye, and to the Hospitall I would have erected, be not suffycyent and good in Lawe by my said Will, then I most hertily also requyre both for God's sake, and for the honour and love my said heyre and Successour bereth unto me, that my said heyre and Successour will supplye the Imperfection of my said will and testament therein, & accomplyshe and fynishe the same accordynge to my trew mynde and intente, for the dooyng whereof my said heire and Successour shall, I dowte not, be rewarded of God, and avoyde thereby his severe justice pronounced and executed ag[t] all such as be violaters and brekers of wills and testaments, and be the better assisted with his specyall grace and favour in the mynistracyon of ther Regall function and office, And the more honored of the world and loved of ther subjects, whose natural zeale and love (as a most precious jewell unto every Prynce) I leve and bequeathe unto my said heire and Successour for a specyall Legacye and bequeste, the which I most humbly beseech our Lord, the same may enjoye and possesse (as I trust they shall) chefely to the advancement of God's glorye & honor, and to the good quyetnesse and Government of this Realme, the which two thynges I most tender. And albeit my said most Dere Lord and Husband shall for defawte of heyre of my bodye have no further government, order and rewle within this Realme and the domynions thereunto belongynge, but the same doth and must remayne, descend, and goo unto my next heyre and Successour, accordyng to the Lawes and Statuts of this Realme, yet I most humbly beseech his Majesty, in recompence of the great love and humble dewtye that I have allwayes born and am bounden to bere unto his Majesty, and for the great zeale and care the which his Highness hath always sens our marriage professed and shew'd unto this Realme, and the Subjects of the same, and for the ancyente amyte sake that hath always ben betwene our most Noble Progenitours and betwene this my Realme and the Low countries, whereof his Majesty is now the enheritour, And finally, as God shall reward hym, and I praye (I hope among the elect servants of God) that yt may please his Majesty to shew hymself as a Father in his care, as a Brother or member of this Realme in his love and favour, and as a most assured and undowted frend in his powre and strengthe to my said heire and Successour, and to this my Country and the Subjects of the same, the which I trust his Highnesse shall have just cause to thynke well bestowed, for that I dowte not, but they will answer yt unto his Majesty with the like benevolence and good will, the which I most hertily requyre them to doo, bothe for my sake, and for the honour and suerty of this Realme. And in witnesse that I have cawsed this Codicell to be made, and that my will & entent ys, that the same shall be annexed and added unto my said former testament & last will, the which my full mynde and will ys shall stonde and remayne in perfytte force and effect, to all intents and purposes, and this Codicell to be accepted taken and declared only as a part and parcell of my said testament and last Will, I have sign'd this Codicell with my Signe Manuell, and have also cawsed my privy Signet to be put thereunto, the day and yere fyrste in this Codicell above written. These beying called to be my wytnesses as well to my said testament and last will as to this Codicell whose names followeth.

MARYE THE QUENE
EDMOND PECKHAM
THOMAS WENDYE
JOHN WILLIS
BARNARD HAMPTON

Source: J. M. Stone *Mary I: Queen of England*, 507–20; from a transcript in the Harleian MSS (6949). The original does not survive. The transcript was made by the Rev. George Harbin in the early eighteenth century, and the underlinings are his. They represent words and passages written in Mary's own hand in the original will.

Bibliographical Abbreviations

APC	*The Acts of the Privy Council*
BL	British Library
Cal.Pat.	*Calendar of the Patent Rolls*
Cal.Span.	*Calendar of State Papers, Spanish*
Cal.Ven.	*Calendar of State Papers, Venetian*
Chronicle	*The Chronicle and Political Papers of King Edward VI* ed. Jordan
L&P	*Letters and Papers of the Reign of Henry VIII*
PRO	Public Record Office
STC	*Short Title Catalogue of Books published ... between 1475 and 1640*
TTC	Loades, *Two Tudor Conspiracies*

References and Bibliography

Manuscript sources

Public Record Office	
State Papers, Domestic	Henry VIII (SP 1)
	Edward VI (SP 10)
	Mary, and Philip and Mary (SP 11)
	Elizabeth (SP 12)
	Supplementary (SP 46)
Foreign	Mary, and Philip and Mary (SP 69)
King's Bench	Plea Rolls (KB 27)
	Ancient Indictments (KB 8)
Exchequer	Accounts various (E101)
	Subsidy Rolls (E179)
	Pipe Office, declared accounts (E351)
	Issues; writs and warrants (E404)
Lord Chamberlain's Office	Robes and special events (LC 2)
	Miscellanea (LC 5)
Lord Steward's Office	Miscellaneous books (LS 13)
British Library	
Cotton MSS	Otho (C.x, E.ix)
	Titus (A.xiv, B.ii, C.vii, C.xvii)
	Vespasian (C.xiv, F.xiii)
	Vitellius (C.i)
Cotton Charters	XIV
Harleian	283, 289, 416, 3504, 6234, 6807, 6949
Arundel	151
Egerton	2986
Lansdowne	3, 170
Royal	17
RP	294
Sloane	1583
Stowe	141, 354, 571

Additional	34320, 41577, 17012
Additional Charters	67534
Archivo General de Simancas	
CMC	E 1184
Estado Inglaterra	E 811
Bodleian Library	
Microfilm 33	Vat. Lat. 5968

Contemporary printed works (London unless otherwise stated)

A supplicacyon to the Queenes Majestie (unknown, 1555).
A warnyng for Englande conteynyng the horrible practises of the Kyng of Spayn in the Kyngedom of Naples... (unknown, 1555).
An epitaphe upon the Death of the Most excellent and oure late vertuous Queene Marie (1558).
Bradford, John, *The copye of a letter sent by John Bradforthe to the right honorable lordes the Erles of Arundel, Derbie, Shrewsburye and Penbroke* (? London, 1556).
Christopherson, John, *An exhortation to alle menne to take hede and beware of rebellion* (1554).
Elder, John, *The copie of a letter sent into Scotlande* (1555).
Forrest, William, *A newe ballade of the Marigolde* (1554)
Glasse of the Truthe (? 1531).
Goodman, Christopher, *How Superior Powers oght to be obeyd* (Geneva, 1558).
Heywood, John, *A balade specifienge partly the maner, partly the matter in the most excellent meetyng and lyke marriage betwene our Sovereigne Lord and our Sovereigne Lady, the Kynges and Queenes highnes* (1554).
Heywood, John, *A breefe balet touching the traytorous takynge of Scarborow Castell* (1557).
Huggarde, Miles, *The displaying of the Protestantes* (1556).
Il felicissimo ritorno del regno d'Inghilterra alla cattolica unione (Rome, 1555).
Knox, John, *The First Blast of the Trumpet against the Monstrous Regiment of Women* (? Geneva, 1558).
La solenne et felice intrata delli serenissimi Re Philippo et Regina Maria d'Inghilterra (Rome, 1555).
Nowe singe nowe springe oure care is exil'd... (1554).
Ponet, John, *A shorte treatise of Politike Power* (? Strasbourg, 1556).
Pownall, Robert, *An admonition to the towne of Callays* (unknown, 1557).
Procter, John, *The Historie of Wyates rebellion* (1554).
Stopes, Leonard, *An Ave Maria in Commendation of oure most vertuous Queene* (1553).
The Determinations of the moste famous and mooste excellent universities of Italy and Fraunce (1531).
Traheron, Bartholomew, *A warning to England...by the terrible example of Calece* (? Wesel, 1558).

Calendars and printed sources (London unless otherwise stated)

Acts of the Privy Council, ed. J. R. Dasent (1890–1907).
Calendar of the Patent Rolls, Edward VI-Philip and Mary (1924–39).
Calendar of the State Papers, Domestic, 1547–80, ed. R. Lemon (1856).

Calendar of the State Papers, Foreign, 1553–8, ed. W. B. Turnbull (1861).

Calendar of the State Papers relating to Scotland, ed. J. Bain et al. (Edinburgh, 1898–1952).

Calendar of State Papers, Spanish, ed. R. Tyler et al. (1862–1954).

Calendar of the State Papers, Venetian, ed. R. Brown et al. (1864–98).

Clifford, H. *The Life of Jane Dormer, Duchess of Feria*, ed. J. Stevenson (1887).

Collection des Voyages des Souverains des Pays-Bas, ed. L. P. Gachard and C. Piot (Brussels, 1874–82).

Fernández Alvarez, M., *Corpus Documental, de Carlos V* (Salamanca, 1973–7).

Feuillerat, A., ed., *Documents relating to the office of the Revels* (Louvain, 1908–14).

Foxe, John, *Acts and Monuments of the English Martyrs*, ed. S. R. Cattley (1837–41).

Gardiner, Stephen, *The Letters of Stephen Gardiner*, ed. J. A. Muller (Cambridge, 1933).

Greyfriars Chronicle, ed. J. G. Nichols (Camden Society, LIII, 1852).

Hall, Edward, *The union of the two noble and illustre famelies of York and Lancaster*, ed. H. Ellis (1809).

Historical Manuscripts Commission, MSS of Lord Montague of Beaulieu; More Molyneux MSS at Loseley.

Kervyn de Lettenhove, J.M.B.C., *Relations politiques des Pays-Bas et de l'Angleterre* (Brussels, 1882–1900).

Letters and Papers, Foreign and Domestic, of the Reign of Henry VIII, ed. J. Gairdner et al. (1862–1932).

The Lisle Letters, ed. m. St Clare Byrne (Chicago, 1981). *Literary Remains of King Edward VI*, ed. J. G. Nichols (Roxburgh Club, 1857).

A Machiavellian Treatise by Stephen Gardiner, ed. P. S. Donaldson (Cambridge, 1975).

Machyn, Henry, *The diary of Henry Machyn*, ed. J. G. Nichols (Camden Society, XLII, 1848).

Malfatti, C. V., ed., *Four Manuscripts of the Escorial* (Barcelona, 1956).

Original Letters relative to the English Reformation, ed. H. Robinson (Parker Society, 1846–7).

Pole, Reginald, 'Pole y Paul IV; una celébre Apología inédita del Cardenal Inglés', ed. J. I. Tellechea Idigoras (*Archivum Historiae Pontificiae*, IV, 1966).

The Privy Purse Expenses of King Henry VIII, ed. N. H. Nicholas (1829).

The Privy Purse Expenses of the Princess Mary, ed. F. E. Madden (1831).

Selve, Odet de, *Correspondance Politique de Odet de Selve*, ed. G. Lefèvre-Pontalis (Paris, 1888).

Short Title Catalogue of books printed in England, Scotland and Ireland and of English Books printed abroad, 1475–1640, by A. W. Pollard and G. R. Redgrave; revised by W. A. Jackson, F. S. Ferguson and K. F. Pantzer (1976–86).

Statutes of the Realm, ed. A. Luders et al. (1810–28).

Strype, J., *Ecclesiastical Memorials* (1721).

Surtz, E. and Murphy, V., eds, *The Divorce Tracts of Henry VIII* (Angers, 1988).

The Chronicle and Political Papers of Edward VI, ed. W. K. Jordan (1966).

The Chronicle of Queen Jane and of the first two years of Queen Mary, ed. J. G. Nichols (Camden Society, XLVIII, 1850).

'The Count of Feria's despatch to Philip II of 14 November 1558', ed. M. J. Rodríguez Salgado, and S. Adams, *Camden Miscellany*, XXVIII, 1984.

The passage of our most dread Sovereign Lady, Queen Elizabeth, through the City of London, ed. A. F. Pollard, in *Tudor Tracts* (1903).
Throgmorton, Sir Nicholas, *The Legend of Sir Nicholas Throgmorton*, ed. J. G. Nichols (1874).
Tres Cartas de lo sucedido en el viaje de su Alteza a Inglaterra (La Sociedad de Bibliófilos Españoles, Madrid, 1877).
Tudor Royal Proclamations, ed. P. L. Hughes and J. F. Larkin (New Haven, 1964–9).
Underhill, Edward, 'The narrative of Edward Underhill', in *Tudor Tracts* ed. A. F. Pollard (1903).
Vertot, R. A. de, ed., *Ambassades des Messieurs de Noailles en Angleterre* (1681–1714).
Watson, Foster, ed., *Vives and the Renasence Education of Women* (1912).
Wingfield, Robert, 'Vitae Mariae Reginae', ed. D. MacCulloch, *Camden Miscellany*, XXVIII, 1984.
Wriothesley, Charles, *A chronicle of England by Charles Wriothesley*, ed. W. D. Hamilton (Camden Society, NS XI, 1875–7).
Wyatt, George, *The Papers of George Wyatt*, ed. D. M. Loades (Camden Society, 4th series, V, 1968).

Secondary works (London unless otherwise stated)

Alexander, G., 'Bonner and the Marian persecutions', *History*, LX (1975), 374–92.
Anglo, S., *Spectacle, Pageantry and Early Tudor Policy* (1965).
Bartlett, K. R., 'The English exile community in Italy and the political opposition to Mary I', *Albion*, III (1971), 223–41.
Bartlett, K. R., 'The misfortune that is wished for him', *Canadian Journal of History*, XVI (1979), 1–28.
Beer B. L., *Northumberland* (Kent, Ohio, 1973).
Braddock, R. C., 'The rewards of office holding in Tudor England', *Journal of British Studies*, XIV (1975), 29–47.
Brandi, K., *Charles V* (1939).
Bush, M. L., *The Government Policy of Protector Somerset* (1975).
Charles Quint et son temps, Colloques Internationaux de Centre National de la Recherche Scientifique (Paris, 1959).
Colvin, N. M., *The History of the King's Works* (1963–76).
Crehan, J. H., 'The return to obedience: new judgement on Cardinal Pole', *The Month*, NS XIV (1955), 221–9.
Davies, C. S. L., 'England and the French war, 1557–9' in J. Loach and R. Tittler, eds, *The Mid-Tudor Polity, 1540–1560* (1980).
Davies, C. S. L., 'The Pilgrimage of Grace reconsidered', *Past and Present*, XLI (1968), 54–76.
Dickens, A. G., *The English Reformation* (1964).
Dodds, M. H. and R., *The Pilgrimage of Grace and the Exeter Conspiracy* (Cambridge, 1915).
Dowling, M., *Humanism in the Age of Henry VIII* (1987).
Dowling, M., 'The Gospel and the court: reformation under Henry VIII' in *Protestantism and the National Church in Sixteenth-century England* ed. P. Lake and M. Dowling (1987), 36–77.

Dugmore, C. W., *The Mass and the English Reformers* (1959).
Elton, G. R., 'Politics and the Pilgrimage of Grace' in *After the Reformation: Essays in Honor of J. M. Hexter,* ed. B. C. Malament (Philadelphia, 1980).
Elton, G. R., *Policy and Police* (Cambridge, 1972).
Elton, G. R., *Reform and Renewal* (1973).
Elton, G. R., *Reform and Reformation* (1977).
Emmison, F. G., *Tudor Secretary* (1971).
Erickson, C., *Bloody Mary* (1978).
Fenlon, D. B., *Heresy and Obedience in Tridentine Italy* (Cambridge, 1972).
Fernández Alvarez, M., *Política Mundial de Carlos V y Felipe II* (Madrid, 1966).
Fisher, F. J., 'Influenza and inflation in Tudor England', *Economic History Review,* 2nd series, XVIII (1965), 120–30.
Frede de, C., *La Restaurazione Cattolica in Inghilterra sotto Maria Tudor* (Naples, 1971).
Froude, J. A., *The Reign of Mary Tudor,* ed. W. L. Williams (1910).
Gammon, S. R., *Statesman and Schemer: William, First Lord Paget, Tudor Minister* (Newton Abbot, 1973).
Garrett, C. H., *The Marian Exiles* (Cambridge, 1938).
Glasgow, T., jun., 'The Navy in Philip and Mary's war, 1557–8', *Mariner's Mirror,* LII (1967), 23–37.
Glasgow, T., jun., 'The maturing of naval administration, 1556–64' *Mariner's Mirror,* LVI (1970), 3–27.
Gunn, S. J., *Charles Brandon, Duke of Suffolk* (Cambridge, 1988).
Guy, J., 'Thomas More and Christopher St. German: the battle of the books' in *Reassessing the Henrician Age,* ed. J. Guy and A. Fox (Oxford, 1986).
Guy, J., 'Thomas Cromwell and the intellectual origins of the Henrician Reformation' in *Reassessing the Henrician Age,* ed. J. Guy and A. Fox (Oxford, 1986).
Haigh, C., 'From monopoly to minority: catholicism in Early Modern England' *Transactions of the Royal Historical Society* 5th series, XXXI (1981), 129–47.
Haigh, C. *Reformation Revisited* (1987).
Haller, W., *Foxe's Book of Martyrs and the Elect Nation* (1963).
Harbison, E. H., *Rival Ambassadors at the Court of Queen Mary* (Princeton, New Jersey, 1940).
Hillerbrand, H.M., 'The early history of the Chapel Royal', *Modern Philology* XVIII (1920).
Hoak, D. E., *The King's Council in the Reign of Edward VI* (Cambridge, 1976).
Hoak, D. E., 'Rehabilitating the Duke of Northumberland' in *Tudor Rule and Revolution: Essays for G. R. Elton from his American Friends,* ed. J. W. McKenna and J. de Lloyd Guth (Cambridge, 1982).
Hoak, D. E., 'Two revolutions in Tudor government: the formation and organisation of Mary I's privy council' in *Revolution Reassessed,* ed. D. Starkey and C. Coleman (1986).
Hoffman, C. Fenno, 'Catherine Parr as a woman of letters', *Huntington Library Quarterly,* XXXIII (1960), 349–67.
Hughes, P. L., *The Reformation in England,* 3 vols (1953–6).
Ives, E. W., *Anne Boleyn* (Oxford, 1986).
James, M. E., 'Obedience and dissent in Henrician England: the Lincolnshire rebellion of 1536', *Past and Present,* XLVIII (1970), 3–78.

James, M. E., *English Politics and the Concept of Honour*, Past and Present Supplement 3 (1978).
Jones, N., 'Elizabeth's first year' in *The Reign of Elizabeth I*, ed. C. Haigh (1984).
Jones, W. R. D., *The Tudor Commonwealth* (1970).
Jordan, W. K., *Edward VI: The Young King* (1968).
Jordan, W. K., *Edward VI: The Threshold of Power* (1970).
Kelly, H. A., 'Kingship, incest and the dictates of law', *American Journal of Jurisprudence*, XIV (1969), 68–78.
Kelly, H. A., *The Matrimonial Trials of Henry VIII* (Stanford, California, 1976).
Kelly, M., 'The submission of the clergy', *Transactions of the Royal Historical Society*, 5th series, XV (1965), 97–119.
Knecht, R. J., *Francis I* (1982).
Knowles, M. C., *The Religious Orders in England*, III (Cambridge, 1959).
Levine, M., *The Early Elizabethan Succession Question* (Stanford, California, 1966).
Levine, M., *Tudor Dynastic Problems, 1460–1571* (1973).
Loach, J., 'Pamphlets and Politics, 1553–1558', *Bulletin of the Institute of Historical Research*, XLVIII (1975), 31–45.
Loach, J., 'The Marian establishment and the printing press', *English Historical Review*, CI (1987), 135–48.
Loach, J., *Parliament and the Crown in the Reign of Mary Tudor* (Oxford, 1987).
Loades, D. M., *Two Tudor Conspiracies* (Cambridge, 1965).
Loades, D. M., *The Oxford Martyrs* (1970).
Loades, D. M., *The Reign of Mary Tudor* (1979).
Loades, D. M., *The Tudor Court* (1986).
Loades, D. M., 'Philip II as king of England' in *Law and Government under the Tudors: Essays presented to Sir Geoffrey Elton*, ed. C. Cross, D. M. Loades and J. J. Scarisbrick (Cambridge, 1988).
MacCaffrey, W., *The Shaping of the Elizabethan Regime* (Princeton, New Jersey, 1968).
McConica, J. K., *English Humanism and Reformation Politics* (Oxford, 1965).
McCoy, R. C., 'From the Tower to the tiltyard: Robert Dudley's return to glory', *Historical Journal*, XXVII (1984), 425–35.
MacCulloch, D., *Suffolk and the Tudors* (Cambridge, 1987).
McLean, J., *The Life of Sir Thomas Seymour* (1869).
Maltby, W. S., *The Black Legend in England* (Durham, North Carolina, 1971).
Mattingly, G., *Catherine of Aragon* (Boston, Massachusetts, 1941).
Miller, H., *The English Nobility in the Reign of Henry VIII* (Oxford, 1986).
Muller, J. A., *Stephen Gardiner and the Tudor Reaction* (1926).
Murphy, J., 'The illusion of decline: the Privy Chamber 1547–1558' in *The English Court*: ed. D. Starkey (1987).
Olsen, V. N., *John Foxe and the Elizabethan Church* (Berkeley, California, 1973).
Parmiter, G. de C., *The King's Great Matter* (1967).
Paul, J. E., *Catherine of Aragon and her Friends* (1966).
Pogson, R. H., 'Revival and reform in Mary Tudor's church: a question of money', *Journal of Ecclesiastical History*, XXV (1974), 249–65.
Pogson, R. H., 'Reginald Pole and the priorities of government in Mary Tudor's church', *Historical Journal*, XVIII (1975), 3–21.
Pogson, R. H., 'Stephen Gardiner and the problem of loyalty' in *Law and*

Government under the Tudors ed. C. Cross, D. M. Loades and J. J. Scarisbrick (Cambridge, 1988), 67–89.

Potter, D. L., 'The Duc de Guise and the fall of Calais', *English Historical Review*, XCVIII (1983), 481–512.

Prescott, H. F. M., *Mary Tudor* (1952).

Ramsey, G. D., *The City of London in International Politics at the Accession of Elizabeth Tudor* (Manchester, 1975).

Ridley, J., *Thomas Cranmer* (1962).

Ridley, J., *The Life and Times of Mary Tudor* (1973).

Robison, W. B., 'The national and local significance of Wyatt's rebellion in Surrey', *Historical Journal*, XXX, 769–90 (1987).

Rodríguez Salgado, M. J., *The Changing Face of Empire: Charles V, Philip II and Habsburg Authority, 1551–1559* (Cambridge, 1988).

Russell, J. G., *The Field of Cloth of Gold* (1969).

Scarisbrick, J. J., *Henry VIII* (1968).

Scarisbrick, J. J., *The Reformation and the English People* (1986).

Schenk, W., *Reginald Pole, Cardinal of England* (1950).

Smith, A. G. R., *The Emergence of a Nation State, 1529–1660* (1984).

Smith, L. B., *Tudor Prelates and Politics* (Princeton, 1953).

Smith, L. B., *The Mask of Royalty* (1971).

Stone, J. M., *Mary I, Queen of England* (1901).

Stone, L., *The Crisis of the Aristocracy, 1558–1640* (Oxford, 1965).

Starkey, D., *The Reign of Henry VIII: Personalities and Politics* (1985).

Strong, R., *The Cult of Elizabeth* (1977).

Strype, J., *Ecclesiastical Memorials* (1721).

Tellechea Idigoras, J. I., 'Bartolomé Carranza y la restauración católica inglesa (1553–1558)', *Anthologia Annua*, XII (1964), 159–282.

Tellechea Idigoras, J. I., 'Pole, Carranza y Fresnada. Cara y cruz de una amistad y de una enemistad', *Diálogo ecuménico*, VIII (1974), 287–393.

Tellechea Idigoras, J. I., *Fray Bartolomé Carranza y el Cardenal Pole* (Pamplona, 1977).

Thorp, M. R., 'Religion and the Wyatt rebellion of 1554', *Church History*, XLVII (1978), 363–80.

Tittler, R., 'The incorporation of boroughs, 1540–1558', *History*, LXII (1977), 24–42.

Tittler, R., *The Reign of Mary I* (1983).

Tittler, R. and Battley, S. L., 'The local community and the crown in 1553: the accession of Mary Tudor re-visited', *Bulletin of the Institute of Historical Research*, LVII (1984), 131–9.

Waldman, M., *The Lady Mary* (1972).

Warnike, R., 'Sexual heresy at the court of Henry VIII', *Historical Journal*, XXX (1987), 247–68.

Weikel, A., 'The Marian Council re-visited' in J. Loach and R. Tittler, *The Mid-Tudor Polity, 1540–1560* (1980).

White, B., *Mary Tudor* (1935).

Willen, D., *John Russell, first Earl of Bedford: One of the King's Men* (Royal Historical Society, 1981).

Williams, P., *The Tudor Regime* (1979).

Woodbury, L., 'Jean Ribault and Queen Elizabeth', *American Historical Review*,

IX (1903–4), 456–9.
Young, A., *Tudor and Jacobean Tournaments* (1987).
Youngs, F. A., *The Proclamations of the Tudor Queens* (Cambridge, 1976).

Unpublished theses

Boscher, P., 'The Anglo-Scottish Border, 1550–1560' (Ph.D., Durham, 1985).
Braddock, R. C., 'The Royal Household, 1540–1560' (Ph.D., Northwestern, 1971).
Brigden, S. E., 'The Reformation in London in the Reign of Henry VIII' (Ph.D., Cambridge, 1979).
Dawson, J. E. A., 'The Early Career of Christopher Goodman, and his Place in the Development of English Protestant Thought' (Ph.D., Durham, 1978).
Lemasters, G. A., 'The Privy Council in the Reign of Mary I' (Ph.D., Cambridge, 1971).
Marmion, J. P., 'The London Synod of Cardinal Pole' (MA, Keele, 1974).
Pogson, R. H., 'Reginald Pole, Papal Legate in England in Mary Tudor's Reign' (Ph.D., Cambridge, 1972).
Took, P., 'Government and the Printing Trade, 1540–1560' (Ph.D., London, 1978).
Tighe, W. J., 'The Gentlemen Pensioners in the Sixteenth Century' (Ph.D., Cambridge, 1983).

Index